The Age of Life on Earth

The Age of Life on Earth

Edited by
LYNDEN J. ROGERS

WIPF & STOCK · Eugene, Oregon

THE AGE OF LIFE ON EARTH

Copyright © 2025 Wipf and Stock Publishers. All rights reserved. Except for brief quotations in critical publications or reviews, no part of this book may be reproduced in any manner without prior written permission from the publisher. Write: Permissions, Wipf and Stock Publishers, 199 W. 8th Ave., Suite 3, Eugene, OR 97401.

Wipf & Stock
An Imprint of Wipf and Stock Publishers
199 W. 8th Ave., Suite 3
Eugene, OR 97401

www.wipfandstock.com

PAPERBACK ISBN: 979-8-3852-4671-7
HARDCOVER ISBN: 979-8-3852-4672-4
EBOOK ISBN: 979-8-3852-4673-1

Copyright Notices

Chapter 1 The Scripture quotations contained in chapter 1 are from the New Revised Standard Version Bible, copyright © 1989, by the Division of Christian Education of the National Council of the Churches of Christ in the U.S.A., and are used by permission. All rights reserved.

Chapters 9–10 The Scripture quotations contained in chapters 9 and 10 are from The ESV Bible (The Holy Bible, English Standard Version), copyright © 2001 by Crossway, a publishing ministry of Good News Publishers. Used by permission. All rights reserved.

Chapter 10 is reproduced by permission of The Association of Adventist Forums. (An earlier version of this paper appeared in Spectrum 51:1 (2023) 60–79).

Dedication
Graham Will (1927–2019)
BSc, MSc, DSc
Soil scientist, church elder, and honest Christian thinker

Graham Melville Will (1927–2019), who has been described as "the Father of Radiata Pine Nutrition,"[1] took his BSc degree in 1949 and his MSc in 1950 at Victoria College, later Victoria University, New Zealand. In 1970, he submitted a substantial collection of published scientific papers to Victoria University, Wellington, and was awarded the prestigious DSc degree.

Most of Graham's professional life was spent engaged in soil research with New Zealand's Forest Research Institute in Rotorua, where he settled in 1953. His work soon produced an extensive body of data from the soils and geological features of the Rotorua caldera that challenged the short chronology of life adopted by the Seventh-day Adventist Church, of which he was a member throughout his life. Mindful of his faith community's lack of familiarity with such problems, he felt unable to discuss them openly, a circumstance which persisted through the decades. However, he was able to share his thoughts with his understanding wife, Vid. During a study itinerary in the United States in 1971–1972, he made contact with some similarly minded Adventist scientists, such as Asa Thoresen and Richard Ritland, and subsequently enjoyed association with Adventist Forums, both in the United States of America and Australia.[2]

Graham remained an active, gracious, and committed Adventist Christian throughout his ninety-two years, functioning at times as head elder at his local church. He also cautiously contributed his perspective to

---

1. Dyck, Bill. "Graham Will – the Father of Radiata Pine Nutrition." *New Zealand Journal of Forestry* 64:1 (2019) 42–43.

2. Will, Graham. "Lynden Rogers' interview with Graham and Vid Will in Sydney," Australia (May 27, 2013).

Dedication

those Geoscience Research Institute tours that visited New Zealand in the 1980s and to a conference on Origins organized by the South Pacific Division of the Seventh-day Adventist Church held in 2003 at Avondale College (Avondale University), NSW, Australia. Some of the material that Graham presented on this latter occasion was subsequently published in *Spectrum* magazine.[3]

---

3. Will, Graham. "What Have Volcanos and Soils Told Me?" *Spectrum* 38:4 (2010) 64–69.

Table of Contents

List of Figures ix

List of Tables xi

List of Contributors xii

Preface xv

Acknowledgments xxi

Chapter 1 The Creation Narrative in Genesis 1:1–2:4a: Towards a Proper Reading and Understanding, Part 1 | 1

Chapter 2 The Creation Narrative in Genesis 1:1–2:4a: Towards a proper Reading and Understanding, Part 2 | 42

Chapter 3 A Brief Review of Design in the Cosmos | 73

Chapter 4 Dating Quaternary Life | 103

Chapter 5 Radiocarbon Dating of Once-living Specimens | 128

Chapter 6 How Far Can a Kangaroo Jump? Plate Tectonics and the Biogeography of Marsupials | 193

Chapter 7 Ice Cores and What They Tell Us About Past Life | 209

Chapter 8 Mary Schweizer and Dinosaur Soft Tissues: Initial Reactions and Current Opinions | 238

Chapter 9 Theological Problems with Old-age Models for Life | 270

Chapter 10 Can a Seventh-day Adventist Hold Non-traditional Views of Origins? | 301

Index | 337

List of Figures

Preface Figure 0.1 Flowchart for questions on Origins. xvi

Figure 1.1 Bridging the separations between the ancient and the contemporary. 3

Figure 3.1 Quantized energy states of the carbon nucleus showing the first excited state to be 4.43 MeV above the ground state and the second excited state to be 7.68 MeV above the ground state. 82

Figure 4.1 Longshore sediment drift on the coast of northern New South Wales and southern Queensland (drawn by B. Timms). 109

Figure 4.2 Two Australian coastal lakes: (A) Myall Lakes, coastal New South Wales, 75 km north of Newcastle; (B) Tuggerah Lake, coastal NSW, 50 km south of Newcastle (drawn by B. Timms). 114

Figure 4.3 Core data from Lynch's Crater on the Atherton Tablelands (modified from Kershaw, 1994). 119

Figure 4.4 Some Australian gnammas and some of their denizens: (A and B) gnammas on two inselbergs in Western Australia; (C) Waterflea (*Ceriodaphnia*), approximately 1 mm in length; (D) Clam Shrimp (*Ozestheria mariae*), approximately 5 mm in length; (E) Fairy Shrimp (*Branchinella longirostris*), approximately 12 mm in length. Also (F) a Brine Shrimp (*Parartemia minuta*), approximately 9 mm in length. These swim upside down (photographs by B. Timms). 123

Figure 5.1 Schematic diagram of a tandem Accelerator Mass Spectrometer (AMS). 143

Figure 5.2 Standard deviation as a percentage of total count. 150

List of Figures

Figure 5.3 The radiocarbon analytical pathway. 156

Figure 5.4 Experimental design for isotopic enrichment. 177

Figure 5.5 The quark process of β- decay where one down-quark (d) changes into an up-quark (u) mediated by the W- boson with the emission of an electron (e-) and anti-electron neutrino. The other up- and down-quarks (at the top) remain unaffected. This transmutes a neutron into a proton. 183

Figure 6.1 Relative positions of the continents in the Oligocene (A) and the Present (B). The continents are shown in approximate outline. The relative levels of land and sea have changed progressively and at various times parts of the continents were submerged. On Map A (Oligocene) arrows show likely routes of migration of marsupials out of North America (see Section 6.4). Map B (Present) shows the location and approximate age of some significant fossils. The presence of a fossil at any location does not preclude the existence of the species in the area earlier or later than the date of the fossil. Most Indonesian islands are not shown, although marsupials have spread westwards from New Guinea as far as Sulawesi (see Section 6.4) (drawn by H. Fisher and L. Rogers). 198

Figure 7.1 Schematic (and non-linear) diagram of the ice column, showing composition at various depths. The base of such an ice column could be on bedrock or soil/sediment (drawn by T. Annable). 215

Figure 7.2 Two-dimensional representation of global air circulation patterns. (Vertical scale in atmosphere greatly exaggerated) (drawn by T. Annable). 216

Figure 7.3 Ice storage at approximately -36°C (photograph taken at the National Ice Core Laboratory, Denver, Colorado in 2002 by Lynden Rogers). 218

Figure 7.4 Ice core with visual banding (photograph taken at the National Ice Core Laboratory, Denver, Colorado in 2002 by Lynden Rogers). 220

Figure 7.5 Lake Vostok Russian drill site section, age of accretion ice at base dated at several Myr. (drawn by T. Annable). 229

Figure 10.1 Spectrum of views on Origins. 303

List of Tables

Table 5.1 Effect of modern carbon contamination on calculated CRAs | 154

Table 5.2 Comparison of ABA and ABOx dates: Grotto di Fumane, Italy | 159

Table 5.3 Collagen measurements from three laboratories | 167

Table 5.4 Background measurements and calculated *LOD*s from several laboratories | 171

Table 6.1 Main Metatherian Groups | 197

Table 6.2 Upper Geological Timescale | 199

Table 8.1 Timeline of Critical Research Publications | 248

Table 8.2 Milestones in the analysis of ancient DNA (data from Morozova et al.) DNA Res 2016) Note: The directions to the publications corresponding to the numbers shown in this table are listed in footnote #38 | 251

List of Contributors

Lynden Rogers, BSc (Hons), MSc, PhD; Senior Lecturer (Physics), Avondale University (Ret.)

Major research interests: Christian Faith and Science

Rudy Van Moere, BTh, M Rel Studs, MTh, PhD; Professor (Biblical Hebrew, OT Theology and Exegesis) Faculty of Protestant Theology in Brussels (Ret.)

Major research interests: OT Exegesis, OT Theology, New Testament, Jewish-Christian Studies

Kevin deBerg, BSc, DipEd, BEd, PhD, MAppSc, MACS; Associate Professor, Avondale University (Physical Chemistry) (Ret.)

Major research interests: Thermodynamics and Kinetics, Chemistry Education, History and Philosophy of Science, Christian Faith and Science

Ewan Ward, BSc (Hons) PhD, Grad Dip Theol, Grad Dip Min; Senior Lecturer, Avondale University (Molecular Biology, Biochemistry, Microbiology) (Ret.)

Major research interests: Christian Faith and Science

Brian Timms, BSc (Hons), PhD, DSc; Adjunct Professor, University of NSW, Assistant Director Sanitarium Research laboratory (Ret.)

Major research interests: Limnology, Lake Geomorphology, Aquatic Ecology, Crustacean Taxonomy

List of Contributors

Geoffrey Madigan, BSc, PhD, MA; Senior Lecturer (Physical Chemistry) at Avondale University, Principal Scientist, Sanitarium Analytical Laboratory (Laboratory report signatory, approved by the *National Association of Testing Authorities*) (Ret.)

Major research interests: Crystal Growth/Dissolution Kinetics, Aluminosilicate Chemistry, Analytical Methods.

Colin Waters, BEd (Science), BSc (Hons), PhD; Professor, University of Newcastle (Physics)

Major research interests: Space Plasma Wave Propagation, the Magnetosphere and Ionosphere, Auroral Currents

Howard Fisher, BScAgr, MScAgr, PhD; Senior Lecturer, Avondale University (Physical Geography) (Ret.)

Major research interests: Biogeography, Ecology, Christian Concern for the Environment

Terence Annable, BSc (Hons), PGCEd, MSc, PhD; Senior Lecturer (Anatomy, Physiology, Ecophysiology), Avondale University (Ret.)

Major research interests: Natural History, Herpetology

Paul U. Cameron, BMedSc (Hons), MBBS, PhD, FRACP, FRCPA; Associate Professor, Doherty Institute, University of Melbourne (Ret.)

Major research interests: Immunology, Cell Biology, Immunopathology

David Thiele, BA, BD (Hons), MTh, MEd, PhD (NT); Associate Professor, Pacific Adventist University (Ret.)

Major research interests: Systematic Theology, New Testament

Preface

THE CHAPTERS IN THIS book began as papers presented at the Sydney Adventist Forum's conference on "The Age of Life on Earth", held in Morisset, NSW, Australia, in 2021. The Origins landscape flowchart shown in Figure 0.1 was used as a guide for the choice of presentation topics. The three main schools of thought on Origins found among contemporary Seventh-day Adventists, as among Christians generally, are *recent creationism, ancient creationism,* and some form of *guided evolution*. Of course, considerable variations exist within all these categories. The flowchart demonstrates that these three views, along with a fourth, *naturalistic evolution*, emerge as responses to the data relevant to addressing three successive questions.

The three questions are shown in the parallelogram boxes. Significant areas of scientific investigation relating to each question are shown on the left. The four schools of thought mentioned above are shown on the far right, as they are differentiated. For each question, significant theological problems that a conservative perspective might identify are shown on the medium right for both "yes" and "no" options.

Note that this flowchart first separates out naturalistic evolution, the only significant atheistic position. Obviously, no Christian would entertain an atheistic option. It must also be recognized that for most individuals a huge range of information besides scientific data is likely to influence their choice on this initial question. Most Christians would never resort to scientific evidence on design to establish their theism. Similarly, avowed atheists might quickly affirm the opposite position, irrespective of design testimony. However, the question certainly can be approached in terms of scientific evidence, as shown by a large body of literature on design. Since, according to our scenario, this broad question of design arises even before the question of age, one conference presentation was allocated to this topic.

Preface

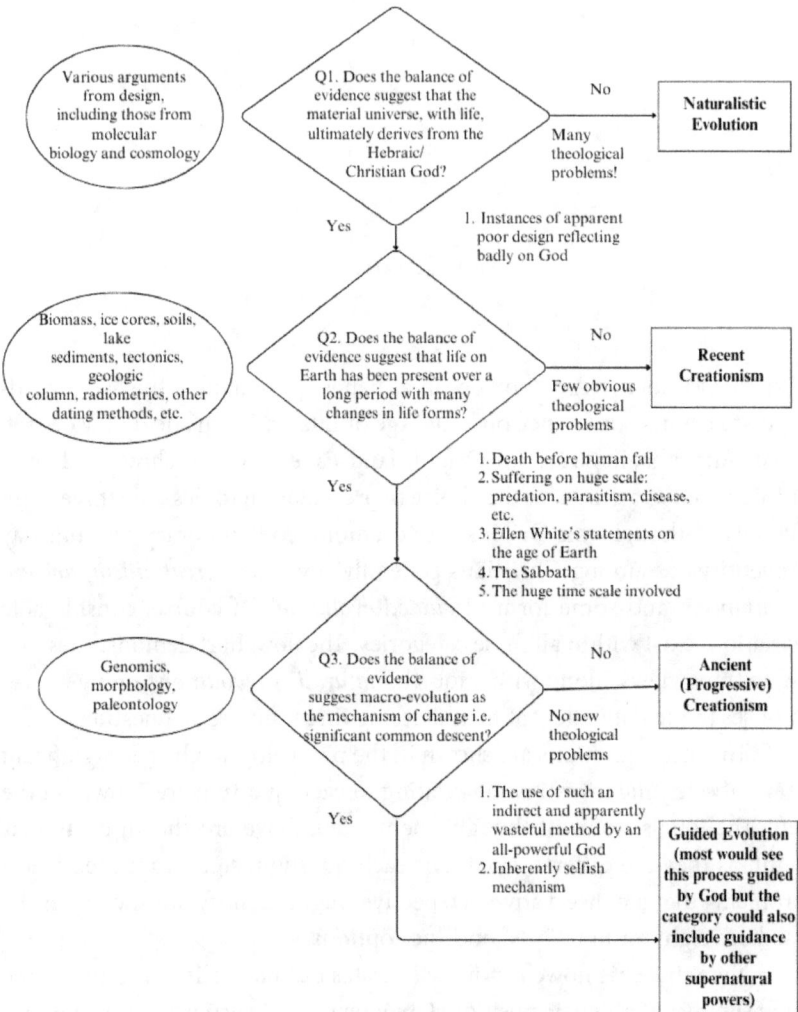

Figure 0.1 Flowchart for questions on Origins.

The remaining options all exist within a theistic framework and represent those available to individuals of Christian faith. It is contended that, logically, the next question encountered *does not* concern evolution, as commonly supposed by recent creationists, but the age of life on Earth. It is also the case that the main theological problems encountered by traditional Christian thought are met in connection with a *long-age* resolution of this question, not in connection with evolution. If it is established that life on Earth is old these theological enigmas remain even if evolutionary ideas are

Preface

cast aside. And there are certainly other old-age options besides evolution, a fact seldom recognized. It also happens that a very large body of independent but interlocking scientific data relates to this age-of-life question. Fortunately, some of these data are readily accessible, since they are not highly technical in nature. The "Age of life on Earth" question is, then, the "elephant in the room." Criticizing evolution without having addressed the data concerning the age of life is to risk the logical error of setting up straw men and then triumphantly knocking them down. This happens frequently among recent creationists. Accordingly, five papers presented at the Forum conference, hence chapters in this book, speak to the issue of the age of life.

Another way of emphasizing the primacy of age-of-life data is to note that, broadly speaking, scientific inquiry is conducted at three levels. In a popular article, Eric Magnusson wrote that science first searches for the data then examines the data for regularities, and lastly searches the regularities for explanations.[1] Of course, this is after an initial hypothesis is proposed. These three stages may be called collective science, descriptive science, and causal science, respectively. We may usefully apply these categories to the scientific study of Origins. Obviously, we first need relevant data. These data can then be examined to establish whether they most coherently support a descriptive model involving a young age for life or an old age. Only then can one enquire meaningfully into the causal stage, in which a mechanism is sought. If our decision is for young life then recent creation is really the only causal option. If the evidence has been seen as supporting the conclusion that life is very old, then the search is on for mechanisms that produce or sustain life over long periods. Here there is a range of possibilities, at least one of which does not involve macroevolution, as earlier noted.

It is important to observe that this concept map does not probe the age of the inanimate universe, the solar system, or our Earth. While these questions are certainly of interest, they do not divide Christians to anywhere near the extent of those relating to the age of life. This is demonstrated by the fact that Adventists who claim that the entire creation took place within a very recent timescale and those who allow longer, even scientifically accepted, ages for the abiotic universe, solar system, or Earth, typically view each other amicably. No one appears to be under threat of church censure over issues related to the age of any part of the inanimate universe. George McCready Price's earlier vacillations on this question appear to have settled

---

1. Eric Magnusson, "Making a Good Rope Out of Air Bubbles: Darwin and the Scientists, 1859 and 1987", Signs of the Times 102:9 (1987) 4–6.

Preface

into a tolerance for a range of views. Furthermore, such questions do not appear to challenge the Christian faith of any Adventists, young or old. It is likely that this is because comparatively few theological problems are encountered by stretching the timescale for non-life.

Although it was noted above that many of these topics are reasonably accessible, others are inevitably somewhat technical in nature, employing difficult concepts and terminology. In such discussions, it is very easy to lose even an informed audience. But too-zealous attempts to overcome this problem can result in over-simplification and distortion. As Einstein is purported to have said,—things should be explained as simply as possible, but no simpler! Accordingly, the authors in this book have attempted to reduce their technical language to a minimum, but also to avoid misleading over-simplifications. This is indeed an impossibly difficult balancing act. Where we have failed, we ask for your forbearance. The most technical chapter (that devoted to carbon dating) is preceded by a brief editor's summary for the benefit of non-technicians.

Our writers do not all speak from the same perspectives, and readers may detect this. In fact, it should be expected. Forum is happy for these differences to emerge. All must recognize and live with the problems associated with their preferred views.

This book is presented in four sections: textual studies of Genesis 1, design, scientific evidence concerning the age of life, and then some systematic theology. The science content is, then, appropriately bookended by biblical studies. The authors of the science chapters are all Australian scientists and readers will detect an unapologetic flavor of Antipodean evidence in places.

In chapters 1 and 2, Rudy Van Moere presents evidence that the Genesis account was carefully crafted to answer existential questions confronting the Jewish nation at various crisis points within its history. Chapter 3, by Kevin de Berg, Lynden Rogers, and Ewan Ward contains a critical review of the various forms of the design argument that have been proffered by apologists, particularly over the last few centuries of Christian history. In chapter 4, Brian Timms argues for ancient life on Earth, largely on the basis of evidence involving water, both moving and still, some of it drawn from his life-long studies of lakes and gnammas. In chapter 5, Colin Waters and Geoffrey Madigan explain the fundamental science and the complex procedures and processes of carbon dating, a method commonly used to date the remains of organisms that lived within the last 50,000 years or so.

Preface

In chapter 6, Howard Fisher describes how the past movements of the continents over very long periods fit neatly with the fossil evidence for the changing distributions of marsupials to provide an explanation for their current geographical distribution. In chapter 7, Terence Annable presents evidence for ancient life on Earth from data obtained from ice-core research undertaken over the last five decades. In chapter 8, Paul Cameron examines the evidence and methodology behind Mary Schweitzer's unexpected claims of having found organic remains in dinosaur fossils and uses this controversy to provide a comment on the scientific method. In chapters 9 and 10, David Thiele evaluates various theological arguments for and against a long age for life on Earth, noting that all origins models have some tension with Scripture and suggesting that old-life models cannot be dismissed easily from biblical evidence.

Lynden Rogers

Acknowledgments

I WOULD LIKE TO thank the authors of the chapters in this book for their initial contribution at the Forum conference on "The Age of Life on Earth" and for the willingness with which they subsequently edited these papers into book chapters. Some of these individuals also refereed, fact checked, and proofread chapters written by other authors, a contribution which was greatly appreciated. I am particularly indebted to Dr Howard Fisher, who extensively refereed a number of the chapters and copyedited them all, some a number of times. The text-processing skill and overall enthusiasm and encouragement provided by Sallyanne Dehn were also much appreciated. Finally, I would like to pay tribute to my wife, Julie, who graciously gave her husband up for the swathes of time necessary to assemble this book.

Every effort has been taken to ensure the accuracy of the material presented. Residual mistakes remain my responsibility.

Lynden Rogers

1

The Creation Narrative in Genesis 1:1–2:4a

Towards a Proper Reading and Understanding

PART 1

RUDY VAN MOERE

1.1 GENERAL INTRODUCTION

MY SOLE PURPOSE IN these two chapters is to share with you what I have come to understand about this most important narrative of the Creation, surely one of the most interesting and intriguing subjects of the Hebrew Bible.[1] Obviously, these two chapters are not enough to present all the available data. But be assured that as a biblical exegete, I try not to superimpose my modern concepts onto the text nor to overlay anachronic agenda onto the biblical writer. It is important to note initially that responsible Bible reading in the twenty-first century necessarily involves at least three elements.

1.1.1 Bridging the Separations Between Old and New

Understanding the biblical narratives requires the bridging of an immense gap between *the here and now* of our postmodern times and *the there and*

---

1. According to Tsumura, "Genesis and Ancient Near Eastern Stories," 27–57.

then of the Ancient Near East in which they were written. Present-day readers will therefore have to be continually conscious of:

- *the geographical distance* between nowadays Australia, Belgium, France, etc., and ancient Egypt, Assyria, Babylonia, Persia, etc.;
- *the linguistic differences* between English, French, Dutch, German, etc., and Hebrew, Aramaic, and Greek;
- the differences in *customs and traditions* and in *social circumstances*;
- the differences in the mental world regarding such matters as *worldview, image of God, and portrayal of man*; and
- differences between the present-day *culture* with its science, philosophy, technology, literature, etc., and the ancient *culture* of storytelling, religion, fine arts, literature, etc.[2]

These differences are represented pictorially in Figure 1.1.

---

2. Every nation or community lives from stories. The Genesis creation narrative is an ancient text with forms of literature addressed to a particular, ancient Hebrew-speaking people. They worshipped the God of Israel, and therefore one should eliminate improper ways of reading with wrong expectations and preconceived ideas. Given the original audience, one should read (so to speak) through their eyes, respecting the basic rule of semantics, namely that the meaning of words depends strongly on their context. It is therefore out of the question to invoke the New Testament. The reason for this is that it neglects the dramatic differences in metaphysical and ontological perspectives between Ancient Israel, Hellenistic Judaism and Christianity under the major influence of the Greek language and the Greco-Roman philosophy.

Biblical times there and then	Responsible Bible reading requires	Postmodern Times here and now
	the bridging of . . . an immense distance	
• Egypt, Assyria, Babylonia, Persia, Greece, Rome . . . • Hebrew, Aramaic, Greek • Customs and traditions • Social circumstances • Mental world: worldview, image of God, portrayal of man • Storytelling culture		• Belgium, France, The Netherlands, Russia, Italy . . . • French, Dutch, German, Spanish • Customs and traditions • Social circumstances • Mental world: worldview, image of God, portrayal of man • Scientific culture

Figure 1.1 Bridging the separations between the ancient and the contemporary.

1.1.2 Using Correct Exegetical Criteria

In order to understand and interpret biblical narratives correctly, one must employ appropriate exegetical criteria. This is particularly so in Gen 1:1–2:4a, which displays many unique features, even within Hebrew narrative. To recognize and honor this uniqueness, and to achieve a close reading, the following features must be absolutely observed and respected:

- the vocabulary, word choice, style, and structures employed within the text;
- the genre of the text;

- its situation within the literary context of the scroll or the collection of scrolls; and
- the literary and aesthetic criteria of the Ancient Near East in general and of Ancient Israel in particular.

As noted in the preceding section, one's approach to this text must not be based on literary, historical, aesthetic, and cultural criteria of the twenty-first century.

1.1.3 Observing the Typical Characteristics of Biblical Narrative

The fact that the Bible narratives are still in existence is due to their excellent quality, and therefore, they justly belong to world literature. These narratives are much more than historical reports or journalistic essays. Biblical authors were neither historians nor journalists. They were pastors, teachers, and educators. Their theology was neither systematic nor philosophical but narrative, a style that has been largely forgotten.

Later, their written storytelling fell under the spell of Greek rational thought and logical reasoning. That language, though suited to certain types of discourse and commonly used in the ancient world, is inadequate to convey the semantic range of Ancient Israel's symbolic language. It was through their narratives that Israelite authors testified of their faith in their God YHWH and made it known to their readers.

To achieve accuracy, it is therefore essential to read biblical narratives in the most reliable translations available—such as the ones employed in this presentation—and define their *genre* and the *context* in which they were written, as mentioned earlier. Mediocre reading leads to poor understanding and, therefore, to poor interpretations.

1.1.4 This Study

Accordingly, this chapter and the next constitute a serious attempt to observe and implement these three cautions. This chapter consists of two main sections:

- a correct reading of the Hebrew text—though in an English translation (mostly the *New Revised Standard Version* [NRSV, 1989] and occasionally *The Jewish Publication Society's Bible Translation* (JPS,

1917)—with a special focus on lexical and structural observations; and
- an examination of the specific genre of the text: grammatically, structurally, and thematically.

The second chapter consists of three main sections:
- an exploration of the international context of Israel's creation narrative, comparing it with Ancient Near Eastern creation texts;
- a contextualisation of Israel's creation narrative within the collection from Genesis to Kings; and
- a distillation of some consequences emerging from the study. Some attempt will be made to identify the most plausible and fitting textual interpretation and to exclude some indefensible appropriations of the text.

1.2 READING THE TEXT CORRECTLY

1.2.1 Introduction

Texts in the Hebrew Bible are witnesses of a narrative culture in which all words, sentences, images, and names have a function and play a role. The storytellers regarded these narratives as enormously important because they encapsulate life lessons. That is why, when writing them down, they used their skills as proficiently and efficiently as possible so that their messages would stay with their hearers, readers, and even with future generations. All aspects of the text must, therefore, be meticulously examined through observation, analysis, and evaluation.

1.2.2 Text Delimitation

To investigate a text properly, its beginning and its end must first be determined. The Israelite narrative of creation, as the very first text in the scroll of $b^e r\bar{e}'s\bar{\jmath}t$—or Genesis as it is commonly called—obviously has a distinct beginning (1:1). However, there is less agreement about its final sentence. While some argue that 2:3 is to be considered as such,[3] most exegetes are

---

3. Arnold, *Genesis*, 2009, 55; Cassuto, *Genesis. Part I*, 96–100; Cotter, *Genesis*, 27;

of the opinion that lexical, structural, and thematic signals in this narrative favor 2:4a.[4] This text has several connections with 1:1. Indeed, the latter opens with the impressive tripartite vocabulary *create–heavens–earth,* and 2:4a ends solemnly with exactly the same words. This is shown below, with the contrasting word usage of 2:4b.

Genesis 1:1 and 2:4a and 4b (NRS) [5]

1:1 In the beginning when God *created the heavens and* and the earth

2:4a These are the generations of *the heavens* and the earth when they were *created*

2:4b In the day that YHWH God *made* earth and heavens

In this way, the opening and the closing sentences function as an inclusion. They embrace the whole narrative and characterize it as a delimited and completed whole. That the first narrative ends with 4a is also evident from the fact that this sentence cannot function as a title for 2:4b–25, since the latter is not a narrative about the origins of the heavens and the earth.[6] Moreover, 4b does not give the impression of being a normal continuation of the preceding narrative, 1:1–2:4a. Indeed, this verse, 4b, introduces a different creation narrative (2:4b–25). This can also be deduced from several differences between these two narratives:

Keil and Delitzsch, *Pentateuch*, 70–76; Waltke, *Genesis*, 83; Walton, *Genesis*, 162; Wenham, *Genesis 1–15*, 49.

4. Alter, *Genesis*, 7; Beauchamp, *Création et Séparation*; Buber and Rosenzweig, *Schrift*, 12–13; de Fraine, *Genesis* (Dutch), 43; Goldingay, *Genesis*, 41; Jagersma, *Genesis 1:1–25*, 11; Sarna, "Book of Genesis," 7: 394–98; Speiser, *Genesis*, 5; Turner, *Genesis* 6; von Rad, *Genesis*, 60; Wénin, *D'Adam à Abraham*, 50–51.

5. Genesis 1:1 together with 2:4a show a chiastic parallelism: created – the heavens and the earth X the heavens and the earth–created.

6. Goldingay, *Genesis*, 41.

The Creation Narrative in Genesis 1:1–2:4a

- the order of the word pair "*the heavens* and *the earth*" changes into "*earth* and *heavens*" (both without definite articles);[7]
- the divine appellation changes—God (*'ᵉlōhīm*) in the first narrative and YHWH God in the second one;
- the verbal form (God) "*created*" (1:1) changes to (YHWH God) "*made*" (2:4b); and
- the fact that the first narrative contains successive chronological days (from day one to the *seventh* day), whereas the second narrative starts with a quite different time indication: "in the day that . . ." (2:4b).

Gen 1:1–2:4a, therefore, can be considered *a well-rounded narrative.*[8] Accordingly, these texts will be the main object of our further investigation.

1.2.3 The Text Itself

The full text of the creation narrative below has been taken from the *New Revised Standard Version* [NRSV, 1989]. Although the *New International Version* [NIB or NIV, 1984] is of splendid quality, the former has the advantage that it consistently translates the words that are repeated in the Hebrew source text into English using the same words. That gives a stiffer language that readers must accept.

This presentation provides the text in simple sentences, which helps the reader to perceive the course and development of the narrative. In fact, these simple sentences correspond to the sentences defined by the punctuation marks in the Hebrew text. The numbered verses are therefore split into several sentences that are conveniently indicated by lowercase letters (a, b, c, . . .). Where the narrator is speaking, the sentences begin at the far left, and where the featured character is given the word or the platform, a full space is indented to the right.

---

7. According to Hebrew language logic, the first creation narrative is told from the perspective of *the heavens*, while in the second creation narrative *earth* appears to be the starting point.

8. Fokkelman defines Genesis 1:1–2:4a as an envelope structure with 1:1 as the heading and 2:4a the conclusion. In *Genesis*, Fokkelman, 36–55, 41.

The Age of Life on Earth

Genesis 1:1–2:4a NRS

1   In the beginning[9] when God[10] created[11] the heavens and the earth,[12]
2a   the earth was[13] a formless[14] void[15]

---

9. In Hebrew, it reads $b^e r\bar{e}$'*sjīt*. Its first letter *bēt* is a preposition and can be translated as *in*, *with*, *by* and *when*.

10. The verb *bārā'* should be translated as "he created." See Joüon and Muraoka, *Biblical Hebrew*, 361. Goldingay states with emphasis that "the text announces with utmost simplicity that it was God—and God alone—who created the cosmos," Goldingay, *Genesis*, 25.

11. Tsumura claims—based on etymological studies (Accadian, Arabic, Phoenician, Aramaic, Ugaritic)—that shaping, fashioning or building constitute the basic idea of *bārā'*. It therefore concerns a functional and material creation. Consequently, it is to be understood as uninhabitable but not chaotic (Isa 45:18b). "God would not create chaos." Tsumura, *Earth*, 14–15.

12. "*Heavens and earth*" represent a merism or the entirety of something by reference to the extreme opposites of that entity.

13. "When God began to create the heaven and the earth" is another translation, whereby this phrase functions as the beginning (i.e., a circumstantial sentence of time) of a long sentence that mentions the raw material that God starts to transform. Wénin therefore concludes that God's action should not be understood as a *creatio ex nihilo*. Wénin, *D'Adam à Abraham*, 27–28. Greenwood refers to Holmstedt's observation in "Restrictive Syntax," 55–66, that a linguistic analysis of similar syntactic structures shows that Gen. 1:1 does not refer to a specific beginning of known chronology but to "the beginning of one particular act of God," Greenwood, *Since the Beginning*, 3. See also Bandstra, *Genesis 1–11*, 41–48.

14. *Tōhū*: *unorderly* (i.e., messy not organic) in Isa 24:10; 34:11; 45:18–19 or *formless*: without form; no order; not yet normal. *Bōhū*: *empty* (without life). In Isa 34:11 *empty* with the idea of uninhabited.

15. Alter tries to approximate the assonance of the French edition: *La Genèse* (Geneva: Labor et Fides, 1949). *Tōhū wāvōhū* with *welter and waste* (Alter, *Genesis*, 3) just as Buber did before him in German with *Irrsal und Wirrsal*. See *fünf Bucher der Weisung*, 9–12. This Hebrew word-pair has been translated in diverse ways: *a formless void* [NRS]; *unformed and void* [JPS]; *waste and empty* [DBY]; *without form and void* [RSV]; *formless and empty* [NIB]; *unordered and empty* (Jagersma, *Genesis*, 23). See, for example, Jeremiah 4:23–25 (*lifeless mass*). Cassuto is of the opinion that the phrase *tōhū wāvōhū* refers to "the unformed material from which the earth was to be fashioned at the beginning of its creation in a state . . . to wit, water above and solid matter beneath, and the whole a chaotic mass, without order or life." Cassuto, *Genesis*, 23. According to Tsumura, the word group points to forming and filling the unproductive and uninhabited. It refers to, "not productive, not functional and of having no purpose," Tsumura, *Earth*, 31. He also questions the legitimacy of using the term *chaos* to describe an impersonal waste, including, not only anti-creation, but non-creation, Tsumura, *Earth*, 168. Goldingay states in an analogous way that the term chaos is "both suggestive and misleading," Goldingay, *Genesis*, 27.

2b		and darkness[16] covered the face of the deep,[17]
2c		while a wind[18] from God swept[19] over the face of the waters.
3a		Then God said,
b		"Let there be light";
c		*and there was light.*
4a		*And God saw that the light was good;*[20]
b		and God separated the light from the darkness.
5a		God called the light Day,
b		and the darkness he called Night.
c		*And there was evening and there was morning, day one.*
6a		And God said,
b		"Let there be a dome in the midst of the waters,
c		and let it separate the waters from the waters."
7a		So God made the dome
b		and separated the waters that were under the dome
c		from the waters that were above the dome.
d		*And it was so.*
8a		God called the dome Sky.
b		*And there was evening and there was morning, the second day.*

16. *Chōsjèkh* is *darkness* and thus not light.

17. *T*ᵉ*hōm* refers to water normally under the earth. Tsumura observes that this term is included in the meaning of the term *'èrèts* (i.e., a case of hyponymy). Hence, the author assumes that God created also the tᵉhōm-water.
Tsumura, "The Doctrine of Creation ex Nihilo," 19. Furthermore, it should be noted that the Septuagint (LXX) does not use the word "chaos."

18. *Rūach* stands for different meanings: 1) breath as source of life (and synonym of nᵉsjāmāh— Job 33:4); 2) wind; 3) *Rūach 'ᵉlōhīm* refers to God's creation activity (Gen 8:1; Exod 14:21) and so is different from seeing it as a wind sent by God. The Hebrew tongue denotes both concepts—wind and (divine) spirit—by the same word, because the two ideas were closely connected in ancient Hebrew thought. Arnold states that its use could be either "wind" or "spirit" or in certain metaphoric contexts, both, Arnold, *Genesis*, 38. Keil and Delitzsch consider it as "the principle of all life working upon the formless waste," Keil and Delitzsch, *Pentateuch*, 49.

19. *Mᵉrachèfèt* denotes a present participle: *hovering* [NIB; DBY] and *moving* [RSV], while other translations go for the past simple tense: *swept* [NRS] and *hovered* [JPS]. One should think of an eagle that stirs up its nest, that flutters over its young, spreading out its wings, catching them, bearing them on its pinions (Deuteronomy 32:9–12). Like birds hovering overhead, so YHWH of hosts will protect Jerusalem (Isaiah 31:5).

20. The Hebrew *thōv* means "good." It expresses the satisfaction of an artist who has finished his work and concludes that the result corresponds exactly to the way he imagined it.

The Age of Life on Earth

9a   And God said,
b   "Let the waters under the sky be gathered together into one place,
c   and let the dry land appear."
d   *And it was so.*
10a   God called the dry land earth,
b   and the waters that were gathered together he called Seas.
c   *And God saw that it was good.*
11a   Then God said,
b   "Let the earth put forth vegetation:
c   plants yielding seed,
d   and fruit trees of every kind on earth
e   that bear fruit with the seed in it."
f   *And it was so.*
12a   The earth brought forth vegetation: plants yielding seed of every kind,
b   and trees of every kind bearing fruit with the seed in it.
c   *And God saw that it was good.*
13a   *And there was evening and there was morning, the third day.*
14a   And God said,
b   "Let there be lights in the dome of the sky
c   to separate the day from the night;
d   and let them be for signs and for seasons and for days and years,
15a   and let them be lights in the dome of the sky
b   to give light upon the earth."
c   *And it was so.*
16a   God made the two great lights
b   —the greater light to rule the day
c   and the lesser light to rule the night
d   —and the stars.
17a   God set them in the dome of the sky
b   to give light upon the earth,
18a   to rule over the day and over the night,
b   and to separate the light from the darkness.
c   *And God saw that it was good.*
19a   *And there was evening and there was morning, the fourth day.*
20a   And God said,
b   "Let the waters bring forth swarms of living creatures,

The Creation Narrative in Genesis 1:1–2:4a

c	and let birds fly above the earth across the dome of the sky."
21a	So God created the great sea monsters
b	and every living creature that moves, of every kind, with which the waters swarm,
c	and every winged bird of every kind.
d	*And God saw that it was good.*
22a	God blessed them, saying,
b	"Be fruitful and multiply
c	and fill the waters in the seas,
d	and let birds multiply on the earth."
23a	*And there was evening and there was morning, the fifth day.*
24a	And God said,
b	"Let the earth bring forth living creatures of every kind:
c	cattle and creeping things and wild animals of the earth of every kind."
d	*And it was so.*
25a	God made the wild animals of the earth of every kind, and the cattle of every kind,
b	and everything that creeps upon the ground of every kind.
c	*And God saw that it was good.*
26a	Then God said,
b	"Let us make humankind in our image, according to our likeness;
c	and let them have dominion over the fish of the sea, and over the birds of the air,
d	and over the cattle, and over all the wild animals of the earth,
e	and over every creeping thing that creeps up on the earth."
27a	So God created humankind in his image,
b	in the image of God he created them;
c	male and female he created them.
28a	God blessed them,
b	and God said to them,
c	"Be fruitful and multiply, and fill the earth and subdue it;
d	and have dominion over the fish of the sea and over the birds of the air
e	and over every living thing that moves upon the earth."
29a	God said,
b	"See, I have given you every plant yielding seed that is upon the face of all the earth,

c		and every tree with seed in its fruit;
d		you shall have them for food.
30a		And to every beast of the earth, and to every bird of the air,
b		and to everything that creeps on the earth, everything that has the breath of life,
c		I have given every green plant for food."
d		And it was so.
31a		*God saw everything that he had made,*
b		*and indeed, it was very good.*
c		*And there was evening and there was morning, the sixth day.*
2:1		Thus the heavens and the earth were finished,[21] and all their multitude.
2a		And on the seventh day God finished the work that he had done,
b		and he rested on the seventh day from all the work that he had done.
3a		So God blessed the seventh day
b		and hallowed it,
c		because on it God rested from all the work
d		that he had done in creation.
4a		These are the generations of the heavens and the earth when they were created.

1.2.4 Eye-catching Repetitions[22]

Readers of this narrative[23] note immediately that there are many eye-catching repetitions. The technique of repetition is very characteristic of Bible narratives. Repetitions were primarily intended to focus the readers' attention on the most important things in the narrative. The narrators had a didactic goal in mind. They wanted to anchor these narratives about the past, containing the experiences of both common people and their heroes, in the memory of their listeners and their descendants.

21. Though better "were already completed" from the Hebrew verb *kālāh* (also in 2a), as in Gen 49:33 and in Exod 40:33. See also Gen 17:22 and 24:19 where it refers to one who had finished speaking.

22. See among others Alter, *Biblical Narrative*, chapter 5; Bar-Efrat, *Narrative Art*. 9, chapter 5 C; Licht, *Storytelling*, chapters 3 and 4; Sternberg, *Biblical Narrative*), chapter 11.

23. Genesis 1 is exalted prose with a highly stylized language with no chapter division, no verse division and a repeated pattern. It shows a symmetry with five components: *introduction-command-report-evaluation-time*. Result? Easy to remember and to memorize.

The Creation Narrative in Genesis 1:1–2:4a

The most striking repetition is, of course, "and there was evening and there was morning,"[24] each time indicating which day it is. Mentioning first the *evening* and then the *morning* has to do with the Hebrew conception of time. It assumed that a new day did not start until the previous day had ended. Seen in this way, "one day" corresponded to twenty-four hours, and that would not be the case if one reckoned from sunrise to sunset.

That the series of *seven* days starts in the text with *day one* instead of with *the first day* has to do with the fact that at that specific moment, the following days were not yet brought up. They appear, but later, and are indicated by ordinal numbers: "second day," "third day," etc.

Then God said, "Let there be light;"
    And God saw that the light was *good*;
        And there was evening and there was morning, day *one*.
And God said, "Let there be a dome in the midst of the waters, . . ."
    And there was evening and there was morning, *second day*.
And God said, "Let the waters under the sky be gathered . . ."
    And God saw that it was *good*.
And God said, "Let the earth put forth vegetation: . . ."
    And God saw that it was *good*.
        And there was evening and there was morning, *third day*.
And God said, "Let there be lights in the dome of the sky . . ."
    And God saw that it was *good*.
        And there was evening and there was morning, *fourth day*.
And God said, "Let the waters bring forth swarms of living creatures, . . ."
    And God saw that it was *good*.
        And there was evening and there was morning, *fifth day*.
And God said, "Let the earth bring forth living creatures of every kind: . . ."
    And God saw that it was *good*.
Then God said, "Let us make humankind in our image, . . ."
    God saw everything that he had made, and indeed, it was *very good*.
        And there was evening and there was morning, *the sixth day*.
And on *the seventh* day God finished the work that he had done,
and he rested on *the seventh* day from all the work that he had done.
So, God blessed *the seventh* day and hallowed it, . . .

---

24. 1:5, 8, 13, 19, 23 and Ch. 3.

The paragraph of the *seventh* day does not have the sentence "there was evening and there was morning." Readers, therefore, should not expect another day to follow. With the *seven* days, therefore, the week is complete. *The sixth* and *the seventh* day have the definite article. They thereby break the repetitive sequence of the former days that lack an article ("second day," "third day," ...). That is why the sixth and seventh days require special attention from readers. Both days, therefore function as the true highlights within the narrative process: the creation of *man* (1:26–31) and *the resting of God* (2:1–3).

Another sentence that comes back repeatedly is "and God saw that it was *good*." The word *good* is the translation of the Hebrew *thōv*. It indicates that something corresponds to the initial intention. God had imagined it exactly like this. The *seventh* time it sounds is when "God saw everything that he had made, and indeed, it was *very good*" (1:31). This translation of *m^eōd thōv* corresponds to our *super-good*. Consequently, all creation receives that qualification, including the creation of man and woman.[25]

1.2.5 The Course of the Narrative

Whoever reads the narrative in one go will soon notice its logical development. After the introduction (1:1) followed by the description of the initial situation (1:2), eight creation works are reviewed in ascending order. As in the following scheme, they are spread over the six days (1:3–31). They commence in the same way with "and God said: ...," after which he acts or lets an action take place.

This structure offers a clear picture of the course of God's creation activities. It starts with *an unordered and empty situation,* meaning without any life (1:2a). In complete darkness that reigns over the bodies of water, God's breath or wind comes into action upon the surface of "the deep," which is the (global) primordial ocean (2b). He *is fluttering* above it like an eagle does above its nest with young to which it transfers life energy (2c). It is the harbinger indicating that God will soon speak (3ab) and that he is preparing the moment when he will provide light in the darkness (3c). This is immediately the start of six consecutive days—each with one or two creation works—during which God builds or expands the world. This is shown below.

---

25. Readers therefore have to qualify both man and woman each as "super good."

The Creation Narrative in Genesis 1:1–2:4a

Genesis 1:1–2:4a—Linear Ascendant Structure[26]

A. Intro: God created the heavens and the earth[27]	1:1
B. Initial situation: unorderly and empty—God's breath fluttering	1:2[28]
C. Day 1: light and darkness	1:3–5
D. 2nd day: water under and water above	1:6–8
E. 3rd day: dry land and seas	1:9–10
vegetation	1:11–13
C' 4th day: lights	1:14–19
D' 5th day: birds and fish	1:20–23
E' *the* 6th day: animals	1:24–25
man and woman	1:26–31
B' Final situation *the* 7th day: completed order—God stops working	2:1–3
A' End: the heavens and the earth created	2:4a

Between the initial and final situation, the narrative has two parts that clearly complement each other. The first part, comprised of C, D, and E, presents the creation of "spaces" which are differentiated in a logical order. Accordingly, the second part, comprised of C', D', and E', introduces the "residents" of these spaces. Figuratively, the carriers of light, C', belong to the light, C. The birds and fish, D', fly and swim respectively in the air and in the water, D. Ultimately, the animals and humans, E', come as the residents on the earth, E. In this way, the second series of three days is closely related to the first series of three days. Both series have the same structure: each series has two days with one creation work each and a third day with two creation works. These consecutive works show a clearly progressive line. Their order can hardly be changed.[29] This creation activity of God (1:3–31)

---

26. God does not speak in the passages 1:2 and 2:1–3. In between them there are the ordering and categorizing of the primordial material into a world suitable for human habitation (1:3–1:31). All in all, this does not mean "that God made things out of nothing" but on the contrary that he *brought differentiation*. Its result is an *orderly and populated* world.

27. Earth and $t^eh\bar{o}m$ are (as mentioned earlier) hyponymous which means that $t^eh\bar{o}m$ is a (subordinate) part of the earth. *The earth* is the antonym of *the heavens*.

28. 1:2 gives a description of the way things were before God executed any specific act of creation.

29. The animals and the humans of the sixth day cannot live without being on the dry earth and are certainly in need of the world of plants. The birds require the air, and the fish cannot live outside water. Clearly, man is the one who brings all the creation works

ended with his cessation of work since he had completed an ordered whole or orderly creation (2:1–3).

1.2.6 Thematic Structural Observations

Besides the linear, ascending course of the narrative that represents its development, it is also worthwhile to look at it from a thematic angle. We have seen that the two series of three days show a clear correspondence in their parallel sections and that the narrative totals two times four, i.e., eight creation works.

The first three stand out as *separations,* respectively between light and darkness (day 1), air and water (day 2), and land and seas (day 3a). The following four creation works are characterized by *demarcations* with each having an enumeration of *three* categories respectively: grass, plants yielding seed and trees bearing fruit (day 3b); greater and lesser light and stars (day 4), marine animals, swarming creatures, and birds (day 5) and the *trio of* cattle, crawling animals, and wild beasts (day 6a). Finally, the *seventh* plus one or eighth creation work introduces the human (i.e., man and woman). By expressing humanity's nearness to God through the expression, God's "image and likeness," the human race is *elevated* above all preceding seven creation works (6b). This thematic structure is shown below.

---

to a climax. This is not only because—as the image of God—he is the only one who has anything in common with God, but also because he must rule over the fish, the birds, the cattle, and everything that creeps upon the earth (1:26). Furthermore, he must subdue the whole earth (1:28).

The Creation Narrative in Genesis 1:1–2:4a

Genesis 1:1–2:4a—Thematic Structure[30]

Prologue: God created heaven and earth (1:1–2)

Act I God creates spaces	Act II God creates residents[31]
Day 1. Light, 1:3–5	Day 4. Lights, 1:14–19
separation: light/darkness	*demarcation*: greater light, lesser light, stars
Day 2. Expanse, 1:6–8	Day 5. Aquatic and flying animals, 1:20–23
separation: water below/water above	*demarcation*: marine animals, swarming creatures, birds
Day 3a. Land, 1:9–10	Day 6a. Animals, 1:24–25
separation: land/seas	*demarcation*: cattle, crawling animals, wild beasts
Day 3b. Vegetation, 1:11–13	Day 6b. Mankind, 1:26–31
demarcation: grass, plants yielding seed, trees bearing fruit	*elevation*: God's image, man and woman, rulership

Act III *God completes creation*

Day 7. God has finished his work, 2:1–3

completion: God ceases, blesses, sanctifies

Epilogue: the heavens and the earth created (2:4a)

Finally, it can be seen that the *seventh* day falls outside the pattern, although it follows very naturally the sequence of the preceding six days. On the last day, God does not create anymore. He has *completed* his creation works. *Three* verbs with God as their subject describe his position: he rests—or better, stops (working)—he blesses it, and he sanctifies it (day 7).

---

30. The parallelism between the first trio and the second trio of creation days has been recognized or mentioned by several exegetes: days 1 and 4 (light//luminaries); days 2 and 5 (sea and heaven//fish and fowl) and days 3 and 6 (earth with plants//land creatures and man) with the culmination of the creation process on the seventh day. Cassuto and Beauchamp were some of the first to present them in a structured frame, Cassuto, *Genesis*, 16 and Beauchamp, *Création*, 71–75. Within a similar structure, Wénin and Goldingay specified that there were two creation works of the third and the sixth day. Wénin, *D'Adam à Abraham*, 21 and Goldingay, *Genesis*, 24. The above structure is similar to the former (see 1.2.5), but it adds a number of distinguishing features: spaces and residents; separations, demarcations, elevation, and completion. It also specifies the creation works on days 4 to 6 and describes how God fills in his leisure time on day 7.

31. Or God creates environments and residents.

1.2.7 More Lexical Repetitions

Readers who are familiar with the Hebrew Bible know that narratives, poems, songs, family trees, legal texts, and oracles can contain quite a few repetitions, which may be single words, expressions, phrases, and even entire sentences.

Threefold Repetitions

The writers of the Hebrew Bible prefer *threefold* repetitions. Frequently, they play the role of keyword or emphasis in the narrative. Narrators use such repetitions as a powerful means of clarifying the meaning of something without spelling it out in words. Their motive(s) then become clear to the readers. These *triple* repetitions occur frequently in this narrative of creation.

- *three times* "heavens and earth" as the object of God's creation (1:1; 2:1, 4a),
- *three times* "all the work he had made" within exactly twice *three* days (2:2, 2,3),
- twice *three times*: "and there was evening and there was morning" as a time indication (1:5, 8, 13, 19, 23, 31),
- *three times* "to divide" (1:4, 6, 14),
- *three times* "to increase in number" (1:22, 22, 28),[32]
- *three times* "to bless" (1:22, 28; 2:3),[33]
- *three times* "cattle" (1:24, 25, 26), "to swarm" (1:20, 20, 21),[34] "living creature" (1:20, 21, 24),
- *three times* "image" as a characterization of man (1:26, 27, 27),
- *three times* "the *seventh* day" (2:2, 2, 3).

There appear also groups of *three* successive items.

---

32. Two times addressing the animals (day 5) and the humans (day 6).

33. About the animals of the fifth day (1:22), to the humans on the sixth day (1:26) and to the *seventh* day (2:3).

34. "Let the waters *swarm* with *the swarm* of living creatures" (Alter, *Translation*, 4).

The Creation Narrative in Genesis 1:1–2:4a

- *three* kinds of respectively: vegetation, luminaries, living creatures, and animals,
- *three* successive verbs describing God's behavior on the *seventh* day.

This *triple repetition of words* and sentences on the one hand and a *triple* grouping of objects, living creatures, and verbs on the other, *together strongly emphasize God's creation activities.*

God considers man as his most important creation. So, he makes *three* pronouncements expressively about or to man:

26a And God said: "Let us make man *in our image*, in our likeness . . ."

28b And God said: "Be fruitful and increase in number; fill the earth *and subdue it*, . . ."

29a And God said: "I give you all the seed-bearing plant on the face of the whole earth . . ."

The second and the third statements underline God's warm interest and care for humankind. The first statement emphasizes that he places man in a relationship with himself. God connects himself in an incredibly distinct way with the one that he made into his "image." The Hebrew word *tsèlèm* for "image" means a copy that shows the original very concretely and fully. The narrator uses a second word that God utters, namely *d^eṁut* or "likeness," which weakens the first word. Consequently, man *is* God's image *but not completely.*

Tenfold Repetitions

In addition to these *three specific statements* about man, the narrator uses *seven more times* "and God said":

3a	And God said, "Let there be . . ."
6a	And God said, "Let there be . . ."
9a	And God said, "Let the waters . . ."
11a	And God said, "Let the earth . . ."
14a	And God said, "Let there be . . ."
20a	And God said, "Let the waters . . ."
26a	And God said, "Let the earth . . ."

That brings its number to *ten*.³⁵ When the Hebrew Bible deals somehow with God's rule or kingship, then this figure *ten* or a *tenfold* repetition appears in a number of instances.³⁶ Also appearing ten times are the phrases "to make,"³⁷ "after its kind"³⁸ and "to yield seed," and "seed."³⁹

Sevenfold Repetitions

Moreover, various words and verbs occur *seven* times:⁴⁰

- "God saw that it was good" as an evaluation,⁴¹ with the superlative "very good" for the *seventh* time,⁴²
- "*and there was (waj^{e}hī) light*" (*'ōr*) plus its Hebrew equivalent "*and it was (waj^{e}hī) so (khēn)*" functioning both as confirming notices,⁴³
- "to create" (*bārā'*), "to make" (*'āśāh*), "to see" (*rā'āh*) in 1:3–31,
- "to creep"/"creeping"; "to fly"/"bird" and "to give light"/"light." Each of these three pairs has the same Hebrew stem.
- or in a multiple of seven:⁴⁴

---

35. "And God said" in 1:3, 6, 9, 11, 14, 20, 24, 26, 28, 29.

36. In addition to these *ten creation words*, Bible readers count, for example, *ten plagues* in Egypt. By them, Israel's God proves his ruling power over Pharaoh and his gods. On Mount Sinai, YHWH communicates his majestic *ten words* (which is a more correct translation of the Hebrew *hadd^{e}vārīm* than the word *commandments*). They summarize the covenant that he offers to Israel in order to constitute his "kingdom" of priests. God's command or reign in the creation narrative is therefore evident. Not only so by his creation acts but also from his *tenfold* speaking.

37. 1:7, 11, 12, 16, 25, 25, 31; 2:2, 2,3.

38. 1:11, 12, 12, 21, 21, 24, 24, 25, 25, 25.

39. 1:11, 11, 11, 12, 12, 12, 29, 29, 29, 29.

40. Readers sometimes simply do not notice this. At the end of God's creation works, the *seventh* evaluation uses the superlative m^{e}ōd thōv or "very good." Overall, this repeated evaluation forms a *sevenfold* chorus that rhythmically underlines God's satisfaction with his own work.

41. *Thōv* or "good" is not to be understood as a moral value but as a functional quality (see 2:18 where man's *being alone* is qualified as "not good").

42. 1:4, 10, 12, 18, 21, 25, 31.

43. 1:7, 9, 11, 15, 24, 30. According to Cassuto the basic meaning of *khēn* is "firm," "like an established thing; so it came to pass, and so it has remained for all time," Cassuto, *Genesis*, 34. This is also the first of four meanings of *khēn* in KBL 442–443.

44. *Seven times*: "to see" (1:4, 10, 12, 18, 21, 25, 31); "good" (1:4, 10, 12, 18, 21, 25, 31); "to create" (1:1, 21, 27, 27, 27; 2:3,4); "to crawl" (1:21, 24, 25, 26, 26, 28, 30); "bird" (1:20,

The Creation Narrative in Genesis 1:1–2:4a

- fourteen times: "day" (*jōm*),
- twenty-one times: "earth" (*'èrèts*), "heaven" (*sjāmajīm*) together with "expanse"(*rāqī'ᵃ*).

It is interesting to note that the phrase "God saw that it was good" appears after each creation work except that of the second day. Similarly, the phrase "and it was so" does not appear in connection with the fifth day. These repetitions and omissions do not appear to be coincidences or mere mistakes. They are simply the narrator's intention. These instances should not be taken as indicating that God was not satisfied with day two[45] or that there was no confirmation of God's activity on the fifth day.[46]

The word that is found by far the most refers to "God" (*'ᵉlōhīm*). The text is full of it. Whoever takes the effort to count them ends up with *thirty-five times*![47] In light of all the previous *sevens*, this multiple of seven can hardly be a coincidence. It draws the readers' full attention to the one

---

21, 22, 26, 28, 29) and "flying" (1:20).

Fourteen times: "day" (1:5, 5, 8, 13, 14, 14, 16, 18, 19, 22, 31; 2:2, 2, 3); thirteen times (almost *fourteen times*) "light" (1:3, 3, 4, 4, 5, 18) and "lights" (1:14, 15, 16, 16, 16) plus "to give light" (1:15, 17) having the same Hebrew stem.

Twenty-one times: "earth" (1:1, 2, 10, 11, 11, 12, 15, 17, 20, 22, 24, 24, 26, 26, 28, 28, 29, 30, 30; 2:1, 4a) and *twelve times* "heaven" (1:1, 8, 9, 14, 15, 17, 20, 26, 28, 30, 2:1, 4a) plus *nine times* "expanse" (1:6, 7, 7, 7, 8, 14, 15, 17, 20), totaling twenty-one times.

45. The above-mentioned clause is mentioned exactly *seven* times, and this harmonizes with other *sevenfold* repetitions (see below). It is also possible that day two was chosen for the omission because the "waters"—related to "the deep" in 1:2b—might not have been considered as good or pleasant by the narrator. This thought harmonizes with the fact that Israelites—who were not sailors and not accustomed to the sea—experienced a certain fear and distrust of the mighty waters. Accordingly, "waters" were often used to symbolize the mighty powers of world empires or hostile kingdoms. The second-century Greek translators of the Hebrew Masoretic text (MT) or what has been called the Septuagint (LXX) inserted right at this spot (between 1:8a en 8b) "and God saw that it was good." In this way, they harmonized the paragraph of the second day with those of the five other days. Some modern commentators consider this Septuagint reading to be correct. It is however very doubtful that the Septuagint translators were right in adapting the Hebrew text in this way (see below 6. More lexical repetitions).

46. Here also the LXX adds "it was so" with the purpose of harmonizing and conforming with the other creation days. But footnote 43 makes it clear that part of the meaning of this phrase is "and so it has remained for all time." One reason why this clause could not be used by the narrator for the creation work on the fifth day is that these great creatures—the great sea monsters (*hattannīnim haggᵉdōlīm*)—did not survive in later times (e.g., Isa 27:1; Ps 74:13; Jer 51:34). Cassuto, Genesis, 49).

47. *Thirty-five times*: "God" (1:1, 2, 3, 4, 4, 5, 6, 7, 8, 9, 10, 10, 11, 12, 14, 16, 17, 18, 20, 21, 21, 22, 24, 25, 25, 26, 27, 27, 28, 28, 29, 31; 2:2, 3.3).

and only figure in the creation narrative who speaks, who acts, and who determines everything.

The fact that the narrator really programmed these *sevens* also becomes apparent from the number of words in the Hebrew source text.[48]

- *seven* words compose verse one,
- *fourteen* words are found in verse two,
- there are *thirty-five* words dealing with the *seventh* day (2:1–3):
  » the three middle sentences each have *seven* words,
  » with *the seventh day* situated in their respective midst.

The writer presents his narrative in "keys" and in waves of *seven* words or groups of words. These seven repetitions and multiples of seven can be considered as a kind of brand name for, or the key characteristic of, this creation narrative. Contrary to the popular idea that the number seven expresses perfection, a word that does not even exist in Hebrew, it refers more precisely to *fullness or plenitude*. Could it be more strongly emphasized? Hardly conceivable! In sum, this narrative not only wants to express in all ways that God's creation is not only achieved *in seven days* but also that *the seventh day* occupies an indisputably significant place.

1.2.8 Observations about the Creation of Man

In terms of representation, the Bible narrator lifts the creation of man to a *threefold* higher (language) level. God's creation activities are described in a telling way, but for man's creation, the narrator switches over to a more elevated style, namely, to poetry. Within the narratives of the Hebrew Bible, it is the highest and most powerful mode of expression.[49]

Not only does the writer emphasize *three* times that God created man, but also *three* times that these beings constitute his image. He does this with *three* parallel lines of poetry (1:27),[50] each subsequent verse clarifies the preceding one.

---

48. Before God starts off with his creation works the Genesis narrator thus uses respectively *seven and fourteen words*. In its beginning paragraph readers count indeed *twenty-one* words (1:1–2). When he describes the *seventh* day wherein God completes his creation, he does this with exactly *thirty-five* words (2:1–3).

49. It distinguishes itself very strongly from (normal) narration.

50. This is called a progressive synonym parallelism with the lack of any rhyme.

After all, the information in the first line of poetry is not entirely clear. To whom does "in *his* image" refer? To God or to man? The second line eliminates that lack of clarity by specifying "in the image of . . . God." But how should readers interpret that expression? The third line takes the plunge: God's image, that is, man and woman (or male and female).

FIGURE 4

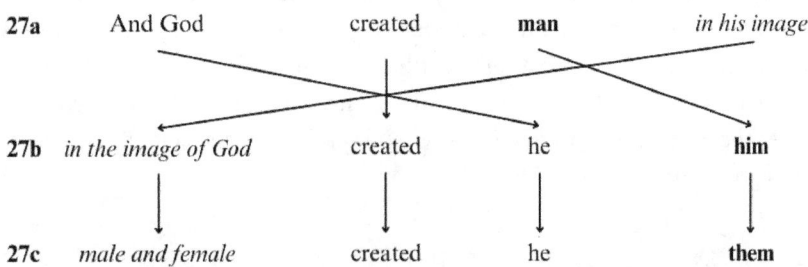

The creation of man thus stands out in the narrative structure far beyond all other works. And quite rightly so, because in his capacity and duties, he really takes the most prominent place. Man is the highlight or zenith of all creation works.[51]

Indeed, the narrator makes it clear that all *seven* previous works are there *for the purpose of preparing an environment for man*.[52] Moreover, he must subdue and populate the earth (the sixth day). Unlike all other works, the human being *'ādām*, while linked with the soil *'ªdāmāh*, has God's "image and likeness" (1:26) and so also has a close relationship with God. He is earthly in origin but also borrows something from God's level, and so is not entirely earthly. In this way, man can represent his creator in the world and pursue his actions. He is given the task of being the ruler of the earth while reflecting God as the ruler of the universe.[53]

---

51. Humans, therefore, should not have a poor opinion of themselves.

52. The light is to see (day 1); the air to breathe (day 2); the dry land to live on and to till. The plants and trees serve as food and, as it were, as furniture (day 3); the luminaries provide light and indicate time and seasons (day 4); man must rule over the fish, the birds (day 5) and over the land animals (day 6).

53. Readers therefore can easily call the human "king of the earth." Essential to this attribution is his multiplying and becoming numerous.

1.2.9 Observations about the Seventh Day

God has completed his creation works, and to conclude, he seals them by ceasing to work on the seventh day. His so-called "resting" means that God stops working. Moreover, he blesses and hallows it.

In this context, the meaning of the verb "to bless" is a bit like "to cause it to multiply." Just as God's blessing of the animals of day five and the humans (day 6) was in order that they multiply, so the seventh day seems to be meant to be repeated again and again![54] God's "hallowing" of that day refers to his assigning it a special place. It has a completely distinctive character when compared to the previous six days. The fact that the narrative emphasizes the seventh day in diverse ways and places it in a special light reflects its significance to God.[55]

1.2.10 Observations about God

God is the Only Acting Figure

In the narrative, God acts as the only player. He occupies and controls the entire stage with his speech and actions. He performs various functions in the execution of creation. As a hydraulic engineer, he separates water and land, as an electrician, he places lights on the sky dome, as a gardener he plants trees and takes care of young greenery and seed-bearing plants. Not only does he invent all life forms—he also creates them into being. Whenever he says that something must be done or that he himself has accomplished something there is the short sentence "and it was (so)."

Remarkably, the reader of the narrative has to go without any information about God. There is no attempt to prove that God exists. The narrator does not even introduce him. The reader must simply presuppose his existence. He also remains in the dark about his method of creating. The

---

54. *The seventh day* does not end in the way the *six* preceding days do. So, readers may assume that it was meant to be repeated . . . ?

55. Given the nature and the destiny of man as being created in God's image, the narrative suggests that man can only imitate God's creation works to a certain extent. He can also perform this role by resting on *the seventh day*. During six days he can perform his duties, but also—just like God—he can stop working on *the seventh day*. By resting every week on that specific day, man blesses and sanctifies it. Through this practice of—what later is called —the sabbath day, he identifies himself with his creator. He is then, as it were, on God's wavelength. Figuratively, readers can therefore speak of an encounter with God on that day. Jewish tradition has turned this into a practice with the aim of considering and honoring *the seventh day* as the queen of days within the week.

The Creation Narrative in Genesis 1:1–2:4a

text says that God creates by speaking. He announces and realizes each work. The narrative uses the verb "to create" for this. No subject other than God is associated with this verb in the Hebrew Bible. So, God makes things that man is incapable of producing.

The reader can only partially infer who God really is and what he is like from his speeches, acts, and evaluations. Only in the creation of man does he come a little closer to being visible. After all, God announces that he will create man in "his image and his likeness." That means that man has something divine and—if one might say so—that God has something in common with man.

God is an Orderly and Superior Creator

The careful structure of the creation narrative depicts God's systematic approach. He creates divisions—between light and dark, water above and below, water and earth—and draws boundaries so that everything has a place. He even divides plants, birds, fish, and animals into various categories, although, of course, not modern, scientific categories. About ten times the narrator uses the expression "according to its nature (kind)." He also gives the sun, the moon, and the stars in the heavens a domain over which they may hold sway. He appoints the "great (*gādōl*) light" to rule over the day and the "small (*qāthōn*) light" to rule over the night. He also gives them the task of setting fixed times of days and years (1:14). It is very interesting for the reader that neither God nor the narrator gives them proper names. This is very revolutionary because these heavenly bodies certainly did have names among all the nations around Ancient Israel and were even worshipped as main gods. The fact that they are not named in the Hebrew Bible means that they deserve no esteem and are simply part of the universe. A greater humiliation could hardly be imagined in the Ancient Near East. Moreover, God makes them appear on the scene of the world only on the fourth day.

Even the great sea monsters (*hattannīnim haggᵉdōlīm*) are no match for the narrator's God. Although he mentions them together with every living creature that moves, of every kind, with which the waters swarm, and with every winged bird of every kind (1:21), they are not part of these general categories of animals. He introduces the former in a special way. While for most of the denizens of water and air, he quotes God as saying: "*Let the waters bring forth swarms of living creatures*," he specifies that "*God created* the great sea monsters." He does that with an evident purpose. In Mesopotamia (and in Egypt), the gods fought with these monsters, whereas the narrator here makes the clear statement that Israel's God is not their opponent but that he created them. In this way, the narrator places emphasis on his sovereignty over them.[56]

God is a Satisfied King of the Universe

As noted earlier, after every work of creation—except for that on the second day—it is stated that God found it good and therefore adequate. The *seventh* time it is the superlative, "very good." However, this does not mean that creation is "perfect" or "finished." After all, this cannot be reconciled with man's command to subjugate creation, to rule over the animals and to populate the earth. For God, the work was done and he then leaves it to his image and likeness to continue the work. From the above, it may rightly be inferred that the biblical narrative argues that God is the king of the universe and transcends all life. He is the unique, undisputed inventor and maker of all that exists.

1.2.11 Partial Conclusion (Part I): A Reading exercise

The first creation narrative (Gen 1:1–2:4a) is a large literary unit in which everything appears to be related to everything else. Its form and its content go hand in hand in a skilled way.[57] The parts of the text are aligned and inextricably linked. The great care exercised in their choice and use creates an internally ordered whole. Words and expressions are well-considered and weighted. The repetition of certain words (or groups of words) *three, seven,* and *ten* times raises them to keywords or expressions. Consequently, they function as signposts, set accents, and bring important data to the surface.[58]

---

56. See Cassuto, *Genesis*, 49–50; Wenham, *Genesis 1-15*, 24. "They represent a specialized subgroup of creatures singled out of the generic crowd." Walton, *Genesis*, 126; "By using the verb "to create" precisely with these animals, the narrator here emphasizes that these so-called primordial monsters are not gods, but only creatures." Jagersma, *Genesis*, 28.

57. Not to be seen as a photo but as a painting on which God's activities are being structured and arranged.

58. The use of key words is one of the characteristics of biblical narrative. They concern words or word stems that are repeated in a meaningful way within a text. Numerous authors point to these characteristic word-repetitions and call them indeed *key words*, following Buber, who introduces them as *leitwörter*. See, *Schrift*, 211. Chopineau defines Buber's *leitwort* as *follows*: "By a guiding word (translated literally from the French *mot-guide*) one should understand a word or a root which, within a text, a series of texts or

The Creation Narrative in Genesis 1:1–2:4a

This reading exercise has been a fascinating experience since the narrative about creation turns out itself to be an impressive "creation" or a literary work of art. The varied form of the narrative stimulates our wonder and admiration for the way it is told. It helps readers to understand its content and meaning, particularly as it focuses on the creating God, his image (i.e., man), and his s*eventh* day.

In sum, the agenda of Gen 1:1–2:4a is three-dimensional for it wants:

- to be experienced as *glorifying God* as the inconceivable creator of the heavens and the earth and the imposing ruler over all elements of nature. It is a confession of faith *that he alone* is worthy to be praised;
- to be seen *as instructing humans*—the crowning piece of God's creation—about who they are: the image of God with an implicit instruction to imitate God; and
- to be understood *as assigning man and woman* the tasks of procreation and caring for the earth.

1.3 A GENRE DEFINITION

Before assessing more precisely the purpose of the first creation narrative, it is important to define its relationship with the rest of the Book of Genesis and, through this process, to qualify its genre.

1.3.1 The Creation Narrative in the Book of Genesis

The compact narrative about the creation of the world (1:1–2:4a) appears to function only as a stepping-stone. Therefore, one should read the book completely. Only then can we identify its central theme, namely, Israel's fertility and resultant increase in population.[59]

The scroll of Genesis contains five narrative acts. They present its five main characters:

---

a set of texts, is repeated in a significant way. To the one who follows these repetitions, a meaning of the text opens or becomes clearer or even becomes strongly evident." Chopineau, "Texte et parole," 57–90 (59). Bar-Efrat clarifies: "In other words, the meaning is not expressed by any supplement to the actual story, through exposition of the ideas or views, but becomes apparent from the story itself, through the repetition of key words." (Bar-Efrat, *Narrative Art*, 212–14); See also Alter, *Art*, 121–23; Seybold, *Poetik*, 76–81, 96, 174–75, 281; Sonnet, "L'analyse narrative," 47–94.

59. Fokkelman, *Genesis*, 42–43.

Adam	Noah	Abram	Jacob	Joseph
1:1–5:32	6:1–11:26	11:27–25:18	25:19–37:1	37:2–50:26

Genesis starts by telling the "primeval narrative"—spread over eleven chapters—with Adam and Noah as the first two main characters. From these arise the peoples of the world in general and the Semitic peoples in particular. The narrator then spends thirty-nine chapters on a progenitor narrative with Abram, Jacob, and Joseph as the main protagonists and Isaac in the background.[60] Only in the last chapters does the real purpose of the book become clear—to present the origin of the people of Israel (49:1–50:26).

The creation of Israel thus begins—long before its own origin—with the creation of heaven and earth and humankind. From this beginning have arisen the peoples of the world in general and the Semitic peoples in particular. Among the latter are Terah and his son, Abram, who is personally called by YHWH. After a first selection, the Ishmaelites (as descendants of his son, Ishmael) drop out of the story. It is the same with the Edomites (descendants of Jacob's son, Esau). The narrative finishes with the Israelites (as descendants of Jacob).

1.3.2 What Kind of History is this Creation Narrative?

What kind of history is represented by the creation narrative? There are plenty of choices.[61] According to the translations of the New Revised Standard Version (NRSV, 1989) and the Jewish Publication Society (JPS, 1917), Gen 2:4a reads as "these are *the generations* of the heavens and of the earth when they were created." It is the meaning of the word "generations" in this sentence that plays a decisive role in the search for a plausible answer to our question. The word "generations" is a favored rendition in English of the word *tōlᵉdōt* in the Hebrew original text. It is a plural form, derived from the verb *jālad*, which means "to beget." Thus, *tōlᵉdōt* is possibly best

---

60. The *tōlᵉdōt*-structuring clauses link these narratives all together with the Primeval Story of Genesis 1–11, suggesting that the diverse stories collected here are really only one story. See also Arnold, *Genesis*, 126.

61. A romantic representation of the creation event? A general, national, or sacred narrative of Israel? A religion narrative with mythical elements? A philosophical or theological treatise? A factual account of events and actions that can withstand the test of historical-scientific criteria? A scientific presentation of how it all played out back then?

represented by the plural of the word "begettings" and, derived from that, by "descendance history."[62]

The word tōl*e*dōt does not appear in the introduction of the narrative about the origin of the world (1:1), but at the end of it. It functions as a postscript (2:4a). Immediately afterwards, the narrator zooms in on other things about that origin (2:4b–25). After the first mention of tōl*e*dōt in Gen 2:4a it occurs another *twelve* times, of which the *twelfth* concerns Jacob, to whom YHWH gives the name Israel, who would have *twelve* sons. The following overview from the JPS version, which translates the word tōl*e*dōt consistently with the Hebrew text, lists these occurrences.

The tōl*e*dōt *in Genesis (JPS)*

2:4a	These are *the generations* of the heaven and of the earth when they were created.[63]
5:1	This is the book of *the generations* of Adam ...
6:9	These are *the generations* of Noah ...
10:1	Now these are *the generations* of the sons of Noah: Shem, Ham, and Japheth ...
10:32	These are the families of the sons of Noah, after their *generations*, in their nations; ...
11:10	These are *the generations* of Shem.
11:27	Now these are *the generations* of Terah ...
25:12	Now these are *the generations* of Ishmael ...
25:13	And these are the names of the sons of Ishmael, by their names, according to their *generations*:
25:19	And these are *the generations* of Isaac, Abraham's son ...
36:1	Now these are *the generations* of Esau - the same is Edom.
36:9	And these are *the generations* of Esau the father of the Edomites ...
37:2	These are *the generations* of Jacob.

---

62. These tōl*e*dōt always relate to the story of the men who were conceived, their experiences and their achievements. However, they always take place within the framework of whether they go about with God.

63. Distinct from the *twelve* sentences with their tōl*e*dōt of X—referring to the humans as the fathers and as subjects of the begetting (i.e., genitive objectivus mode or direct object)—the heavens and earth are the objects of the begetting (i.e., genitive subjectivus mode subject). Fokkelman, "*Genesis*," 41.

By the time the narrator of Genesis introduces the actual genealogy of Adam (5:1) and elaborates it (5:2–32), he had already introduced his readers to this first man (Genesis 2–4). The word *tōlᵉdōt* thus seems to function there (5:1) as a literary (narrative) hinge connecting two related parts of the text,[64] just as 2:4a does it between the first and the second creation narratives (1:1–2:4a and 2:4b–4:26).[65]

1.3.3 Natural and Unnatural Begettings

The *twelve* (!) *tōlᵉdōt* or "begetting" narratives are like genealogies and family trees.[66] The genre of *tōlᵉdōt* narratives does not aim at literary aesthetics but intends to contribute to the central theme of the Genesis scroll, namely *fertility and becoming numerous.*[67]

Nine of the *twelve* *tōlᵉdōt* narratives concern natural begettings or generations. What else could one expect? Procreating is the normal thing. However, *three* *tōlᵉdōt* narratives present unnatural begettings. Over three generations, there are no natural births from father to son since there are three successive barren wives: Sarah, Rebekah, and Rachel. These are significant obstacles to procreation. However, YHWH intervenes these three times "creatively" by removing the obstacle, and these women then give birth to sons. Therefore, as a matter of speech, he becomes the progenitor.

---

64. Genesis 2:4a represents a transitional technique. It joins successive textual units (i.e., 1:1–2:4a and 2:4b–25) together. These *tōlᵉdōt* sentences either indicate the overture of a list or function as its end.

65. This means that the stories about persons on the list which readers get to know—before the mention of this word *tōlᵉdōt*—do not stop. The earlier information helps them to evaluate better the later experiences in the follow-up stories.

66. The Hebrew word *tōlᵉdōt* is thus related to family trees, descendances and genealogies as the result of the fertility of the human figures mentioned therein. Other choices for its translation are: "lineage" (Alter, *Translation*, 2 2); "descendants" (Arnold, *Genesis*, 51); "history" (Cassuto, *Genesis*, 273); "lines of descent" (Goldingay, *Genesis*, 110); "account" (Walton, *Genesis*, 274) and "family history" (Wenham, *Genesis 1–15*, 117). Sometimes they tell a few things about the experiences of their most prominent figures. Central to this is always the lesser or the greater relationship of these figures with their God YHWH.

67. While progressing in Genesis, readers become spectators of the various and not-always-successful choices, initiatives and activities of its main figures, but they find that God always remains in control.

Furthermore, he promises the husbands, Abraham, Isaac, and Jacob (alias Israel), numerous offspring.[68]

These three procreations by God are also, in a sense, his works of creation. So, not only the heavens and the earth owe their being to God's creation work, but also the people of Israel. Without YHWH's deliberate creation, Israel would not even have existed.

The neighboring nations of Ancient Israel considered the contribution of their gods to the births of people as an ordinary matter. They saw the growth of crops and the pregnancies of animals and humans as the result of the sexual activities of their gods. These were aroused by, among other things, the sexual intercourse of their priests and priestesses with their believers. The births of Isaac, Jacob, and Joseph might superficially appear to fit into that frame, but readers hear (so to speak) the Bible narrator protesting vigorously against this view, asserting that "our God is absolutely not a fertility god," but a God who creates by *himself*. This is conveyed by the preceding narrative in which the word *to create* is strongly emphasized.[69]

---

68. To Abraham: "I will indeed bless you, and I will make your offspring as numerous as the stars of heaven and as the sand that is on the seashore. And your offspring shall possess the gate of their enemies" (21:17). To Isaac: "I will bless you and make your offspring numerous for my servant Abraham's sake" (26:24). To Jacob: "I am God Almighty: be fruitful and multiply; a nation and a company of nations shall come from you, and kings shall spring from you" (35:11).

69. Neighboring peoples had fertility gods, but their fertility had to be initiated through human sexual activities giving rise to the begetting of children. In a way YHWH "begot" the heavens and the earth but the Genesis' narrator claims that he is not a fertility but a *creating* God and therefore he adds: "when they were created" (2:4a). Conclusion: the heavens and the earth only exist because of God, and this is also the case for the people of Israel. Fokkelman develops this idea in a really interesting way. It deserves to be quoted in full: "The exceptional usage attracts the reader's attention. Everywhere else "the *tōlᵉdōt* of X" refers to human beings as fathers and as subjects of begetting, but 2:4a raises the radical question whether heaven and earth may be objects of God's begetting. The word *tōlᵉdōt* is, then, a metaphor which, approaching the boundaries of the taboo in Israel's strict sexual morals, carries the oblique question that the cosmos may have originated in a sexual act of God. It becomes evident how daring a game the writer is playing when we consider the world from which Israelite belief wished to dissociate itself: a world characterized by natural religion, fertility rites, cyclic thinking and sacred prostitution; a world in which the idea of creation as the product of divine intercourse was a commonplace." Fokkelman, *Genesis*, 41.

1.3.4 General Similarities Between the *Tōlᵉdōt* of Creation (1:1–2:4a) and the *Tōlᵉdōt* of Terah (11:27–25:11)

Beginning with Gen 11:27, the *tōlᵉdōt* of Terah[70] presents the experiences of his son Abram in *twenty-one* narratives, henceforth called "Abram narratives" and indicated as (B). These are shown below.

1. 11:26–32 Prologue: Abram's birth and background,[71]
2. 12:1–3 God invites Abram to leave Haran,
3. 12:4–9 God promises Abram the land for his descendants,
4. 12:10–20 Abram cheats Pharaoh,
5. 13:1–18 Abram and Lot separate. God's renewed promise (Land and Offspring),
6. 14:1–24 Abram's victory and meeting with the kings of Salem and Sodom,
7. 15:1–24 Promise, covenant and sign,
8. 16:1–16 Hagar's flight and birth of Abram's son Ishmael,
9. 17:1–27 Promise of posterity, covenant and circumcision,
10. 18:1–16 Announcement of Isaac's Birth,
11. 18:17–33 YHWH involves Abram in his plan to destroy Sodom and Gomorrah, whereupon Abram pleads for the righteous in these cities,
12. 19:1–29 Destruction of Sodom and Gomorrah,
13. 19:30–38 Lot's daughters bear him sons,
14. 20:1–18 Abraham cheats on King Abimelech,
15. 21:1–21 Birth of Isaac and expulsion of Hagar and Ishmael,
16. 21:22–34 Abram's covenant with King Abimelech,
17. 22:1–19 Abraham tested and blessed,

---

70. "Terah took his son Abram and his grandson Lot son of Haran, and his daughter-in-law Sarai, his son Abram's wife, and they went out together from Ur of the Chaldeans to go into the land of Canaan" (Genesis 11:31 NRS) but when they came to Haran, they settled there. So, it was a good initiative, but he does not reach his goal. The narrative of 11:27–32 functions as the introduction or prologue of the act or cycle of Abram.

71. Hamilton states that the focus in these verses is on Terah and his three sons and their wives. Hamilton, *Genesis*, 362.

18. 22:20–24 Abraham's brother Nahor begat twelve sons,
19. 23:1–20 Sarah dies, and Abraham buys a piece of land,
20. 24:1–67 Isaac's marriage to Rebekah,
21. 25:11 Epilogue: Abram's final stage of life and death.

These run parallel with the creation *tōlᵉdōt*, henceforth indicated as (A), which accounts for only *thirty-five* verses in the Masoretic Text. Despite this quantitative disproportion, there are many similarities in terms of text delimitation, main figure(s), prologue, and epilogue. As shown earlier, the creation narrative (A) highlights the number *seven* and *sevenfold* word repetitions. Also noted earlier, "sevens" can be regarded as its key characteristic or brand name. This also applies to the *twenty-one* Abram narratives (B), although proportionately their frequency is not quite so high. Interestingly, one can notice quite a few other parallel and corresponding elements between these two *tōlᵉdōt* narratives. These are dual theme, course, sequence, structure, entry, climax, and ending, as represented below.

	Creation narrative (A)	**Abram narratives (B)**
Tōlᵉdōt of:	heaven and earth	Terah
Narrative:	1 narrative of 35 verses	21 narratives
Theme:	works: spaces & habitats	promises: land & offspring
Course:	7 linear ascending days	7 linear ascending episodes
Sequence:	logical & not to be altered	logical & not to be altered
Structure:	thematically parallel	thematically parallel
Entry:	unordered & empty	Ur of Chaldeans & sterility
Climax:	"be fruitful and numerous"	innumerable offspring
Ending:	creation completed	descendants assured
Brand name:	number 7 & 35x ELOHIM	number 7 & 42x YHWH

The Abram narratives (B) also turn out to have a linear ascending series of *seven* scenes with *seven* divine encounters clearly situated in time and place, which is clearly analogous to the creation narrative.[72] These seven scenes show a path in which the dual theme of *land* and *offspring* unfolds in *seven* steps. YHWH, whose name appears *forty-two* times (or six times seven), makes himself known *seven* times to Abram. Each time

---

72. Buber calls these episodes *sieben Offenbarungen* (i.e., *seven* revelations). Buber, "Abraham der Seher," 871–95.

he addresses him with a *promise*. Furthermore, *seven* times YHWH makes him to *see,* and he *speaks* to him about his future *offspring*. The creation narrative (A) and the Abram narratives (B) thus each present *seven* logically consecutive episodes, as shown below.

day 1 about *space* (parallel to)
encounter 1: from Ur to a *land* (for?) your great nation (or offspring)
    day 2 about *space* (parallel to)
    encounter 2: this *land* for your offspring
        day 3 about *space* (parallel to)
        encounter 3: *the whole land* for your innumerable offspring
            day 4 about *residents* (parallel to)
            encounter 4: *your offspring* in *this land* between Nile and Euphrates
                day 5 about *residents* (parallel to)
                encounter 5: your *offspring* will get the whole Canaan forever
                    day 6 / about *residents* (parallel to)
                    encounter 6: your *offspring* in a year's time
                        day 7 about *completion* (parallel to)
                        encounter 7: *your mega countless offspring*

The similarities between (A) and (B) are obvious:

- The sixth day and "the sixth" encounter each lead respectively to an impressive climax: the creation of man as the image of God and the long-awaited birth of Abraham's physical son. Both are prepared by *seven* previous creation works and *seven* previous experiences and are effectively rounded off,

- All the narrated events culminate respectively in a *seventh* creation day (A) and Abraham's *seventh* encounter (B),

- So, God's creation works are completed on the *seventh* day (2:1-3) and Abraham's interactions with YHWH reach their intended goal during the *seventh* encounter (22:1-19): Abraham will have an innumerable offspring whereby all nations will be blessed.

The Creation Narrative in Genesis 1:1–2:4a

1.3.5 A Thematic Examination of the Abram Narratives

Further evidence that the Abram narratives (B)—which are part of the *tōlᵉdōt* of Terah—run remarkably parallel with those of the *tōlᵉdōt* of heaven and earth (A) is provided by a closer examination of internal structures and themes. Between prologue and epilogue, two main parts, or acts, followed by a third concluding act, can be distinguished. The narrator's focus on the promised *land* in the first act (chapters 12–14) shifts from the fourth revelation to the promised *offspring* in the second act (chapters 15–21). Between these *seven* specific contact moments, other experiences are mentioned, which are related to a lesser and greater extent to YHWH's promises expressed in this regard.

The first act (hereafter known as *Act I*) consists of four episodes about the *land* that YHWH promises to Abram (12:1–14:24).

- Episode 1: Abram has to say goodbye to his past and is assigned a *land* by YHWH, in which he builds two altars to YHWH (12:1–9),
- Episode 2: His wrong choice to go to Egypt results in Abram's material gain, but not in God's blessing (12:10–20),
- Episode 3a: After Abram's return to the *land*, Lot goes to live near Sodom and Gomorrah. Abram remains in the land, whereupon God shows him all the *land* that he promised him (13:1–18),
- Episode 3b: After Abram's liberation raid, he is blessed and celebrated, and his presence in the *land* is assured. On that occasion, he distances himself completely from the king of Sodom (14:1–24).

The second act (hereafter known as *Act II*) also has four episodes, this time about his future *generation* (15:1–21:34).

- Episode 4: YHWH promises Abram a son. Moreover, he indicates the country in which his numerous *offspring* will live (15:1–21),
- Episode 5: It turns out to be a wrong choice to acquire his *offspring* through an Egyptian slave girl (16:1–16),
- Episode 6a: Ishmael does not qualify as the promised *offspring* of Abram. YHWH appoints a son from his own wife (17:1–27),
- Episode 6b: YHWH assures Abram that about a year later, Sarah will give birth to *his son* (18:1–21: 34).

In addition to the above, a thematic structure can also be distinguished. The ideas of *separation, demarcation,* and *elevation* are found in this later narrative, as in the creation narrative. This is shown below.

Tōlᵉdōt of Terah—Genesis 11:27–25:11 (B) - Thematic Structure

Prologue: Terah's children and Abram's childlessness (Gen 11:27–32)[73]

Act I: YHWH promises a land	Act II: YHWH promises an offspring
Episode 1. land allocated, 12:1–9	Episode 4. offspring allocated, 15:1–21
separation: away from Haran to Canaan where two altars are constructed	*demarcation*: not Damascene but own son; in Canaan between Nile and Euphrates
Episode 2. wrong chosen country, 12:10–20	Episode 5. wrongly chosen offspring, 16:1–16
separation: not Egypt but Canaan	*demarcation*: not through Egyptian slave girl
Episode 3a. land designated, 13:1–18	Episode 6a. offspring designated, 17:1–27
separation: Lot at Sodom, Abram in Canaan	*demarcation*: not Ishmael but Sarah's son
Episode 3b. land assured, 14:1–24	Episode 6b. offspring assured, 18:1–21:34
demarcation: blessing (Abram) + rejection (Sodom) tithe of all possessions	*elevation*: Isaac is celebrated, but Ishmael is not *seven* lambs of sheep and cattle

Act III: YHWH blesses Abraham and his offspring

Episode 7. offspring promise confirmed – 22:1–19

completion: God provides – knows – blesses

Epilogue: Sarah's death, Abraham's extra begotten, Isaac's marriage, and Abraham's death (Genesis 22:20–25:11)

In the third act (referred to as III), it appears to Abram and to the readers that all YHWH's promises are being jeopardized (Gen 22:1–19). The supreme test, because of Abraham's obedience, ends in YHWH's greatest promise and most abundant blessing. YHWH confirms this with a

---

73. The overall theme in Genesis is "fertility," which means that the dual mention of Sarah's barrenness at the start of the Abram narratives catches the eye and gets full emphasis. See also Arnold, *Genesis*, 28.

sworn oath (Gen 22:17). YHWH says literally: *to bless, yes I will bless you* and *to multiply, yes I will multiply* your offspring. This way of wording is the strongest confirmation imaginable in Hebrew. That is how it will really happen.

Making his future offspring "as numerous as the stars of heaven and as the sand that is on the seashore" is added as an extra reinforcement. The fact that YHWH adds that all the nations of the world will be blessed through Abraham's offspring is a confirmation of his very first promise to Abram (Gen 12:1–3). So, on Mount Moriah, he meets a God who has now truly become his. It is a God who provides for him, knows him, and blesses him.

The thematic repetitions within the Abram narratives, which allow readers of later episodes to link back to earlier episodes, facilitate their placement within the whole of the twenty-one Abram narratives.

1.3.6 Summary of Parallels Between the Creation Narrative and the Abram Narratives

We have seen that the narrator of the Genesis scroll appears to have arranged his presentation of *Terah's tōleḏōt*, particularly its Abram narratives (B), in such a way that their structure gives the impression of imitating the earlier *tōleḏōt of the heaven and the earth* (A). Readers who have an eye for their respective presentations—of prologues and epilogues, demarcation of acts, and organization of the episodes—notice interesting similarities. Some of these are easy to identify, like the matching distribution of God's creation works and Abram's experiences. Others need more focused attention, such as concerning motives, implicit connections, and sometimes also vocabulary.

A comparison of the structure of the two *tōleḏōt* narratives given in sections 1.2.5, 1.2.6, and 1.3.5 seems to confirm and strengthen their mutual relationship. This is due in part to their parallel narrative lines and literary structure, and in part to multiple similarities which occur in all kinds of ways. These include:

- prologues and epilogues with analogous data,
- *three* acts:
    » the first: creation of spaces (A) and promise of the land (B)

- » the second: creation of residents (A) and promise of posterity (B)
- » the third: God completes his creation works (A) and YHWH confirms his offspring's promise (B),
- series: *twice three* days (A) and *twice three* episodes (B),
- a pivot point: at the *fourth* day (A) and at the *fourth* episode (B),
- *eight* creation works within *six* days (A) and *eight* episodes in the framework of *six* revelations (B):
  - » pattern: one creation work + one creation work + two creation works (A), one episode + one episode + two episodes (B)
  - » *two* related works of creation on the third and on the sixth day (A), *two* related events during the third episode (about Sodom), and during the sixth episode about Sarah's son (B).
- *three* separations accomplished respectively on the first, second, and third day,[74]
- *four* completed demarcations:
  - » between species of plants on the third day, between light carriers on the fourth day, between animals on the fifth day, between animals on the sixth day (A); between blessing (Abram) and rejection (Sodom's king), between Eliezer of Damascus and his own son, offspring not via an Egyptian woman, between Ishmael and Sarah's son (B).
- *one* striking elevation:
  - » prepared by *seven* works (A) and by *seven* episodes (B)
  - » as the eighth creation work: man as God's image on the sixth day (A) and during the eighth episode: Isaac's birth as Abraham's son at the occasion of the sixth encounter (B).
- *seventh* day (A) and *seventh* revelation (B)
  - » these follow on the previous six days (A) and on the previous six episodes (B)
  - » these occupy a separate position, as they are not linked to (A2 or B2)

---

74. (A): light and darkness; waters below and waters above; sea and land; (B): Haran and Canaan; Egypt and Canaan; Sodom and Canaan.

> » they function as a pinnacle in the completion of creation (A) and in the confirmation (with an oath) of Abraham's future progeny (B)
> » They are respectively accompanied by God's blessing (A) and YHWH's blessing (B). :

All days and episodes are connected in such a way as to form a harmonious textual network. Changes in their respective order, interrelation, and position would mean that they no longer highlight the purposeful intent of the narrator.

1.3.7 Partial Conclusion: Definition of Genre

1. Based on the *twelve* other uses of the term in Genesis, the text of 1:1–2:4a is to be identified as *a tōlᵉdōt (or "begetting") narrative*. Nine of these other twelve describe the coming into being of people through natural begettings. However, *three* of them are quite unnatural since they are due to God's removal of the obstacle of barrenness on the part of the founding mothers of Israel. This people, would not have existed without his special intervention. Consequently, God emerges not only as the creator of the heavens and the earth but also, in an incredibly special and unparalleled way, of the people of Israel.[75] Amidst all the other nations, Israel really stands out for its special divine origin.

2. Furthermore, the literary presentation of the Abram narratives also demonstrates that in many aspects, Israel's creation is tightly connected with the first creation narrative. The mutual similarities and resemblances are very telling. *Both creations are not the result of a natural process but of effective creation works of Israel's God, YHWH.*

3. Rather than standing alone as an ancillary to the main message of Genesis, the *tōlᵉdōt* of the heavens and the earth introduces the central theme of the book: *fertility followed by posterity*. So, by the end of Genesis, Israel has fulfilled God's commission to man (in Gen 1:28) to be fruitful and to multiply.

4. The creation narrative therefore functions *as a blueprint to understand Israel's origin* and existence.

75. Arnold puts this as follows: "cosmic beginnings and Israel's beginnings are tied together theologically as one story," Arnold, *Genesis*, 126.

BIBLIOGRAPHY

Alter, Robert. *The Art of Biblical Narrative*. New York: Basic Books, 1981.
———. *Genesis. Translation and Commentary*. New York: Norton, 1997.
Arnold, Bill T. *Genesis*. Cambridge: Cambridge University Press, 2009.
Bandstra, Barry. *Genesis 1-11. A Handbook on the Hebrew Text*. Waco, TX: Baylor University Press, 2008.
Bar-Efrat, Shimon. *Narrative Art in the Bible*. Sheffield: Almond, 1989.
Beauchamp, Paul. *Création et Séparation. Etude exégétique du chapitre premier de la Genése*. Paris: Aubier-Montaigne, 1969.
Buber, Martin. "Abraham der Seher." In *Werke, Zweiter Band, Schriften zur Bibel*, 871-95. Heidelberg/München: Kösel/Lambert Schneider, 1964.
———. *Die fünf Bücher der Weisung: Die Schrift. Verdeutscht von Martin Buber gemeinsam mit Franz Rosenzweig*, 1. Heidelberg: Verlag Lambert Schneider, 1976.
Buber, Martin, and Franz Rosenzweig. *Die Schrift und Ihre Verdeutschung*. Berlin: Schocken, 1936.
Cassuto, Umberto M. D. *Commentary on the Book of Genesis. Part I. From Adam to Noah*. Jerusalem: Magnes, 1978.
Chopineau, Jacques. "Texte et parole. L'art du récit dans l'histoire d'Abraham." In *Quand le texte devient parole. Analecta Bruxellensia*, 6:57-90. Bruxelles: FUTP, 2001.
Cotter, David W. *Genesis*. Collegeville, MN: Liturgical, 2003.
de Fraine, Jean. *Genesis*. Roermond en Maaseik: Romen & Zonen, 1963.
Fokkelman, Jan P. "Genesis." In *The Literary Guide to the Bible*, edited by Robert Alter and Frank Kermode, 36-55. Cambridge: Harvard University Press, 1987.
Goldingay, John. *Genesis*. Grand Rapids: Baker Academic, 2020.
Greenwood, Kyle. *Since the Beginning: Interpreting Genesis 1 and 2 through the Ages*. Grand Rapids: Baker, 2018.
Hamilton, Victor P. *The Book of Genesis, Chapters 1-17*. Grand Rapids: Eerdmans, 1990.
Holmstedt, Robert D. "The Restrictive Syntax of Genesis 1:1." *Vetus Testamentum* 58 (2008) 55-66.
Jagersma, Henk. *Genesis 1:1-25:11*. Baarn: Callenbach, 1995.
Joüon, Paul, and Takamitsu Muraoka. *A Grammar of Biblical Hebrew*. Rome: Pontificio Istituto Biblico, 2000.
Keil, Carl F., and Franz Delitzsch. "The Pentateuch." In *Commentary on the Old Testament*, 1. Grand Rapids: Eerdmans, 1980.
Licht, Jacob. *Storytelling in the Bible*. Jerusalem: Magnes, 1978.
Sarna, Nahum M. "The Book of Genesis." In *Encyclopaedia Judaica*, 7:394-98. Jerusalem: Keter, 1978.
Seybold, Klaus D. *Poetik der erzählenden Literatur im Alten Testament*. Stuttgart: Kohlhammer, 2006.
Sonnet, Jean-Pierre. "L'analyse narrative des récits bibliques." In *Manuel d'exégèse de l'Ancien Testament*, edited by Michaele Bauks and Christophe Nihan, 47-94. Geneva: Labor et Fides, 2008.
Speiser, Ephraim A. *Genesis*. Anchor Bible 1. Garden City, NY: Doubleday, 1964.
Sternberg, Meïr. *The Poetics of Biblical Narrative. Ideological Literature and the Drama of Reading*. Bloomington: Indiana University Press, 1983.
Tsumura, David T. "The Doctrine of Creation ex Nihilo and the translation of *tōhû wābōhû*." In *Pentateuchal Traditions in the Late Second Temple Period: Proceedings*

of the International Workshop in Tokyo, August 28–31, 2007. Supplements to the Journal for the Study of Judaism 158, edited by Akio Moriya and Gohei Hata, 3–21. Leiden: Brill, 2012.

———. *The Earth and the Waters in Genesis 1 and 2: A Linguistic Investigation*. Sheffield: Sheffield Academic, 1989.

———. "Genesis and Ancient Near Eastern Stories of Creation and Flood: An Introduction." In *Ancient Near Eastern, Literary, and Linguistic Approaches to Genesis 1–11*, edited by Richard S. Hess and David T. Tsumura, 27–57. University Park: Eisenbrauns PSU Press, 1994.

Turner, Laurence A. *Genesis*. Sheffield: Sheffield Phoenix, 2009.

von Rad, Gerhard. *Genesis. A Commentary*. The Old Testament Library. Philadelphia, PA: The Westminster, 1973 (French edition: *La Genèse*. Geneva: Labor et Fides, 1949).

Waltke, Bruce, K. *Genesis. A Commentary*. Grand Rapids: Zondervan, 2001.

Walton, John H. *Genesis*. Grand Rapids: Zondervan, 2001.

Wenham, Gordon J. *Genesis 1–15*. Word Biblical Commentary 1. Nashville: Zondervan Academic, 1987.

Wénin, André. *D'Adam à Abraham ou les errances de l'humain. Lecture de Genèse 1.1–12.4*. Paris: editions du Cerf, 2013.

2

The Creation Narrative in Genesis 1:1–2:4a
Towards a Proper Reading and Understanding

PART 2

RUDY VAN MOERE

2.1 A CONTEXT EXPLORATION: THE ANCIENT NEAR EAST

ISRAEL'S LITERARY HERITAGE IS dwarfed by the huge literary, religious, and cultural products of the ancient world powers of Egypt, Assyria, and Babylonia. Is it then to be disregarded in favor of the many hieroglyphic narratives on Egypt's imposing buildings and the texts on the countless clay tablets left by the writers from Mesopotamia? Does the Israelite locust vanish in comparison with the Egyptian hippopotamus and the Assyrian-Babylonian lion? In order to be able to give an adequate answer, some comparison and reflection are necessary.

2.1.1 Creation Texts in the Ancient Near East[1]

It might be asked how special is Israel's creation narrative, particularly since it is only available on one of Israel's written scrolls. After all, in the world of the Ancient Near East,[2] it stands alongside other narratives about the

---

1. Speiser and Grayson, "Akkadian Myths and Epics," 62–67, 501–03.
2. Frendo clarifies this terminology by pointing out that nowadays Egypt is politically

origin of the world and humanity.³ How much does it resemble and differ in turn from their conceptions of creation? What image of God, the world, and man predominates in these other narratives? To what extent are they similar to, or different from, Genesis 1:1–2:4a? What does the introduction to the Book of Genesis want to convey to its readers about God, the world, mankind, and . . . Israel?

Present-day readers of creation texts from Ancient Egypt and from Assyria-Babylonia encounter views of God, man, and the world that are alien to them.⁴ Therefore, they need to know something about the geography,⁵ history, culture, and religion of both empires if they are to appreciate these texts at more than face value.

2.1.2 Egyptian Creation Texts⁶

In general, the gods of Egypt can be said to relate to those entities that turn out to be the strongest politically,⁷ and where the natural elements most clearly affect the life of the population.⁸ Thus, the sun functioned as the main, general god, with the privilege of having many names. The creator gods Ra (partly in the form of a falcon, also both god and man) and Atum (the self-created antediluvian god) were the most important of these. The god most popular with the population was Osiris. The god Ptah of

---

and economically not considered as being included in the Middle East. Nevertheless, Egypt played an important role in the history and culture of the ancient Near East, and therefore—according to him—the latter term seems justified. See Frendo, "Israel Princeton 2016, in the Context of the Ancient Near East," 86–105.

3. Arnold considers the ancient cosmogonies of Egypt and Mesopotamia as "the interpretative context for Gen 1." See Arnold, *Genesis*, 29.

4. See e.g., Ringgren, *Religionen des Alten Orients*.

5. *The Macmillan Bible Atlas* revised ed., by Yohanan Aharoni and Michael Avi-Yonah, Macmillan, New York, chart 82.

6. Wilson, "Egyptian Myths, Tales, and Mortuary Texts."

7. Such as Heliopolis, Memphis, Hermopolis and Thebes.

8. The different Egyptian creation myths have some elements in common. They all held that the world had arisen out of the lifeless waters of chaos, called Nu (or Nun) and they also included a pyramid-shaped mound, called the benben, which was the first thing to emerge from the waters. These elements were inspired by the flooding of the Nile River each year. The receding floodwaters left fertile soil in their wake, and the Egyptians may have equated this with the emergence of life from the primeval chaos. The imagery of the pyramidal mound derived from the highest mounds of earth emerging as the river receded.

the influential city of Memphis had the reputation of being a divine sculptor and life provider. Usually, the temples of Egypt pictured the cosmos, in which heaven, earth, and sea each have their place. Following are two examples of Egyptian creation narratives, in which a few gods play a leading role. These illustrate some of the character traits of these gods.

Creation by Atum

In a text from about 2400 BCE, the god Atum rises from the waters of chaos in the form of a prehistoric hill. From that primeval hill, he creates the cosmos and brings forth the first gods, including air, moisture, heaven, and earth. In another version of this narrative, some 400 years later, Atum comes to life by himself from the waters of chaos. He also says:

> "I am the great god who came to life by himself.
> Who is he?
> The great god who came to life by himself.
> It is water.
> He is Nun (or Re), the father of the gods . . .
> Who is he?
> He is Atum, who is in his sun disk."

Creation of Man by the Sun God Ra

In a text from around 2000 BCE, the sun god Ra makes all people equal in their access to the basic needs of life:

> "I made the four winds, that every man might breathe in his time . . .
> I made the great inundation, that the humble might benefit by it like the great . . .
> I made every man like his fellow; and I did not command that they do wrong. It is their hearts which disobey what I have said . . .
> I have created the gods from my sweat, and the people from the tears of my eye."

It is obvious that these texts exude a very different atmosphere and present a completely different content than Israel's creation narrative. This observation also applies to creation narratives from Mesopotamia.

2.1.3 Mesopotamian Creation Texts

Mesopotamia has also contributed to the Ancient Near Eastern arsenal of creation texts. Three important texts deserve attention:

- the epic narrative of *Athrahasis* (different versions between the seventeenth and the eighth centuries BCE),[9]
- the creation narrative *Enuma Elish* from about 1900 to 1800 BCE,
- the epic narrative of Gilgamesh from about 2000 BCE.

Due to limited space, this paper only shows a fragment of the second-mentioned creation narrative.

The *Enuma Elish*,[10] is a work of art contained in *seven* tablets, each of 150 lines. It tells a myth or a prehistoric narrative about the origin of the gods and their bloody battles.

> "When in the height heaven was not named,
> And the earth beneath did not yet bear a name,
> And the primeval Apsu, who begat them,
> And chaos, Tiamat, the mother of them both.
> Their waters were mingled together,
> And no field was formed, no marsh was to be seen;
> When of the gods, none had been called into being,
> And none bore a name, and no destinies were ordained;
> Then were created the gods in the midst of heaven."

In the beginning, there are only the male freshwater ocean Apsu, and the female saltwater ocean Tiamat. These two gods beget so many gods that neither of them can sleep anymore. Therefore, they want to destroy their offspring, but the god Marduk successfully fights Tiamat. He cuts her body to pieces and brings about creation. He makes the sky in the form of a temple with stories and determines the trajectory of the stars and the division of the year. Furthermore, he also creates the moon, the sun, day, and night. He makes clouds, winds, rain, and cold from Tiamat's saliva. He makes one-half of the earth out of Tiamat's head and the other half from her body. In addition, the invincible Marduk expresses his plan to establish a sanctuary on earth called Babylon for himself and his helpers. After this, he creates the animals and the plants, and ends with man. Marduk creates

---

9. Dalley, "Atrahasis," 9–35.

10. King, *Enuma Elish: The Seven Tablets of Creation*; Lambert and Parker, *Enuma Elish. The Babylonian Epic of Creation*, 6–7, 62–63.

him from the blood and bones of a slain rebel god and for the purpose of serving the gods. With his extraordinary strength, he succeeds in creating order in the world.

Every year at the New Year's Eve festival, the *Enuma Elish* was recited to Marduk, the hero of the narrative and the most important god of Babylon.[11]

The Birth of Marduk, the God of Babylon

> "In the chamber of fates, the abode of destinies,
> A god was engendered, the most able and wisest of gods. (line 80)
> ...
> In the heart of Apsu was Marduk created,
> In the heart of holy Apsu was Marduk created.
> He who begot him was Ea, his father;
> She who bore him was Damkina, his mother.
> The breast of goddesses he did suck.
> The nurse that nursed him filled him with awesomeness.
> Alluring was his figure, sparkling the lift of his eyes.
> Lordly was his gait, commanding from of old.
> When Ea saw him, the father who begot him,
> He exulted and glowed, his heart filled with gladness." (line 90)

Whoever compares Genesis with the Egyptian and Mesopotamian creation texts shown above will find that Israel's creation story stands out as a sober narrative in plain language[12] and without superfluous imagery. It is structured very logically and without contradictory data.

2.1.4 Comparison with Israel's Creation Narrative

Without much difficulty, readers will notice similarities and differences between these texts and the first creation narrative of the Hebrew Bible.[13]

---

11. According to Lambert there "is no evidence of Hebrew borrowing from Babylon." Lambert "New Look at the Babylonian Background of Genesis," 287–300.

12. Talon claims that the study on the contextually Ancient Near Eastern and the literary use of the language of the time proves that the temporal language of time in Genesis 1–11 does not refer to the time periods in which the events are described. Such an explanation is therefore according to him, really misguiding. Talon, *Standard Babylonian Creation Myth_ Enuma Elish-Neo-Assyrian Text Corpus Project*.

13. Römer suggests that the deported Judean intellectuals acquired knowledge of the

The Creation Narrative in Genesis 1:1–2:4a

The limitations of this study do not permit the comparison of Gen 1:1–2:4a with each of these narratives separately. However, several general remarks will suffice and provide a sufficiently clear picture.

Similarities between Ancient Near Eastern Creation Myths and Israel's Creation Narrative:

- Both the world and humankind are created by divine power(s).
- The creation activity takes place through their spoken word,
- The creator lives (creators live) eternally,
- The world is created from water,
- A demarcation is made between water and the dry land,
- The mutual equality of all people is underlined,
- Humans are assigned tasks,
- The number seven features prominently: seven tablets; seven gods; seven men and seven women; seven days.

Differences Between the Ancient Near Eastern World and Israel's World:

While there are some similarities, the differences are more noticeable.

- In the Ancient Near East, there is a general polytheism. In Israel, on the other hand, the belief in one God is stubbornly held.[14] Humanity owes its origin to that one God,
- In the A.N.E. texts, the creation of the cosmos (i.e., cosmogony) arises from the previous origin of the gods (i.e., theogony),

---

Babylonian creation texts and therefore the knowledge of the biblical writers can be easily explained. Römer, "Narrative Books in the Hebrew Bible," 118. He also notices that "the major difference between the biblical and the Ancient Near Eastern narratives is the fact that the different epics, novellas, and stories in Genesis-Kings have been compiled into one mega-narrative and have in a lengthy process become *Holy Scripture*. Römer, "Narrative Books in the Hebrew Bible," 120.

14. Wenham notices that Genesis 1 insists that "the powerful deities: sun, moon, stars and sea monsters are merely creatures." Wenham, *Genesis 1–15, Volume 1, Word Biblical Commentary*, XLIX.

- In these texts, the gods fight with each other and with the elements of nature. They are even connected to it organically. For Israel's Bible writers, the elements of nature are completely subject to their one God. He transcends them and he is separate from them,
- In Mesopotamian and Egyptian texts, man is subjected to slave labor, while in the Genesis narrative, he is assigned the role of ruler. Full dominion over nature is allotted to him,
- In the former texts, people function as a plaything of the fighting gods. The biblical creation narrative, on the other hand, is completely devoid of political traits and presents man as a ruler with the status of "image of God,"
- In Babylonian society, the weeks count *seven* days, bearing the names of their *seven* planetary gods. In the Hebrew creation narrative, the first week also counts *seven* days. A new day begins at sunset and not at sunrise and is marked with an ordinal number (i.e., first day, second day, etc.),
- The *seventh* day is also regarded as a special or holy day. However, this day has an unfavorable or dire character in Babylonia. While the *seventh* day in the Israelite narrative is also given a specific place and treatment in the seven-day week, it has a completely opposite quality. This holy day is seen as a blissful day of rest,
- Israel's creation narrative is structured very logically, without contradictory data. The Egyptian and Mesopotamian texts, on the other hand, have a distinctly epic character with a passionate and dramatic style. They are also laced with mythical and sometimes contradictory data.

Within the Ancient Near Eastern context of widespread polytheism, Israel's YHWH is thus an out-of-class God. He had hardly anything in common with the gods of Babylonia (especially) or with those of Ancient Egypt. The narrator of the creation narrative, which acts as an introduction to the Genesis scroll, is absolutely convinced of this. He offers the members of his people a completely different view of the world, of God, and of humanity.

2.1.5 Israel's Subtle and Unmistakable Narrative

The way in which the narrator does this commands admiration. He neither ridicules nor criticizes the ancient Egyptian or Babylonian gods. He does not argue with their believers or their priests. Nor does he set up any evidence to dissuade his compatriots from adopting the Egyptian or Babylonian faith.

The Judean narrator simply presents his people with a sober creation narrative. He wants to teach his people that their God is of a completely different order. Being confronted day in and day out with the Babylonian religion, his fellow citizens in exile will readily recognize his implicit allusions to those gods and their activities.[15] Current readers cannot do that unless they are familiar with that religion and culture. If so, they will also recognize the same allusions in the Babylonian creation texts as they read the Israelite creation narrative.[16]

1. The narrator straightforwardly presents his own God as the sole creator of the universe (1:1) without mentioning any family tree or origins of this God. No trace of other gods is to be seen. In this creation narrative, he uses the universally known generic name *'elōhīm* (God) and then his Israelite proper name, *jhwh or JHWH*; in the second creation narrative.

2. He introduces the initial situation at creation (1:2) with no mythological features but with neutral material images having neither unrest nor conflict. The God in the narrative does what he wants with the matter created by him. So, there is no creation from nothing or *creatio ex*

---

15. Arnold points out that Genesis 1 is not genetically related to the Enuma Elish, nor is it necessarily a direct polemic against it, since the author has a positive agenda. Considering the biblical creation account as a polemic against Egyptian and Mesopotamian accounts is, according to him, "a too negative assessment." Arnold, *Genesis*, 31–32.

16. The majority of biblical scholars see a stronger relationship between the Genesis creation account and the Babylonian creation texts than with the Egyptian ones. These typically choose the Babylonian exile as the time of writing and editing the Enneateuch. A minority hold the converse belief and typically defend the idea that the Pentateuch was written by Moses, who would have possessed knowledge of Egyptian beliefs.

The Age of Life on Earth

nihilo,[17] but a creation out of God: so *creatio ex deo*.[18] God is indepen-

17. 1) this phrase does not appear in the Hebrew Bible and its concept is also absent in Egyptian and Mesopotamian texts. The dogma of *creatio ex nihilo* was also not shared by the Babylonians and Assyrians. Heidel, *Babylonian Genesis*, 37 n. 73.

2) Speiser remarks that if the first clause is considered as an adverbial phrase, the notion of creation from nothing implied in Gen 1:1-3 disappears. The translation then becomes: "When God set about to create heaven and earth—the world being then a formless waste, with darkness over the seas and only an awesome wind sweeping over the water—God said, "Let there be light." Speiser, *Genesis*, 3. See also Alter's translation: "When God began to create heaven and earth, and the earth *then (italics supplied)* was welter and waste and . . ." Alter, *Genesis. Translation and Commentary*, 3.

3) the verb *bārā'* is also used for the creation of the great sea monsters (1:21a), of man (27ab) and even of Israel (Isa 43:15). Consequently, it does not point exclusively to a creation out of nothing. Wenham observes that "the text never states *what God creates out of* (italics ed.)." Wenham, *Genesis 1-15*, 14.

4) Paul correctly points out that *bārā'* does not imply *creatio ex nihilo* but that "it denotes, as it does throughout the Bible, a divine activity that is effortlessly effected." Shalom M. P. Paul, "Creation and Cosmology in the Bible." In *Encyclopaedia Judaica*, 5 (Jerusalem: Keter, 1972), 1059-63.

5) Tsumura makes a quite interesting observation about the theological term *creatio ex nihilo*. According to him, it must be understood "as describing the situation where nothing exists without God's creative activity." "In other words," he says, "anything that exists, except God himself, exists as the result of God's creative activity." Tsumura, "Chaos and Chaoskampf in the Bible," 963-69.

6) The phrase *creatio ex nihilo* appears only for the first time in 2 Maccabees 7:28 and then, of course, not in Hebrew but in Greek: "I beseech you, my child, to look at the heaven and the earth and see everything that is in them and recognize that God did not make them out of things that existed" (RSV).

7) The Latin expression *creatio ex nihilo* became important much later than in biblical times.

18. 1) See the explanation about 2:4a, which represents the end of God's creation works. Grammatically, the *tōlᵉdōt* or "begettings" function thereby as the subject of the heavens and the earth (i.e., genitive objectivus). It implies that God is their "begetter," the one from whom they owe their existence.

2) "I am YHWH, who made all things" (Isa 40:24) and "for he is the one who formed all things" (Jer 10:36).

3) According to Ps 139:7-10 God is omnipresent. Omnipresence is one of God's attributes and according to Rice "it describes God's involvement in the world spatially . . . and it means that there is no part of the universe from which God is excluded." Rice, *Reign of God*, 73. Consequently, why should Bible readers restrict this concept to the time after his action that is described in Gen 1:1-2?

4) The rabbis Eisenberg and Abecassis advance the following interesting thesis which therefore deserves to be quoted in full: "One could say: 'In the beginning was God' since it is he who created the world. . . . What is certain, however, is that he had a history before the beginning: it is the history of God" (23). The word *bārā'*—"he created"—derives from a verb which has a double meaning. On the one hand, it means "to cut." God cut the world, he shaped it, in a way, he sculpted it. That would send us back to the problem

dent of matter. He brings forth from within himself. He calmly creates and arranges whatever he pleases. Furthermore, he does not have any rival power opposite or next to him with which he must deal. He is a transcendent God who rules the whole scene. Readers can hardly imagine a greater, although passive, attack on polytheism in the narrator's time. He degrades the great gods of the Ancient Near East to impotent pawns! The narrator mentions a material earth, describing an initial neutral situation with three elements: (a) *a disorderly* (unstructured) *and desolate* (empty) *situation,* (b) *the darkness,* and (c) *the* (global) *primordial ocean*. For the Mesopotamians, the latter represents particularly negative forces (including sea monsters), which cause strife and unrest.

3. Over this inactive matter, the breath or wind of this independent God appears to be fluttering (and thus generating energy), as does a bird above the nest of its young. After this, God transforms the initial situation into an orderly whole with spatial boundaries and fills it with all kinds of distinct life forms (1:3–31).

4. The great primordial ocean (i.e., $t^eh\bar{o}m$)[19] around the world had extremely negative connotations among the Babylonians. The God of Israel divides these into waters above and waters below, between which he arranges a firmament in the form of a canopy, which he calls "sky" or "heaven" (1:6–8). What a difference from the way the god Marduk cuts Tiamat into two halves. From one half of this goddess, he creates the sky, and from the other half the earth.

---

of raw material ... On the other hand, the verb *bārā'* is related to the adverb *bar* which means "out of"... It means that another reading of the biblical text can be proposed to us: God put the world "out of himself." He kind of expelled or ejected it. So, "In the beginning God expelled heaven and earth" (31-32). "Also, with all due respect to theologians, it should not be said that the world was drawn from nothingness but drawn from God. And even more precisely, pushed, pushed back, expelled by God from the very bosom of God. We can see it clearly: everything, in this language, evokes childbirth. God gave birth to the world by a creative expulsion" (33). Eisenberg and Abecassis, *Bible Ouverte*, 23, 31-33.

19. Tsumura in thoroughly re-examining $t^eh\bar{o}m$ from a linguistic point of view concludes that it is phonologically impossible that $t^eh\bar{o}m$ "ocean" would have been borrowed from Tiamat, the goddess of the sea in the Assyrian-Babylonian texts. Tsumura, "Genesis and Ancient Near Eastern Stories of Creation and Flood," 31.

5. With a masterly statement, God creates light in the darkness, which he does not really make disappear (1:3). He only limits its presence to a period he calls night.

6. God makes the unordered or unstructured and empty or desolate situation disappear, for he lets the waters flow together – which he calls "seas" – so that dry land appears (1:9–10). God then gives rise to plant life in three categories, each of which he divides into innumerable independent species (1:11–13).

7. God hangs two important light bearers in the sky. He does not give these names, like the Babylonians,[20] but a threefold task, which demonstrates their functional use: separating day and night, acting as signs for seasons, days, and years, and shining their light on the earth. God also gives a place to the stars (1:14–19). He gives these innumerable Babylonian gods a mere functional existence.

8. On the fifth day, God subdues, among other things, *the large aquatic animals* – which Babylonians considered to be dreaded sea monsters – as if they were fish in a large aquarium (1:20–23).

9. God makes *all* people in his own image. Very democratic! In contrast, the Babylonians see only their own king as an image of their god. Since they are images of God, the people of the Genesis narrative are all rulers of this world and do not have to work as slaves for him (1:26–31).[21]

10. By affirming all mankind as being in God's image the narrator teaches his readers that they do not need to visit him in a set place, such as a temple. They can do that in time: on the auspicious *seventh* day of each week (2:1–3).

2.1.6 Partial Conclusion: A Context Exploration: The Ancient Near East

A literary comparison between the Genesis' creation narrative and the other Ancient Near Eastern creation accounts reveals how completely different

---

20. The Babylonian sun and moon god are called respectively Shamash and Sin.

21. The multiplication of humans occurs in the creation account in Genesis 1 as well as in the Athrahasis epic. But God institutes it in the former while in the latter the gods try to prevent it. Römer, "*Narrative Books*," 117.

Israel's God is from the gods of the Egyptians and Babylonians. The writer of the first creation narrative in the Hebrew Bible presents his God in a terse manner without using a conflicting or polemic[22] tone, or using defensive, apologetic language. He does not attack the beliefs of the Babylonians or of the Egyptians but talks very calmly about how he sees the God of his people, Israel.[23] Undoubtedly, he thereby encourages his fellow citizens in their belief in their God YHWH and strengthens them in their differentness and in their identity. He seems to be urging them to trust their God.

Within the Ancient Near Eastern context of widespread polytheism, Israel's YHWH is thus an out-of-class God. The narrator of the creation narrative—which acts as an introduction to the Genesis scroll—offers his people a completely different view of the world, God, and mankind.

2.2 A CONTEXT EXPLORATION: GENESIS-KINGS

To understand the true meaning of Israel's first creation narrative, readers need to know to which literary collection the Book of Genesis belongs and to get some idea of the period and situation in which it was written and the intended recipients.

2.2.1 When was Israel's Creation Narrative Written?

Substantive Anchoring and Connecting Elements

The narratives in the scrolls from Genesis to Kings very extensively present the history from the creation of the world to the exile of YHWH's people.[24] Specialists have given this collection of Nine Scrolls – Genesis through Kings – the name *Enneateuch* (i.e., literally "nine books") by analogy with

---

22. According to Arnold, the polemic nature of Genesis 1 over against the Egyptian and Mesopotamian has been overstated and "is not the primary *raison d'être* for the chapter." Arnold, *Genesis*, 30.

23. Current readers must understand the cognitive environment of ancient Israel in order to be able to assess its significance and relevance.

24. In the Masoretic Text (MT) and the Septuagint (LXX) the scrolls Joshua, Judges, Samuel and Kings always follow the Pentateuch. Other versions also present Genesis through Kings (the so-called Enneateuch or "nine-part work") in the same order. The Jewish canon, which has become, as it were, the standardized book order, also does this. The canon prompts a reader to a *lectio continua* (i.e., continuous reading) within over 42 percent of the BHS standard edition (1966/77).

the name *Pentateuch* for the first five scrolls. They connect chronologically in a seamless fashion.[25] This is also evident from the fact that the subject, or theme, with which each scroll ends reappears at the beginning of the next scroll. Thus, the narrative thread of a scroll is not broken off at the end of it, but simply continues in the next scroll, as shown below.[26] It can hardly be otherwise than that there is an editorial structure at the basis of this collection of texts.[27]

A Collection of Nine Scrolls

Scroll	Text and theme	Text and theme	Scroll
	End of scroll	Start of scroll	
Genesis	ch. 46–50 Jacob + 70 persons to Egypt	1:1–7 Jacob + 70 persons in Egypt	Exodus
Exodus	*location*: Sinai ch. 39 priestly garments ch. 40 inauguration of tabernacle	*location*: Sinai ch. 1–7 offering in the tent ch. 8–9 ordination	Leviticus

25. Gosse presents this as the time span between the loss of Eden and the loss of Jerusalem. In Gosse, "L'inclusion de l'ensemble Genèse – II Rois, entre la perte du jardin d'Eden et celle de Jérusalem," 118–211. Fokkelman considers Genesis as a part of a grand design uniting the books of the Torah with Joshua, Judges, Samuel and Kings in one configuration. Fokkelman, "Genesis," 40. Goldingay states that "Genesis 1 is the beginning of the long narrative extending from Genesis to 2 Kings, . . ." Goldingay, *Genesis*, 21.

26. According to Gordon these books are not only grouped in a chronological order, but they are very closely related. He specifies: "Where the Pentateuch ends, the book of Joshua begins, where the book of Joshua ends, the book of Judges begins, and this continues with the books of Samuel and Kings." Gordon, *Vóór de Bijbel. Het gemeenschappelijk verleden van de Griekse en de Hebreeuwse beschaving*, 252–53.

27. Römer points out that Spinoza actually launched the idea of the Enneateuch in 1670 in his *Tractatus theologico-politicus*. In it, he stated that the five books of the Pentateuch and the Early Prophets show such a coherence that they must have belonged to the same historian. Its purpose was to describe Jewish antiquities from the most remote times to the first destruction of Jerusalem. He noted, among other things, that these books are "so closely connected that it is noticeable from this point of view that they are absolutely one story, unquestionably composed by one historian." Römer, "L'historiographie deutéronomiste (HD). Histoire de la recherche et enjeux du débat," 15–16. Rendtorff and Houtman hold an analogous opinion. Rendtorff, *Introduction à l'Ancien Testament*, 225; Houtman, "De Pentateuch," 327 (Dutch).

Leviticus	*location*: Sinai ch. 27 vows – ordination – redemption	*location*: Sinai ch. 3 firstborns replaced by Levites ch. 6 vows – ordination	Numbers
Numbers	ch. 35–36 Commandments via Moses to Israel in the plains of Moab	ch. 1–4 Torah via Moses to Israel in the land of Moab	Deuteronomy
Deuteronomy	31:1–8 Joshua encouraged 34:1–12 Moses' death 34:9–12 Joshua's investiture	1:1–9 Joshua encouraged 1:1 Moses' death 1:2–9 Joshua's investiture	Joshua
Joshua	24:29–30 Joshua's death	1:1 Joshua's death	Judges
Judges	ch. 19–20 Benjamin's misdeeds 21:25 Shiloh – no king in Israel	ch. 1–2 Shiloh – hint for a king Eli's sons' misdeeds ch. 8 demand for a king	Samuel
Samuel	24:18–25 end of David's reign David sacrifices	ch. 1 end of David's reign Adonijah sacrifices	Kings

Moreover, it is noticeable that within the whole of these Nine Scrolls, a number of related themes are being discussed: the promise of a land and living in one's own land, the location of the sanctuary, Torah reading, exile, and return, (from Genesis to Joshua) and tensions between the tribes concerning the monarchy (from Judges – Samuel to Kings).[28] These are elaborated below.

Narrative and thematic lines within the collection

1. *YHWH's promise of a land to Abram* that will reach from the river of Egypt to the river Euphrates (Genesis 15) is presented to Israel by Moses as referring to the promised land (Deuteronomy 32). Joshua realizes the first phase of it (Joshua 24). David achieves the unified kingdom of Israel (2 Samuel 8), and under Solomon, it does indeed reach its maximum extent from the Nile to the Euphrates (1 Kings 4).

2. *The successive placement of the tent sanctuary and the ark of the covenant* in a number of locations. These first occur at Sinai (Exodus 40).

---

28. Römer mentioned at a colloquium in Lausanne in 2005, the following proponents of the Enneateuch hypothesis: P. Weimar and Erich Zenger; H. Chr. Schmitt; Th. Krüger; K. Schmid; E. Aurelius and P. Sacchi.

Later, David places them in his city, Jerusalem (2 Samuel 6). His son, Solomon, builds a temple to replace YHWH's tent (1 Kings 5–7) and installs the ark of the covenant in it (1 Kings 8).

3. *The reading of the Torah* is first undertaken under Moses (Deuteronomy 31). Within the Nine Scrolls, this happens a few more times, and for the last time under Josiah (2 Kings 22).

4. *The exile* is announced several times, and on separate occasions (Leviticus 26; Deuteronomy 28; Joshua 23; 1 Kings 8). This takes place in two stages: for Israel in 2 Kings 17 and for Judah in 2 Kings 25.

5. *The tension between the tribes* concerns the monarchy (Judges – Samuel – Kings).

The Dating of the Final Editing of the Enneateuch

As shown, together these Nine Scrolls form one large literary corpus (or collection of texts). Because of this unity, it strongly appears to have been produced by one writer or by a group of writers and editors (i.e., scholars and priests). The latter option may be the most likely. It can hardly be otherwise than that this was completed after the year 586 BCE. In that year, the events which are described at the end of the scroll of Kings took place. The last chapter talks about the capture of Jerusalem by King Nebuchadnezzar and about the Judean people which he carried away to Babylonia (2 Kgs 25:1–17).[29]

Several texts and parts of the Enneateuch may, of course, have already existed.[30] The author (or authors) of the Nine Scrolls also draws (draw) on a large reservoir of oral traditions from various times and environments. These include parables, legends, sagas, myths, sayings, poems, and songs. Sometimes they make use of temple and palace documents, legal texts, admonitions and prophetic speeches, blessings, and curses. However, the lion's share of the lyrics are folk narratives. During the exile, they were given

---

29. Goldingay is of the opinion that the internal relationship within Genesis – Kings suggests a literary creation at the beginning of the Babylonian exile. Even occasional notes fit in that period of time. Goldingay, *Genesis*, 8.

30. Parts of the narratives in Genesis to Kings were first passed on orally and only later received their written record in which were also inserted reworked materials. The result bears witness to an excellent literary quality, in which traces of this telling event can still be seen.

The Creation Narrative in Genesis 1:1–2:4a

a place in this mega narrative of Israel's history. The above situation in time helps to determine why, and for whom, these Nine Scrolls—including that of Genesis—were written. The most obvious reason will have to do with the experiences of the people who ended up in Babylonian captivity.

2.2.2 The Addressees of the Nine Scrolls

So, it appears that the narrated history in the Nine Scrolls is intended for the deported and traumatized people of Judah.[31] It does not take much imagination—even for current readers—to envision the kilometres-long convoys of Judean prisoners after a long, murderous siege and famine in the city. Under appalling conditions, they must cover about 1,150 km in just four months. Those who survive this misery of fear and deprivation[32] do not have it easy after their arrival. Only after some time can they pursue their own or another profession and build a new life for themselves and their surviving relatives.[33]

A Feeling of Huge Loss

Being uprooted and displaced causes colossal depression among the exiles. Their losses are very drastic. These are summarized below.[34]

- They are far away from family, neighbors, and fellow villagers.
- They have lost home, property, and money.
- They have hardly any hope of a return to their distant homeland.
- It looks like the end of Judah as a nation.
- Jerusalem's walls have been demolished, and many houses destroyed.

---

31. Houtman defines this history as "an explanation for the catastrophe of Jerusalem in 586 with a continuous call to repentance, to faithfulness to the LORD and to his commandments." Cees Houtman, "Geschriften van het Oude Testament." In *Bijbels Handboek, Deel IIA*, ed. Abraham S. van der Woude (Kampen: Kok, 1982), 329 (Dutch).

32. Abecassis, *Pensée juive. 3. Espaces de l'oubli et Mémoires du Temps*, 27.

33. On behalf of YHWH Jeremiah encourages the exiles with the words: "Build houses and live in them; plant gardens and eat what they produce. Take wives and have sons and daughters; take wives for your sons, and give your daughters in marriage, that they may bear sons and daughters; multiply there, and do not decrease" (Jer 29:5–6 NRS).

34. Soggin, *Histoire d'Israël et de Juda*, 318; Lods, *Prophètes d'Israël et les débuts du judaïsme*, 218; Bright, *History of Israel*, 48; Porten, "Exile, Babylonian," 1038.

- The royal palace has been burned, and their king is in the palace prison in Babylon.
- David's dynasty has been broken.
- The temple vessels have been taken to Babylon.
- YHWH's temple has been razed to the ground.
- There has been a cessation of temple services for the remission of sins and reconciliation with YHWH.

The consequences would have been an emotional climate of desperation, despair, and unbelief.[35]

Pressing Questions and Missing Answers

The geographic and ideological uprooting of the exiles understandably raises many questions for them.[36]

- How did this catastrophe happen (to us)?
- Did our God, YHWH, suffer defeat against Marduk, Nebuchadnezzar's Babylonian god?
- What are we to do with YHWH's unconditional promise to David about a lasting dynasty?
- Where is YHWH, actually?
- Where does he reside now that his house in Jerusalem has been destroyed?
- Has he forsaken us? Or ... does he even *not* exist?
- How are we going to continue?
- Will we merge into the Babylonian society and disappear as a people? Who and what are we then?

---

35. Despair, fear, tears and cries are some of the words that describe the catastrophe that they experienced. Some were afraid that YHWH had cut their people off and cancelled their destiny. See, for example, Ezek 33:10 and 37:11 (NRS).

36. Liverani mentions among the several traumatic experiences of the people the destruction of the temple in Jerusalem as a major problem. According to him, problems were not only of theological and moral nature but also of a strictly technical nature: where to situate God? With the destruction of the temple in Jerusalem, the Judeans were no longer able to locate God. Liverani, *Bible et l'invention de l'histoire*, 309.

- Can we ever return to our country?
- What does the future hold for us?

In this emotional climate of desperation, despair, and unbelief, the voices of the prophets Jeremiah and Ezekiel resound. Both blame this catastrophe on the violation of the people's relationship with YHWH.[37] The first one writes his letters of encouragement from Judah, urging them to start a new life. The second of these voices sounds from among them, in Babylon. On the one hand, Ezekiel tries to point out with speeches, visual acts, and texts that they should not put their trust in Babylonia and its god Marduk, nor become infatuated by the idolatrous practices of the Babylonians. On the other hand, he wants to offer them concrete hope from a YHWH perspective.[38]

Explanation Desperately Needed

Doubts about their identity and the reason for their existence occur as the Israelites are rapidly confronted by other religions and gods, including those of the Babylonians. All this means that the exiles are much in need of a solid theological explanation.[39]

They receive it from the writer or the group of writers of the Nine Scrolls, who tell about the history of their people. The narratives remind them of YHWH's actions in the past and talk about who he really is, compared to the Babylonian gods, among others. Thanks to their sublime narrative art in the scrolls, their readers learn to see the history of their people, Israel, from the perspective of their God, YHWH. They learn how he is foundational for the Israelite people because he created them and also how he has traveled with them for hundreds of years without departing from their side.

The telling of their history and the assertion that they are important to their God, YHWH helps the exiles. The authors do not give a doctrinal exposition or some theoretical treatise, but an explanation in the form of

37. Jagersma, *Geschiedenis van Israël in het oudtestamentische tijdvak*, 254.

38. After 586 BCE, Ezekiel's task was no longer to predict the collapse of the state, but to announce and prepare for the future recovery of the nation.

39. Zenger considers the "Exilisches Geschichtswerk" (i.e., exilic history work) (Gen 2:4b–2 Kings 25) as its literary result "which compiled the historic-theological and legal traditions at that time into a single large work." Zenger et al., *Einleitung in das Alte Testament*, 177–78.

narratives, in other words, narrative theology. Much of this material was already known to the readers because it had been circulating within their nation for centuries, passed on orally from generation to generation. The Nine Scrolls thus deal with major events and with prominent figures. They tell about the very beginning with the patriarchs and about the origin of the twelve tribes who form a union around their tent sanctuary. Under the guidance of YHWH, they become a kingdom with a dynasty, a capital, and a temple building. Later, it splits into two separate kingdoms.

The Abram and Jacob narratives, for example, give the exiles a view of their potentialities and their options. Thanks to his father Terah, Abram left the Babylonia of that time, namely Ur of the Chaldeans. In Haran, YHWH asks him to leave again, this time for the land he has in mind for him. Abram acts as a role model for the exiles, and so does Jacob. Just like them, Jacob ended up extremely far from home, in his case in Haran. He lived and worked there and . . . experienced the closeness of their God, YHWH. While traveling back to his native land, that same God did not leave his side and continued to protect him.

2.2.3 Narratives with a Prophetic Character

The narratives in the Nine Scrolls therefore do not represent the products of historians, chroniclers, or reporters, but of *pastors, teachers, and educators.* These priests and sages pursue much the same goal as that of the priestly prophets Jeremiah and Ezekiel and have much the same effect. Prophets encourage their listeners and readers to reflect on their relationships with God, their fellow citizens, other inhabitants of their land, or even the surrounding peoples. Among other things, they call on the people to put their trust in their God YHWH, and to come to terms with him. The writers of the Nine Scrolls do just that, but through narratives. In a sense, these can also be labeled as prophetic. They are clearly not intended to entertain, but to convince, guide, and educate their hearers and readers.

In Jewish tradition, the scrolls from Joshua through Kings are referred to as "Early (or Earlier) Prophets" so as to distinguish them from all the writing prophets, i.e., Isaiah through to Malachi. That description also applies to the first five scrolls, which are in Moses' name. According to his own words and those of YHWH, he, too, is a prophet (Deut 18:15, 18). Certainly, the narratives of the Pentateuch are written from a prophetic perspective, with a focus on the quality and depth of the people's relationship with YHWH. It is important for modern readers to read these narratives carefully (i.e., close reading), as it were, through the glasses of the writers who shared the fate of the Babylonian exiles. This entails some awareness of the political, cultural, and religious history of that period. Failure to do this inevitably results in a mediocre understanding of the message.

Not Purely Historical Narratives

The narratives in Genesis are clearly not eyewitness testimony, nor are they exact accounts of the events related. This also applies to all the narratives in the first eight scrolls and to most of the ones in the King's scroll. Readers soon notice that as they progress through that final scroll, the events recounted take on an increasingly accurate historical character. The account of Jerusalem's siege by Nebuchadnezzar has a comparatively high historical value because of the many details recorded. Furthermore, the facts presented correspond well to other, extrabiblical reports. The same cannot be said, for example, of David's capture of the city Jebus and certainly not for the Joshua-induced fall of Jericho.

The Nine Scrolls thus do not provide their readers with an accurate or complete historical account of all events in the successive periods from Abraham to the captivity. They cannot tell everything or report fully about this period of about 1,200 years. These narratives, therefore, do not claim historical accuracy since historical details were largely inaccessible to the writers. They did not hear about most of the events first or second-hand. Their narratives thus present a very limited selection of events from the life of, for example, Abraham. The way in which the twenty-one narratives unfold and the manner in which they are related to each other demonstrates this clearly, as shown in chapter 1.

This implies that the Genesis narrator has very carefully and specifically fitted well-known traditions into his scroll. For example, readers sometimes come across nearly identical accounts (so-called duplications) or even contradictory narratives. It is remarkable that the compilers do not filter out the similarities or resolve the contradictions, thus bringing them into harmony with each other. This is true for the entire Enneateuch. The fact that they give place to different traditions that circulated among the people shows their profound respect for what they have received. The traditions about Abraham and Isaac (in Genesis) or about Saul and David (in Samuel) are wonderful examples of this.

These folktales generally do not provide an accurate account of what exactly happened. They contain elements that arise from the imagination of the writer. This input is strongest when they put the thoughts of the actors into words. Of course, that also applies when the writers put words into a character's mouth since exact words would rarely have been handed down. These beautifying elements enliven the narratives, making them more colorful, also more powerful. They help fix the stories in the memories of their exiled readers and hearers. Such storytelling traditions and skills were deeply ingrained features of Israelite culture. Moreover, these elements in no way prevent the intended and authentic message from being delivered. The recipients would not have wondered, as might modern readers, about whether every detail was historically correct. Given their circumstances, they would, however, have felt encouraged to trust in their God, YHWH, and to look forward to returning to their country of origin.

Truthfulness and Reliability?

Of course, modern readers might understandably wonder whether such narratives can be regarded as truthful or reliable. Modern times are based on a more rational worldview, or so we like to think, where all is submitted to historical, scientific, and philosophical scrutiny. Clearly, the narratives within the Nine Scrolls should not be subjected to such analysis. On the other hand, neither should they be regarded as either fiction or fantasy in historical dress. They are a unique literary oeuvre, in which some details of real, historical events have been selected or added for very specific, and very valid, theological reasons. In this sense, they can be regarded as being both truthful and reliable. Readers should pay close attention not only to the history of the Ancient Near East (particularly Israel) but its aesthetic, literary, and cultural dimensions as well.

Narratives with an Educational and Pedagogical Purpose[40]

All in all, with the creation narrative and the rest of Genesis, the narrator tries strongly to counteract the Babylonian religious influences.[41] As

---

40. Römer clarifies the usefulness of narratives. They are not only of universal application but entertain audiences by teaching, legitimizing and criticizing and by creating cohesion among a group. Römer, "*Narrative Books,*" 113.

41. Soggin describes the strong Babylonian influence that the exiles underwent. It

The Creation Narrative in Genesis 1:1–2:4a

pastor, teacher, and educator, the narrator wants to encourage, teach, and strengthen readers by making them remember and understand[42] the following pivotal points:

1. They do not need to feel intimidated by the power of the Babylonians or of their gods, including the chief god Marduk. Their YHWH is the only God. He is also the creator of, and the ruler over, the entire world and over all nations, including their Babylonian rulers.

2. As stated in the scroll of Genesis, as a people, they are a unique creation of God. If YHWH was able to form them into a nation back then, then he could realize that end again, even with them as scattered exiles.

3. YHWH escorted their ancestors Abram and Jacob from ancient Babylonia to the land of Israel. If he did that, then he could do it again.

4. As taught in the creation and Abram narratives, the right choices (separations and demarcations) culminate in beautiful climaxes and elevations (namely, man as God's image and Isaac as Abram's son). The exiles can therefore trust that once back in their country of origin, they too can reach such highlights, provided they do not mix with the people living there.

5. The elements of nature are not to be feared. Furthermore, they are absolutely not gods, because it was their own God who created them.

6. They do not need to be concerned about the (so-called) very unfavorable effect of the *seventh* day in Babylonian society, because the creation narrative teaches them just the opposite. They may nevertheless fully experience that day as a blessed time.

7. As a people, they have a specific place and commission among the peoples of the world.

8. As a people, they should be proud of their identity because YHWH is there for them, and they can trust him.

---

consisted for example of the Mesopotamian calendar, the Babylonian anthroponyms, the so-called square alphabet and the use of the Aramaic language which then became the international language. Soggin, *Histoire*, 318–19.

42. Liverani explains that the Judean priests and scribes found in Babylon a fertile ground to consolidate their own "philosophy of history" (i.e., Deuteronomist ideology) from before the fall, based on the sin-punishment relationship. Liverani, *Bible*, 315.

9. Each one of them is an image of God, while in Babylonia that privilege belongs only to the king.
10. As a people (Israel) they are called in all respects, in their limitation and dependence (on God) to function as a role model for the nations of the world.

2.2.4 Back to Genesis and the First Creation Narrative

Creator of the World

Undoubtedly, Genesis presents God as the creator of the world and everything in and around it. But some readers of the book of Genesis fixate on the account of the creation of this world, from which they want answers to their modern questions. Some read up to the chapters on the mega-flood. Why don't they read further? It may be because they are more interested in the origin of mankind generally, with whom they identify more easily than in the ancestors of the Israelite people. But the previous chapter shows that the creation of the world and the narratives of Israel's origin are closely linked. They should then, therefore, be read together. A primary focus on the first few chapters of Genesis not only does injustice to Israel's creation but gives rise to contradictory interpretations of the beginning of all things.

Creator of all People

We have noted that anyone who reads the entire book of Genesis will soon notice on the basis of its content that the narrator's interest is more in human history than in that of the physical world. The Gen 1:1–2:4a creation narrative presents YHWH as the creator of *all* people. The narrator appears to use a three-dimensional approach. Firstly, he affirms his huge admiration for this creative God. The account is a hymn of praise to this God who is the only creator. Secondly, he introduces man, both male and female, as being in the image of this God and clearly urges this awareness upon humanity. Humanity is the pinnacle of God's creation. Thirdly, there is the stated implication of this status, namely that humans are intended as responsible rulers over this earth and all the life created on it. Furthermore, humans are to multiply God's image through procreation. Praise, true human status and awareness, and its attendant responsibility.

The Creation Narrative in Genesis 1:1–2:4a

Genesis begins with Adam and his descendants, whose relationship with God is shipwrecked, culminating in a mega-flood. Although Noah makes a fresh start, the relationship with God is quickly broken by his descendants. This primeval history is covered in just eleven chapters (1:1–11:25).

Creator of the Israelite People and the Judean Exiles

The narrator's interest quickly moves from primordial history to the ancestors of Israel. The primeval history seems to function as a background for the patriarchal history, which continues for some forty chapters (11:26–50:26). A third beginning comes with Abraham. Like him, his descendants make many mistakes but slowly develop a positive relationship with YHWH, so that by the end of Genesis, one can speak of a people of YHWH. This origin of Israel involves far-reaching interventions in the lives of three founding mothers, as earlier discussed. In a sense, this is the main focus of Genesis, for which the creation of the world serves as the introduction.

However, not only does the creation account not stand alone, but the entire book of Genesis does not stand alone. This first scroll introduces the history of the people of Israel. It is therefore improper to interpret its contents separately and thereby disconnect it from the other eight scrolls. The fact that these scrolls come to readers of all ages in Hebrew is another indication that their primary intended readership was Israel. As has been noted, non-Jewish readers have some work to do in order to contextualize and understand the important messages they contain.

While reading the Nine Scrolls, the Judean deportees are urged to feel connected to their past, to stand together in the present of the exile, and to look ahead to a new dawn. Their resilience is fuelled or boosted by it. These scrolls also help them understand the usefulness and meaning of YHWH's guidelines regarding the Sabbath, circumcision, Torah study, and purity laws.[43] When they are applied again – as these narratives encourage them to do – their identity as a people will be strengthened. Thus, however small their community may be within this all-powerful Babylonian world empire, they can still be proud of who they are.

---

43. Noth, *Histoire d'Israël*, 206; Bright, *History*, 349–350.

2.2.5 Partial Conclusion: A Context Exploration: Genesis – Kings

All in all, the creation narrative (Gen 1:1–2:4a) is a teaching narrative about God's role as creator of the world and humanity. Nevertheless, it only serves as an introduction to what comes after: a limited piece of primordial history about the nations of the world, followed by very extensive narratives about God's role in the creation and development of the people of Israel. Since the first narrative of the creation of the world and the narratives of Israel's origins are strongly linked, they should therefore be read together. Concentrating chiefly on the creation narrative does injustice to the narratives concerning Israel's creation. It also leads to an inadequate and even contrary interpretation of the first creation narrative.[44]

It has been shown that the scroll of Genesis does not stand alone. Furthermore, it is, therefore, inappropriate to refer to its content separately, cutting it loose from the other eight scrolls. Genesis functions as an introduction to the complete collection, which is about the origin and history of the people of Israel. Because of their content and of the fact that they are written in Hebrew, these Nine Scrolls—the first creation narrative included—are not addressed directly to other peoples, nor is it really intended for them. It is specially written for the Judean exiles.[45]

Most non-Jewish readers do not approach the Hebrew Bible, including these Nine Scrolls, as a separate section. They see these passages merely as *one part* of the Old Testament, with the Greek (New) Testament as *the second section*. In general, such readers understand the first part in the light of the second. This has a lot of consequences for discerning the meaning of the Nine Scrolls in general and Genesis and its creation narrative in particular. There is thereby a danger that the identity, purpose, and meaning of the latter may be overlooked and or even altered.[46]

---

44. Wenham writes in the same sense: "Though Christian theologians have devoted most of their attention to Gen 1–11 or more precisely Gen 1–3, the rest of the book has been comparatively neglected, although it is about four times as long as the opening chapters. The balance of material in Genesis shows where the editor's interest lies, with the patriarchs rather than with the primeval history. Clearly Gen 1–11 serves simply as background...," Wenham, *Genesis 1–15*, xlv.

45. The Hebrew Bible in general and the Enneateuch in particular belong to the Jewish people. Therefore, they should not be appropriated by Christians or by the Churches. These have no right to do whatever they want with them. They should ask them permission and ask their opinion about how to read and interpret them.

46. To attain an as close as possible initial reading and interpretation of the Hebrew Bible, the latter should remain free from any ecclesiastical, dogmatic, Christological,

2.3 GENERAL CONCLUSION

At the end of our discussion of these four parts of this reading exercise of the Hebrew creation narrative in Gen 1:1–2:4a it is time to come to a general evaluation. The proposed approach has been followed, and the required steps have been taken in order to respect the authenticity and uniqueness of this creation narrative. A repetition of our four partial conclusions would be superfluous. Several concluding remarks will suffice:

1. The austerity and didactic nature of the creation narrative in Gen 1:1–2:4a in the context of the Judean exiles means that it cannot be characterized as, or degraded to, a religious myth from a nebulous past, nor to a childish representation of the beginning of world history.[47] On the other hand, the ingenious narrative-telling style and structure also invalidate the idea that it should be read as if things went exactly like that in the very beginning.

2. The narrative does not provide much information to satisfy the reader's curiosity over issues he/she may see as important. Instead, it lets readers discover the narrator's view. This is what one calls *narrative theology*.[48]

3. The narrator demonstrates a clear account of his faith in God, devoid of any scientific data or theoretical statements, and shares this faith with his Judean people in Babylonia. It is obvious that his creation myth is not intended for paleontologists, biologists, physicists, chemists, geologists, archaeologists, psychologists, sociologists, philosophers, dogmaticians, and mystics.

4. The Genesis narrator seems not so much interested in the "how" and the "when" of the creation event. He does not provide detailed

systematic theological or philosophical input.

47. The evaluation of Vriezen is worth quoting in full: "Genesis 1 shows signs of deep reflection in the field of religion and "natural science" and cannot simply be interpreted as a naive, copied, old mythological representation; it does represent a deeply thought-out worldview. It is certainly the most "modern" of all creation narratives known from the Ancient East. But its real significance lies in the attempt to place cosmology entirely in the light of the belief in the one God." Vriezen, *Hoofdlijnen der theologie van het Oude Testament*, 363.

48. The narrative contains important lessons that the reader—if he/she reads carefully—can dig up from under the surface of the text. This narrative about the magnificent creation turns out to be an impressive "creation," a genuine literary work of art. In any case, a biblical narrative transcends any historical document.

information about the "begetting" and creation mechanisms. He limits God's action to create, make, say, name, separate, and see. As to the "when," readers must be content with the general indication of "in the beginning" and the division of the time into *seven* days. The narrator focuses these verbs completely on God, without proving that he exists. He presents him as the undisputed creator of *all* life, man, and time. He also makes it clear that God rules over *all* the forces of nature in the universe. His *modus operandi* is one of separating, demarcating, elevating, and completing. From an initial unordered and empty situation, God brings forth well-ordered spaces, filling them with life.

5. Besides the above-mentioned emphasis that God is the creator, the narrative development and the narrative structure point the way to the "why" and the "what for" of creation. God creates for the sake of human beings. That is the answer to the "why" question. Man functions as a climax because God elevates him as his image bearer above all that has gone before. He assigns man the role of not only representing him in the world but also multiplying his image in it through procreation.

6. The answer to the "what for" question boils down to the charge that God gives man—as it were, as his partner—to continue the creation by ruling over the earth, plants, and animals. At the same time, readers can infer from the way God defines man as being *in his image* that not only are *all* people created equal, but also that man and woman are *both* in God's image. After the completion of the entire creative event, he completes this by resting on the *seventh* day. The impression is given that man, as his image, will also imitate him in this respect.

7. Gen 1:1–2:4a has all the characteristics of a faith narrative, and therefore it makes absolutely no sense to use it against scientific theories or *vice versa*.[49] Rather than debate between religion and science, it makes much more sense to ask to what extent the creation narrative can still be relevant in the twenty-first century.[50]

---

49. According to Spiekermann the critical investigation of the creation narrative and natural science have developed their own methods and belong to different realms. There is no need for rivalry, but conversation. Spiekermann, "Creation. God and World," 271.

50. Lucas is of the opinion that Genesis 1–11 should be read "as the theological text as it is, instead of 'mining' it for scientific information." Lucas, "Interpreting Genesis in the 21st Century," 1–4.

The Creation Narrative in Genesis 1:1–2:4a

All in all, the creation narrative, and the other narratives within the Nine Scrolls should not be screened or assessed based on aesthetic, literary, and scientific criteria of the twenty-first century. Imposing an anachronic agenda onto the creation narrative is out of the question. Today's criteria do not apply to Israel's storytelling culture, in which the narratives from Genesis to Kings[51] belong. Their writers are not historians, but pastors, teachers, and educators. Thus, current readers should be very attentive to the historical, literary, aesthetic, and cultural criteria of the Ancient Near East in general and of Ancient Israel in particular.

Within the setting of this conference, "The Age of Life on Earth," the following concluding remarks deserve attention:

1. The creation narrative should not be approached by using scientific tools, nomenclature, and concepts, since it has no scientific pretensions, and it does not present the mechanisms or time scales through which God created. The preceding reading exercise of the text, the definition of its genre, the contextual exploration (Ancient Near East and Genesis to Kings), and a philological, literary, and contextual examination of the text—through analysis, observation, description, and evaluation—have contributed to valid theological conclusions.

2. Science and the Hebrew Bible belong to two completely different spheres.[52] They have nothing in common and should therefore not be merged. The purpose of science is to understand the natural world. The Hebrew Bible in general, including the creation narrative, acquaints us with the inspired messages of meaning addressed to the deported Judeans and all those who identify themselves with them. Neither should position itself in a superior way to the other.[53]

3. The Hebrew Bible should not be approached by scientific questions, nor should the field of sciences be approached by the biblical texts.

---

51. These scrolls are about Israel's heritage, and therefore they are never clinical, objective, or comprehensive. They are moving, subjective and eclectic.

52. Link clearly states that the modern interest in uncovering a simple basic structure in all reality is alien to the biblical texts. According to him the Bible and natural science represent two different perspectives. A competition between them leads to a pointless and hopeless impasse. Link, *Schöpfung. Ein theologischer Entwurf im Gegenüber von Naturwissenschaft und Ökologie*, 128.

53. Lucas sees Genesis "as a theological text, expressed in symbolic stories addressed to ancient Hebrews, and not as a scientific text." Lucas, *Interpreting Genesis*, 1.

4. Nowhere in the Hebrew Bible have its authors revealed scientific data beyond that known by the ancient Israelite culture. It is then absolutely inappropriate to ask modern scientific questions of this text.

Finally, the preceding investigation has made clear that the creation narrative is concerned mainly with the genesis or origin of Israel and not about planet Earth's history. It is written *for* and *by* Israel and belongs *to* Israel.[54] Given the findings presented in the partial conclusions of the four parts of this presentation, the creation narrative does not contribute to the debate about the age of life on Earth. So, a debate based on the biblical text between the proponents of Young Earth Creationism and those who accept an old age for life is pointless. Similarly, there is also no textual ground for a debate between creationists and evolutionists. Finally, in these kinds of debates, wouldn't it be wise to learn from the way the creation narrative in Gen 1:1–2:4a is written: not to criticize, nor to polemize, nor to convince with arguments, but simply to present one's own insights?

BIBLIOGRAPHY

Abecassis, Armand. *La pensée juive. 3. Espaces de l'oubli et mémoires du temps*. Paris: Librairie générale française, 1989.
Aharoni, Yohanan, and Michael Avi-Yonah. *The Macmillan Bible Atlas*. Revised ed, chart 82. New York: Macmillan, 1968.
Alter, Robert. *Genesis: Translation and Commentary*. New York: Norton, 1997.
Arnold, Bill T. *Genesis*. Cambridge: Cambridge University Press, 2009.
Bright, John. *A History of Israel*. London: SCM-Canterbury, 1972.
Dalley, Stephanie M., ed. "Atrahasis." In *Myths from Mesopotamia: Creation, The Flood, Gilgamesh, and Others*, 9–35. Oxford: Oxford University Press, 1989.
Eisenberg, Josy, and Armand Abecassis. *A Bible Ouverte*. Paris: Albin Michel, 1991.
Fokkelman, Jan P. "Genesis." In *The Literary Guide to the Bible*, edited by Robert Alter and Frank Kermode, 36–55. Cambridge: Harvard University Press, 1987.
Frendo, Anthony J. "Israel in the Context of the Ancient Near East." In *The Hebrew Bible. A Critical Companion*, edited by John Barton, 86–105. Princeton: Princeton University Press, 2016.
Goldingay, John. *Genesis*. Grand Rapids: Baker Academic, 2020.
Gordon, Cyrus H. *Vóór de Bijbel. Het gemeenschappelijk verleden van de Griekse en de Hebreeuwse beschaving*. Utrecht/Antwerpen: Het Spectrum,1966. (*The Common Background of Greek and Hebrew*. New York: Norton Library, 1962).

---

54. The main focus of the narrator of the scroll of Genesis, as noted above, is focused on Israel's history rather than on the background of the primordial history of the world and mankind. More specifically, it fulfils two functions at the same time (i.e., does double duty).

The Creation Narrative in Genesis 1:1–2:4a

Gosse, Bernard. "L'inclusion de l'ensemble Genèse – II Rois, entre la perte du jardin d'Eden et celle de Jérusalem." *Zeitschrift für die alttestamentliche Wissenschaft* 114 (2002) 118–211.

Heidel, Alexander. *The Babylonian Genesis*. Chicago: University of Chicago Press, 1951.

Houtman, Cees. "De geschriften van het Oude Testament." In *Bijbels Handboek, Deel IIA*, edited by Abraham S. van der Woude, 279–335. Kampen: Kok, 1982.

———. "De Pentateuch." In *Bijbels Handboek II A*, edited by Abraham S. van der Woude, 279–335. Kampen: Kok, 1982.

Jagersma, Henk. *Geschiedenis van Israël in het oudtestamentische tijdvak*. Kampen: Kok, 1979. Dutch edition and translated into English: *A History of Israel in the Old Testament Period*. Minneapolis: Fortress, 1983.

King, Leonard W., ed. *Enuma Elish: The Seven Tablets of Creation; the Babylonian and Assyrian Legends Concerning the Creation of the World and of Mankind*. Whitefish, MT: Kessinger, 2010.

Lambert, Wilfred G. "A New Look at the Babylonian Background of Genesis" *The Journal of Theological Studies* 16:2 (October 1965) 287–300.

Lambert, Wilfred G., and Simon B. Parker. *Enuma Elish. The Babylonian Epic of Creation*. Oxford: Clarendon, 1966.

Link, Christian. *Schöpfung. Ein theologischer Entwurf im Gegenüber von Naturwissenschaft und Ökologie*. Neukirchen: Neukirchen-Vluyn, 2012.

Liverani, Mario. *La Bible et l'invention de l'histoire*. Paris: Bayard, 2008.

Lods, Adolphe. *Les Prophètes d'Israël et les débuts du judaïsme*. Paris: Albin Michel, 1969.

Lucas, Ernest. "Interpreting Genesis in the 21st[set superscript st] Century." In *The Faraday Papers*, 1–4. 2007. www.faraday-institute.org.

Noth, Martin. *Histoire d'Israël*. Paris: Payot, 1970. French translation of *Geschichte Israels*. Berlin: Evangelische Verlagsanstalt, 1968.

Paul, Shalom M. "Creation and Cosmology in the Bible." In *Encyclopaedia Judaica*, 5:1059–63. Jerusalem: Keter, 1972.

Porten, Bezalel. "Exile, Babylonian." In *Encyclopaedia Judaica*, 6:1036–41. Jerusalem: Keter, 1978.

Rendtorff, Rolf. *Introduction à l'Ancien Testament*. Paris: Les Éditions du Cerf, 1989.

Rice, Richard. *The Reign of God*. Berrien Springs, MI: Andrews University Press, 1986.

Ringgren, Helmer. *Die Religionen des Alten Orients*. Göttingen: Vandenhoeck & Ruprecht, 1979.

Römer, Thomas. "L'historiographie deutéronomiste (HD). Histoire de la recherche et enjeux du débat." In *Israël construit son histoire. L'historiographie deutéronomiste à la lumière des recherches récentes*, edited by Albert De Pury, et al. 9–120. Genève: Labor et Fides, 1996.

———. "Narrative Books in the Hebrew Bible." In *The Hebrew Bible. A Critical Companion*, edited by John Barton, 271–92. Princeton: Princeton University Press, 2016.

Soggin, Jan A. *Histoire d'Israël et de Juda*. Bruxelles: Lessius, 2004.

Speiser, Ephraim A. *Genesis*. Yale Anchor Bible 1. Garden City: Doubleday, 1964.

Speiser, Ephraim A., and Albert K. Grayson, "Akkadian Myths and Epics." In *Ancient Near Eastern Texts relating to the Old Testament*, edited by James B. Prichard, 60–67, 501–03. Princeton: Princeton University Press, 1950.

Spiekermann, Hermann. "Creation. God and World." In *The Hebrew Bible. A Critical Companion*, edited by John Barton, 271–92. Princeton: Princeton University Press, 2016.

Talon, Philippe. *The Standard Babylonian Creation Myth - Enuma Elish-Neo-Assyrian Text Corpus Project*. Helsinki: Helsinki University, 2005.

Tsumura, David T. "Chaos and Chaoskampf in the Bible." In *Creation, Chaos, Monotheism, Yahwism: Conversations on Canaanite and Biblical Themes*, edited by Rebecca S. Watson and Adrian H. W. Curtis, 963–69. Berlin: Gruyter, 2022.

———. "Genesis and Ancient Near Eastern Stories of Creation and Flood: An Introduction." In *I Studied Inscriptions from Before the Flood: Ancient Near Eastern, Literary, and Linguistic Approaches to Genesis 1–11*, edited by Richard S. Hess and David T. Tsumura, 27–57. University Park, PA: Eisenbrauns, 1994.

Vriezen, Theodorus C. *Hoofdlijnen der theologie van het Oude Testament*. Wageningen: H. Veenman en Zonen, 1977. English translation: *An Outline of Old Testament Theology*. Oxford: Blackwell, 1970.

Wenham, Gordon J. *Genesis 1–15*. Word Biblical Commentary 1A. Nashville: Zondervan Academic, 1987.

Wilson, John A. "Egyptian Myths, Tales, and Mortuary Texts (Text and translation)." In *Ancient Near Eastern Texts relating to the Old Testament*, edited by James B. Pritchard, 3–37. Princeton: Princeton University Press, 1969.

Zenger, Erich, et al. *Einleitung in das Alte Testament*. Stuttgart: Kohlhammer, 1995.

3

A Brief Review of Design in the Cosmos

KEVIN DE BERG, LYNDEN ROGERS AND EWAN WARD

3.1 INTRODUCTION

ARGUMENTS FOR THE EXISTENCE and attributes of God based on the grandeur, complexity, and apparent purposefulness of nature go back to Scripture. These apologetics were used in apostolic times, and they have re-emerged repeatedly during Christian history. At various times, these arguments appear substantially to have carried the day in intellectual circles while at other times they seem to have withered under savage critique, only to reappear in other incarnations, like the mythical phoenix. They have been presented by theists in a number of different, sometimes conflicting, forms, and it is apparent that Christians have often seriously disagreed over just how nature's attributes can best be mustered in support of the idea of a Creator-God. The gradual appearance of modern science in Western Europe from the sixteenth century appears to have increased this diversity of viewpoints. In this chapter, some of the most substantive developments in the long history of the design argument are documented, right down to the present day.

3.2 EBBS AND FLOWS: KEPLER TO DARWIN

When Johannes Kepler (1571–1630) penned his three laws of planetary motion, he considered that "God himself has waited six thousand years for his work to be seen."[1] Later, when Isaac Newton (1642–1727) was able to derive these three laws from first principles using his new universal law of gravitation and three laws of motion, he also gave glory to the Christian Creator God. He declared:

> This most elegant system of the sun, planets, and comets could not have arisen without the design and dominion of an intelligent and powerful being . . . He rules all things, not as the world soul, but as the Lord of all. And because of his dominion, he is called Lord God *Pantokrator*, that is, universal ruler . . . The supreme God is an eternal, infinite, and absolutely perfect being.[2]

Four hundred years earlier, the Catholic theologian and priest Thomas Aquinas (1225–1274) had used the concept of design as one of his arguments for the existence of God. Using the ideas of Aristotelian science, he saw that, "things achieve their end not by chance but through design . . . Therefore some intelligent being exists by whom all natural things are ordered to their end; and this being we call God."[3] That Aquinas urged his case for a designer God on the basis of a geocentric model of the universe while the post-Copernican Kepler and Newton presented a similar argument on the basis of their heliocentric view indicates that the design argument can transcend significant changes in scientific understanding. This foreshadowed a similar phenomenon in the twentieth century when Christians were first presented with the steady state theory[4] of the universe (a universe with no beginning) by Bondi, Gold, and Hoyle in 1948[5] and then a sophisticated version of the Big Bang theory (a universe with a beginning) by Guth in 1981.[6] Both of these scenarios enabled Christians in general to maintain a strong belief in God as designer and creator.

One possible explanation for the situation just described is the understandable tendency of Christians to give precedence to revelation over empirical data. Indeed, some Christians have carried this so far as to dismiss completely all arguments for God based on order and system in nature. According to Poe, the Christian philosopher and mathematician, Blaise Pascal (1623–1662), "had little regard for the attempt to prove the existence

1. Kepler, *Harmonices Mundi*, Book V, 197.
2. Newton, *Principia Mathematica*.
3. Aquinas, *Summa Theologica*, Part 1.
4. Bondi and Gold, "Steady State Theory," 252.
5. Hoyle, "New Model for the Expanding Universe," 372.
6. Guth, "Inflationary Universe."

of God from nature. One either knows intuitively through revelation that God made all of nature, or one does not."[7] Speaking of those who glibly use the design argument, Pascal wrote:

> I admire the boldness with which these persons undertake to speak of God. In addressing their argument to infidels, their first chapter is to prove Divinity from the works of nature. I should not be astonished at their enterprise, if they were addressing their argument to the faithful; for it is certain that those who have the living faith in their hearts see at once that all existence is none other than the work of God whom they adore. But for those in whom this light is extinguished, and in whom we purpose to rekindle it, persons destitute of faith and grace, who, seeking with all their light whatever they see in nature that can bring them to this knowledge, find only obscurity and darkness; to tell them that they have only to look at the smallest things which surround them, and they will see God openly, to give them, as a complete proof of this great and important matter, the course of the moon and planets, and to claim to have concluded the proof with such an argument, is to give them ground for believing that the proofs of our religion are very weak. And I see by reason and experience that nothing is more calculated to arouse their contempt.[8]

Of course, Pascal expressed this rather negative view of the design argument as a devout Christian, so it comes as no surprise that his skeptical sentiments were shared in larger measure by unbelievers. One such influence, Scottish philosopher, David Hume (1711–1776), strongly attacked the attempt to support the conclusion that the God of Christianity exists from a study of nature. Hume outlined his objections to the "design in nature" argument for the existence of God largely through the mouthpiece of Philo in his *Dialogues Concerning Natural Religion* (1779).[9] In the *Dialogues*, the character Cleanthes attempts to defend the establishment of religious principles on the basis of observed facts about the natural world. The character Demea also defends religious belief, although not on the grounds of a study of nature, and Philo comes closest to representing Hume as the philosophical skeptic.

Hume was particularly critical of the attempt to argue the existence of God as the designer and creator of the universe by using the analogy

---

7. Poe, "Design Argument," 49.
8. Pascal, *Pensées*, Section 4.242.
9. Hume, *Dialogues*.

of constructions designed and built by human agents. At one stage in the dialogue, Cleanthes suggests a parallel involving the building of a ship. But Philo countered by admitting that one can legitimately infer the existence of a designer and builder of a ship because of the many examples one can draw upon as solid evidence. But a ship, he claimed, is vastly different from our universe; no one has ever seen even a single universe, much less many universes, being built and designed by God to provide similar, solid evidence. Here is his challenge:

> And will any man tell me with a serious countenance, that an orderly universe must arise from some thought and art, like the human; because we have experience of it? To ascertain this reasoning, it were requisite that we had experience of the origin of worlds; and it is not sufficient surely, that we have seen ships and cities arise from human art and contrivance.[10]

According to Hume, even if one could draw upon the ship analogy, one would have to infer the existence of many gods, since many builders are associated with building a ship. Not surprisingly, this idea was not acceptable to Demea and Cleanthes, whose belief in a monotheistic God of infinite power, infinite wisdom, and infinite goodness remained strong. Hume, however, through his mouthpiece Philo, challenged these qualities of their God, given the solid, observational evidence seen in the world, such as natural disasters and the existence of evil. Cleanthes responds:

> The only method of supporting divine benevolence (and it is what I willingly embrace) is to deny absolutely the misery and wickedness of man. Your representations are exaggerated: Your melancholy views mostly fictitious: Your inferences contrary to fact and experience. Health is more common than sickness: Pleasure than pain: Happiness than misery. And for one vexation which we meet with, we attain, upon computation, a hundred enjoyments.[11]

Whereupon Philo taunts Cleanthes with this response:

> But allowing you, what never will be believed; at least, what you never possibly can prove, that animal, or at least, human happiness in this life exceeds its misery; you have yet done nothing: For this is not, by any means, what we expect from infinite power, infinite wisdom, and infinite goodness. Why is there any misery at all in

---

10. Hume, *Dialogues*, 60.
11. Hume, *Dialogues*, 110.

the world? Not by chance, surely. From some cause then. Is it from the intention of the deity? But he is perfectly benevolent. Is it contrary to his intention? But he is almighty. Nothing can shake the solidity of this reasoning, so short, so clear, so decisive; except we assert, that these subjects exceed all human capacity, and that our common measures of truth and falsehood are not applicable to them; a topic, which I have all along insisted on, but which you have, from the beginning, rejected with scorn and indignation.[12]

Hume concluded that design in nature could equally arise from within nature itself as from a divine intelligence, with the evidence tipped in favor of the former.

This view was to meet strong opposition from William Paley (1743–1805), Archdeacon of Carlisle. In his magnum opus of 1802, *Natural Theology*, he challenged comprehensively this view, beginning with his famous "watchmaker" analogy:

> In crossing a heath, suppose I pitched my foot against a *stone*, and were asked how the stone came to be there; I might possibly answer, that, for anything I knew to the contrary, it had lain there for ever; nor would it perhaps be very easy to show the absurdity of this answer. But suppose I had found a *watch* upon the ground, and it should be enquired how the watch happened to be in that place; I should hardly think of the answer which I had before given, that, for anything I knew, the watch might have always been there. But why should not this answer serve for the watch as well as for the stone? Why is it not as admissible in the second case as in the first? For this reason, and for no other, viz. that, when we come to inspect the watch, we perceive (what we could not discover in the stone) that its several parts are framed and put together for a purpose, e.g., that they are so formed and adjusted as to produce motion, and that motion so regulated as to point out the hour of the day.[13]

Paley countered skeptics like Hume with a litany of specific examples from biology to show that such features as eyes cannot be understood as simply randomly generated forms. Paley's book was enormously influential and was read and appreciated, for example, by the young Darwin, whilst a university student at Cambridge.

---

12. Hume, *Dialogues*, 111–12.
13. Paley, (1802), cited in Le Gros Clark, *Paley's Natural Theology*, 9–10.

However, the argument swung back in support of Hume in 1859 with the appearance of Charles Darwin's (1809–1882) *Origin of Species*, containing his causal theory of *natural selection*, an evolutionary mechanism to explain biological diversity. This quieted significantly those voices declaring that design in nature was a signature for the existence of God. According to Poe, this subdued attitude was to last until about the middle of the twentieth century:

> Though interest in the design argument faded significantly in the new theological/philosophical/ scientific climate of the early twentieth century, a major revision of the design argument appeared in Britain at Cambridge at the same time the philosophers of Oxford were capitulating to naturalism.[14]

It is fascinating to note that the data most relevant to the revival of the design argument during the twentieth century emerged from two very divergent fields, cosmology and molecular biology. We examine each of these areas in turn.

3.3 TWENTIETH-CENTURY DEVELOPMENTS IN COSMOLOGY

3.3.1 A Fine-tuned Universe

The twentieth century witnessed revolutionary developments in physics (particularly nuclear physics and relativity), chemistry (particularly biochemistry and genetics), geology, astronomy, and cosmology. Much more precise measurements of universal constants, such as the mass and charge of the electron and proton, the mass of the neutron, and the speed of electromagnetic radiation, became available. It also became possible to identify and measure the four fundamental forces which operate in our universe: the strong nuclear force which holds neutrons and protons together in the nucleus of the atom; the weak nuclear force which is related to radioactive decay; the electromagnetic force which binds electrons and protons into atoms; and the gravitational force which acts over much longer distances and which, for example, governs the orbits of the planets about the sun in our solar system. Nuclear reactions in the stars were shown to be capable of synthesizing the elements of the periodic table. It was recognized, to

---

14. Poe, "Mechanical Universe," 66.

universal surprise, that these constants and forces of nature were incredibly finely tuned and, furthermore, that life on Earth was only possible because of this delicate balance. This awareness has led to the field of cosmic teleology. Nature's constants and forces appear to have been designed for the purpose of supporting life.

The idea that the universe seems to have been designed for life is sometimes called the Anthropic Principle. Unquestionably, these cosmological discoveries have breathed new life into the design argument. So much so, in fact, that the last four decades have seen the appearance of a plethora of highly acclaimed books on this topic by well-known figures of science and astronomy, by no means all of them Christians. Astronomer Royal, Martin Rees (born 1942), presents what he sees as the most striking six of these apparent coincidences in his book, *Just Six Numbers: The Deep Forces Which Shape the Universe*.[15] Two relate to basic nuclear and atomic forces, where the ratio of the strength of gravity to that of the electromagnetic force has dramatic implications for the lifetime of stars. Another two fix the size and overall texture of the universe. Rees' last two numbers fix the properties of space itself, one of which concerns the fact that we live in a 3D physical world. It transpires that this seemingly innocuous reality carries profound implications. Paul Davies (born 1946), in *The Goldilocks Enigma*, presents another very readable discussion of these and other relevant data.[16]

The excitement of this new field of cosmology has elicited a range of responses from scientists. Martin Rees, for example, does not see it as suggesting a Divine designer. He responds in the following way:

> Is this tuning just a brute fact, a coincidence? Or is it the providence of a benign Creator? I take the view that it is neither. An infinity of other universes may well exist where the numbers are different. Most would be stillborn or sterile. We could only have emerged (and therefore we naturally now find ourselves) in a universe with the "right" combination. This realization offers a radically new perspective on our universe, on our place in it, and on the nature of physical laws.[17]

However, there is no supporting scientific evidence for the existence of multiverses.

---

15. Rees, *Just Six Numbers*.
16. Davies, *Goldilocks Enigma*.
17. Rees, *Just Six Numbers*, 4.

In contrast, the new discoveries in cosmology have led scientists such as F. R. Tennant (1866–1957) to believe that one could legitimately employ them as the very strongest evidence in support of the existence of an intelligent creator or designer. According to Poe, "Tennant believed that empirical evidence provided the only legitimate basis for the establishment of theistic religion."[18] As shown previously, Pascal would have had great difficulty with this statement.

3.3.2 The Proton-Neutron Mass Difference

The kind of empirical evidence upon which Tennant drew, to take one example, was the mass difference between the neutron (1.6749×10^{-27} kg) and the proton (1.6726×10^{-27} kg). According to Greenstein, "There seems to be no fundamental reason why the neutron should be the more massive of the two. Furthermore, the mass difference is quite small, a mere tenth of a percent. One might think it would make no difference. But it does make a difference. Indeed, it is crucial."[19] It turns out that neutrons undergo radioactive decay, but protons do not. If the proton was slightly more massive than the neutron and underwent decay while the neutron did not, then this would have major implications for the existence of hydrogen, which has just one proton in its nucleus and one electron surrounding the nucleus. Hydrogen is important for carbon-based life, so the implications for life are enormous. According to Davis, ". . . if protons decayed rather than neutrons, stars would exhaust their fuel within a century, which is too short a time frame for life to form."[20]

3.3.3 Carbon (the Basis of Life) Formed in the Stars

According to Giberson and Collins, the best example of fine-tuning is the production of carbon nuclei in the stars, without which carbon-based life could not exist.[21] The process is called the triple-alpha process because it involves the fusion of three alpha particles (helium nuclei) in a two-step

---

18. Poe, "Mechanical Universe," 66.
19. Greenstein, *Symbiotic Universe*, 93.
20. Davis, "Fine-Tuned Universe," 72.
21. Giberson and Collins, *Language of Science and Faith*, chapter 7.

process as follows in reactions (1) and (2). The equations only show the nuclei involved.

$$^4_2He + ^4_2He \rightarrow ^8_4Be \tag{1}$$

$$^8_4Be + ^4_2He \rightarrow ^{12}_6C \tag{2}$$

Helium nuclei contain two protons and two neutrons and so are charged (2+). Reaction (1) requires the strong nuclear force to fuse these two nuclei together. The resultant beryllium nucleus is very unstable, with a half-life of about 10^{-15} seconds. If a third alpha particle combines with the beryllium nucleus in the brief interval before it decays away, a carbon-12 nucleus can form, but only if the combined energy of the beryllium and helium nuclei is just equal to the energy of an excited state of carbon. The ground and excited energy states of a nucleus are quantized like those of the electron, and the chances of such a match in energies between reactants and products in reaction (2) is fairly slim. However, it turns out that the combined nuclear energies of beryllium and helium is only 4 percent below the energy of the second excited state of carbon (7.68 MeV). With the addition of the kinetic energies of the beryllium and helium atoms to their nuclear energy, the formation of carbon-12 in the excited state can occur. The carbon atom in the excited state then readily transitions to one in the stable ground state (see Figure 3.1). Early in 1953, Fred Hoyle[22] had predicted an excited state of carbon having an energy of around 7.68 MeV and, remarkably, this was experimentally confirmed later in 1953.[23] The nature of this fine-tuning is discussed by Giberson and Collins in terms of the values of the fundamental forces involved:

> The strong and electromagnetic forces collaborate to enable fusion. The electromagnetic force opposes the fusion reaction by trying to keep the positively charged nuclei away from each other. Because of the intense heat in the stars, the nuclei move about rapidly with the possibility that they might overcome this repulsion and smash into each other. If they do, then the "glue" of the strong force has a chance to hold them together permanently. The slightest change to either the strong or electromagnetic forces alters the relevant energy levels, resulting in greatly reduced production of carbon. And carbon, of course, is essential to life, so reducing its

---

22. Hoyle et al., "State in C12 Predicted from Astrophysical Evidence," 1095.
23. Dunbar et al., "7.68-MeV State in C12," 649–50.

production dramatically reduces the probability that the universe will turn out to be habitable.[24]

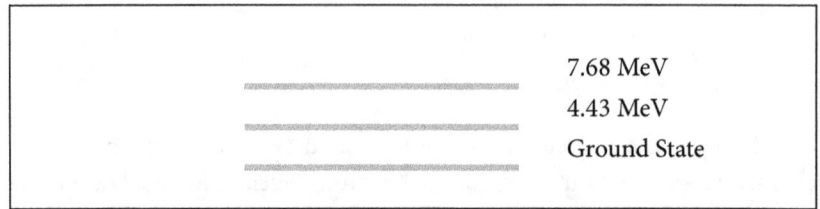

Figure 3.1 Quantized energy states of the carbon nucleus showing the first excited state to be 4.43 MeV above the ground state and the second excited state to be 7.68 MeV above the ground state.

Oberhummer et al.[25] have calculated that a change in the nucleon-nucleon interaction as small as 0.5 percent would make carbon-based life impossible.[26]

However, some scientists have disagreed with the religious overtones sometimes attached to the so-called fine-tuning, teleological, anthropic principle. Livio et al. have calculated that an energy level of the excited state of carbon, anywhere between 7.596 MeV and 7.716 MeV could produce the abundant level of carbon-12 observed in nature. They question whether this could be classified as an example of fine-tuning.[27] Steven Weinberg focuses on the energy difference between the beryllium and helium nuclei when together at rest and the carbon resonance energy (0.25 MeV), rather than the carbon resonance energy itself (7.65 MeV) and concludes, "This energy misses being too high for the production of carbon by a fractional amount of 0.05 MeV/0.25 MeV, or 20 percent, which is not such a close call after all."[28] Others accept the fine-tuning argument but claim that in a system of multiverses, one would expect, according to the laws of probability, one of these universes to have properties just like ours. It may be seen that the opinion on whether or how best to apply a design argument based on these data is divided. Astronomer Fred Hoyle was certainly impressed, writing the following, well-known statement:

24. Giberson and Collins, *Language of Science and Faith*, 182.
25. Oberhummer et al., "Triple-alpha Process and its Anthropic Significance," 119–23.
26. Oberhummer et al., "Fine-tuning Carbon-based Life in the Universe," 197–206.
27. Livio et al., "Anthropic Significance," 281–84.
28. Weinberg, *Facing Up*.

A Brief Review of Design in the Cosmos

> A common sense interpretation of the facts suggest that a super-intellect has monkeyed with physics, as well as with chemistry and biology, and that there are no blind forces worth speaking about in nature. The numbers one calculates from the facts seem to me so overwhelming as to put this conclusion beyond question.[29]

We have seen that the formation of carbon nuclei within giant red stars involves a somewhat delicate balancing act, whatever one thinks of the anthropic principle. The formation of the numerous compounds of carbon, which leads ultimately to information bearing molecules like DNA which encode life, must be orders of magnitude more complex again.

3.4 DESIGN IN BIOLOGICAL SYSTEMS

3.4.1 Apparent Design in Biology: Good, Sub-optimal, and Macabre

Not only did the twentieth century witness great advances in physics and astronomy, it greeted corresponding advances in the fields of biology and life chemistry. Investigations into the chemistry, biochemistry, physiology, and anatomy of organisms have also provided data that have been used as evidence of design. For the purposes of the following discussion, it is possible to differentiate three broad classes of apparent design in biological systems: *good*, *poor*, and *macabre*.

Good design may be recognized where the goal of the system under consideration appears to have been achieved with few mistakes: the components of the system work well together and experience few breakdowns. The overall system displays the hallmarks of efficiency and functionality. Such features leave us feeling satisfied that the intelligence behind it all has got it right or at least nearly right. A system like this is in keeping with what would be expected of an intelligent and benevolent designer. And so much of the biosphere appears to display these characteristics. It is worth noting that we have avoided the use of the term "perfect design," as all biological systems appear to have flaws to varying degrees and so cannot really be considered perfect. Instead, the term *good design* will be employed. The DNA molecule— its structure, function, and associated proteins—has been chosen as an example of good design.

However, not all biological systems appear to be optimally designed. Evidence of *poor design* is provided by features that lead to inconsistent

---

29. Hoyle, "Universe: Past and Present Reflections," 16.

performance or seemingly unnecessary component failures and breakdowns. Such characteristics suggest that there is room for improvement and refinement in the design parameters. In such cases, questions might legitimately arise concerning the intelligence behind such designs. The human eye and spine have been chosen as examples of design at the organ and structural level that may be said to demonstrate such deficiencies.

Even worse for the design argument, however, are those many cases in which the design appears to be brilliantly and incredibly suited for purpose but which is downright macabre, as in many mechanisms of predation. After all, in his famous letter to the American biologist, Asa Gray, Darwin referred to the wasps (*Ichneumonidae*) that lay their eggs in other living organisms as evidence that a beneficent God could surely have had nothing to do with the development of living organisms. The *Cordyceps* parasitic fungus genus has been chosen here as an example of, as it would seem, macabre, predatory design. This organism not only exhibits what appears to be a highly contrived interaction between two distant species, but one that affects an entire ecosystem.

Any argument used to infer an intelligent creator behind the universe and, more particularly, the originator of carbon-based life on this planet, needs to address these last two categories as well as the first. Would not a divine intelligence provide perfectly designed organisms, ones without weak spots? And why would this same benevolent intelligence design the horrifying intricacies of some predatory mechanisms? For that matter, why design predators at all? This paper includes a brief articulation of these problems for design.

3.4.2 Good Design – DNA and Molecular Systems

All life forms begin as single cells, which are themselves far from simple, and which increase in the diversity of their molecular interactions as they mature. This multi-level complexity allows the organism to be responsive to environmental stimuli, to maintain homeostasis, to have a functioning and coordinated metabolism, to assimilate nutrients, and to reproduce—allowing genetic traits to be passed on to offspring. Design may be examined at any of these levels, from the molecular to the entire physiological system or anatomical structure.

This staggering complexity is perhaps most evident when one considers apex life forms, such as humans. Our bodies are collections of organic molecules, including DNA, proteins, and lipids, that allow the cellular development and coordination that build digestive, reproductive, neural, endocrine, circulatory, and respiratory systems. This extraordinary collection of molecules can move around, interpret environmental data, search for food, react to positive and negative stimuli, integrate and interpret data, communicate, and display thought processes along with a range of complex emotions. Among all the species on this planet, humans appear to be uniquely equipped to consider the origin of life and their place in the universe. Describing the wonder of this circumstance from a naturalistic, evolutionary viewpoint, Carl Sagan remarked:

> We have begun to contemplate our origins: starstuff pondering the stars; organised assemblages of ten billion billion billion atoms considering the evolution of atoms; tracing the long journey by which, here at last consciousness arose.[30]

The microscopic cell, the basic unit of life, extraordinarily varied in form and function, is a molecule-packed, membrane-bound sac of watery protoplasm. It is a fantastic miniature factory. Its DNA molecule is carefully coiled and packaged in the nucleus, which is located near the center of the cell (although some cells, such as bacteria, do not have a nucleus, their DNA being free to float inside). Then there are the enzymes and proteins whose existence, structure, and function are dependent upon the genetic information coded along the DNA molecule. Enzymes are a specialized group of proteins that act as molecular tools, performing tasks on specific target molecules that alter their chemistry, structure, and function.

Certain specific enzymes access the genetic information contained in the DNA, reading its chemical language of four nucleotide bases as one reads the words and sentences in a book. These instructions are then used to manufacture more enzymes and proteins from small molecules called amino acids found in the cell. In many cases, the cell manufactures these amino acids by complicated biochemical pathways, themselves controlled by a host of specific enzymes also produced from information held in the DNA. Amino acids are connected and ordered in very specific ways to form chains that determine the overall three-dimensional shape of the molecule. In turn, the shape of the "active site" of the enzyme very specifically determines the type of chemical reactions it will control in its target molecules, known as "substrates."

---

30. Sagan, *Cosmos*, 364.

The interactions between enzymes and substrates allow cellular metabolism to occur. These involve complicated pathways in which one substrate is enzymatically converted to a product, which in turn is a substrate for another enzyme. Enzymes operate in chaotic systems with interactions with substrates being dependent on random collisions, producing the correct orientation of the target substrate molecule, so it can interact with the active site of the enzyme. Ultimately, it is the genetic information held in the DNA molecule that determines the metabolic output of the cell and also the function of the physiological system to which it belongs. The cell, and hence the whole organism, is directed by blocks of information known as genes that stretch along the DNA molecule. If all this sounds complicated, it's because it is!

Reproduction of the organism necessarily involves cell division. It transpires that prior to cell division, the DNA molecule must be replicated in its entirety. This magic is performed by another set of specialized enzymes, themselves coded for by the same DNA. Any mistakes made during the replication of DNA (or chemical damage to DNA sustained at any other time for that matter) are corrected by complicated enzymatic machinery known as DNA repair mechanisms. Some false transcriptions still slip through, but these complex error-detecting provisions are amazingly successful. Thus, the fidelity of the genetic code is preserved and, in the case of non-gamete cells, each newly replicated cell is genetically an exact copy of its predecessor. Of course, sperm and ova are in a different category. The fact that these cells are not genetically identical to the cells from which they are derived, having only half the amount of the parent DNA, allows for the formation of genetically non-identical offspring.

However, despite the self-correcting mechanisms described above operating in most cases, there are some genes that not only allow random mutations but actually encourage them, and this is for very good reasons! Examples of these "hypermutable" genes are those DNA segments responsible for the organism's "armed forces." No organism can possibly predict the individual structure of the 10^{17} or so antigens (protein venoms, bacterial toxins, viruses, etc.) that will invade and threaten it over a lifetime. Furthermore, there are only about 22,000 genes in human DNA, most of which code for other functional purposes. This means that our bodies have nowhere near enough genetic information to formulaically produce the number of different antibodies required. And even if we did, there is no saying that an unforeseen antigen might present.

Accordingly, higher organisms cleverly use random mutations and recombinations within specialized cells of the immune system to produce the hugely diverse range of protective antibody molecules we may need. These antibodies, armed to the teeth, so to speak, are then released into the blood and other body fluids following infection or vaccination. If they encounter "their" pathogen, they eliminate it before it can do harm.

Of course, things do go wrong in this complex picture. Despite the elaborate DNA repair processes, mistakes do occur during DNA replication, and not all of these are corrected. Such mistakes allow for mutations to arise in newly synthesized daughter DNA molecules, which may alter the function of the cell. These mistakes allow for variation in base sequences in either genes or non-coding DNA regions that may produce either new genes or altered gene products that may or may not be an advantage to the organism. Unfortunately, these mistakes also play a role in the development of cancers and other diseases that result from altered information in DNA, particularly that affecting the control and expression of other genes.

But despite the fact that it does not always work perfectly, this fantastically intricate and finely balanced relationship between DNA (information) and proteins/enzymes (structure and function) which is fundamental to cell function, and hence the propagation of all higher life forms, is seen by many Christian biologists as a supreme example of *good design*. The probability of such a complex system of cybernetic control and information structures arising spontaneously, without any intelligent input at all, would seem vanishingly small to this group.

3.4.3 Poor Design

In contrast to *good design*, there are several important anatomical and physiological systems that appear to show evidence of *poor design (dysteological design)*. These organs are not dysfunctional to a large degree but seem to display sub-optimal features. The human eye and the spine are often cited as examples.

The eye is a marvelous structure that allows light from objects near and far to enter with controlled intensity and then pass through a lens that refractively focuses a sharp, inverted image on the retina. A combination of chemical and electrical signals then conveys information about the image via the optic nerve to the brain, where it is interpreted.

Design theorists argue about the efficiency of the design evident in the human eye. It is now known that the retina has several layers through which light rays must pass before striking the photoreceptors, the rod, and cone cells. These are the neural layers, which contain the cells that relay information to the brain and also the capillaries that supply blood to retinal cells. Obviously, this arrangement has the potential to cause some interference with the light which is eventually received by the receptor cells. If the neural cells are considered equivalent to "wiring," surely good design would dictate that they should be behind the photoreceptor layer, rather than in front. Interestingly, the retina of the cephalopods (squids and octopuses) does have this neural "wiring" behind the photoreceptor cells, where it might be expected. Does this make the octopus eye better than ours?

Another point of consideration concerns the placement of the optic nerve. At the back of the human eye, the optic nerve and a vascular bundle (retinal artery and vein) exit the retina at a point referred to as the optic disc. The optic disc lacks photoreceptor cells, resulting in what is sometimes referred to as the "blind spot." It would seem from a design perspective that the optic disc is in the wrong position and would be better located at the side of the retina so that the image formed by the lens falling on this area is not compromised. There is no obvious reason why this could not have been so.

Remarkably, these apparently poor design features of the eye are compensated by our stereoscopic vision. The images formed from each eye are overlapped in the brain, and many discrepancies are resolved. Perhaps the sub-optimal design of our eye is good enough for most purposes. Still, the question remains.

However, in some instances, sub-optimal design does lead to widespread problems. Given the prevalence of back problems in the human population, the spine may also be considered an example of *poor design*. The spine consists of twenty-six vertebrae separated by intervertebral discs that allow forward and backward movement, as well as sideways and rotational mobility. The spine supports the head and also provides the various points of attachment for the ribs, pelvis, and muscles of the upper and lower limbs. The vertebral column protects the spinal cord and allows for the branching of spinal nerves to various parts of the body.

Given the importance of this anatomical structure, one would expect to see a very good design indeed. Any serious damage to the spinal cord and the structure of the vertebral column can have very serious consequences.

The intervertebral discs, which keep the vertebrae separated, consist of a tough fibrocartilage with a soft elastic center that compresses under load, acting as a shock absorber for the vertebral column. Herniation (bulging) of these discs, which is a common cause of human spinal problems, results from trauma, excessive load bearing, poor posture, and disc degeneration. Disc herniation may lead to compression of spinal nerves, with accompanying pain of great severity and also compromised sensation and limb function. Unfortunately, the discs have a poor blood supply. This reduces the amount of oxygen and nutrients received, which has a negative and limiting effect on healing and repair. Given the critical importance of the spine, why does this overall structure not have better design features? Could not a benevolent creator have alleviated a lot of suffering by producing a better design for the spine in the first place?

Further examples of poor/sub-optimal design in the human body include the fallopian tubes that allow for the fertilized ova occasionally to be retained, leading to potentially life-threatening ectopic pregnancy, rather than migrating to the uterus. Another is the small size of the female pelvic bones that sometimes prevents the passage of the baby's head during childbirth. Human birth problems appear to be much more prevalent than is the case, for instance, with other primates.

In all the above examples, it must be appreciated that the various types of cells making up these intriguing structures all have the superb molecular design in their DNA, enzymes, and proteins noted earlier, and yet the structures and systems they form seem to display non-ideal features. Such cases are often used to discount a divine intelligence behind creation on the assumption that a perfect Creator would have employed nothing but optimal design.

3.4.4 Macabre Design

Predation

When considering design within the complexity of biological life on this planet, it is all too easy to be awed by the nice bits: the design in colorful flowers that give off perfume, birdsong in the morning, the playful kitten (which really is just practicing predatory moves), or the delicate fawn treading warily through the sun-dappled glade to mention but a few. However, nature seems to be mostly about where the next meal is coming from:

the deadly game of predation and the subsequent assimilation of the prey's molecules into the biological structure of the predator. Predation appears as a central feature of life—eat or be eaten.

The success and efficiency of predatory design cannot be ignored, particularly when one considers the streamlined design of sharks and killer whales, the inwardly curved claws and teeth of large cats such as lions, and the rapidly paralyzing venom of a taipan, which simultaneously attacks its victim's life processes in at least three ways.

Parasitism and the Cordyceps Fungus

But it is not just the large and powerful predators that apparently exhibit design features that make them so successful. Consider the fungal genus, *Cordyceps*, whose 600 species seem to have taken predation to truly macabre levels. It is almost as if these fungi are flaunting their parasitic behavior.

Species in the genus *Cordyceps* are parasites that target insects, anthropods, and in a few cases, other fungi. The fungus is made up of a mycelial network of individual filaments called hyphae. Specialized hyphae produce spores that are then spread by air currents and on the bodies of insects that come in contact with the fungus. The brain of infected ants is so affected by the chemicals produced by the fungus as to cause the ant to climb nearby vegetation and eventually to lock its jaws around a stalk in a vice-like death grip. When the ant dies the fungus continues to spread through its body, with specialized hyphae growing from the ant's head and then releasing spores into the environment, the dissemination of the fungus spores being enhanced by the height to which the ant managed to climb. The many species of *Cordyceps* fungi are each specific to an individual host species.[31] It is believed that such targeting of specific populations of insects helps to control their numbers, ensuring that any one insect species does not become predominant. Such controls have important environmental and ecological implications.

From the viewpoint of molecular biology, a number of intriguing questions are raised by this parasitic story. For instance, from whence came the toxins of *Cordyceps* which interact with molecular receptors in the brain of the ant, altering its behavior? How did this match come to be? The information for manufacturing these toxins is contained within

---

31. Hughes et al., "Behavioral Mechanisms." Also, de Bekker et al., "Species-Specific Ant Brain Manipulation."

specific genes in the DNA of the fungus. These genes have no interaction with the ants, yet the design of the toxin molecule must match that of the receptor in the ant's brain, a totally different type of organism to the fungus. When it comes to the world of predators and parasites, it does indeed look like design, but it would certainly appear that the designer behind it all had a devious imagination!

It is sometimes argued that such macabre design features could be the result of changes in the original design plans beyond the control of the designer, as sin entered the world. However, others regard the attribution of such extensive powers to Satan as unbiblical. For example, Giberson and Collins observe that this would imply the attribution of considerable creative ability to forces in opposition to the designer.

> Where did these sinister designs originate? Some respond too quickly that they come from Satan, but this is too glib a response from a Christian perspective. To ascribe the creation of *anything* in nature to Satan is to elevate Satan from a *creature* to a co-creator of the world with God. This claim is quite heretical from a technical point of view. No distortion of Christian theology can accommodate the idea that Satan created portions of the world.[32]

3.5 TWO CONTRASTING FORMS OF THE MODERN DESIGN ARGUMENT

Quite apart from issues of apparently good and bad design, it is important to note that the design arguments advanced by Christians have bifurcated into two subtly different forms over the last four decades.

3.5.1 Mainstream Approach to Design

This form of the design argument is painted with broad, comprehensive strokes. For these theists, the hand of the designer is seen primarily in the incredible balances (some of which are noted above) and creative potential observed within the natural laws undergirding the universe and life within it rather than in specific details of such. At a conference in 2003 convened at Grafton, NSW (New South Wales), physicist Sir John Polkinghorne developed his articulation of the design argument by reference

---

32. Giberson and Collins, *Language of Science and Faith*, 133.

to such features of our universe as its anthropic nature, the fact that it exhibits complex systems, the highly relational nature of its physical building blocks, its unexpected intelligibility to humans and the fact that it contains consciousness, values, and aesthetics.[33] Unfortunately, space does not allow further elaboration of these arguments.

It is important to note that this group sees evidence for design principally in what *can* be understood by science rather than in what *cannot*. This variant of the design argument may be regarded as the generic form, and most closely matches that offered in earlier centuries.

Christian biologists such as Darryl Falk, Francis Collins, Simon Conway Morris, and Alistair McGrath are among those who have argued for design in these general but powerful terms. Irrespective of whether one agrees with this position it is apparent that among its adherents are some of the most articulate and effective contemporary Christian apologists. They are found among many faith groups including the Anglican, Lutheran, Baptist, and Catholic churches, and in the Jewish community.

One area from which these broad design inferences are drawn concerns what is called "evolutionary convergence," where very similar solutions to the same problem appear to have evolved more than once across a range of unrelated organisms. Simon Conway Morris mentions several of these apparent convergences, such as the highly-developed eyes of cephalopods and vertebrates. It turns out that, while the various components of these two eyes differ significantly at the molecular level, their mode and efficiency of function are similar.[34] Such indications of convergence would still be in harmony with the anthropic principle. Michael Denton suggests that the mechanisms that have led to the development of carbon-based life with its complex biological structures depend upon some deep biological and molecular programming, as yet not understood, at the level of "natural" law.[35] Denton goes further by suggesting that such a recognition represents by far the best option for those wishing to ascribe nature's order to a Divine creator.[36]

---

33. Polkinghorne, "Cosmic Richness."
34. Morris, *Life's Solution*.
35. Denton, *Nature's Destiny*.
36. Denton, "Anti-Darwinian Intellectual Journey," 153–76.

3.5.2 Intelligent Design

Another form of the design argument emerged during the 1990s. This is known as Intelligent Design (ID) and argues for design on the basis of specific instances, mainly in the biosphere, for which science is currently *unable* to offer an explanation. For many, it is perhaps the most visible Christian design viewpoint. It became Australian national news in October 2005, when the then Federal Education Minister, Brendon Nelson, partially endorsed the DVD, "Unlocking the Mystery of Life."[37] This glossy production, which was being widely circulated by the Campus Crusade for Christ, Australia, was part of an ID promotional program.

Most correctly and usefully, the term "Intelligent Design" should be applied to the viewpoint of the Intelligent Design Group, or "The Wedge" movement, probably best represented by the Centre for Science and Culture (CSC), which began as the Centre for the Renewal of Science and Culture (CRSC) in 1996.[38] The CSC is closely associated with the Discovery Institute, based in Seattle, Washington. Phillip Johnson, a law professor at the University of California (Berkeley), is usually regarded as the founder of the ID movement.[39] He commenced his attack on the scientific establishment with the publication in 1991 of his book *Darwin on Trial*.[40] In the DVD, "Unlocking the Mystery of Life," it is suggested that it was the gathering in 1993, at Johnson's invitation, of a number of sympathetic scientists at Pajaro Dunes, California, which marked the beginning of the ID movement as such. Works by several authors who were present at that initial meeting have contributed significantly to the following currently enjoyed by the ID movement.[41] Behe's notion of "irreducible complexity" and Dembski's "explanatory or causal filters" and "specified complexity" are considered to be important identifiers of such instances of design and are discussed below.

ID proponents insist that what they do is authentically scientific and cannot be dismissed as religious dogma. Typically, they perceive design very much as taking place at the organism level rather than at the more fundamental level of the setting up of natural laws capable of nurturing

---

37. Illustra Media. *Unlocking the Mystery of Life.*

38. Forrest and Gross, *Creationism's Trojan Horse*, 7–21.

39. Forrest and Gross, *Creationism's Trojan Horse*, 7–21. Also see Gibson, "Intelligent Design Movement, Part 2," 13.

40. Johnson, *Darwin on Trial.*

41. See Behe, *Darwin's Black Box*; Dembski, *The Design Inference*; Dembski, *Mere Creation*; and Wells, *Icons of Evolution.*

life. This important point may be further illustrated by noting that causality in nature may arise from either natural law or contingency (intervention). While the ID movement presumably regards natural law as originating in the Divine Mind, it also insists that these laws provide inadequate explanations for some phenomena, and hence sees God acting contingently, as well as through natural processes.

However, while there is coherence among ID exponents to this extent, individual differences in emphasis and viewpoint make it difficult to identify a characteristic stance on other issues. For example, no time scale for life on Earth is spelled out by most exponents within this group. Although many adherents would espouse a recent life history, some definitely do not. Correspondingly, evidence suggests that this group includes some special creationists and some theistic evolutionists. Another point to note is that some prominent ID purists make a point of *not* attempting to identify the designer, being content to concentrate simply on seeking evidence for design.

Behe's Irreducible Complexity

A hallmark of Intelligent Design is the concept of irreducible complexity.[42] Here it is urged that there exist systems in nature for which all the components must be present in order for the system to operate and that these could not have been added gradually as part of a long developmental process. Examples cited include the eye, the blood-clotting cascade, and the bacterial flagellum, often used as the flagship example of irreducible complexity.

However, this argument has been assailed.[43] Opponents have advanced what they see as plausible evolutionary mechanisms for the development of these seemingly irreducibly complex systems.[44] It has been noted that the various stages of development of such features as eyes could have useful functionalities, even if different from that of the final form. In a similar fashion, many of the protein components of bacterial flagella, have been

---

42. Behe, *Darwin's Black Box*.
43. Macnab, "Bacterial Flagellum."
44. Le Page, "Evolution Myths."

shown to be parts of other bacterial systems,[45] and proposed evolutionary mechanisms for the development of flagella have been described.[46]

Dembski's Design Filters

Intelligent Design proponents have also attempted to establish objective criteria by means of which the presence of design could be inferred legitimately. Perhaps some of the best work in this area has been done by William Dembski.[47] Dembski noted that there are three possible modes of causality for any outcome. First, there are those outcomes that occur with absolute reliability, as, for example, a consequence of natural law. Second, there are outcomes, like winning the lottery, which are by no means certain, but which occur within well-understood bounds of probability. Third, there are events that are so unlikely to occur spontaneously that when they are observed, we can legitimately infer deliberate, outside intervention and design. Furthermore, Dembski suggests that increasing complexity is associated with a decreasing probability of the event occurring spontaneously. The more complex, specific, and ordered the result, the greater its improbability. A discussion of Dembski's explanatory filters is beyond the scope of this chapter but can be found elsewhere.[48]

3.5.3 Negative Responses to ID from Other Theists

Many mainstream Christian scholars tend to view ID with some suspicion. This stance is articulated by Owen Gingerich, a number of whose ancestors were Amish bishops. In his lecture, "Dare a Scientist Believe in Design?," Gingerich recalled participating some years ago in a scientific conference at Dallas during which a group of Christian biochemists led by Charles Thaxton argued that aspects of evolution were untenable. Gingerich comments:

> I soon found myself in the somewhat anomalous position that to me, the atheists' position was much more interesting than the theists'. That particular group of Christian biochemists had concluded that ordinary science didn't work . . . and they attempted

---

45. Musgrave, "Evolution of the Bacterial Flagellum."
46. Pallen and Matzke, "From the Origin of Species to the Origin," 784–90.
47. Dembski, *Intelligent Design*.
48. Ward, "Mechanics of Intelligent Design."

to delineate an alternative "origin science" in which the explicit guiding hand of God could make possible what was otherwise beyond probability. The reason I admired the atheist biochemists so much was that they hadn't given up . . . "Let us not flee to a supernaturalistic explanation," they said, "let us not retreat from the laboratory." Now it might be that the chemistry of life's origins *are* forever beyond human comprehension, but I see no way to establish that scientifically. Therefore, it seems to me to be part of science to keep trying . . . But meanwhile, a new generation has re-clothed some of these same ideas under the name "intelligent design" . . . My theological presuppositions incline me to be sympathetic to this point of view, but as a scientist I accept methodological naturalism as a research strategy.[49]

John Polkinghorne introduced his Grafton paper on design with the words:

I want to propose a worldview that takes absolutely seriously all that science can tell us about the universe in which we live, and then deepens that understanding by viewing it in the wider and more profound setting of theistic belief. *Of course, I am not supposing that the world is full of objects stamped "made by God"* (italics supplied). While it would be perplexing to theistic belief if there were no footprints of the Creator found at all, it would be surprising if they were of so unambiguous a kind as to overwhelm the free exploration of the human mind into the nature of reality. On this basis, we might anticipate that we will find God to be neither totally hidden nor totally revealed in His works.[50]

From the context of this remark, it seems most likely that this is a shot across the bow of the ID movement in Polkinghorne's signature style of mannerly British understatement.

Echoing these sentiments, Nobel-Prize-winning physicist, Eric Cornell, wrote in *Time* magazine:

But as exciting as intelligent design is in theology, it is a boring idea in science . . . The thrill is that our ignorance exceeds our knowledge; the exciting part is what we don't understand yet. If you want to recruit future scientists, you don't draw a box around

---

49. Gingerich, "Dare a Scientist Believe in Design?"
50. Polkinghorne, "Cosmic Richness."

all our scientific understanding to date and say, "Everything outside this box we can explain *only* by invoking God's will."[51]

About 350 years ago, Robert Boyle bequeathed funds to sponsor an annual lecture for the purposes of "proving the Christian religion against notorious infidels."[52] After a long lapse, these lectures have been recommenced recently. The 2005 Boyle Lecture was presented by Prof Simon Conway Morris, who suggested that "science reveals unexpected depths to Creation while religion informs us what on earth (literally) we are going to do about it." A little later in his lecture, he asserted that:

> ... it is easy to appreciate the intellectual attraction of the quasi-scientific/quasi-theological movement known as intelligent design (ID). Before you react with consternation and dismay at the prospect of Intelligent Design's having gained another recruit, let me hasten to assure you—not a bit of it! In my opinion ID is a false and misleading attraction.[53]

Richard Colling writes in connection with ID:

> As a devout Christian and university biology professor, I can certainly appreciate the sincere efforts of school officials: the possibility of an intelligent creator should not be patently excluded from science classroom discussion! However, as a measure that promotes sound science while also preserving the long-term viability of faith, intelligent design fails both tests ...
>
> Intelligent design is not a recognized process within the general scientific community—even among conservative Christian biologists. It ... leads to no testable hypotheses ...
>
> If the goal of religious conservatives is to preserve an element of faith, intelligent design ideas provide but a temporary solution by positing an intelligent designer to explain perceived gaps in current scientific understanding. This approach is fraught with liability, and actually counterproductive to the stated purpose. If history teaches any lesson, it is this: as understanding in science and biology inexorably march on the perceived mysteries of today will inevitably give way to well-understood processes, and science will systematically erase the prospects of a designer—one data point at a time.[54]

---

51. Cornell, "What Was God Thinking?" 72.
52. Coulson, *Science and Christian Belief*, 23.
53. Morris, "Boyle Lecture 2005: Darwin's Compass," 5–22.
54. Colling, "Intelligent Design Has No Place in Science Classes."

The Age of Life on Earth

In his book, *Random Designer*, Colling also states that "Ironically, at the precise moment we scientifically proved or disproved God's existence, our definition of God would have to be changed."[55]

Interestingly, all these responses appear to be in close agreement with sentiments expressed by C. A. Coulson FRS some fifty years ago, well before the appearance of ID. He regarded the attempt to define boundaries for science within the natural order as "a fatal step to take." He cited the example of Newton himself, who once wrote that since the diurnal rotations of the planets could not be derived from gravity, a Divine arm must be impressing it on them. Coulson took the view that this was not Newton's finest hour! Using the wave-particle duality of the electron as an example, Coulson stressed that when we encounter the edge of our knowledge we should not regard it as the "gateway of religion" but be led to "think a little more deeply about our science."[56] Along the same lines, Bonhoeffer made the following observation:

> If in fact the frontiers of knowledge are being pushed back (and that is bound to be the case), then God is being pushed back with them, and is therefore continually in retreat. *We are to find God in what we know, not in what we don't know; God wants us to realise his presence, not in unsolved problems but in those that are solved* (italics added).[57]

Mainstream theist scholars clearly view the ID movement as straying perilously close to the old "God of the Gaps" approach, in which advances in science inevitably reduce the need for a God until, like Carroll's Cheshire Cat, only his benign smile remains. They endorse the ID movement's opposition to the philosophical naturalism of contemporary science but maintain that it is possible, in fact essential, to practice science from a perspective of methodological naturalism. In other words, a Christian should actually *do* science in a manner indistinguishable from that of his/her secular colleagues. According to this view, the processes actually happening in the universe and the laws governing them comprise one level of reality. The ultimate metaphysical and religious significance of it all represents another. This distinction is nicely illustrated in C. S. Lewis's Narnian children's story, *The Voyage of the Dawn Treader*. Eustace meets Ramandu, a retired star of the Narnian skies, and comments that back in his world a star was a huge

---

55. Colling, *Random Designer*, 18.
56. Coulson, *Science and Christian Belief*, 32–38.
57. Bonhoeffer, cited in Venema and Knight, *Adam and the Genome*. 67.

ball of flaming gas. Very insightfully, in the context of our current discussion, Lewis has Ramandu reply: "Even in your world, my son, that is not what a star is but only what it is made of."[58]

Another reason for the caution shown by these scholars concerns the language of definite proof and disproof often encountered within ID. As Owen Gingerich points out, modern science chooses between competing theories on the basis of the hypothetico-deductive method, which stresses cohesion, coherence, and consistency.[59] Accordingly, this group of scholars prefers to make a cautious statement to the effect that, all things considered, the theistic option fits the primary data better and more easily than naturalistic alternatives. However, to go beyond this and seek to identify specific instances of design against a background of "natural" phenomena they would see as both futile and unnecessary. As evidence of the difficulty of correctly identifying irreducible complexity, they cite the very considerable advances made by modern science in establishing mechanisms whereby often-quoted features, such as the bacterial flagellum, could have evolved.

3.6 CONCLUSION

Can one be sure that there is a designer at all? One could ask what the biological world would look like if it were the product of pure chance. As we earlier noted, David Hume long ago suggested that it might easily look as if it were designed, when it really wasn't. Darwin said similarly.

The authors of this chapter think differently, but it is obvious that the design argument must be used somewhat tentatively and with care. The staggering complexity and functionality at the molecular level (DNA, proteins, and enzymes), whilst enormously impressive and suggestive of design, sometimes appears to result in poor or even macabre end products. Can the one designer be responsible for all this? The picture may also be complicated by changes in the original design plans, as Christians have frequently urged. Perhaps, too, there is some degree of freedom and self-determination built into this design process. It is also clear that among Christians, the design argument is conceived in very diverse forms, and we must display tolerance for those who think differently from us.

---

58. Lewis, *Voyage of the Dawn Treader*, 159.

59. Gingerich, "Is There a Role for Natural Theology Today?"; Gingerich, "Truth in Science: Proof, Persuasion and the Galileo Affair," 85.

Perhaps the best evidence for design comes from consideration of the anthropic principle with which we began, namely the fine-tuning of our universe for the support of carbon-based life. It would then be reasonable to assume that in some way the designer had a hand in the development of that life as well. Freeman Dyson remarked,

> The more I examine the universe, and the details of its architecture, the more evidence I find that the Universe in some sense must have known we were coming.[60]

BIBLIOGRAPHY

Aquinas, Thomas. *The Summa Theologica*, Part 1, Question 2, Article 3 (written between 1265 and 1274). Translated by Fathers of the English Dominican Province. Rome: Benzinger Bros., 1485.

Behe, Michael. *Darwin's Black Box: The Biochemical Challenge to Evolution*. New York: Simon & Schuster, 1996.

Bondi, Hermann, and Thomas Gold. "The Steady State Theory of the Expanding Universe." *Monthly Notices of the Royal Astronomical Society* 108 (1948) 252.

Bonhoeffer, Dietrich. Cited in Dennis R. Venema and Scot Knight. *Adam and the Genome: Reading Scripture after Genetic Science*. Grand Rapids: Brazos, 2007.

Colling, Richard. "Intelligent Design Has No Place in Science Classes." *The Institute for the Study of Christianity in an Age of Science and Technology* 1 (2005). https://iscast.org/wp-content/uploads/attachments/Colling_R_2005-08_Intelligent_Design_In_Schools.pdf.

———. *Random Designer*. Bourbonnais, IL: Browning, 2004.

Cornell, Eric. "What Was God Thinking? Science Can't Tell." *Time* (USA) 45 (2005) 72.

Coulson, Charles. *Science and Christian Belief*. London: Collins, 1955.

Davies, Paul. *The Goldilocks Enigma: Why is the Universe Just Right for Life?* London: Penguin, 2007.

Davis, Jimmy H. "A Fine-tuned Universe." In *Chance or Dance: An Evaluation of Design*, edited by Jimmy H. Davis and Harry L. Poe. West Conshohocken, PA: Templeton Foundation, 2008.

de Bekker, Charissa, et al. "Species-Specific Ant Brain Manipulation by a Specialized Fungal Parasite." *BMC Evolutionary Biology* 14:166 (2014). https://bmcecolevol.biomedcentral.com/articles/10.1186/s12862-014-0166-3.

Dembski, William. *The Design Inference: Eliminating Chance Through Small Probabilities*. Cambridge: Cambridge University Press, 1998.

———. *Intelligent Design: The Bridge Between Science and Theology*. Downers Grove, IL: IVP, 1999.

———. *Mere Creation: Science, Faith and Intelligent Design*. New York: InterVarsity, 1998.

---

60. Dyson, *Disturbing the Universe*, 250.

A Brief Review of Design in the Cosmos

Denton, Michael. "An Anti-Darwinian Intellectual Journey: Biological Order as an Inherent Property of Matter." Cited in *Uncommon Dissent: Intellectuals Who Find Darwinism Unconvincing*, edited by William A. Dembski, 153–76. Wilmington, DE: ISI, 2004.

Denton, Michael. *Nature's Destiny: How the Laws of Biology Reveal Purpose in the Universe*. New York: The Free Press, 1998.

Dunbar, David N. F., et al. "The 7.68-MeV State in C12." *Physical Review* 92 (1953) 649–50.

Dyson, Freeman. *Disturbing the Universe*. New York: Basic Books, 1979.

Forrest, Barbara, and Paul Gross. *Creationism's Trojan Horse*. Oxford: Oxford University Press, 2004.

Giberson, Karl W., and Francis F. Collins. *The Language of Science and Faith: Straight Answers to Genuine Questions*. Downers Grove, IL: IVP, 2011.

Gibson, Jim. "The Intelligent Design Movement, Part 2." *Ministry* 78:2 (2006) 13.

Gingerich, Owen. "Dare a Scientist Believe in Design?" Presented at the ISCAST COSAC (Conference on Science and Christianity), Adelaide, Australia, 2001.

———. "Is There a Role for Natural Theology Today?" In *Science and Theology: Questions at the Interface*, edited by Murray Rae et al., 43. Edinburgh: T & T Clark, 1994.

———. "Truth in Science: Proof, Persuasion and the Galileo Affair." *Perspectives on Science and Christian Faith* 55:2 (2003) 85.

Greenstein, George. *The Symbiotic Universe: Life and Mind in the Cosmos*. New York: William Morrow, 1988.

Guth, Alan. "Inflationary Universe: A Possible Solution to the Horizon and Flatness Problems." *Physical Reviews D* 23:2 (1981) 347–56.

Hoyle, Fred. "A New Model for the Expanding Universe." *Monthly Notices of the Royal Astronomical Society* 108 (1948) 372.

———. "The Universe: Past and Present Reflections." *Annual Review of Astronomy and Astrophysics* 20 (1982) 1–36.

Hoyle, Fred, et al. "A State in C^{12} Predicted from Astrophysical Evidence." *Physical Review* 92 (1953) 1095.

Hughes, David P., et al. "Behavioral Mechanisms and Morphological Symptoms of Zombie Ants Dying from Fungal, Infection." *BMC Ecology and Evolution* 11:13 (2011). https://www.biomedcentral.com/1472-6785/11/13.

Hume, David. *Dialogues Concerning Natural Religion* (1779). London: Penguin, 1990.

Illustra Media. *Unlocking the Mystery of Life*. Illustra Media, 2005.

Johnson, Phillip. *Darwin on Trial*. Downers Grove, IL: IVP, 1991.

Kepler, Johann. *Harmonices Mundi*, Book V, Introduction (1618). Cited in David Brewster, *The Martyrs of Science; or the Lives of Galileo, Tycho Brahe, and Kepler*. New York: Harper & Brothers, 1841.

Le Page, Michael. "Evolution Myths: The Bacterial Flagella is Irreducibly Complex." *New Scientist* (2008). https://www.newscientist.com/article/dn13663-evolution-myths-the-bacterial-flagellum-is-irreducibly-complex/.

Lewis, Clive, S. *The Voyage of the Dawn Treader* (1952). London: Fontana, 1981.

Livio, Mario, et al. "The Anthropic Significance of the Existence of an Excited State of ^{12}C." *Nature* 340 (1989) 281–84.

Macnab, Robert M. "The Bacterial Flagellum: Reversible Rotary Propeller and Type-III Export Apparatus." *Journal of Bacteriology* 181 (1999) 7149–53.

Morris, Simon Conway. *Life's Solution: Inevitable Humans in a Lonely Universe*. New York: Cambridge University, 2003.

———. "The Boyle Lecture 2005: Darwin's Compass: How Evolution Discovers the Song of Creation." *Science and Christian Belief* 18:1 (2005) 5–22.

Musgrave, Ian. "Evolution of the Bacterial Flagellum." In *Why Intelligent Design Fails: A Scientific Critique of the New Creationism*, edited by Matt Young and Tanet Edis, 72–84. Piscataway, NJ: Rutgers University, 2005.

Newton, Isaac. *Principia Mathematica-Mathematical Principles of Natural Philosophy*. 3rd ed. (1726). Translated by I. Bernard Cohen and Anne Whitman. London: The Folio Society, 1999.

Oberhummer, Heinz, et al. "Fine-tuning Carbon-based Life in the Universe by the Triple-alpha Process in Red Giants." In *The Future of the Universe and the Future of Our Civilization*, edited by Vladimir Burdyuzha and Grigory Khozin, 197–206. Singapore: World Scientific, 2000.

Oberhummer, Heinz, et al. "The Triple-alpha Process and its Anthropic Significance." In *Nuclei in the Cosmos V*, edited by Nikos Prantzos and Sotiris Harrissopulos, 119–23. Paris: Editions Frontières, 1998.

Paley, William. Cited in Frederick Le Gros Clark. *Paley's Natural Theology*. (1802). London: The Christian Evidence Committee of the Society for Promoting Christian Knowledge, 1885.

Pallen, Mark J. and Nicholas J. Matzke. "From the Origin of Species to the Origin of the Bacterial Flagella." *Nature Reviews Microbiology* 4:10 (2006) 784–90.

Pascal, Blaise. *Pensées*, Section 4.242 (1670). Translated by William F. Trotter. *Great Books of the World*, 33. Chicago: Encyclopedia Britannica, 1955.

Poe, Harry L. "The Design Argument." In *Chance or Dance: An Evaluation of Design*, edited by Jimmy H. Davis and Harry L. Poe, 49. West Conshohecken, PA: Templeton Foundation, 2008.

———. "The Mechanical Universe." In *Chance or Dance: An Evaluation of Design*, edited by Jimmy H. Davis and Harry L. Poe, 66. West Conshohecken, PA: Templeton Foundation, 2008.

Polkinghorne, John. "Cosmic Richness." Presented at the *Third International Philosophy, Science and Theology Festival*. Grafton, Australia, 2003.

Rees, Martin. *Just Six Numbers: The Deep Forces that Shape the Universe*. London: Phoenix, 2000.

Sagan, Carl. *Cosmos*. New York: Random House, 1980.

Ward, Ewan. "The Mechanics of Intelligent Design – Good Enough to Teach?" *Teach Journal of Christian Education* 2:2 (2008) 40–47.

Weinberg, Steven. *Facing Up: Science and its Cultural Adversaries*. Cambridge: Harvard University Press, 2001.

Wells, Jonathon. *Icons of Evolution*. Washington, DC: Regnery, 2000.

4

Dating Quaternary Life

Brian V. Timms

4.1 INTRODUCTION

THERE IS NO DOUBT that an essential element of the evolution story is time, lots of it! However, it must be recognized that considerable evidence of a long age for life on Earth appeared before Darwin's theory and much more has emerged since. It is also important to note that these data are largely independent of one's views on evolution.

It is convenient when discussing the age of life to differentiate between what is sometimes called shallow time and what is referred to as deep time. The former embraces a period from tens of thousands to hundreds of thousands of years, while deep time refers to much longer ages, generally hundreds or even thousands of millions of years. In this chapter, I attempt to conduct a walk through time. First to be considered are those domains of life that are widely agreed to provide evidence for a life history of tens of thousands of years. Even these ages are unpalatable for many conservative Christians, including most Seventh-day Adventists. I then move on to features of Earth's life history which appear to speak first of hundreds of thousands of years and eventually of a million years or more.

In essence, under examination is what is called the Quaternary period, which includes both the Holocene epoch (the last 12,000 years) and the Pleistocene epoch (to ca 2.6 Myr BP). The evidence examined in this paper is very accessible and relates to well-understood scientific processes. While in many cases, radiometric dating is used to quantify the dates claimed, it is important to note that approximations of these ages may be obtained by using a range of other, independent methods.

Much of the material presented in this chapter is not new and is widely known. Furthermore, many of the associated dating methods have enjoyed wide acceptance for decades. The consistency and reliability of their stories undergirds many global industries, such as mining. However, this testimony is frequently omitted from conservative discussions on Origins. Much of the additional data presented here has grown out of my personal and international research as a lake geomorphologist over the last five decades.

4.2 DENDROCHRONOLOGY

Dendrochronology is the technique of dating growth rings in trees to the year they were formed. Trees, particularly conifers in temperate climates, continually form distinct new layers of cells under the bark. Small dark cells are laid down in winter, and many larger and lighter-colored ones in summer. Each such pair forms a yearly growth ring. Good seasons generally form thicker rings and bad seasons thinner rings, so past climatic conditions can be inferred from growth ring patterns. This is one reason for their study.

But practical dendrochronology is not as easy as simply cutting down or coring a tree, counting the rings, and obtaining a direct age result. Variations are sometimes found to exist even between adjacent trees. For this reason, where possible, several trees from the same region are studied, thus increasing the measure of confidence in the results. Furthermore, there may occasionally be double growth rings or possibly none at all in a severe drought year. Complex mathematical pattern-recognition algorithms are sometimes required to identify a consistent pattern, although this is not generally the case. The oldest living trees are commonly considered to be the Bristlecone pines in the White Mountains of California, with the oldest tree, the Methuselah Tree, 4,852 years old.[1] However, older dates can be obtained by comparing inner growth ring sequences from living trees to outer sequences from fossilized trees, many of which still clearly display the growth ring patterns, although silicas have largely displaced carbon compounds in the cell matrix.

---

1. "Methuselah Tree."

I had some exposure to dendrochronology during the 1980s when helping with the program of an honors student at the University of Newcastle who used this method of dating on *Callitris* pines in my Paroo study area, northwest of Bourke, New South Wales. The biggest trees there were found to be about 300 years old. The best trees in Australia for dating are the native pines of the east coast, particularly Tasmania's Huon Pine. While individual Australian trees have not been dated beyond 3,000 years, a clonal colony of Huon Pine on Mt Read has been dated at 10,500 years by overlapping evidence from various living and dead stems.[2] Clonal tree colonies arise from root systems that are often much older than the living trunks currently above ground.

Oak chronology is understood to extend to 6,939 years in Ireland and 7,429 years in England. The record in the Californian Bristlecone pines goes back some 8,500 years. A cross-matched study of pines and oaks in central Europe indicated ages of 12,580 to 13,900 years.[3] None of these dates relies on any evidence other than the counting of growth rings. This therefore constitutes straightforward evidence that life on Earth goes back at least some 14,000 years. It is also important to note that these techniques present an essentially consistent picture of age across a range of species, growth habitats, and continents. Accordingly, the widely accepted dates from tree-ring sequencing have been used to calibrate some other dating methods.[4] Dates older than those mentioned above are sometimes claimed in connection with dendrochronology methods,[5] but since these generally involve more sophisticated and contentious procedures, they are not considered in this chapter.

4.3 SOIL PROFILES

Soils are vitally important to us all since most plants require a soil environment in which to grow. Many soils are formed from rocks under the action of physical, chemical, and, importantly, biological processes acting over considerable periods of time. These soils are multilayered, consisting of an uppermost A horizon, usually dark because of the high proportion of organic humus they contain; the B horizon or subsoil, usually a mixture of

2. "Huon Pine Growth of Mount Read."
3. Reimer et al., "INTCAL 13 and Marine 13 Radiocarbon."
4. Mitton and Grant, "Genetic Variation and the Natural History."
5. Pakenham, *Remarkable Trees of the World*.

some humus and the broken-down parent rock; the C horizon, a layer of weathered but unconsolidated rock particles having little biological activity; and lowermost, the R horizon consisting of the underlying bedrock.[6]

Soils show great variation in their characteristics depending on climate, land relief, biological activity, and the time since formation began. It is believed that most soils take several tens of thousands of years to develop, though occasionally (in certain restricted tropical conditions) somewhat less time is required. In most places, the earth is covered with just one set of soil layers, but sometimes there can be two or more of these layered sets, those underneath being known as "paleo" or fossil soils. These occur in places where the land surface has been modified, mainly by moving dunes or by the deposition of more layers of mineral matter by volcanic activity.

Graham Will, well-known to Australian Adventist scientists, studied New Zealand soils all his professional life and has suggested that there is no better place to study fossil soils than the volcanic country around Rotorua, situated on the North Island of that country.[7] There, the timing of various eruptions is well known from independent methods, including the use of radiometric indicators, rates of chemical weathering, and rates of landscape evolution. While the warm, moist New Zealand climate favors relatively quick soil development, the process still usually takes thousands of years. Successive eruptions have formed distinctive layers of tephra (volcanic ejecta), the new material arriving aerially. In some cases, the soil profiles formed from these do exhibit the classic A, B, and C layers mentioned above. In other places, evidence suggests that soils were buried by the next eruption before they had had time to differentiate into these layers. One such soil sequence in the caldera near Rotorua has ten distinct soil profiles, one upon the other, each with varying degrees of maturation and layering, each corresponding to a distinctive volcanic eruption, the oldest of which is thought to have occurred some 14,700 years ago.

Will reported on several New Zealand soils, including the basalt soils in the Auckland district. Basalt eruptions deposit lava over quite a small area, typically producing mound-like geographical features. In contrast, pumice eruptions distribute tephra over much wider regions. Within the region of Auckland city, there have been some forty basalt eruptions, each leaving what is now a hill.

---

6. Molloy, *Living Mantle*.
7. Will, "What Have Volcanoes and Soils Told Me?"

Dating Quaternary Life

The last of these formed Rangitoto Island near the entrance to Auckland harbor. Although there is tree cover over much of this island, not much soil is present, and in order to find nourishment, tree roots penetrate the scoria and shallow organic debris found between the rocks. Evidence from dendrochronology and archaeology suggests an age of between 500 and 700 years for this island.

One Tree Hill, located within the city region, is clearly much older. While there remain basalt boulders near the crater and on lower levels the cone is largely covered by young soils that support a ground cover of grass, although the shallow depth of the soil prevents mechanical cultivation. A range of independent techniques suggests an age of at least 15,000 years for One Tree Hill.

In clear contrast to these two examples are the well-rounded Bombay Hills, situated to the south of Auckland. These are covered in rich, red soils derived from the basalt rocks, which originally formed these hills. The soils are meters deep and easily cultivated mechanically. It is thought that continuous cultivation over many decades has already resulted in the loss of about a meter of this abundant topsoil. An assigned age of 100,000 years seems consistent with our knowledge of soil formation and development through weathering.[8]

Will notes that the clay content of soils is also an important indicator of age. Clays are the finest particles found in soils, small sand grains being one hundred times larger. The clays formed in pumice soils are mineral precipitates from the dissolved ash particles. The clay content of soils formed from the extensive Mt Taupo eruption some 2,000 years ago is found to be just 2 percent of the total mineral component. Other ash-derived soils have been found to contain up to 80 percent clay, speaking of much greater ages indeed.[9]

The same incremental story is told by a number of other soil types, such as those formed in loess, the fine material produced by glacial rock weathering. This material is transported by rivers and later blown out of their floodplains by strong winds. This material is then deposited, sometimes many kilometers away, where it accumulates, often slowly forming soils. Such soils are found on the eastern side of New Zealand's South Island.[10] On the face of such multi-stranded evidence, it seems reasonable to

---

8. Will, "What Have Volcanoes and Soils Told Me?" 65, 67.
9. Will, "What Have Volcanoes and Soils Told Me?" 65.
10. Will, "What Have Volcanoes and Soils Told Me?" 67, 68.

conclude that much longer periods of time are required to explain many soil structures than are available within a recent-life chronology.

4.4 RIVER DELTAS

The formation of deltas is frequently shoehorned into a post-Genesis-Flood scenario by recent-creationist authors and presented as evidence for a young Earth.[11] The Mississippi Delta (area 12,000 km^2) is often cited in this connection, even though it contains sediments that are up to six kilometers thick. According to classical geology, the huge Mississippi Bay formed in the Cretaceous, about 100 Myr ago, with the building of the delta itself taking place from the Miocene (23 Myr) onwards and particularly in the last 7,500 years of the Holocene (last 12,000 years). This ancient delta exhibits multiple dateable horizons. For example, old progradational shorelines of various ages are detectable from northern Arkansas (of Paleocene age) to far southern Mississippi (Pleistocene age), each marking major ancient depositional stages (deposodes).[12] It is only the comparatively recent depositions that have been the focus of short-term chronologists' interest.

Before proceeding with a discussion of deltas, it is necessary to explain what they are and how they relate to the age of life on Earth. Deltas are formed on flood plains as rivers enter the sea or large lakes, depositing their sediment load as the water flow decreases. We see this process in action in many places around our globe today. As would be expected, the sediments carried by rivers include particulate matter, such as soils and sand, but also organic material, such as leaves and pollens. However, owing to the turbidity of rivers and the irregular rearrangement of the sediments by subsequent events, such as floods, the organic remains are much more mixed up than, for example, organic remains found in the lake-core deposits discussed in Section 4.6. For this reason, deltaic sediments are cored less frequently than lake beds and fewer studies have been made of them. That being said, a number of investigations have been made into the organic content of deltaic sediments. Keil et al, for example, found in their study that some 70 percent of river-borne organics are lost or broken down before sedimentation occurs. Approximately 30 percent are deposited.[13] Perhaps unsurprisingly, sediments with high organic content have been found to be

11. Coffin and Brown, *Origin by Design*.
12. Galloway, "History of Cenozoic North American Drainage."
13. Keil et al., "Loss of Organic Matter."

Dating Quaternary Life

more highly susceptible to compaction.[14] Bianchi and Allison studied the transport and transformation of carbon in deltaic flows.[15]

Compared to the mouth of the Mississippi, Australia has no large deltas presently being constructed. This is partly because of its aridity and hence our lack of very large rivers. These circumstances result in relatively low erosion rates. In addition, the influence of the high-energy wave environment on the east coast discourages deltas from projecting seawards from that coast. Potentially the most active area with respect to delta formation is the north coast of New South Wales, as shown in Figure 4.1, where there are a number of quite large river valleys (e.g., the Hunter, Manning, Macleay, Clarence, and Tweed Rivers).

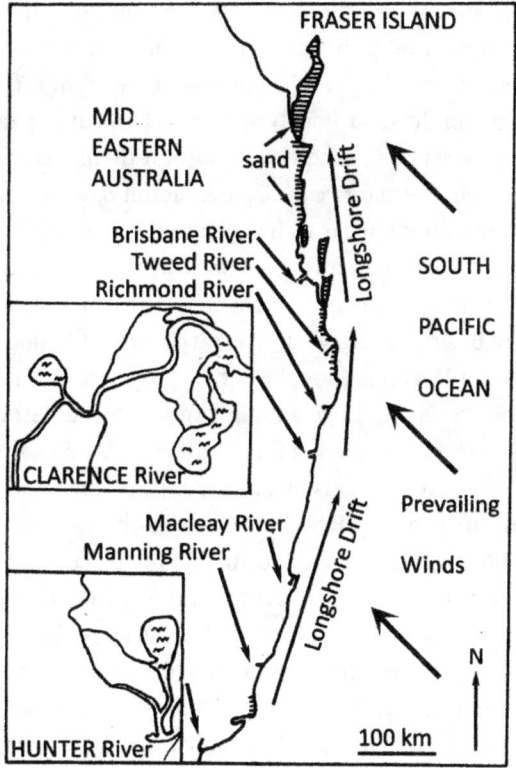

Figure 4.1 Longshore sediment drift on the coast of northern NSW and southern Queensland (drawn by B. Timms).

14. Keogh et al., "Organic Matter Accretion, Shallow Subsidence."
15. Bianchi & Allison, "Large-river Delta-front Estuaries."

The presence of estuarine lakes associated with these east coast delta formations, such as Fullerton Cove in the Hunter River, Wollowayah Lagoon in the Clarence River, and the Terranora Lakes in the Tweed River, may appear to imply that the respective rivers have not yet have had time to fill them with sediment, and hence that their deltas are quite young. However, as can be seen in the figure, these lakes and swamps are far from the main channels, and the regional topographies are such that flood flows largely miss them, passing directly out to sea. But instead of the sediments they carry being dropped to form off-shore *deltas in situ* they have been moved northwards by the strong, longshore drifts shown in Figure 4.1 to form the great sand islands of southern Queensland (e.g., Moreton and Fraser Islands), which appear to date back a few hundred thousand years.[16] This scenario demonstrates that each delta should be assessed on the basis of its topographic layout, and not just on its degree of infilling. While these Australian deltas might superficially appear to be young, a more complete analysis of the data reveals a much longer age for them. An additional complication is the well-attested rise in sea level about 6,000 years ago.[17]

But Australia does appear to have had mighty deltas in the past. Although thought to date much further back in time than the Quaternary Period under primary focus in this chapter, it is worth noting in passing that the Sydney Basin, a massive down-warped area (44,000 km^2) in mid-coastal New South Wales, is thought to be a large ancient delta and shows evidence of once receiving huge amounts of sediment.[18] Stratigraphic evidence suggests that it originated in the Permian (299 Myr), firstly as a series of deltaics interrupted by extensive forests, now coalbeds, which are found at depths of up to five km. Evidence suggests that almost all these coal beds formed autochthonously (i.e., formed in the place where found) from these swampy forests, with little allochthonous organic material washed in. (Allochthonous deposits are composed of material which has been transported some distance from the location in which they are found.) This coal is of excellent quality. The deltaic sand is thought to have been deposited during the Triassic (252–201 Myr) by an ancient river larger than the Amazon, bringing in large volumes of sediments from a once huge mountain massif southwest of Broken Hill. It is thought that the end of the Triassic

---

16. Davies, *Geographical Variation in Coastal Development*.
17. Henderson and Johnson, *Geology of Australia*.
18. Branagan et al. *Outline of the Geology and Geomorphology*.

was marked by various faulting and uplift processes that formed the Blue Mountains west of Sydney, among other features.

According to this scenario, these consolidated deposits were severely eroded in the Jurassic and Cretaceous and became dominated by deep, steep-sided valleys, as well as a few volcanic intrusions (such as Mt. Warrawolong in the Watagan Mountains to the west of Lake Macquarie, New South Wales). During the Cenozoic Era (66 Myr to the present), the Botany Basin is understood to have developed in its southeast, and this was filled by reworked sands. In the Holocene (last 12,000 years), the lower parts were flooded by rising sea levels after the last ice age, to form Sydney Harbour, Botany Bay, and the Hawkesbury River estuary, among other geographical features seen today. While it might be urged that these deposits were laid down during the biblical Flood, there is nowhere near enough time available in the last 4,000 years or so for them to have consolidated into rock and then be severely eroded to their present state. This is especially so in the case of reworked rocks where the process appears to have been repeated more than once.

Furthermore, the sedimentary rocks of the Sydney Basin contain abundant fossils, either in the coal measures or in the surmounting strata. Even if the conventionally accepted geological dates cited above are questioned, it is difficult to imagine how the complex cycles of geological activity required to produce these extensive, fossiliferous geographical features can be compressed into just a few thousand of years. These data do not speak only of great age but also of a complex history.

Concluding our digression, there are also thought to be many old, former river basins across Australia. One (now almost gone) is represented by the Kata Tjuta and Uluru residuals in central Australia.[19] On the basis of good evidence, these are identified as isolated remnants of extensive sandy alluvial fans once flowing in an easterly direction from former, massive mountains, the remains of which are the current Petermann and Musgrave ranges to the southwest. It is significant that "upstream" Kata Tjuta is composed of coarse conglomerate, being nearer the sediment source, while "downstream" Uluru is composed of sandstone, the sediments having suffered further corrasion (mechanical wear of rock by movement). There has also been considerable action by tectonic forces over the ages so that the strata of Kata Tjuta are dipping and the sandstone beds of Uluru are now almost vertical. For the typical tourist visiting Uluru, this explanation may

---

19. Henderson and Johnson, *Geology of Australia*.

seem far-fetched, as there is no other evidence of residuals from a delta, nor of a huge, ancient stream bed, nor of the massive mountain range from which it must have come. In a sense, this is a common problem in the Australian Outback — the landscape is so old that most of it has been eroded to a more-or-less level peneplain. Thus, the interpretation of remaining features is not as straightforward as in more recently formed landscapes, such as those of North America or Europe.

There are many rock pools (i.e., gnammas — see section 4.6.3— on top of Uluru and they are deeper than on most other rocks, such as granite outcrops. This could be attributed to the supposed great age of Uluru, and hence extra time for corrosive forces to work, but it could also be a result of the softer sandstone of Uluru *vis-à vis* hard granite. In a paper on this subject published recently, I argued that the near-vertical bedding planes of this huge rock have allowed easier access to water and hence have accelerated the rotting of the rock.[20] Again, this demonstrates the need for care when interpreting geological features. The multifactorial nature of landscapes precludes easy, amateur analysis.

Recent creationists typically offer a different explanation for the origin of Kata Tjuta and Uluru, couched in the supposed turmoil of the Genesis Flood.[21] According to this view, quick erosion of the nearby Petermann and Musgrave uplands during the Flood would have resulted in massive deposits of conglomerate upstream and sandstones downstream, as in the scientifically accepted model, but accumulating in vast depressions in the landscape and then consolidating quickly into the landscape we see today. But this fails to take into account the thousands of thin layers in Uluru and the hundreds of layers in the thicker, coarser Kata Tjuta sediments. These would appear to indicate multiple deposits over long periods of time rather than a single catastrophe or even a few such events. Another significant, and frequently raised objection to this explanation is that, as mentioned earlier, 4,000 years or so is insufficient time for the conversion of the unconsolidated sediments into hard rock.

20. Timms, "Pan Gnammas (weathering pits) across Australia."
21. Snelling, "Uluru and Kata Tjuta."

4.5 COASTAL LAKES

These are similar to the side lakes of the deltas discussed previously and, generally, are also recent landscape features, although not quite as recent as short-term creationists might wish. The New South Wales coastline, as for much of southeastern Australia, is one of drowned valleys and embayments that have been modified since glacial times by changes in sea level. Core samples have been taken from sediments in some of the lakes formed in this way, so we know more details of their past history than that of the deltas of northern NSW. Two examples near Newcastle are instructive.

The first of these, the Myall Lake system (Figure 4.2 a), is thought to go back to early post-glacial times (20,000 years ago), when a series of inner barriers, essentially a series of former beaches, developed seaward of what is now Myall Lakes proper. The sediment which was deposited came from the steady northward movement of sand from the Sydney area and beyond, and not from local rivers. Later, a more complex "outer barrier" developed seaward of this, and a lake developed, now called the Broadwater, ca 8,000 to 6,000 years ago.[22] There is a distinct break between the systems to the northeast of Myall Lake, as evidenced by a swamp and the freshwater Eurunderee Lagoon.[23] Many of the lakes of this system are brackish, owing to indirect contact with the oceanic water around Port Stephens, to the south. These lakes have not filled in because there is a lack of big rivers in the region. Cores have recorded comparatively recent changes due to white settlement, mainly in the amount of material deposited and sedimentation type. The precision with which the dating of these sudden changes in the core corresponds to historical data strongly suggests the overall reliability of the dating methods used and the dates quoted.

---

22. Thom et al., "Late Quaternary Evolution of Coastal Sand Barriers." See also Timms, *Lake Geomorphology*.

23. Timms, "Freshwater Lagoon, Myall Lakes National Park."

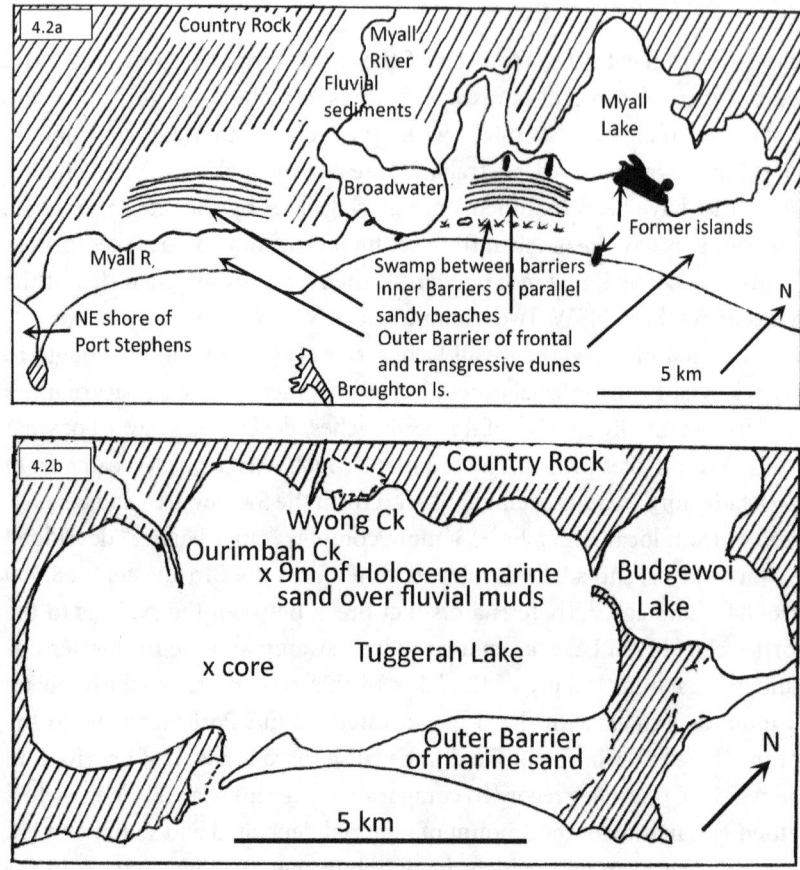

Figure 4.2 Two Australian coastal Lakes: (a) Myall Lakes, coastal NSW, 75 km north of Newcastle; (b) Tuggerah Lake, coastal NSW, 50 km south of Newcastle (drawn by B. Timms).

The second example is Tuggerah Lake (Figure 4.2 b), a large, former marine embayment now virtually cut off from the sea by an outer barrier to form a brackish lake. Cores of sediments reveal a thick, sandy overlay above organic sediments with base dates of 8,500 years ago. The outer barrier was built from 7,000 to 4,000 years ago.[24] Higher river flows during this time and local sand contributed, but again the outer sand barrier formed mainly from marine sand transported northwards. Lower river flows since then and periodic cut-offs from the ocean initiated a complex interaction

---

24. Macreadie et al., "Holocene Record of Tuggerah Lake."

between fluvial and marine-dominated conditions. Considerable mixing of bottom sediments was found, as evidenced by some sediments having ages of 7,000 years according to ^{14}C being found on top of some with ^{14}C ages of only 3,350 years. This mixing was reasonably attributed to storm waves when the embayment stage was exposed to oceanic storms. Major hydrological disturbances occur in Tuggerah Lake to this day, as evidenced by the floods of the recent La Niña years, 2020 to 2022. However, despite these irregularities, which were carefully reported by the researchers, the main distributions of the sedimentary data were very consistent with independently known data on, for example, sea-level changes over that period. Again, this correspondence indicates the overall dependability of the dating methods used.

4.6 FRESHWATER LAKES

Freshwater lakes have been the primary focus of my professional life. Over the last fifty years, I have visited most of the big ones across the world, mapped many of those in Australia, written a book entitled *Lake Geomorphology*,[25] and contributed a number of articles relating to lakes to scientific encyclopedias and journals.[26]

Coffin et al.[27] maintained that the presence of so many lakes in the global landscape, which have seen considerable infilling within living memory, constitutes evidence for a young Earth. I proceed to examine some of the evidence relating to this claim.

4.6.1 Different Types of Lakes

It is true that lakes are often claimed by conventional geologists to be temporary landscape features. This is not surprising, since it is certainly true for the numerous shallow lakes formed as a result of recent glaciation. It is also true for floodplain lakes, coastal lakes, and lakes formed by wind deflation (blowing out of unconsolidated sediments) in drylands. However, mainland Australia has few glacial lakes, so evidence of quick filling is largely lacking here. We do, though, have many relict billabongs, also known as

---

25. Timms, *Lake Geomorphology*.
26. 182 at last count.
27. Coffin and Brown, *Origin by Design*.

oxbow lakes, such as those along the Murray River. These are filling with sediment slowly, not nearly as fast as Coffin's shallow glacial lakes. Australia also has many inland lake beds that are now always dry, a consequence of Pleistocene (2.6–0.01 Myr) climate change, e.g., Lake Mungo in western New South Wales.

But one must consult all the available data before generalizations are made. If, in addition to Australian lakes, the big lakes of the world are considered there emerges a large body of evidence which cannot easily be explained by rapid processes. Lakes formed by tectonic earth movements are generally very old.[28] Uganda's Lake Victoria was formed by a complex of earth movements and volcanism and is thought to be 400,000 years old. Lake Superior (USA/Canada) is thought to have started as a mid-continental rift around 1.2 Myr ago. It was then much enlarged by continental glaciation during the last 100,000 years. In Africa, Lake Malawi (1.3 Myr), Lake Turkana (4 Myr), and Lake Tanganyika (10 Myr) provide other examples showing earlier rifting. There is reason to suppose that Lake Titicaca in the Altiplano (high plateau) of South America also has a tectonic origin dated at about 14–18 Myr. Since its origin, it has formed many elevated beaches that have datable features, such as organics (shells, wood) in old beaches or terraces. Lake Baikal (in southern Siberia) is similarly thought to owe its origin to plate rifting about 30 Myr ago.

Evidence suggests that Australia's Lake Eyre has existed in some form for at least two million years, as indicated by dated, old shorelines.[29] It is also thought that Australia's Lake George, near Canberra, was formed 4 Myr ago by faulting and has dated, elevated shorelines dated up to 27,000 years ago.[30]

Again, while many of these specific dates are derived from radiometric dating methods, which are not accepted by some Young-Earth-Creationists, the evidential stories told by these phenomena speak of interesting and varied histories, including life histories, which have taken place over long periods of time.

---

28. Burgess and Morris, *Natural History of Lakes*.
29. Timms, *Lake Geomorphology*.
30. Timms, *Lake Geomorphology*.

4.6.2 Lakes as Biological Time Recorders

Deep lakes are ecological sinks, accumulating sediments that often provide clues to past conditions in the lake and within its catchment. The simplest evidence is provided by alternating layers of contrasting thickness and color on the lake bottom. In mountain regions where there is an accumulation of snow over the winter, the following summer melt washes considerable amounts of coarse sediments, and occasionally of organic matter, into the deep lakes often found in the valleys. Many of these lakes were, in fact, formed by earlier glaciers. This material forms a thick, dark deposit. In winter, these lakes freeze over and the finer sediment of very small sand grains, silts, and clays settles out to form a thin, light-colored layer on the lake bottom. This pair of layers is called a varve.[31] Thousands of these layers can sometimes be identified, their relative thickness indicating weather conditions at the time each varve was formed. For recent layers, these weather patterns can sometimes be confirmed, at least qualitatively, from medieval records.

In some geologically recent lakes, up to 20,000 varve-pairs can be detected, supposedly indicating some 20,000 years of sedimentation. Young-Earth-Creationists argue strongly that most varves are not annual features, but that many layers are formed each year. Even geologists sometimes argue in specific cases about whether these varves are annual deposits or simply multiple laminations formed during a given calendar year. In very shallow lakes, for example, wind may disturb sediments or, in the case of lakes receiving irregular inflow, many varves may be laid down in some years. Occasional unusual weather disturbances may also result in the doubling of a varve or in a missing pair. It is also true that comparisons with ^{14}C dating of the same sediments sometimes result in a narrower time span for varve sets. However, large numbers of varve sets cannot easily be squeezed into a very short period, and the one varve pair per year remains a workable hypothesis in most circumstances. The warm-season component of a varve-pair often contains pollens from surrounding vegetation, from which changes in vegetation over time can be determined.

While discussing varves, it should be noted that the much-cited laminations of Eocene sediments (50 Myr) in the Green River formation in the USA appear to have resulted from a different scenario.[32] In this deposit there

---

31. Morris and Whitcomb, *Genesis Flood*.
32. Bradley, "The Varves and Climate of the Green River Epoch."

are very many thin sediment layers that have accumulated to a thickness of some 800 m, supposedly deposited over six million years. But these laminations are very thin, and, furthermore, seem to have been deposited quickly and repeatedly in shallow conditions. Fossil fish are common, together with a variety of other organic materials.[33] Accordingly, it would seem that these laminations are not classical varves.[34]

The organic sediments in various types of lakes also provide clues to the past. Volcanic crater lakes are particularly useful because of their closed catchments. Glacial lakes are also very important because of the great changes wrought by several glacial and interglacial periods in their history. The dating of sediments is often extended further back by other methods, including examination of their mineralogy, studies of pollens and other fossils, and the identification of stable isotopes. Using these techniques, many European glacial lakes have been found to have a well-established history dating back 100,000 years or more.

Shallow lakes can be cored simply with a length of PVC pipe, but deep lakes require expensive drilling gear. Cores are then analyzed, centimeter by centimeter, for layering and also for various components, including pollen grains, animal microfossils, coarse organic matter (such as leaves), and various chemicals. Volcanic minerals sometimes occur at spaced intervals in a core—for example, lakes on the North Island of New Zealand have many volcanic layers in their sediments. The chemical signatures of volcanic eruptions mean that such layers can usually be linked to specific eruptions.

Many Australian lakes have been cored. I shall consider two examples. Some sixty-meter cores have been studied from Lynch's (volcanic) Crater, on the Atherton Tablelands in Queensland. The crater originally contained a lake but it was drained when the wall was breached by natural erosional processes.[35] These cores were dated using a variety of methods, including ^{14}C, other radiometric methods, and mineralogical patterns. A number of pollen grains and charcoal fragments have also been identified and counted. The results are consistent between cores and indicate successive periods of different vegetation types around the lake: sclerophyll (eucalypts and wattles) woodland, araucarian (southern conifers, e.g., Hoop Pine) rainforest, and complex rainforest, as shown in Figure 4.3.

33. Morris and Whitcomb, *Genesis Flood*.
34. Green River Formation.
35. Kershaw, "Pleistocene Vegetation of the Humid Tropics."

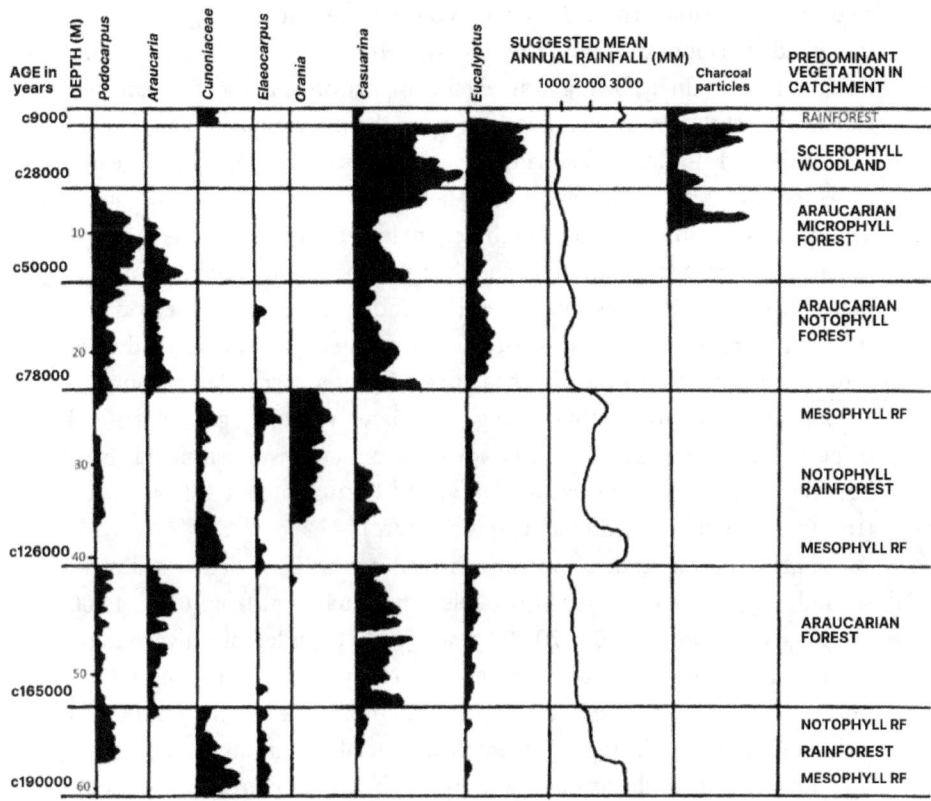

Figure 4.3 Core data from Lynch's Crater on the Atherton Tablelands (modified from Kershaw, 1994).

The ultimate causes of the variation in fossils found in the bottom mud are minor climate changes, mainly expressed in rainfall variations. It can be seen that there is a marked increase in charcoal at about 38,000 years BP, thought to be caused by the firestick-farming methods of Aboriginals, following their arrival in this region about that time.

The second Australian example is Lake Selina on the west coast of Tasmania. It was formed by glaciation, but was unoccupied by ice during the last (Wisconsin) glaciation, as indicated by a geomorphic study of the site. The nearest glacier at that time flowed down from the Tyndall Range and covered Lakes Huntley and Rolleston with an outwash area beyond their terminal moraines. Colhoun et al[36] studied a 400 cm core from the 6.5

36. Colhoun et al., "Late Pleistocene Vegetation and Climate History."

m deep Lake Selina. The sedimentary column was dated using ^{14}C by two independent laboratories and the base rock by U/Th. The dating was difficult to resolve finely, owing to uneven compaction, and more recent ages were found at the lowest depths, contrary to the usual expectation.

This study indicates that dates are not always easy to interpret. The unexpected initial ^{14}C results mentioned here were reported in the literature. The authors, personally known to myself, made no attempt to hide their apparent problem. Scientists are generally open about unexpected results. A plausible explanation was subsequently found and the dating method was refined as a result. This age inversion was attributed to humic groundwater movement through the base of the core. This water carries large, spurious amounts of new carbon, thus giving anomalous younger ages, which had to be ignored. The real age of the lowest sediments was estimated to lie between 70,000 years (by extrapolation of ^{14}C curves) and 160,000 years (from U/Th dating of sediment below the core).

Palynological studies (pollen analysis) of the Lake Selina sediment strongly suggest that rainforest occupied the catchment from 0 to 14,000 years ago and from 45,000 to 70,000 years ago. In the interval between these rainforest communities, the catchment was clothed with alpine vegetation. This is exactly what would be expected from the change in temperature and sedimentation rate during the Wisconsin glacial maximum in a lake not directly affected by glaciers at that time. In fact, I am confident that sediments in this lake are older than 70,000 years and that this lake was formed before that date by an earlier, more severe glaciation.

Lake Malawi provides a final, non-Australian example. A great deal of evidence suggests that this lake is very different from the Australian examples and, at 1.3 Myr, it is much older.[37] Its age was determined by radiometric dating of flood basalts on either side of the lake. Put simply, these flows split as Africa was pulled apart by the forces of plate tectonics. It is the most southerly of the Rift Valley Lakes in Africa and, with a depth of 700 m, is the fourth-deepest lake in the world. It is unusual in that the basal 500 m is anoxic (no oxygen) so that sediments settle but do not decompose. The rainy season occurs during summer, so most sediment is delivered then. This is also the season during which biological production is highest. However, some sediments are also laid down during winter. Accordingly, the lake forms two layers of sediment each year, neither of which decomposes. These are easily identifiable as many thousands of pairs. Primary dating is

---

37. Duff, "Lake Malawi Sediment."

by ^{14}C back to 50,000 years, i.e., at sediment depths down to about twenty meters.

At a depth of twenty-eight meters in the sediments, there is a layer of volcanic glass. Chemical evidence relates this deposit to the world's largest-ever volcanic explosion, in Toba Lake, Sumatra. This eruption affected much of the world and has been dated by various methods and at different sites at ~74,000 years. The ^{14}C age of 50,000 years cited immediately above for sediments found at a depth of 20 m is clearly consistent with an age of 74,000 years for sediments found at a depth of twenty-eight meters. (Dating after this time is confirmed by magnetic pole reversals and finally by U series elements, but this is secondary to the argument here.) As well as demonstrating broad coherence between the different dating methods used, these data suggest that the sedimentation rate was fairly constant over a long period when the lake was stable. The present sediment rate is 0.3–0.4 mm per year, the rate over the years datable by ^{14}C is 0.3 mm/year, and the mean rate over the last 74,000 years is 0.38 mm per year (after compression and removal of water). These convergent data provide convincing evidence that the dating methods are accurate over the last 74,000 years. Young-Earth-Creationists appear to ignore this lake.

Deeper into the Lake Malawi core, at 400 m, the layers are compacted and dating is more complicated. Additionally, the lake apparently went through some convulsions attributed to droughts that occurred roughly every 100,000 years. These durations are estimated by organic C analysis and ^{18}O determinations (used as a proxy for temperatures). As a result of these studies, it is estimated that the sedimentary history goes back 1.3 Myr.[38]

It is obvious to scientists that lake muds are excellent recorders of Earth's history and that while this history may be short in shallow, recent lakes, it extends back to a million years or more in older, deeper lakes. Moreover, the age of the geological setting correlates well with the age of the muds and the characteristics of life recorded in them.

Most importantly for the age of life, one must recognize that, as discussed, the sediments within all these lakes contain microfossils (for example, pollen grains, insect and crustacean parts, and snails) with those at the bottom of the sedimentary profile necessarily having ages close to that of the lake. Again, most recent creationists do not appear to appreciate this point.

---

38. Lyons et al., "Continuous 1.3-million-year Record."

4.6.3 Evidence of Longer Lake Ages from Speciation

Another aspect of evidence associated with long ages of lakes involves speciation. It is now generally accepted by Young-Earth-Creationists, including the Geoscience Research Institute (GRI), that maybe all species in a genus and even within a family may have developed since Noah's flood.[39] After all, many families have thousands of species and they couldn't possibly have all fitted into the ark. The speed with which species can change and form a different species varies tremendously with the type of organism and habitat it occupies. For instance, in plants, new species can form almost instantaneously by polyploidy, e.g., by doubling the number of chromosomes at cell division. However, evidence suggests that usually populations of a species slowly drift apart genetically, especially if they are isolated, over a time scale ranging from 1,000 to 100,000 years or more, so considerable time is required to form a new species.

Gnammas

The first of these speciation studies involves gnammas, which I have studied over the last twenty years. These are isolated rock pools, generally on granitic hilltops. Figure 4.4 A–E shows some Western Australian gnammas and some of their small inhabitants. Gnammas are of two basic types: (a) shallow pan gnammas (about 20 cm deep) which dry regularly each year, the inhabitants surviving by depositing drought-resistant eggs in the bottom muds; (b) deeper pit gnammas (about one m deep), which generally contain water much or all of the year and support ordinary pond fauna. These are generally not as diverse. Pan and pit gnammas are formed by a range of physicochemical processes which need not concern us here.

In order to survive in a pan gnamma, species require various life-history specializations, which take time to develop and accumulate in the genetic code. The older the gnamma, the more likelihood there would be that such specializations would occur as new species develop. These specializations involve microevolution, with only a few families of crustaceans involved, but there are many genera and a host of closely related species. Of course, the isolation of populations in this process is important, and it so happens that these pan gnammas are effectively isolated across the

---

39. Coffin and Brown, *Origin by Design*.

countryside, often in groups, on various rock outcrops. Pan gnammas are then ideal sites to encourage speciation over long time periods.

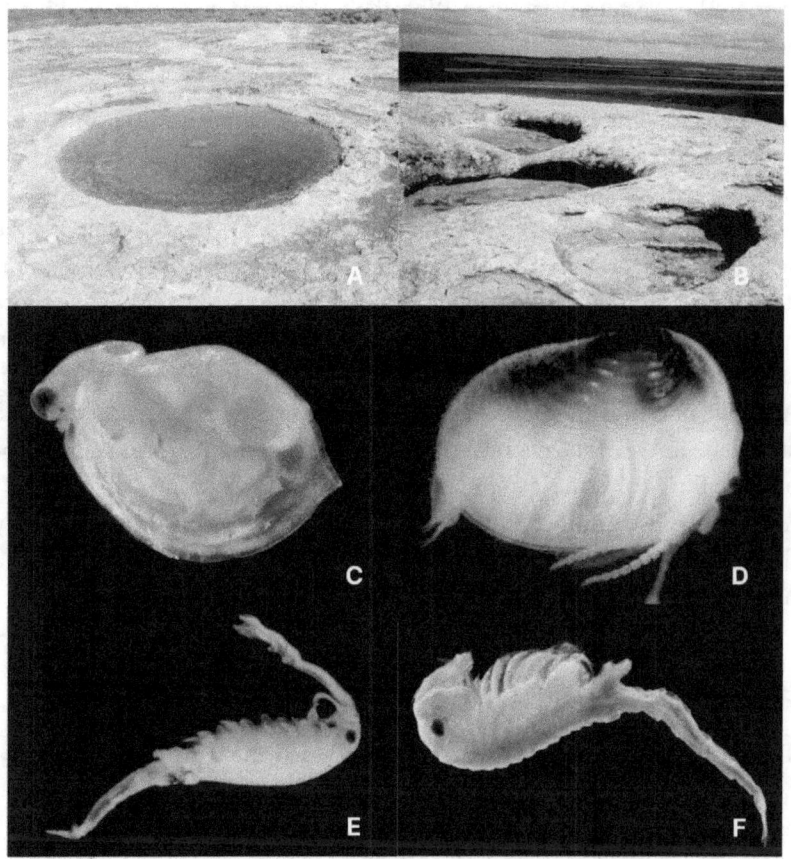

Figure 4.4 Some Australian gnammas and some of their denizens: (A and B) Gnammas on two inselbergs in Western Australia; (C) Waterflea (*Ceriodaphnia*), approx. 1 mm in length; (D) Clam Shrimp (*Ozestheria mariae*), approx. 5 mm in length; (E) Fairy Shrimp (*Branchinella longirostris*), approx. 12 mm in length. Also, (F) a Brine Shrimp (*Parartemia minuta*), approx. 9 mm in length. These swim upside down (photographs by B. Timms).

Gnammas in North America, Europe, and Africa rarely support more than ten species per pool, although this number can rise to twenty or thirty if on a mountain. The small pools found near the summits of high country in central Victoria are typically found to contain about eight species of invertebrates on any one sampling date. This is called the alpha diversity. If all the pools on a particular peak are examined the figure rises to about thirty-five species—the beta diversity. For all outcrops in the vicinity, some fifty species have typically been identified—the gamma diversity.[40] However, in the Western Australian Wheatbelt, there are many scattered inselbergs (rocky hills) of granite, and the small pools found near their summits typically each have twenty-five to thirty species of invertebrate present on any one sampling date.[41] If all the pools per inselberg are examined, the figure rises to about sixty species,[42] and for such outcrops across the whole wheatbelt, a gamma diversity of some 220 species is found.[43]

While local ecological conditions contribute to these differences, the age of the rocks themselves is also a major contributing factor. The granites in Victoria are thought to be about 400 million years old, while those in Western Australia are thought to be much older, at around two billion years old.[44] The implication is that pools are likely to be older in Western Australia and thus there has been more time for speciation. Moreover, the landscape in Western Australia is one of the oldest in the world, and appropriately, the pool fauna is found to be the most diverse in the whole world.[45] In fact, scientists from various overseas research laboratories come to study the unique biology of the gnammas of Western Australia. I have shown a number of them around this region and contributed to their research.

Brine Shrimp Diversity

The second study of speciation is provided by brine shrimps in continental salt lakes. A specimen is shown in Figure 4.4 F. Australia has its own endemic genus, *Parartemia*, with eighteen known species, ten of which I discovered, named, and described. Thirteen of these occur in Western Australia, seven in South Australia, and only one each in Victoria, New South Wales, and Queensland (with some sharing of species).[46] This also accords with the notion of greater opportunity for speciation events in the much older landscapes of WA (up to ca. two Byr) than in the volcanic plains of western Victoria (as young as 6,000 years).

40. Timms, "Study of the Gnammas (rock pools)."
41. Timms, "Seasonal Study of Aquatic Invertebrates."
42. Timms, "Seasonal Study of Aquatic Invertebrates."
43. Pinder et al., "Granite Rock Outcrop Pools."
44. Timms, "Study of the Gnammas (rock pools)."
45. Brendonck et al., "Invertebrates in Rock Pools."
46. Timms, "Review of the Biology of Australian Halophilic."

Biodiversity in Deep Lakes

Another related issue is the biodiversity found in large, deep lakes. Tasmania's Lake St Clair is relatively large and, at 163 m deep, is Australia's deepest lake. All the evidence suggests that it was formed by a series of glaciations during the ice ages, some 20,000 to 100,000 years BP. There has never been a count of its invertebrate species richness (I analyzed the bottom-mud-dwelling animals in 1972), but I would be surprised if there were more than 150 invertebrate species in the whole lake. European glacial lakes of similar age, such as those in Switzerland, have been studied in more detail and have been found to have from 200 to 300 species. By contrast, Lake Tanganyika in Africa has ca. 1,000 species of invertebrates, including 200 crustaceans, and displays high levels of endemism (i.e., uniqueness to the site). All the geological evidence suggests that this lake is the second oldest in the world, at 10 Myr. It is certainly the second largest (18,900 km^3) and the second-deepest (1,471 m) in the world. Even if the large space available for speciation is taken into account, the species count is perfectly consistent with such a great age for this lake.

Lake Baikal (Siberia) is thought to be the world's oldest lake at 30 Myr. It is also the deepest (1,642 m) and largest lake (23,615 km^2 area) on the planet. It is known to support at least 2,300 species of plants and animals, of which 80 percent are endemic.[47] For instance, there are 300 species of amphipod crustaceans (sidehoppers), all endemic. The most parsimonious explanation given for this unrivaled diversity is in terms of its isolation and gigantic size, but also the great length of time that has been available for speciation to take place.

4.7 CONCLUSION

I have marched through the Quaternary and occasionally beyond and I hope not to have lost too many readers along the way. The dendrochronological evidence for trees having lived on Earth for about 14,000 years is difficult to refute. It is based on the simple arithmetic of counting yearly growth rings and requires no reliance on various other dating methods. The soil data also provide very direct evidence for similar and somewhat longer ages.

---

47. Burgess and Morris, *Natural History of Lakes*.

The Age of Life on Earth

It is true that much of the evidence cited later in this chapter does rely to some extent on radiometric dating. I have been involved peripherally in projects that used these dating methods. I can only say that, while there can be problems in sample preparation and in the interpretation of data, the overall results I have seen are generally consistent and meaningful. Furthermore, I have found that my extensive studies of deltas and lakes all over the world point unambiguously to a much older age for life on Earth than I was taught to believe in my youth.

BIBLIOGRAPHY

Bianchi, Thomas S., and Mead A. Allison. "Large-river Delta-front Estuaries as Natural Recorders of Global Environmental Change." *Proceedings of the National Academy of Sciences of the United States of America (PNAS)* 106:20 (May 19, 2009) 8085–92.

Bradley, Wilmot H. "The Varves and Climate of the Green River Epoch." *U.S. Geological Survey Professional Paper* 158 (1929) 87–110.

Branagan, David F., et al. *An Outline of the Geology and Geomorphology of the Sydney Basin.* Sydney: Science, University of Sydney, 1976.

Brendonck, Luc, et al. "Invertebrates in Rock Pools." In *Invertebrates in Freshwater Wetlands,* edited by D. Baxter and D. Boix, 25–53. New York: Springer, 2016.

Burgess, Mary, and Pat Morris. *The Natural History of Lakes.* Cambridge: Cambridge University, 1987.

Coffin, Harold, and Robert H. Brown. *Origin by Design.* Hagerstown, MD: Review and Herald, 2005.

Colhoun, Eric A., et al. "Late Pleistocene Vegetation and Climate History of Lake Selina, Western Tasmania." *Quaternary International* 57–58 (June, 1999) 5–23.

Davies, Jack L. *Geographical Variation in Coastal Development.* London: Longman, 1977.

Duff, R. Joel. "The Lake Malawi Sediment Chronometer and the Toba Super Eruption." *Naturalis Historia* (2019). https://thenaturalhistorian.com/2019/11/11/the-lake-malawi-sediment-chronometer-and-thetoba-super.

Galloway, William. "History of Cenozoic North American Drainage Basin Evolution, Sediment Yield and Accumulation in the Gulf of Mexico Basin." *Geosphere* 7:4 (2011) 938–73.

Green River Formation. https://en.wikipedia.org/wiki/Green_River_Formation.

Henderson, Robert, and David Johnson. *The Geology of Australia.* 3rd ed. Port Melbourne, Australia: Cambridge University, 2016.

Huon Pine Growth of Mount Read. Wondermondo Wonders of the World. https://www:wondermondo.com/huon-pine-growth-of mount-read/.

Keil, Richard G., et al. "Loss of Organic Matter from Riverine Particulates in Deltast." *Geochimica et Cosmochimica Acta* 61:7 (April 1997) 1507–11.

Keogh, Molly E., et al. "Organic Matter Accretion, Shallow Subsidence and River Delta Sustainability." *Journal of Geophysical Research: Earth Surface* 126:12 (2021).

Kershaw, A. Peter. "Pleistocene Vegetation of the Humid Tropics of Northeast Queensland, Australia." *Palaeogeography, Palaeoecology & Palaeoclimatology* 109 (1994) 399–412.

Dating Quaternary Life

Lyons, Robert P., et al. "Continuous 1.3-million-year Record of East African Hydroclimate, and Implications for Patterns of Evolution and Biodiversity." *Proceedings of the National Academy of Sciences of the United States of America (PNAS)* 112 (2015) 15568–73.

Macreadie, Peter, et al. "Holocene Record of Tuggerah Lake Estuary Development on the Australian East Coast: Sedimentary responses to sea level fluctuations and climate variability." *Geographical Research* 5 (2015) 57–73.

Methuselah Tree, https://en.wikipedia.org/wiki/Methuselah_(tree). Also https://www.google.com/search?q=historic+mysteries+oldest+tree.

Mitton Jeffry B., and Michael C. Grant. "Genetic Variation and the Natural History of Quaking Aspen." *Bioscience* 46:1 (1996) 25–31.

Molloy, Les. *The Living Mantle: Soils in the New Zealand Landscape*. Wellington, NZ: Mallison Rendel, 1988.

Morris, Henry M., and John C. Whitcomb. *The Genesis Flood*. Philadelphia: The Presbyterian and Reformed, 1963.

Pakenham, Thomas. *Remarkable Trees of the World*. New York: Norton, 2002.

Pinder, Adrian M., et al. "Granite Rock Outcrop Pools in South-western Australia: Foci of diversification and refugia for aquatic invertebrates." *Journal of the Royal Society of Western Australia* 83 (2000) 149–61.

Reimer, Paula J., et al. "INTCAL 13 and Marine 13 Radiocarbon Age Calibration Curves 0–50,000 Years CAL BP." *Radiocarbon* 55 (2013) 1869–87.

Snelling, Andrew A. "Uluru and Kata Tjuta: A Testimony to the Flood." *Creation* 20:2 (1998) 36–40.

Thom, Bruce, et al. "Late Quaternary Evolution of Coastal Sand Barriers in the Port Stephens – Myall Lakes Area, Central NSW, Australia." *Quaternary Research* 15 (1981) 345–64.

Timms, Brian V. "The Freshwater Lagoon, Myall Lakes National Park." *Hunter Natural History* 4 (1972) 6–10.

———. *Lake Geomorphology*. Adelaide, Australia: Gleneagles, 1992.

———. "Pan Gnammas (weathering pits) across Australia: Morphology in Response to Formative Processes and its Influence on Biological Diversity." *International Journal of Geosciences* 12 (2021) 984–93.

———. "A Review of the Biology of Australian Halophilic Anostracans (Branchiopoda: Anostraca)." *Journal of Biological Research – Thessalonika* 21 (2014) 1–8.

———. "Seasonal Study of Aquatic Invertebrates in Five Sets of Latitudinally Separated Gnammas in Southern Western Australia." *Journal of the Royal Society of Western Australia* 95 (2012) 13–28.

———. "A Study of the Gnammas (rock pools) in Some Granitic Outcrops in Central Victoria, with Comparisons of Their Invertebrate Communities Across Southern Australia." *Journal of the Royal Society of Victoria* 129 (2017) 21–36.

Will, Graham. "What Have Volcanoes and Soils Told Me?" *Spectrum* 38:4 (2010) 64–69.

5

Radiocarbon Dating of Once-living Specimens

Geoffrey A. Madigan and Colin L. Waters

EDITOR'S NOTE

THIS IS THE LONGEST and perhaps the most technical chapter in this book, and it was thought useful to justify this complexity. Carbon dating is one of the most widely employed methods used to date the remains of organisms thought to have lived within the last 50,000 years. It has developed enormously since the invention of the method by Willard Libby in the 1940s and now involves complex instrumentation and extensive and complicated processes. Popular attempts to discredit this dating method by opponents of old life face a high risk of oversimplification, and this can lead to serious misunderstanding. The authors of this chapter have attempted to provide sufficient information about the theory, the techniques of carbon dating, and the principles of analysis to identify how and where these misunderstandings have occurred.

Sections 5.1 and 5.2 present a summary of the fundamental Physics undergirding carbon dating. These equations are now more than one hundred years old and are not really in dispute. While it is important to state these, non-mathematical readers can read quickly through this material.

The following sections detail the historical development of calibration conventions (5.3), instrumentation and reporting conventions (5.4), practicalities of measurement, including sample preparation (5.5), the important role of background samples (5.6), studies on the stability of decay rates (5.7) and a summative conclusion (5.8). Admittedly, this can be difficult to follow in places, but a close reading will reward toilers with a much more comprehensive understanding than is available in most popular evaluations of this dating method.

5.1 INTRODUCTION TO RADIOACTIVITY

5.1.1 History and Basics of Radioactivity

The term *radioactivity* was introduced to science by Marie Curie in 1898. Her work on the discovery and isolation of radioactive elements (radium and polonium) in pitchblende, a mining waste product, earned her two Nobel prizes, added new elements to the periodic table, and challenged the longstanding idea of the time that the atom was indivisible. Until the late 1890s, the atom was thought to be the fundamental unit of matter. This entity had been proposed and labeled *atomos* (meaning indivisible) by Democritus of Abdera around 430 BC.[1] Over the last 120 years, experimental and theoretical developments in atomic theory have resulted in the abandonment of most of the original Greek ideas about the properties of the atom, such as its being uniform, solid, incompressible, and indestructible. However, the concept of the atom remains in language and literature.

Radioactivity is a natural process involving changes in the internal arrangement of atoms, producing different atoms as well as radiation. These are called *by-products* or *daughter* products. This is the stuff of nuclear physics and has nothing to do with chemical reactions. Like many other areas of science, this topic has its fair share of imprecise explanations, confusion of measurement units, and out-of-context claims. Many of these are discussed in the following sections, with an emphasis on presenting a balanced appraisal of the scientific literature on the subject.

Why does radioactivity occur? A common response explains the root cause of radioactivity as a preference for a lower energy state of an atom. However, radioactive processes conserve many properties, one being energy, so this response is imprecise at best. Radioactivity, like every other natural process, follows the rules of entropy which imply that it is more likely that a system will transition to a less-ordered state. Hence we see in radioactivity the more probable outcome. More detailed explanations of

---

1. Bertsch et al., "Atom," in Encyclopedia Britannica.

these processes require quantum mechanical descriptions of fundamental interactions between very small bits of matter, a topic which is revisited in Section 5.7.

The present scientific understanding of matter is known as the *Standard Model* and describes how the fundamental units of matter relate in synergy with fundamental "forces" (or interactions). This model has developed from theoretical and experimental findings over the last ~150 years, including a focused effort during the atomic research program of World War II. The model broadly assumed its current form in the 1960s, identifying two categories of fundamental particles: quarks and leptons. Quarks and their interaction fields (called gluons) combine to form bound states (called hadrons) such as protons and neutrons. Leptons (e.g., electrons, muons, neutrinos) interact with the electroweak force (and gravity), providing the nuclear mechanism responsible for radioactivity. Quantum field theory (QFT) and quantum electrodynamics (QED), which emerged around the 1960s as well, also contribute to our understanding of radioactivity.

Each element listed in the Periodic Table is comprised of atoms having a unique number of protons in the atomic nucleus. It is possible for the atoms of a particular element to contain different numbers of neutrons, the other common particle found in nuclei. This differing number of neutrons gives rise to what are called *isotopes* of the element. Details of the known elements are available from an interactive chart.[2]

Radioactivity is often described as radioactive *decay*. The reality is closer to radioactive *transmutation* whereby internal atomic processes trigger a change from one element into one or more different elements. However, common use has popularized the less accurate term "decay," so "transmutation" and "decay" of atoms are often used interchangeably. Radioactive transmutation is an internal atomic process that is usually independent of external conditions such as pressure, temperature, and chemical environment.[3] One example of radioactive transmutation which *is* initiated by an external circumstance is the special mechanism that allows electron or neutron capture by a nucleus. High-intensity magnetic fields in some stars are also known to influence nuclear dynamics. However, for the purposes of radiometric dating, radioactive processes are considered to be

2. Airey et al., "Scientific Basis," in *Radioactivity in the Environment*. An interactive Periodic Table chart available, see Periodic Table.

3. By 1930, after extensive experimentation, Rutherford announced that "the rate of transformation of an element has been found to be a constant under all conditions." See Rutherford et al., *Radiations from Radioactive Substances*.

independent of external influence. Some recent discussions about this topic are summarized in Section 5.7.

To quantify nature consistently, the scientific community has agreed upon a standard system of units and measures known as the *SI system* (International System of Units) established (in 1960) and maintained by the General Conference on Weights and Measures.[4] Quantitative properties of nature are conventionally expressed in terms of *SI units*. The SI unit of time is the second (s) of length is the meter (m), and of mass is the kilogram (kg). The SI unit of radioactivity (or just *activity*) is the becquerel (Bq) where 1 Bq is the activity level at which one nucleus decays per second. *Specific activity* is the activity per unit mass of the radioactive material, with the SI unit becquerel/kilogram (Bq/kg).

Radioactive isotopes are often described as *unstable*, but this can be an imprecise term. The number of isotopes considered to be unstable depends on a number of factors such as the definition of *stable*: whether only those elements that occur naturally on Earth are included and on advances in measurement techniques. For example, Marcillac et al. have reported a half-life of $(1.9 \pm 0.2) \times 10^{19}$ yr for ^{209}Bi (bismuth), which was previously considered to be stable.[5] The half-life is the time taken for half of the parent atoms to transmute into the daughter product(s). Not surprisingly, radioactive isotopes having long half-lives tend to have low activity and vice versa. Radioactive elements have a wide range in *activity* and half-lives, the latter ranging from 10^{-24} s to 10^{30} s. The most active isotope known is polonium-210 (^{210}Po), an alpha-emitter that glows blue. It has a half-life of 138 days and an activity of 166 TBq/g (tera-becquerel per gram) where the "tera" prefix represents a multiplying factor of 10^{12}. The isotope of carbon used in dating has eight neutrons in the atom along with the required six protons and so is described as carbon fourteen and often written as ^{14}C. It has a half-life of approximately 5,700 years, although much more will be said on that topic later.

These example data show the range of units employed in the literature and illustrate that, unfortunately, SI units are not always used in reporting. Half-lives of radioactive substances may be quoted in years, days, seconds, or other units of time. Specific activity can be given in Bq/g (per gram) rather than Bq/kg (the SI unit), disintegrations per minute per gram of carbon (dpm/gC), or even curie per gram (Ci/g). For reference, the curie

---

4. The website is part of the Bureau International des Poids et Mesures.
5. Marcillac et al., "Experimental Detection of α-particles."

is the older (non-SI) unit for radioactivity. One curie (Ci) corresponds to 3.7×10^{10} Bq (decay per second). Furthermore, there are at least three general protocols for reporting ^{14}C activities, as discussed by Mook and Plicht.[6] These are the absolute activity, activity ratio, and relative activity. Unfortunately, the scientific community has not eradicated all the confusion resulting from the use of non-SI units, so readers must be sufficiently agile in unit conversions. Some of the consequences of using non-standard (SI) measures are discussed in Sections 5.4 to 5.6.

Our growing understanding of the internal composition, dynamics, and energy configuration of atomic nuclei has given rise to modern applications of nuclear processes. These include electricity generation using nuclear energy, nuclear medicine, and more importantly for this chapter, the estimation of the ages of various rocks and some remains of life forms from the current relative abundance of various radioactive isotopes. Of these dating methods ^{14}C, introduced by Willard Libby and his colleagues in the late 1940s, is perhaps the best known to the popular mind and is used to directly date the remains of once-living organisms. This method currently returns ages of up to about 50,000 years, much greater than the few thousand years with which many Christians feel comfortable.

Accordingly, the methodology of the ^{14}C dating method has attracted a great deal of conservative criticism. One idea proposed by critics to reduce what are to them unacceptably old ^{14}C ages questions the fundamental notion, affirmed by physics, of the constancy of the radioactive half-life. An informed discussion of this objection requires some understanding of the mechanism of radioactivity, the Standard Model, and aspects of Quantum Field Theory. This objection, along with some others, is taken up in Section 5.7. Similar criticisms are leveled at other radiometric dating methods. It should be remembered that there are over forty different radiometric techniques used for establishing historical dates as well as many non-radiometric methods.[7]

5.1.2 ^{14}C Production and Transmutation

Carbon has fifteen isotopes ranging from ^{8}C to ^{22}C, but only ^{12}C and ^{13}C are stable. Apart from these two stable isotopes, the only carbon isotope with a

---

6. Mook and Plicht, "Reporting ^{14}C Activities and Concentrations," untangles the absolute and relative measures, conventions and symbols used to report radiocarbon data.

7. Wiens, "Radiometric Dating: A Christian Perspective."

lifetime longer than one year is carbon-14 (^{14}C) having a nucleus comprising, as we noted, six protons and eight neutrons.

Carbon-14 is naturally produced in Earth's atmosphere by incident cosmic rays. While details of the origins of cosmic rays are a topic of ongoing research, their general properties have been identified. The majority are high-energy (10^{10}–10^{15} eV) particles of galactic origin known as Galactic Cosmic Radiation (GCR), comprising ~90 percent protons (hydrogen ions) and ~9 percent helium nuclei. The incoming cosmic ray flux is modulated by the solar and geomagnetic fields. Inbound nuclei that encounter Earth cascade through various energy loss interactions with atoms in the atmosphere (10–15 km altitude) to produce thermal neutrons (n) which are absorbed by nitrogen atoms (N), producing ^{14}C and protons (p) according to the process written as

$$n + {}^{14}_{7}N \rightarrow {}^{14}_{6}C + p \tag{1}$$

In Earth's environment, ^{14}C mostly appears as ^{14}CO$_2$ and is incorporated into plants during photosynthesis.[8] The radiocarbon dating of any specimen requires a knowledge of the amount of ^{14}C present at death. This depends on the production rate at that time and hence on the spatial and temporal variation of the cosmic ray flux. It also relies on information concerning any other variability in ^{14}C levels over tens of thousands of years.

The global production rate of ^{14}C is ~1.4 PBq (1.4x10^{15} Bq) with a total atmospheric stock of about seventy-five tons.[9] The 2009 measurement of the specific activity of atmospheric ^{14}C (as CO$_2$) is 238 Bq/kg. This has reduced from over 400 Bq/kg, found during the nuclear weapons testing period of the mid-1960s. Therefore, dates that are estimated from ^{14}C measurements are referenced to years before 1950, known as *cal BP*. Nuclear power stations add an activity of ~1 percent due to a combination of facility release products, usually in the form of CH$_4$, which plants do not assimilate (see footnote 8), and the management of these releases. Fossil fuel combustion products, which contain very little ^{14}C, add CO$_2$ to the atmosphere, diluting the specific activity by ~3 percent (over the period 1900–1970).

---

8. Garnier-Laplace and Roussel-Debet, "Carbon-14 and the Environment."

9. United Nations Scientific Committee on the Effects of Atomic Radiation (UNSCEAR).

Carbon-14 transmutes (or decays) into stable nitrogen-14 (^{14}N) plus an electron (e-) and an electron antineutrino (v_e). This process is written succinctly as

$$^{14}_{6}C \rightarrow {}^{14}_{7}N + e^- + v_e \qquad (2)$$

This transmutation process has a half-life of 5,700±30 years and an activity of ~0.23 Bq/g.[10] The electron is called a beta particle (β^-). As noted earlier, this transmutation involves the electroweak nuclear force. This electron has relatively small energy (average ~50 keV, rest mass decrease = 156 keV), which allows penetration of only ~0.3 mm into body tissue.

5.1.3 Radioactive Uranium and Beryllium

The transport pathways from the production of ^{14}C in the atmosphere to absorption by living things at the ground are components of what is known as the carbon cycle and are quite complex. Comparisons between ^{14}C transport pathways and those of some other radioactive elements present are used to mitigate uncertainties in the carbon cycle arising from environmental factors, thus enhancing the accuracy of ^{14}C dating methods. Of particular interest in this respect are radioactive beryllium (^{10}Be) in ice-core samples and the uranium (^{234}U) -thorium radioactive sequence.

Beryllium-10 (half-life of 1.39×10^6 yr) is naturally produced by the interaction of cosmic rays with atmospheric nitrogen and oxygen, similar to the production of ^{14}C. However, the dwell time of ^{10}Be in the atmosphere is much shorter (only a few years) compared with the dwell time of ^{14}C. Furthermore, beryllium has a more direct pathway from atmospheric aerosol to the ground and can be extracted from polar ice sheets. This reduces complexities derived from the combined effects of the cosmic ray input flux plus changes in transport and deposition in Earth's environment that are involved in the carbon cycle. Comparisons with ^{10}Be data can isolate the system (Earth's biosphere) from the temporal input variations in cosmic ray flux. Steinhilber et al. combined ^{10}Be concentrations obtained from ice cores extracted in Greenland and Antarctica and ^{14}C from tree ring data to reveal the temporal variation of solar activity and cosmic ray intensity over the past 9,400 years.[11] Adolphi et al. extended this record to the pe-

---

10. See "Nuclear Data."
11. Steinhilber et al., "9,400 Years of Cosmic Radiation."

riod 10,000 to 22,500 years BP. (before 1950).[12] BenZvi et al. described an approach based on direct measurement of ^{14}CO in ice cores that minimizes the influence of uncertainties in transport and deposition associated with both ^{14}C and ^{10}Be.[13] The interest in this research field arises from possible links between solar activity and Earth's climate variability. The ^{10}Be (and ^{18}O) concentration data obtained from ice core samples improves the reliability of determinations of the temporal changes of cosmic ray flux and hence the ^{14}C production rates and concentration values in the Earth system over tens of thousands of years.

The nuclear transmutation sequence of uranium-234, (half-life of 2.45x10^5 yr)) to thorium-230 (^{230}Th) is a subset of the longer ^{238}U to ^{206}Pb (lead) sequence, well known in nuclear fission reactor technology. The ^{234}U to ^{230}Th process produces an alpha particle (helium ion) and the ^{230}Th/^{234}U ratio can be used to provide estimates of the age of materials that retain these elements. These include carbonates from once-living organisms, such as bones, teeth, and corals. Derived ages can be compared with dates obtained from ^{14}C measurements.[14]

The physical models of the ^{14}C method have been greatly refined and tested, and experimental techniques used have become much more sensitive and sophisticated. The aim of this paper is to provide an overview of current ^{14}C dating methods and research, the observations on which they are based, and relevant aspects of the scientific model, in addition to measurement and detection protocols. Section 5.2 outlines the equations of radioactivity and how these are used for estimating ^{14}C dates. Section 5.3 considers the manner in which time periods based on the ^{14}C radioactive half-life are used to determine calendar dates. Of great importance is the amount of ^{14}C remaining in a sample. The difficulties associated with the measurement of this quantity are discussed in Sections 5.4 and 5.5, while Section 5.6 describes aspects of *dead carbon* and background counts in measurement systems.

---

12. Adolphi et al., "Persistent Link Between Solar Activity."
13. BenZvi et al., "Obtaining a History of the Flux of Cosmic Rays."
14. See, for example, Bard et al., "Calibration of the 14C Timescale."

5.2 A SCIENTIFIC MODEL FOR RADIOACTIVITY

5.2.1 The Equations of Radioactivity

Radioactivity is a random process. Specifically, it is not known when a particular atom will transmute. However, statistical metrics such as the mean, median, expected values, and variance may be used to predict and extract information from a radioactive atom population. If p is the probability that a ^{14}C atom transmutes within a given time interval, then the key idea is that p is proportional to the time interval, Δt. For N radioactive atoms, the probability that ΔN of these transmute in a time interval, Δt, is given by

$$p = \frac{\Delta N}{N} = -\lambda \Delta t \tag{3}$$

with λ being the proportionality constant. Moving Δt to the left-hand side gives

$$\frac{\Delta N}{N \Delta t} = -\lambda \tag{4}$$

This is the origin of the assertion that the transmutation rate per atom, λ, is constant. The *rate* or *activity* is $\Delta N/\Delta t$ (decays per second). Equations 3 and 4 are *finite difference* equations which for small Δt may be written as the *differential* equation

$$\frac{dN}{N} = -\lambda dt \tag{5}$$

where N is the number of radioactive atoms at time, t and λ is the (decay) constant. Dating samples using radioactive methods is based on this first order differential rate equation, which has the solution.

$$N = N_0 e^{-\lambda t} \tag{6}$$

Given an initial number of radioactive atoms, N_0, the *half-life* ($t_{1/2}$) is, as earlier noted, the time taken for one half ($N_0/2$) of the radioactive atoms to transmute and can be shown from equation (6) to be given by

$$t_{1/2} = \frac{\ln 2}{\lambda} \tag{7}$$

where ln is the natural logarithm operation. As we have seen, the half-life for ^{14}C is close to 5,700 years, although different values are sometimes used, as discussed in Section 5.2.3.

Equations 6 and 7 show how radioactive atom populations provide a "clock" for dating past events. Critics of the method have raised questions about the assumptions made when determining values of N and $N0$, in addition to the properties of λ. In order to assess the validity of such questions it is instructive to review some statistical aspects of a radioactive atom population.

5.2.2 Statistics of Radioactivity

Prediction values involving random processes are often available from probability distribution functions (e.g., binomial, Poisson, Gaussian) and the discipline of statistics. The choice of probability distribution function depends on the characteristics of the random process. A radioactive event is a *Bernoulli trial*— either it happens or it does not. Therefore, the counting of radioactive events involves natural numbers (the positive integers). Such processes are described by the binomial distribution function in statistics.

From equation 7, the probability of transmutation of a ^{14}C atom per unit time is $\lambda = \ln(2)/5700 = 1.216 \times 10^{-4}$/year $= 3.8 \times 10^{-12}$ s^{-1}, which is very small. For a time interval, Δt, the average (mean) number of atoms that transmute is $\mu = N\lambda$ (decays/sec). Therefore, we have a very small probability compared with the number of atoms, N. These properties mean that the binomial is more like a Poisson probability function given by

$$P(k) = \frac{\mu^k}{k!} e^{-\mu} \tag{8}$$

for k (uncorrelated) events counted in a given time interval. The standard deviation, $\sigma = \sqrt{\mu}$, is used to quantify the measurement uncertainty of counts. The suitability of using Poisson compared with the related binomial statistics for radioactivity was discussed by Sitek and Celler.[15] For example, a binomial probability basis for radioactive atom population dynamics is used in nuclear medicine because of the relatively short half-life of the isotopes used in that field. A plot of experimental data from a radioactive source often shows transmutation counts per time interval on the vertical

---

15. Sitek and Celler, "Limitations of Poisson Statistics in Describing Radioactive Decay."

with time on the horizontal axis. For conditions relevant to equation 8, the "counts" in a given Δt interval are samples from a Poisson distribution.

5.2.3 Principles of ^{14}C Dating

During the late 1940s, the ^{14}C half-life was measured a number of times, using the sampling and measurement technology available at that time. Libby et al.[16] cited the value of Engelkemeir et al.,[17] which was 5,720±47 years, quite close to the modern value. Half-life values for ^{14}C obtained by various researchers around that time were combined to give a value of 5,568±30 years.[18] This value was used by Libby and is now referred to as the *Libby half-life*. Subsequent, more sensitive measurements have led to today's accepted value 5,700±30 years.

The principles of ^{14}C-based dating methods are described in most undergraduate physics textbooks.[19] Plants and animals maintain levels of ^{14}C in equilibrium with environmental concentrations while living. An exception is now made for aquatic environments where ^{14}C appears in carbonate forms that alter the water pH, requiring extra care when interpreting samples from these systems.[20] At death, metabolic uptake of ^{14}C ceases and the amount reduces via nuclear transmutation. Thus, ^{14}C dating can yield an estimate of the time since death provided that the half-life is known, the amount of ^{14}C present at death can be estimated and the sample has not been contaminated from other sources, i.e., changes have occurred only by nuclear transmutation according to equation 5. These are the assumptions for ^{14}C dating estimates and much effort has been devoted to investigating whether they are reasonable (or not).

Estimating the amount of ^{14}C in a sample at death requires an understanding of the uptake of ^{14}C in specimens at ground level. The estimate for this initial amount is linked to the history of cosmic ray flux, a research area of interest to space and solar physicists, and also to those researching climate variability. Linking the production of ^{14}C in the atmosphere to concentrations in specimens at the ground requires an understanding of Earth's carbon cycle dynamics. The ^{14}C produced in the atmosphere is transported

16. Libby et al., "Age Determination by Radiocarbon Content."
17. Engelkemeir et al., "Half-life of Radiocarbon."
18. See, for example, Libby, "Radiocarbon Dating."
19. See, for example, Krane, *Introductory Nuclear Physics*.
20. See, for example, Bao et al., "Dimensions of Radiocarbon Variability."

to plant and animal life via rapid oxidation to $^{14}CO_2$, photosynthesis, the food chain, and the complex carbon cycle. The carbon exchange reservoir is described by Aitken,[21] while a diagram of the carbon cycle in soil, plant, and animal systems is given by Garnier-Laplace.[22] The concentration of ^{14}C in terrestrial specimens depends on the production rate (input) and the carbon cycle that determines distribution and uptake into land-based organisms and the ocean. This is known as the *system* response. Studies that focus on understanding the transport of ^{14}C throughout the biosphere and separating the input from system responses are a significant component of ^{14}C dating and climate variability research.[23]

5.3 FROM RADIOCARBON TO CALENDAR DATES, INTCAL (INTERNATIONAL RADIOCARBON CALIBRATION)

Since the 1950s it has been known that high-precision measurements of ^{14}C in a sample do not necessarily translate to high-precision estimates of calendar dates. Kennett et al. list a number of possible reasons for erroneous dates, including varying ^{14}C concentrations over time due to a range of causes such as vertical transport in sedimentary sequences, improper sample handling, and uncertainties in ^{14}C calibration curves.[24]

The first calibration curves were published in the 1960s. Calibration curves before 1993 were based on dendrochronology, the method of dating the past from the annual growth increments of specific tree species in addition to measurements of ^{14}C and or ^{18}O in the same tree ring samples. Suitable species include Irish, English, and German Oak and Elm, Sequoia, and Bristlecone pine (*Pinus longaeva*) from the western USA. This calibration curve spanned approximately 12,000 years. The technique is to analyze growth rings of suitable trees and align these with periods of time (e.g., years). The material at different depths inside the tree can also be analyzed for ^{14}C.

---

21. Aitken, *Science-Based Dating in Archaeology*, 1st ed.
22. Garnier-Laplace and Roussel-Debet, "Carbon-14 and the Environment."
23. See, for example, Tomizuka, "Is a Box Model Effective for Understanding the Carbon Cycle?"
24. Kennett et al., "Bayesian Chronological Analyses."

However, there are recognized limitations when obtaining dates using dendrochronology. *New World Encyclopedia* (2020)[25] lists many factors that affect the appearance of tree rings. These are categorized as geographical, climatic, non-climatic, and non-linear effects. The sources, sample treatment, and careful selection of tree ring data included in the latest calibration curves are discussed by Reimer et al.[26]

Data from the uranium-thorium (U-Th) radioactive series used to date corals were added to the calibration database around 1993, and by 1998 the data set also included varved sediments from Venezuela and covered the time span back to 24,000 BP.

From 2001, the IntCal Working Group has released internationally recognized calibration curves, known as IntCal curves, referenced to 1950, that capture natural variations of ^{14}C in the atmosphere and oceans which are known to depend on both time and space.[27] The calibration curve update in 2004 (SHCal04) recognized differences between the Southern and the Northern Hemispheres. The Southern Hemisphere has a larger proportion of ocean surface area and it was recognized that for this region the air-sea exchange of CO_2 resulted in smaller ^{14}C oceanic concentrations, as described by Marsh et al.[28]

Obtaining an estimate of the calendar age of a sample and its uncertainty involves consideration of the variability in the IntCal curve. Given the data-derived curve, numerical methods (OxCal or CALIB) are used to deduce the range of a date for a sample of known ^{14}C content at the one standard deviation confidence level. The Wikipedia page on radiocarbon calibration describes the details of this calculation using the output from IntCal13 as an example.[29]

The most recent calibration software is IntCal20, published in *Radiocarbon* in August 2020.[30] IntCal20 applies to the Northern Hemisphere, SHCal20 to the Southern Hemisphere, and Marine20 to marine samples.[31] Tree-ring data (e.g., Bristlecone, Sequoia, and Oak) from 220 data sets were

---

25. "Dendrochronology," New World Encyclopedia.
26. Reimer et al., "IntCal20 Northern Hemisphere Radiocarbon Age Calibration."
27. See, for example, McCormac et al., "Calibration of the Radiocarbon Time Scale for the Southern Hemisphere."
28. Marsh et al., "IntCal, SHCal, or a Mixed Curve?"
29. Radiocarbon Calibration, Wikipedia.
30. Reimer et al., "IntCal20 Northern Hemisphere Radiocarbon Age Calibration."
31. Marsh et al., "IntCal, SHCal, or a Mixed Curve?"

rigorously assessed for inclusion. The development and dissemination of these calibrations are accomplished by international working groups. The improvements include new Bayesian statistical methods for calibration curve reconstruction and tree-ring database comparisons, and discussion of the strengths and weaknesses of using tree rings, varved and sediment marine reservoir ages, U-Th, and ^{10}Be ice-core data. In addition, the IntCal20 data are compared with previous IntCal results. Improvements in the calibration curve arise from using a greater diversity of sources (tree, varve, ice core, etc.), thus increasing the number of input data points (see for example, Reimer et al.[32]), and from advances in data-fitting methods.

Many research papers describe the dendrochronological process, time sequencing from known anomalous events (e.g., rapid increase in ^{14}C, volcanic events), and the subsequent derivation of dates. The interested reader might begin with references listed by Reimer et al., who also summarized data from macrofossils, speleothems (caves), and marine environments.[33]

A debated topic in ^{14}C-dating estimates is the validity and accuracy of measurements of the ^{14}C amount in specimens and whether contamination is a serious hurdle to obtaining reliable dates. These aspects require an appreciation of the highly technical and precision measurement methods and innovations developed over the past seventy-plus years. These aspects are discussed in the following sections.

5.4 MEASURING ^{14}C: INSTRUMENTATION, DEFINITIONS AND METROLOGY

The analytical task in radiocarbon dating is to measure the amount of ^{14}C remaining in a sample. In this section, the determination of ^{14}C is approached from the perspective of quality control in analytical chemistry and the insights that come from metrology, the science of measurement.

5.4.1 Instrumentation

Early measurements of the ^{14}C content in a sample were made using modified Geiger counters to detect the beta particles produced by the decay of the residual ^{14}C. These counters were non-specific, hence relatively insensitive

---

32. Reimer et al., "Selection and Treatment of Data for Radiocarbon Calibration."
33. Reimer et al., "Selection and Treatment of Data for Radiocarbon Calibration."

because, even when the samples were shielded, they also counted the comparatively high levels of ambient background radiation. This meant that large samples and long counting times (days) were required to boost the ^{14}C count and thus to acquire statistically meaningful data. The sensitivity of radiation detection was improved somewhat by the development of liquid scintillation counters.

But it was the application of mass spectrometer technology that proved a game-changer. The discovery that charged atomic or molecular particles (ions) are deflected in different ways by electric and magnetic fields led to the development of the mass spectrometer around 1910. This instrument allowed charged particles to be separated according to their mass. The use of mass spectrometry to count the ^{14}C atoms directly, rather than counting the decay events, promised greater sensitivity. However, a persistent barrier to this method of measuring the number of ^{14}C atoms was interference from ^{14}N, an atom of similar mass to ^{14}C, which is prevalent in biological molecules and comprises about 80 percent of the atmosphere.

Refinements in mass spectrometer design leading to the development of the accelerator mass spectrometer (AMS) in the 1970s have been well described.[34] It was found that if carbon atoms were introduced as negative ions, the analysis was not subject to ^{14}N interference because the negative ions of nitrogen are not sufficiently stable to reach the AMS detector. An AMS schematic is shown in Figure 5.1.

Under these conditions, the sensitivity of an AMS measurement for ^{14}C was about 10,000 times greater than that of a radiation counter. This made it possible to reduce sample sizes and decrease counting times while improving precision. A tandem AMS, first used to measure ^{14}C content in the late 1970s, is the current instrument of choice for radiocarbon dating.[35] Subsequent developments have concentrated on decreasing the sample size from grams to sub-milligram amounts, and the size of the instrument footprint has reduced from that of a small house (200 m^2) to a large benchtop (7 m^2).[36]

In general, AMS measurements cannot be made directly on specimens as found. For clarity, the term *specimen* will be used for the object that is to

---

34. See Budzikiewicz and Grigsby, "Mass spectrometry and Isotopes"; Synal, "Developments in Accelerator Mass Spectrometry" and Kutschera, "Applications of Accelerator Mass Spectrometry."

35. Kutschera, "Accelerator Mass Spectrometry."

36. Kutschera, "Accelerator Mass Spectrometry," 573.

be dated. The term *sample* will refer to a portion of the specimen taken for analysis or to any component of that sample that is isolated as the material to be analyzed. The sample generally needs to be converted into a chemical form that is a suitable *target* for AMS radiocarbon dating.

The two most common substances presented as targets to the instrument are graphite (a form of solid carbon) and carbon dioxide gas. Graphite has been the favored target because of its stronger signal and smaller sample memory effects.[37] The more recent development of compound-specific analyses means that gas ion sources are now receiving more attention.[38] Aerts-Bijma et al. foreshadowed a report on the performance of a gas ion source on their instrument.[39] While the following focuses on the use of graphite targets similar principles apply to carbon dioxide ion sources.

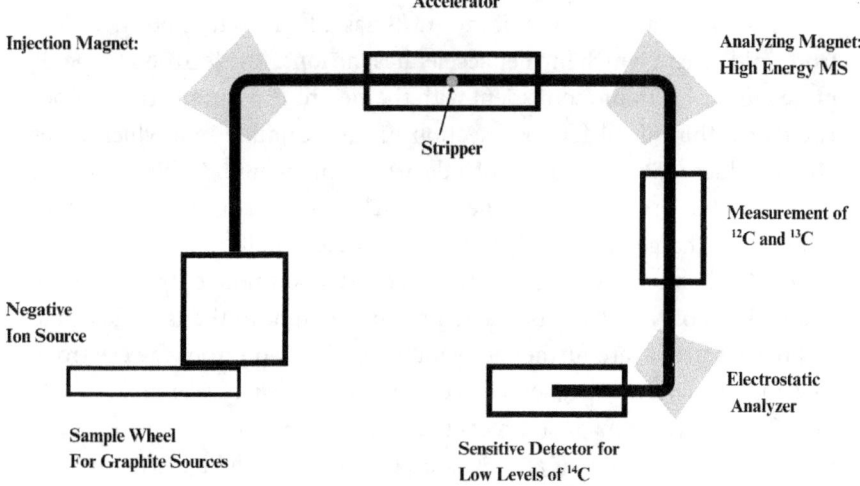

Figure 5.1 Schematic diagram of a tandem Accelerator Mass Spectrometer (AMS).

Graphite targets, mounted in a sample wheel, are presented successively to the negative ion source where negative ions (as well as some neutral atoms) are sputtered from the sample by bombardment with cesium

---

37. Memory effects occur when there is carry over of carbon from one sample into the analysis for the following sample or samples.

38. Kutschera, "Accelerator Mass Spectrometry," 575, 576.

39. Aerts-Bijma et al., "Independent Assessment of Uncertainty for Radiocarbon Analysis," 3.

ions.[40] The beamline (the path followed by the accelerated particles through the instrument) is kept under high vacuum, and the mechanics of the sample wheel enable multiple samples to be analyzed successively in what is termed an *analytical run.*

Between the ion source and the injection magnet (see Figure 5.1), the negative ions are accelerated and focused by an electric field. They are then fed through the injection magnet, which filters by mass according to their momentum to charge ratio. Rapid switching allows for fast cycling through masses 12, 13, and 14, enabling these three carbon isotopes and their ratios to be measured. It should be noted that in addition to the negative $^{14}C^-$ ion, the mass-14 beam may also contain the molecular ions $^{12}CH_2^-$ and $^{13}CH^-$, either as by-products of the graphitization or contaminants introduced from the vacuum pumps.

The accelerator portion of the AMS has a high voltage positive electrode mid-length which further accelerates the ions. An electron stripper is placed in the beamline coincident with the electrode position. The stripper is either a thin metal foil or a section of the beamline into which gases are introduced. Stripper gases include argon and helium. Collisions of the beam with the stripper convert the negatively charged atoms and molecules to multiple-charged positive ions.[41] Under these conditions, the molecular ions ($^{12}CH_2$ and ^{13}CH) largely dissociate and so do not contribute to the count. The positive ^{14}C ions, carried by momentum to the far side of the positive electrode, are further accelerated by repulsion from the electrode toward the analyzing magnet. Hence, the term *tandem accelerator.*

The analyzing magnet directs the mass 12, 13, and 14 ions to the appropriate detector. The ^{12}C and ^{13}C ions, being at a much higher concentration than ^{14}C, are directed to separate detectors for measurement.[42] The ^{14}C beam, which is much less intense and requires more sensitive detection, is

---

40. It might help to think of sputtering as an atomic scale "sandblasting" where the high energy cesium ions knock carbon atoms from the surface of the graphite targets, the majority being negatively ionized in the process.

41. Depending on the instrument, accelerator voltages can vary from several hundred kV to about 5 MV. The lower voltage instruments tend to produce singly positive ions while at the high end up to triply charged ions are produced. The decision on voltage influences the size of the instrument and also the separating power of the second magnet and therefore involves trade-offs.

42. Faraday cups or velocity (time of flight) detectors are examples of detectors used by AMS instruments to detect ^{12}C and ^{13}C.

directed through the electrostatic analyzer, which filters on the basis of the energy to charge ratio, to a sensitive detector.[43]

5.4.2 Definitions, Reporting Conventions and Calculations

Over the years, radiocarbon results have been reported in a variety of ways depending on whether the radioactivity or the number of atoms present was measured. Different conventions have been used, and to further complicate matters, there are instances in which the same name has been given to quantities that are defined differently.[44] Readers who wish to follow calculations in detail need to be aware of these pitfalls. There is a long history of calls (not always heeded) for a standard format for reporting the results of a radiocarbon age determination.[45] It is recommended that quantitative results of all radiocarbon age determinations should be reported either as percent modern carbon (pMC), or as the conventional radiocarbon age (CRA).

Percent Modern Carbon

Modern carbon is a carbon sample in which the $^{14}C/^{12}C$ ratio is equal to that of the atmosphere in 1950 adjusted in a way that cancels out the impact of burning fossil fuels during the twentieth-century.[46] Its value was determined by measuring the $^{14}C/^{12}C$ ratio of an 1890s Oak sample and then adjusting for the decay that occurred between 1890 and 1950.

Experimentally, modern carbon is defined as being 0.95 times the $^{14}C/^{12}C$ ratio of a particular batch of oxalic acid extracted from a 1955 beet crop. By 1955, the atmospheric level of ^{14}C had risen unnaturally as a result of the use and testing of nuclear weapons. The factor of 0.95 reduced the value to make it equal to the notional 1950 value. Given reference values

---

43. This filter removes lower energy mass-14 ions that have originated in the beam line rather than in the ion source.

44. Stenström et al., *Guide to Radiocarbon Units and Calculations*"; Stuiver, "Workshop on ^{14}C Data Reporting," and Oxford Radiocarbon Accelerator Unit, Reporting Radiocarbon Dates.

45. Stuiver, "Workshop on ^{14}C Data Reporting"; Millard, "Conventions for Reporting Radiocarbon Determinations" and "Oxford Radiocarbon Accelerator Unit, Reporting Radiocarbon Dates."

46. 1950 was chosen as a date close to the publication of the first radiocarbon dating in homage to the pioneering work of Willard Libby.

and their uncertainty are determined from the results obtained from several high-expertise laboratories under the oversight of a Standards Authority, in this case, the United States National Institute of Standards and Technology (NIST). The reference material is known as NIST HOX I.

The use of analytical reference materials is standard analytical practice and is not controversial. There are accepted protocols for establishing secondary standards for everyday use and for the characterization of a replacement reference material when stocks of the original diminish. This enables all laboratories to calibrate their instruments to a common base. Thus, *pMC* data determined by different laboratories are calibrated to the same standard. In AMS determinations of the radiocarbon content of a sample, it is necessary (as a minimum) to measure a background sample, a modern carbon standard, and the unknown sample.

The isotopes of carbon fractionate as they move through the biosphere. Lighter molecules diffuse faster than heavier ones so the diffusion rates of the isotopic forms of carbon dioxide are in the order $^{12}CO_2 > {}^{13}CO_2 > {}^{14}CO_2$. Therefore, because diffusion of CO_2 from the atmosphere into living tissue is a factor in the rate of photosynthesis, the $^{14}C/^{12}C$ and $^{13}C/^{12}C$ ratios in plants will be smaller than the corresponding ratio in the atmosphere and this effect is then passed on through the food chain. Changes to these ratios can occur during other processes, including the preparation of samples and targets for an AMS measurement. Therefore, the AMS-measured $^{14}C/^{12}C$ ratio for a sample being dated is affected by two processes: fractionation and radioactive decay. Both reduce its value compared to the atmospheric value during the specimen's lifetime. Radiocarbon dating depends on knowing the change that is caused by radioactive decay alone.

Fortunately, ^{13}C and ^{12}C are both stable isotopes, so any reduction in the $^{13}C/^{12}C$ ratio is due to fractionation only. This change can be measured by the AMS, and these data then enable a mathematical adjustment to the $^{14}C/^{12}C$ ratio to the value it would have had if only radioactive decay had occurred. The equations are complex, but the logic is straightforward.

Percent modern carbon for the sample is calculated from

$$pMC = R_S/R_{MS} \times 100 \qquad (9)$$

where R_S and R_{MS} are the $^{14}C/^{12}C$ ratios, appropriately adjusted for background and fractionation of the sample and modern standard, respectively.

Radiocarbon Dating of Once-living Specimens

Conventional Radiocarbon Age

The conventional radiocarbon age (*CRA*) is obtained from equations (6) and (7) as

$$CRA = -5568/\ln2 \times \ln(pMC/100) \qquad (10)$$

Where 5568 is the half-life in years of ^{14}C as used by Libby. Given that ln2=0.693 we obtain

$$CRA = -8033 \times \ln(pMC/100) \qquad (11)$$

The *CRA* is the number of radiocarbon years before 1950. When *pMC* is less than 100, the *CRA* is a positive number. If *pMC* is greater than 100, as is possible for post-1950 samples, then *CRA* is a negative number.

The *CRA* determination is based on the following:

1. An agreed radiocarbon standard,
2. An agreed method of adjustment for sample isotopic fractionation,
3. The use of 1950 AD as 0 BP,
4. A half-life of 5,568 years (Libby) and
5. The assumption is that all ^{14}C reservoirs have remained constant through time.[47]

*CRA*s are therefore expressed as years before the present (BP), the "present" being 1950. Conditions 1 to 3 are non-controversial.

However, conditions four and five are known to be incorrect to some degree. The accepted half-life of ^{14}C is now taken to be 5,700 years, and there is experimental evidence that carbon reservoirs have varied over time with differences between the Northern and Southern Hemispheres and between land and marine environments. So why does science persist with using *CRA*s?

First, because many *CRA*s had already been published using the Libby half-life, it was decided to continue with that convention. Changing it, midstream so to speak, could lead to confusion over what value (5,568 or 5,700) actually had been used in the calculation of any given *CRA*. Furthermore, *CRA*s would cease to be directly comparable.

---

47. A reservoir is a part of the environment where it is considered that the carbon dioxide content is well mixed. Three examples are the northern hemisphere atmosphere, the southern hemisphere atmosphere, and marine environment(s) where the ^{14}C levels change more slowly than in the atmosphere.

Second, to allow for reservoir changes, calibration curves need to be constructed and refined in an ongoing process as more data are accumulated. The simplest way to correct for the currently accepted half-life is to include it as one factor in the calibration curve. Within the uncertainties of those curves, the real value of the half-life and the variation in the ^{14}C levels in the reservoirs are all accounted for. Calibration curves convert *CRAs* to calendar years. Calibrated ages are expressed as cal years BP, cal years AD (or CE), or cal years BC (or BCE).

When calibration curves are revised from time to time, the reported *CRAs* can be relatively easily recalibrated only if they have a common base. Therefore, *CRAs* continue to be calculated using the Libby half-life and the assumption of invariant reservoirs. How calibration curves are developed and the results obtained by calibration were discussed in Section 5.3

Another reason for reporting results as *pMC* and/or *CRA* is that these quantities are independent of the date on which the measurement was made. This is because the oxalic acid standard and the sample itself decay proportionally to one another. The use of these quantities allows for the direct comparison of *CRAs* measured at different times. Unless otherwise stated, ^{14}C levels are reported in this chapter as *pMC* and/or *CRA*. If different units have been used in the cited publications, then they have been converted to *pMC* or *CRA* as appropriate in order for a simple comparison.

The half-life of ^{14}C places a theoretical upper limit on the values of *CRA* that can be determined. A 1mg sample of carbon from a specimen with a notional *CRA* of 145,000 years BP would be unlikely to contain any residual radiocarbon. Practicalities reduce this limit further to about 100,000 years BP. However, attaining this goal remains technically out of reach for the reasons discussed below.

5.4.3 Insights from Metrology

Confidence in the results of an analysis and their subsequent interpretation is underpinned by metrology, the science of measurement. Metrological principles apply to all instrumental analyses, and the measurement of ^{14}C for radiocarbon dating is no exception. In Australia, metrology is the responsibility of the National Measurement Institute, with the National Association of Testing Authorities, Australia (NATA) given the responsibility of accrediting laboratories and providing criteria by which testing methods must be validated.[48] Perhaps because many radiocarbon laboratories have been associated with universities and research projects, they have not been subject to such accreditation. It is interesting to note a recent call for certification, particularly when analyses are performed as a customer service.[49] There are several metrological concepts that are relevant to the present discussion.

Precision, Accuracy, and Uncertainty

Precision is related to the scatter of a large number of replicate results about a *mean* (m) (or average) value: the narrower the scatter, the more precise the result. The width of the scatter is indicated by the *standard deviation* (sd), which is an indication of the *measurement uncertainty* of a result. Standard deviations are calculated from the spread of multiple determinations on the same specimen. The analyses of *pMC* are reported as $m \pm sd$. If sufficiently large numbers of determinations are made, it is expected that 67 percent will fall within $1sd$ of the mean, 95 percent within $2sd$ of the mean, and 99.7 percent will fall within $3sd$ of the mean (assuming that the distribution of values is normal or bell-shaped).

Accuracy is how close the measurement is to the true result. Accuracy must be distinguished from precision. For example, a result may be precise but inaccurate, or vice versa. The best results are both precise and accurate. Assessing the accuracy of a measurement depends on what is being measured and whether independent checks on its value are available.

As pointed out by Taylor et al., *accuracy* in radiocarbon dating is a measure of how close a radiocarbon age estimate is to the actual calendar age of the sample.[50] However, ^{14}C *content* is what is measured in the analysis. The calibration curve links this measurement to calendar dates, and considerable effort has been expended to improve the accuracy and reduce the uncertainty related to calibration. Therefore, calibration quality depends on the accuracy and precision of other methods of determining the age, such as historical records, the direct counting of annual events (e.g., tree rings and varves), and other independent methods of age determination.

---

48. NATA Technical Circular.

49. Herrando-Pérez, "Bone Need Not Remain an Elephant in the Room," 1.

50. Taylor et al., "Misunderstandings Concerning the Significance of AMS Background ^{14}C Measurements," 728.

The following discussion focuses on the uncertainty in the measurement of ^{14}C. Quantifying this is a time-consuming, meticulous process. Measurement uncertainty varies according to sample preparation methods, the type of apparatus used, and the measurement technology employed. Therefore, it is not the same for all radiocarbon laboratories or for the measurement of different matrices in the same laboratory. Measurement uncertainty arises from the statistics of counting, the reproducibility of methods used to prepare a sample for analysis, and from the process of analysis itself.

A detailed description of the process of determining measurement uncertainties is beyond the scope of this chapter. Interested readers can consult studies such as one reported by the University of Groningen.[51]

Analytical methods based on counting (e.g. AMS) have an inherent uncertainty proportional to the square root of the total count. The standard deviation can be expressed as a percentage of the total count. This percentage decreases as the total count (in this case of ^{14}C atoms) increases, as shown in Figure 5.2.

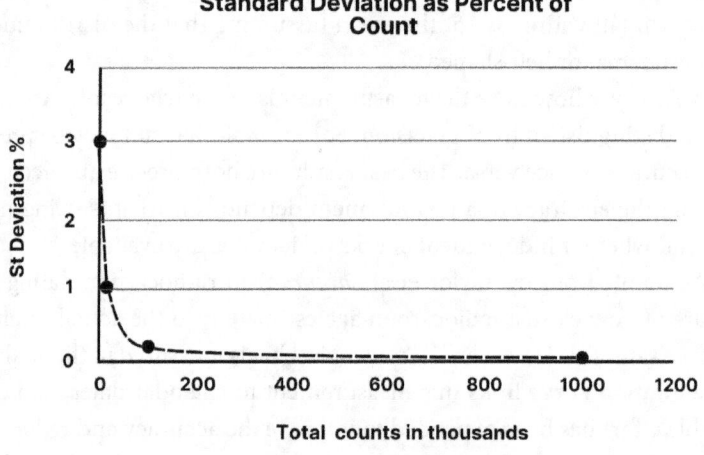

Figure 5.2 Standard deviation as a percentage of total count.

After the total counts exceed 200,000, there are only limited precision gains for hugely increased counts. These gains are offset by increased uncertainties from instrument calibration and detector instabilities during a longer count time. Furthermore, the effect of long count times has obvious commercial implications. The Groningen laboratory has optimized its

51. Aerts-Bijma et al., "Independent Assessment."

count times to forty minutes, which for a modern carbon sample generates a count of about 500,000 (sd 0.14 percent) on their instrument.[52] On that basis, 200,000 counts (sd 0.22) would be achieved in forty minutes for a sample of 40 *pMC*, corresponding to a radiocarbon age of 7,400 years BP. A typical background sample (0.2 *pMC*) would generate a count of 1,000 with a standard deviation of 3 percent.

Experimentally determined measurement uncertainties are found to be larger than those predicted by counting statistics alone, which means there are other factors affecting the overall measurement uncertainty of the analysis. Some of these will be highlighted in the description of the analytical pathway.

Background Signals and Limits of Detection

All instrumental methods of analysis produce a residual signal when a *blank sample*, considered free of the analyte[53] in question, is put through the full analytical process. This is *not* the same as running the analytical instrument without a sample in the sample holder. Metrology has established that for a blank sample to be meaningful, it must be put through each of the steps or processes to which the corresponding analytical sample will be subjected.

For historical reasons, a radiocarbon dating blank is often referred to as *background*. A background sample is one for which it is assumed (based on its geological age) that any ^{14}C initially present would have completely decayed. For simplicity, this is often referred to as *dead carbon*. This assumption will be examined later.

The natural amount of ^{14}C is very small compared to the amount of ^{12}C in the atmosphere and hence in living organisms. For modern carbon, there are approximately 1×10^{12} (one million million) atoms of ^{12}C for every atom of ^{14}C. For samples of specimens that were once living, the ^{14}C content reduces with time following the death of the specimen. Extending the range of carbon dating requires the ability to measure increasingly small ^{14}C amounts with sufficient precision to be useful.

Good analytical practice requires that a *limit of detection* (*LOD*) must be established for any method "intended to measure analytes at

---

52. Aerts-Bijma et al., "Independent Assessment," 16.

53. The analyte is a generic term for what is being analyzed. In radiocarbon dating it is ^{14}C.

concentrations close to zero."[54] An understanding of the implications of *LOD*s is therefore essential for the interpretation of results at the long-age end of the radiocarbon scale. Multiple measurements of the background sample provide a mean value and standard deviation. The *LOD* is defined as the lowest level of analyte that is statistically different from the background. The NATA criterion places the *LOD* at the mean background plus three standard deviations (99.7 percent confidence that the result is different from the background).[55]

However, the convention used for radiocarbon dating is to consider the *LOD* as the mean background of ^{14}C plus two standard deviations, i.e., 95 percent confidence limit that the result is different from the background.[56] This is a lower limit that allows samples of older age to be assigned a date. However, the use of a lower radiocarbon *LOD* increases the possibility of reporting false positives. *LOD*s (and their associated standard deviations) should be determined independently for each different sample matrix type, whenever there is a variation in analytical procedure (including any pretreatment), and for each analytical instrument used. Examples of different matrix types encountered in radiocarbon dating include wood, bone, and shell. *LOD*s may be expressed as either the minimum amount of ^{14}C that can be detected or the maximum *CRA* that can be meaningfully reported.

Some conventional radiocarbon ages are reported as, for example, >48,000 years BP. This reads as "greater than 48,000 years BP." The first thing that this tells us is that the *LOD* for the method used in the measurement was 48,000 years BP. This calculates to a radiocarbon equivalent of 0.25 *pMC*.[57] The second thing it tells us is that the radiocarbon measurement on the sample was less than the *LOD* and therefore indistinguishable from the background. Therefore, the radiocarbon age must be greater than 48,000 years BP, but the analysis cannot determine by how much the age exceeds that figure. It could be a few years greater. Equally, it could be thousands or millions of years greater.

54. NATA, Technical Circular, 17.

55. NATA, Technical Circular, 18.

56. Beta Analytic, *Introduction to Radiocarbon Determination by the Accelerator Mass Spectrometry Method*, 12; Nadeau et al., "Carbonate ^{14}C Background: Does it Have Multiple Personalities?" 169.

57. Such a limit of detection would result from a background count of, say, 0.15 *pMC* with a standard deviation of 0.05 *pMC*. These are values in the range of experimentally determined backgrounds.

Since the measurement of ^{14}C has an associated limit of detection it follows that i) it is not possible to prove experimentally that ^{14}C *is not present* in a sample and ii) it is only logically valid to assert that ^{14}C *is present* in a sample if its quantity is greater than the *LOD*. These concepts should be kept in mind when evaluating background levels in radiocarbon dating.

5.5 PRACTICALITIES OF ^{14}C MEASUREMENT

A majority of radiocarbon measurements are performed on wood (including charcoal and other plant material) and bone (including teeth, antlers, and horns). The Centre for Isotope Research at Groningen University reported that for the period September 2017 to August 2018, 87 percent of their radiocarbon analyses fell in those categories,[58] while the radiocarbon accelerator unit (ORAU) at Oxford University (UK) reported in 2010 that these matrices accounted for 82 percent of their output.[59] It was not clear from the context whether these statistics were just from the previous year or based on their output since 1980. Given the preponderance of wood and bone samples, we shall limit our discussion to those two matrices.

Material suitable for radiocarbon dating is derived from specimens whose date of death extends from the present day back through archaeological and recent geological time. All specimens have been at a greater or lesser risk of contamination from carbon contained in the mineral and organic material of the environment (e.g., groundwater and soil). The structural molecules will also have been subject to varying degrees of diagenesis: that is, the progressive degradation and/or lithification of the specimen after death as it interacts with its environment. Diagenetic processes have the potential to effect the exchange of environmental carbon with that of the specimen. For any post-death contamination of carbon to affect the measured radiocarbon age of a specimen, it must have occurred more recently than the *LOD* expressed in *CRA*. If earlier, it would also have become non-detectable.

Two types of ^{14}C contamination can occur. The first type occurs when substances containing modern carbon are deposited on the surface of the specimen or in cracks and crevices without chemically interacting with the structure of the specimen. Depending on the chemistry, it may be possible to remove these impurities selectively without destroying the sample. The

---

58. Dee et al., "Radiocarbon Dating at Groningen," 63–74.
59. Brock et al., "Current Pre-treatment Methods for AMS Radiocarbon Dating."

second type of contamination occurs when substances containing modern carbon chemically interact with the material in the specimen either through modern carbon exchange with its structural carbon or by reactions leading to chemical addition to its structural material as it undergoes diagenesis.

The extent of change varies with time and with the conditions of the surroundings: whether wet or dry, hot or cold, the chemical character of the environment (e.g., acidic, neutral, or basic), and so on. Contamination that is structural is much more difficult (impossible for some matrices) to remove. Opportunities for contamination also arise during and after discovery. The specimen might have been unearthed in a landslide or as a cliff face eroded. It might have been discovered by a passing hiker or excavated by a painstaking archaeologist. It might have spent time forgotten in someone's shed or have been carefully stored in a museum collection and subjected to preservation and repair by dutiful curators before radiocarbon dating was developed and the need to avoid exposure to reagents containing modern carbon was recognized.

5.5.1 The Effect of Impurities on a Radiocarbon Date

Before considering specific cases, it is worth looking at the theoretical impact that small levels of contamination have on samples of various hypothetical ages. Table 5.1 shows that the presence of a constant small amount of impurity in hypothetical samples has a much larger effect on the age of older specimens than it does on younger ones.

Table 5.1 Effect of modern carbon contamination on calculated CRAs				
Age of Hypothetical Clean Sample	Following 0.2 pMC Contamination		Following 1 pMC Contamination	
CRA Years BP	Apparent CRA Years BP	Difference Radiocarbon Years	Apparent CRA Years BP	Difference Radiocarbon Years
0	0	0	0	0
2500	2494	-6	2471	-29
5000	4986	-14	4931	-69
10000	9960	-40	9804	-196
25000	24662	-338	23438	-1562
50000	44401	-5599	35555	-14445

The addition of modern carbon results in a younger age estimate for what is being measured, hence the negative difference. During analysis, measurements are made on the sample of interest and a background sample. The impact of contamination depends on the difference in contamination of the sample and of the background. If the sample and background are equally contaminated the effect of the contamination on the calculated *CRA* cancels but the *LOD*, which depends on the background value and its uncertainty, still applies.

Samples more contaminated than the background samples would be given erroneously younger ages. Samples less contaminated than the background samples would be given erroneously older ages. When we discuss background samples, we will note that care is taken to select specimens with low contamination for background samples, so an overestimation of age, although possible, is unlikely.

From Table 5.1 we see that the magnitude of the change on *CRA* caused by a positive difference in the sample of 0.2 *pMC* compared to the background is insignificant up to about 10,000 years BP. The effect is larger for older and more highly contaminated samples and such results become unreliable for establishing calibrated dates. However, such results still may be germane to the general question of whether the age of life on Earth exceeds 6,000 years.

Contamination caused by the addition of dead carbon is possible for specimens found in limestone and volcanic environments and from sample contamination by laboratory reagents derived from dead carbon. This type of contamination has a much smaller effect, of about eighty years per 1 percent of dead carbon contamination, irrespective of the radiocarbon age of the specimen. This contamination makes the sample appear slightly older.

The reason why the effect is so small is that the dead carbon impurity is a small addition compared to the large amount of ^{12}C already in the sample. The reason for its virtual constancy across the date range is that in the relevant equations, the amount of ^{12}C appears in the denominator in calculating the $^{14}C/^{12}C$ ratio. Complex pre-treatment procedures have been developed to remove contamination from samples to enable accurate age determinations for older samples.

Before discussing the implications of background results, it is necessary to be aware of the steps in the pathway from specimen discovery to measurement of the ^{14}C graphite target. The generic steps in the analytical pathway are shown in Figure 5.3. The use of a gas phase ion source will not be discussed specifically.

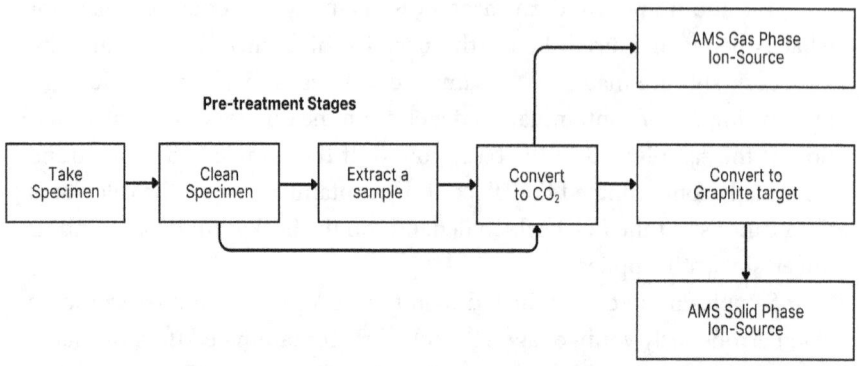

Figure 5.3 The radiocarbon analytical pathway.

The aim during the pre-treatment stages is to remove as much as possible of the CO_2 contamination and to accomplish this without adding modern carbon. It may be decided to extract a component from the sample that is least likely to have been chemically altered.

5.5.2 Cleaning and Sampling Introduction

Specimens showing signs of dirt, rootlets, discoloration, or preservatives may be washed with water and have their surfaces abraded. Small specimens such as seeds and grains may be taken whole as samples. If specimens have scientific, historical, and cultural significance apart from their age, a decision to date them will depend on whether the value of establishing their age directly warrants the damage that will be caused by sample removal. If so, as small a portion as practicable will be removed to be used as the sample. Sampling is another factor that contributes to measurement uncertainty because some parts of the specimen may be more contaminated than other parts and therefore present greater analytical challenges.

If prior preservation and/or repair procedures are suspected, the sample cleaning will be attempted with a succession of organic solvents derived from dead carbon. Wood and bone samples are then usually, but not always, treated with an acid-base-acid sequence (ABA). The first acid treatment is designed to remove inorganic carbonates deposited from groundwater. The base treatment is to remove soil acids (humic and fulvic acids), and the final acid treatment is to remove any modern carbon dioxide that has been taken up during the treatment with the base. This treatment is aimed at the first type of contamination mentioned above.

Fragile samples may need to be treated more gently, with perhaps only washing and a dilute acid treatment, with the recognition that some forms of contamination might remain. Many results have been obtained over the years following ABA pre-treatments.

5.5.3 Component Extraction and Purification

Following the ABA treatment, a single component is often extracted from the sample. Exogenous[60] polymers, because of their large molecular size, are unlikely to have diffused as impurities into a crystalline sample. For this reason, bio-polymers characteristic of the sample, such as cellulose from wood and collagen from bones, are favorites for extraction. The extent of breakdown in the extracted polymers may be assessed chemically. The lower the breakdown, the higher the quality of the sample for age determination.

Higham, writing in 2011 about European archaeological dates between 28,000 and 47,000 years BP, suggested "that as many as 70 percent of the oldest radiocarbon dates in the literature may be too young, due to contamination by modern carbon." and "what was surprising was that these determinations were mostly obtained in the last ten years."[61] His conclusion that these dates might be too young was based on archaeological considerations. Radiocarbon dates obtained on stratified sites were inconsistent between and within strata and showed no clear relation to depth. Strata whose ages were constrained by optically stimulated radiation (OSL) age determinations and/or argon-argon age results contained specimens whose radiocarbon dates were anomalously younger. He noted that a new pretreatment for bone analysis produced older ages than those based on longstanding pretreatments. He also drew attention to the fact that charcoal-derived radiocarbon ages were found to be older if additional steps were included in their pretreatment.

Higham advocated improved pre-treatment as a principal means of bringing radiocarbon dates into harmony with archaeological considerations and other dating techniques. He re-dated specimens using the

---

60. "Exogenous" refers to material external to the living specimen itself. In contrast "endogenous" refers to integral components of the specimen.

61. Higham, "European Middle and Upper Palaeolithic Radiocarbon Dates." This paper by Higham is more readable than some of the other works quoted in this chapter.

new pretreatments and found a better correlation with the archaeological information.

5.5.4 Pre-treatment of Wood and Charcoal Samples

Southon and Magana compared the initial ABA treatment of wood samples with two methods designed to extract cellulose fractions.[62] The first method removed lignins, leaving holocellulose, a mixture of wood polysaccharides, including cellulose. The second method isolated α-cellulose, a high-molecular-weight fraction of cellulose having high stability.

The methods were tested on five well-preserved old wood samples, and the ^{14}C content was measured. For four of the five samples, there was found no significant difference between the extraction methods, with results ranging between 0.6 and 3.1 pMC.[63] For the fifth sample, which had previously been reported to yield high backgrounds even with rigorous ABA treatment, the ABA results were also anomalously high at 4.4 to 5.2 pMC but fell within the low portion of the range of the other five samples when the holocellulose and α-cellulose fractions were measured (range 0.13 to 0.2 pMC).

It is not unusual to find a sample in a group that is resistant to decontamination by simple methods without any indication of why this might be so. Hence, there are some samples for which the ABA treatment will be inadequate.

Dee recommended using α-cellulose extracts when high-precision results on single tree rings are required for calibration.[64] In support, he noted that of thirty-three duplicate measurements made on single growth rings, thirty-one of the duplicates were indistinguishable at the 95 percent probability level.

For poorly preserved samples, such harsher pre-treatments may so reduce the amount of extract that an analysis is not possible. As a result, the choice of pre-treatment may become a compromise between extract quantity and purity.[65]

62. Southon and Magana, "Comparison of Cellulose Extraction and ABA Pretreatment Methods."

63. These results were estimated by eye from a medium resolution graph in the published work.

64. Dee et al., "Radiocarbon Dating at Groningen," 68–69.

65. Cercatillo et al., "Exploring Different Methods of Cellulose Extraction for ^{14}C dating."

The improvement of radiocarbon measurements on charcoal (mentioned by Higham) involved adding a chemical oxidation agent to the second acid step in the older ABA treatment. This is designated as ABOx. Furthermore, the single combustion step prior to graphitization was replaced by three steps in which the sample was heated in a rising temperature sequence at three different temperatures. The carbon dioxide given off at each temperature was collected separately. When converted to graphite targets the carbon dioxide from the highest temperature combustion step was found to result in lower ^{14}C levels and therefore higher *CRAs* than if all the sample was processed at once.[66] This is attributed to the impurities being less stable than the charcoal and therefore burnt off at lower temperatures. A comparison of Higham's ABOx dates with earlier ABA dates for charcoal samples from the site of Grotta di Fumane, Italy, is shown in Table 5.2.

Table 5.2 Comparison of ABA and ABOx dates: Grotto di Fumane, Italy[67]			
Layer 2		Layer 5	
ABA date BP	ABOx date BP	ABA date BP	ABOx date BP
30,650	35,640	33,700	40150
33,380	35,850	36860	(a)
32,120	34,180	34500	41650 (b)
32530	34,940	38800	40460
31,830	35,180	38250	
		39500	
		39490	

Notes on table:
    a. Cells within the columns separate results for subsections of the layer, as grouped by Higham.
    b. The sample corresponding to this result had an unexpectedly low level of carbon for a sample of that nature. The ORAU laboratory code indicated less confidence in this result than the others in the table.

The fact that the ABOx dates are grouped more closely within each layer and reflect the differentiation in age between layers is given as a reason

66. Bird et al., "Radiocarbon Dating of 'Old' Charcoal."
67. Based on Higham, "European Middle and Upper Palaeolithic Radiocarbon Dates," Table 5, 243.

for considering them to be more accurate, as does a comparison with an Ar-Ar date on an "identical cultural horizon" at another site.

5.5.5 Pre-treatment of Bone Samples Based on Collagen Extraction

In a recent paper Herrando-Perez, citing articles published between 1952 and 2009, pointed out that "Fossil bone has been historically regarded as one of the most difficult and unreliable materials for ^{14}C dating due to contamination, degradation and carbon-exchange issues . . . Bone contamination occurs because both the protein (predominately collagen) and the mineral phase (carbonate hydroxyapatite or bioapatite) are chemically reactive with enclosing or overlying soils and sediments, rain and groundwaters."[68] While noting that this is most problematic for Late Pleistocene[69] specimens, he cautioned that scientists should not ignore the possibility of contamination in the case of younger bones.[70]

Collagen is the major bone protein and consists of three intertwined long chains of amino acids. In order to extract collagen from the bone mineral an ABA treatment is applied to the bone sample, preferably whole or in large fragments. The collagen yield for powdered samples is generally lower: the powdering is suspected of allowing more degradation of the collagen during extraction.[71] The first acid treatment is continued until the bone mineral has dissolved. This takes at least twenty-four hours at room temperature and much longer for large bones.

When a bone with high-quality collagen is dissolved the collagen pieces remain structurally intact, maintaining the shape of the original bone (or its fragments), but are translucent and soft. These are sometimes referred to as bone "phantoms."[72] Being able to separate the bone collagen physically in this way from the treating solution was an important step in obtaining quality collagen and, in fact, gave initial meaning to the term "quality collagen."

---

68. Herrando-Perez, "Bone Need Not Remain an Elephant in the Room," 2.

69. For the range covered by radiocarbon dating, the Late Pleistocene includes all ages greater than about 12,000 years.

70. Herrando-Perez, "Bone Need Not Remain an Elephant in the Room," 14.

71. Fewlass et al., "Pretreatment and Gaseous Radiocarbon Dating of 40–100 mg Archaeological Bone."

72. Sealy et al., "Comparison of Two Methods of Extracting Bone Collagen for Stable Carbon."

If the collagen physically collapses and leaves no phantoms, it is indicative of diagenesis. In this case, the collagen may be mixed with other organic material in the dissolving solution. In much of the radiocarbon literature, the term collagen is used to describe the total collagen fraction with other bone protein and lipid material and whatever contaminants might be present. As a reminder that the isolated material may contain more than just the collagen, we will use the term "collagen fraction."[73] With specimen conservation in mind, it became common for much smaller samples to be taken from bone specimens for AMS measurements. This made the assessment of the progress of the treatment from bone to phantoms difficult so more steps were added to the pre-treatment.[74]

Following ABA, the collagen phantoms or collagen fractions are denatured in hot dilute acid, enabling collagen to dissolve. The dissolved material is filtered to remove any remaining particulate matter, washed, and dried, with the crystalline residue stored for further processing.

Many laboratories use the collagen fraction at this point to make their AMS targets. This is expected to be satisfactory for good collagen samples. Therefore, establishing the quality of collagen is an important factor to be considered when interpreting results.

Collagen Structure, Diagenesis and Quality Assessment

Each strand of collagen contains about 900 amino acids. The chemical bond that joins amino acids together involves a nitrogen atom. Collagen contributes 22 percent of the weight of a fresh, dry bone,[75] while the C:N atomic ratio of collagen in fresh bone is about 3.2 and is a function of its amino acid makeup.[76] A significant change to this ratio indicates that chemical changes have occurred, providing an opportunity for modern carbon addition. Despite claims that values of the ratio between 2.9 and 3.6 indicate that the collagen fraction is suitable for radiocarbon analysis, caution is now being urged. At Groningen, samples outside this range are

---

73. Another term used for this fraction is gelatin.

74. Sealy et al., "Comparison of Two Methods of Extracting Bone Collagen," 65.

75. Talamo et al., "'Here We Go Again': the Inspection of Collagen Extraction Protocols," 62.

76. Do not confuse with the C:N atomic ratio of whole bone that is reported in other contexts.

failed, and a warning is issued if the C:N ratio is not between 3.1 and 3.3.[77] The ratio is a more reliable guide for younger samples than for older ones because quantities of modern carbon impurities that are too small to alter the C:N ratio may well have a significant impact on the measured ages of very old samples.

In the normal process of diagenesis, the collagen content decreases and so collagen yield is a useful quality marker. A dry-bone collagen content above 1 percent is offered as a minimum both from experience[78] and from the results of accelerated diagenesis studies.[79] Results from bones containing less than 1 percent collagen are generally considered unreliable. Extracting collagen and purifying the fraction is a long and expensive process. Therefore, it is useful to have a screening test to assess the extent of diagenesis and hence the likelihood that there will be sufficient collagen present for a useful analysis. For example, it is relatively quick and inexpensive to perform an elemental analysis on a small sample of bone. A whole bone nitrogen threshold of 0.7 percent N was found to have a success rate of over 70 percent in predicting whether the standard collagen extraction would yield greater than 1 percent of the bone mass for bones worldwide with ages greater than about 8,000 years BP.[80] The majority of failures were attributable to incorrect inclusions rather than incorrect exclusions.

The same study presented evidence from an anomalous site where a nitrogen threshold of 1.1 percent was needed to achieve the same success rate in predicting whether the bones contained at least 1 percent collagen. This higher value suggested nitrogen contamination at the site, and some evidence of that was presented. For this and other reasons a screening test is not considered to be a universal or an infallible indicator of collagen content and the threshold may need adjusting for some sites, depending on the nature of the contaminants present.

Rather than limit a quality assessment to a single marker, it has been noted that a range of quality indicators should be considered.[81] The C:N ratio of the collagen fraction, as well as its C and N content compared to the mass of the extract, are relevant. The collagen content of the bone, in

---

77. Dee et al., "Radiocarbon Dating at Groningen," 72.

78. Brock et al., "Reliability of Nitrogen Content (%N) and Carbon," 880.

79. Dobberstein et al., "Archaeological Collagen: Why Worry about Collagen Diagenesis?" 38.

80. Brock et al., "Reliability of Nitrogen Content (%N)."

81. Talamo et al., "'Here We Go Again': the Inspection of Collagen Extraction," 64.

addition to the bone's C and N content, also enables judgments to be made about the likely quality of extracted collagen.

Further Treatment of the Collagen Fraction

Herrando-Perez reported that "many authors acknowledge that gelatinization [ABA followed by denaturation] alone fails to remove mild to severe carbon contamination from Pleistocene-age bone."[82] This is also the age range (> 10,000 yrs) where small amounts of contamination can have a large impact on the reported age. There are three main processes that are used to purify the collagen fraction further in attempts to remove contamination and achieve better results.

While "better results" often appears (with some justification) to mean "older dates," there are objective comparisons with which to assess results obtained by different pre-treatments. They include:

- Consistency within an archaeological context.
- Agreement with other dating techniques, including the radiocarbon ages of associated wood.[83]

The three most commonly used additional pre-treatments separately involve ultrafiltration, the use of an XAD resin, and the separation of an amino acid that is common in collagen but rare in other proteins. Each of these processes aims to remove non-collagen material from the collagen fraction.

---

82. Herrando-Perez, "Bone Need Not Remain an Elephant in the Room," 2.

83. Radiocarbon ages of wood require careful interpretation to link them to a given archaeological context. It is possible for wooden artefacts to have been constructed from wood that was already old. Short lived species and seeds are helpful in making archaeological correlations. However, determinations of the age of wood samples have their own significance for the age of life on Earth independent of the archaeological context.

A. ULTRAFILTRATION   It is chemically reasonable to assume that the incorporation of modern carbon into the collagen occurs at breakages of the polymer strands: the shorter the broken strands, the higher the possible relative contamination. It is also known that many, but not all, of the soil contaminants of bone are small molecules. Therefore, a process that can separate small molecules from larger ones ought to improve the quality of the sample. Ultrafiltration is such a process. Molecules of greater size than the filter's cut-off value are retained on the filter, and smaller ones pass through and are discarded.

The collagen fraction is re-dissolved and filtered through a commercial cartridge designed to retain molecules larger than about one-third of a collagen strand length. Small impurities and collagen which has been degraded to less than a third strand length are expected to pass through. The retained fraction is processed for ^{14}C measurement.

This method has been used since 2000 as the standard collagen pretreatment at the Oxford Radiocarbon Accelerator Unit. Their researchers have reported on its performance.[84] On the positive side, they point out that:

- the dates of the retained fraction are older than those of the eluted fraction,
- ultrafiltration improves the C:N ratios,
- the retained sample is lighter in color (suggesting removal of colored soil contaminants) and non-hydroscopic (suggesting removal of salts),
- sometimes (but not always), ultrafiltration improves the dates of Pleistocene[85] samples, making them older. A Pyrenean ibex bone, given as an example, was dated at 33,000 years BP without ultrafiltration. This date was questioned because its archaeological context implied an unexpectedly late Neanderthal presence in the area. After ultrafiltration, it dated > 46,700 years BP.

On the cautionary side, they noted that the portion retained on the filter and processed for AMS measurement still consisted of more than collagen. They report an aggregate of proteins, including collagen, with associated inorganic complexes and non-protein organic substances. Collagen

---

84. Brock et al., "Analysis of Bone 'Collagen' Extraction Products for Radiocarbon Dating."

85. The authors used the cultural term *Paleolithic* rather than the geological term *Pleistocene*. In the context of radiocarbon dating they are essentially equivalent.

appeared to "cross-link" with soil impurities, which resulted in the retention of some of that impurity on the filter. It is still unclear precisely what substances ultrafiltration does remove. As a consequence, it is not possible to identify in advance those samples that will benefit from ultrafiltration.

In another study, ultrafiltration appeared to do well in removing humic acid contamination but failed to remove conservation chemicals.[86] Clearly, ultrafiltration should not be relied upon to remove all humic contaminants. Any humic contaminant larger than the filter cut-off that has not been removed prior to ultrafiltration will be retained with the longer strands of collagen. This effectively concentrates the large molecular contaminant.

B. XAD-2 Resin Treatment[87] In this option, the dissolved collagen is hydrolyzed to its individual amino acids and the solution is passed through an XAD-2 column. Breaking down the collagen to its building blocks releases any crosslinked compounds. The resin in the column is chosen to allow amino acids to pass through but retain soil acids and other materials. The eluted amino acids are then processed for ^{14}C measurement.

This method does not separate contaminating proteins from the collagen and other bone proteins. Amino acids from other bone proteins should not affect the radiocarbon age determination as they are contemporary with the collagen. Contamination with modern proteins could be an issue, but other soil contaminants will be removed. This method will be evaluated in conjunction with the third option.

C. Isolation of Hydroxyproline (HYP)[88] As in the previous option, collagen is hydrolyzed to its constituent amino acids, again releasing crosslinked impurities. The amino acid HYP is chosen for analysis because it has a relatively high abundance in collagen (it contributes about 12 percent of collagen's carbon) but is rare or absent in other proteins and potential contaminants.

A preparative HPLC[89] column is used to separate HYP amino acids from other amino acids present. As HYP reaches the end of the column it

---

86. Devièse et al., "Increasing Accuracy for the Radiocarbon Dating of Sites." Comparing data from Tables 1 and 3.

87. XAD-2 is the registered name of a commercial resin that can be used in chemical separations.

88. Devièse et al., "New Protocol for Compound-specific Radiocarbon Analysis."

89. HPLC is short for High Performance Liquid Chromatography. The rate of passage

is collected, converted to CO_2, and fed into an AMS with a gas ion source, or converted to graphite for use in a solid-state ion source. The theoretical C:N ratio for HYP is 5.0 and the eluting HYP fraction can be analyzed to determine this parameter. Reported C:N ratios have been noted in the range 4.9 to 5.1.

Specific component analysis (for which HYP is the frontrunner) is considered by many to be the most promising method of eliminating contaminants because it isolates a specific molecule. However, such an analysis is several times more expensive, requires highly skilled operators, and is not yet widely offered. Because HYP is a small fraction of the collagen, analysis requires larger samples to be taken from specimens to obtain sufficient carbon for the target. This can be a problem with curators who take into consideration the cultural and other significance of the specimen being dated and who may be reluctant to sacrifice a large sample.

Wood and others have stressed that "with the increasing complexity and length of pre-treatment, the potential for laboratory-derived contamination itself increases. Laboratory contamination is normally assumed to be modern in age . . . and so it is of the utmost importance that these sources are limited and characterized to ensure that the potential of these longer and more rigorous pre-treatment methods are realized."[90]

Sources of radiocarbon contamination have been identified in the equipment used for ultrafiltration and HYP separation. Processes to minimize and correct for this have been described for ultrafiltration[91] and bleed from the HPLC column.[92] Marom and colleagues reported on HYP determinations on two bones that had a history of returning variable radiocarbon dates ranging from about 3,700 to 13,600 years BP.[93] Three dates had been obtained previously on collagen fractions without further pre-treatment.

---

of a molecular species, in this case, an amino acid, through an HPLC column is a balance between the solubility of the amino acid in the solvent and the chemical attraction between the amino acid and the surface of the column packing material. Those amino acids that stick most to the surface move the slowest. By a careful choice of solvent and column packing it is possible to have the target molecule HYP elute from the column free of the other amino acids.

90. Wood et al., "Refining Background Corrections for Radiocarbon Dating of Bone Collagen," 600.

91. Brock et al., "Quality Assurance of Ultrafiltered Bone Dating."

92. Devièse et al., "New Protocol for Compound-specific Radiocarbon Analysis."

93. Marom et al., "Single Amino Acid Radiocarbon Dating of Upper Paleolithic Modern Humans."

These samples had high collagen C:N ratios. Museum conservation or site-based organic contaminants were suspected.

Marom's group took a new bone powder sample and ultrafiltered the collagen fraction. The collagen residue's C:N ratio was found to be 3.8. Rather than analyze it, they took that residue and performed a HYP separation prior to analysis. The HYP returned a C:N ratio of 5.1 (theoretical value = 5.0). The radiocarbon determination yielded a *CRA* of 33,250 ± 500 years BP for the bone.[94] Although very much older than the previous determinations, this result was consistent with dates based on stratigraphy, including direct ^{14}C dates of other materials from the same cultural level of the site.

This paper also reviewed earlier results obtained from a collection of bones from another site. They came from two individuals S2 and S3, "known to be contemporaneous burials and who were interred together," as well as from a mammoth bone from the "same occupation level" of the site. Previous results had been obtained by three radiocarbon laboratories using collagen directly from the collagen fraction, and separately from the ultrafiltered collagen fraction. The results, based on Table 2 from Marom (see Table 5.3), varied between labs and between bones and are compared with new results obtained using HYP analyses.[95]

Table 5.3 Collagen measurements from three laboratories				
Sample	Laboratory	Collagen Fraction CRA	Ultrafiltered Collagen CRA	HYP Fraction CRA
S2	Arizona	27210 ± 270		
		26,200 ± 640		
	Oxford	23,830 ± 220	25,020 ± 120	30,100 ± 550
S3	Arizona	26,190 ± 640		
	Oxford	24,100 ± 240	25,430 ± 160	
			24,830 ± 110	30,000 ± 550
	Kiel		26,000 ± 410	
Mammoth	Oxford	27,460 ± 310	29,640 ± 180	
			29,450 ± 180	30,100 ± 400

94. This situation illustrates a recurrent issue for the dating of old bones. There may not be sufficient material to perform a systematic set of experiments and choices need to be made on the optimum use of the limited material available.

95. Marom et al., "Single Amino Acid Radiocarbon Dating of Upper Paleolithic Modern Humans."

The authors commented that the internal consistency of the HYP results for the two human remains and the mammoth bones from the same cultural level "provides some support for their accuracy." The spread of the mammoth bone dates across the different pre-treatments is narrower than that of the human bones and is attributed to the absence of curatorial contamination.

Devièse et al. compared results obtained by ultrafiltration, HYP, and XAD on samples from a set of animal bone specimens.[96] Of six cases where ultrafiltration and HYP pre-treatments were both performed on the same sample, three cases displayed discrepancies between the results obtained for ultrafiltered collagen and the HYP fraction. The authors cite other researchers who have made similar observations with regard to Paleolithic specimens. In these cases, the ultrafiltered ages were statistically younger than the HYP result. XAD results in all cases were close to the HYP values. The authors claim their results show that only XAD and HYP methods consistently remove all contaminants. Other methods sometimes produce similar results to HYP, but in other cases return younger ages. On the basis of their results, they claim that it is "impossible to predict analytically to a high degree of confidence when methods other than XAD and HYP are able to remove all the contaminating carbon in dated bones."[97] Their claims are reasonable with regard to the contamination they identified.

The results reviewed in this section are additional examples of different pre-treatments providing different ages. For bone, as the chemical pre-treatments isolated material that was increasingly specific to collagen, the measured ages became larger. For wood samples, extraction of α-cellulose produced older dates, as did ABOX treated charcoal. In the cases presented, independent observations supported the conclusion that the older results were more accurate.

5.5.6 Pretreatment of Bone Samples Based on Bone Mineral – Bioapatite

Since a high proportion of older bones have little or no usable collagen, there have been many attempts to date bones using the carbon within their mineral component, most recently using the method outlined by Cherkinsky.[98]

---

96. Devièse et al., "Increasing Accuracy for the Radiocarbon Dating."
97. Devièse et al., "Increasing Accuracy for the Radiocarbon Dating," 178.
98. Cherkinsky, "Can We Get a Good Radiocarbon Age from 'Bad Bone'?"

After physical cleaning, the bone is treated overnight with acetic acid (a weak acid) to remove secondary or diagenetic carbonates. After rinsing it is dried and then a sample is taken and broken into fragments. A cycle of treatments with acetic acid continues until no further CO_2 is released. The remaining bioapatite fragments are then treated with hydrochloric acid (a strong acid) to release CO_2. This CO_2 is collected and converted to graphite and the radiocarbon content is measured.

Cherkinsky warned that if there had been prior modern carbon exchange with the bioapatite mineral structure itself the added modern carbon would not be removed by the pre-treatment.[99] The pre-treatment is designed to remove calcium carbonate inclusions in the bone while (of necessity for the analysis) leaving the bioapatite portion intact, along with any modern carbon that may have chemically exchanged with it.

5.5.7 Comparison of Collagen and Bone Mineral Dates

Cherkinsky and Chatainger examined cases where both collagen and bioapatite-based dates were measured on the same bone and discrepancies observed.[100] Some mineral dates were found to be younger than collagen dates and vice versa. These differences were explained in terms of the geological context of the samples and whether that context was more likely to contaminate the collagen or the apatite fraction of the bones. In some cases, both the collagen and apatite results were younger than the archaeological context in which the bones were found. On the basis of the report by Cherkinsky and Chatainger, bone ages determined solely from bioapatite should not be regarded as definitive and require further interpretation based on context.

Zazzo studied a wider range of samples from different geographical areas and across a broad time range. He included data from the work of other researchers.[101] The study compared ages from bioapatite analysis against a reference age determination for the specimen. Quality ratings from one to four (high to low) were given to each reference age. Quality one required that the collagen and bioapatite ages were determined on the same individual. Quality two applied when the reference age was determined on

99. Cherkinsky, "Can We Get a Good Radiocarbon Age from 'Bad Bone'?" 647.

100. Cherkinsky and Chataigner, "^{14}C Ages of Bone Fractions from Armenian Prehistoric Sites."

101. Zazzo, "Bone and Enamel Carbonate Diagenesis: A Radiocarbon Prospective."

a collagen, charcoal, or shell measurement from specimens at the same excavation level. Quality three reference dates were averages of dates from the strata above and below the stratum containing the specimen. Quality four had no reference dates, but compared the results from bone apatite, enamel, and/or dentine apatite from the animal.

The following conclusions were drawn from the results for specimens designated quality one or quality two. For younger bones, there was little diversion of the apatite dates from the reference ages. However, for older bones apatite ages diverged from (and were younger than) the reference date. The age reduction varied both within and between sites, as is reasonable if contamination of bioapatite was the cause. The observed age differences were between 300 and 1,500 radiocarbon years at a 9,500 years BP site. At another site, age differences varied with the age of the layers from approximately 6,000 radiocarbon years at the 22,000 years BP level to about 10,000 radiocarbon years at the 34,000 years BP level. The ^{14}C contamination of the apatite fraction corresponding to the age differences ranged up to 7 *pMC*. If this level of contamination was to be added to a carbon-dead sample, it would register a *CRA* of 21,100 years BP.

Based on the results of Zazzo it can be concluded that a bone mineral result is not definitive but provides a minimum age rather than an absolute age for a bone. It is possible, on the basis of XAD and HYP analyses reported above, that the collagen reference ages used may also have been younger than the real ages of the bones and thus the contamination levels of bioapatite might be underestimated.

5.5.8 Sample Conversion to Graphite via Carbon Dioxide for AMS Targets

When the desired component has been isolated, it is then converted to carbon dioxide, usually by heating in the presence of copper oxide. The carbon dioxide may be fed straight to an AMS gas phase ion source or converted to graphite over a catalyst, commonly finely divided iron, which becomes coated with the graphite. The graphite-coated iron is pressed into a sample holder, which is fitted as the target into the sample wheel of the AMS for analysis.

An analytical run may consist of many samples depending on the size of the instrument and the geometry of the target holder.[102] Samples of inter-

---

102. For example, the NEC-AMS at the Scottish Universities Environmental Research

est are interspersed with reference samples for modern carbon, standards that cover the expected age range of the samples included in the run, plus background or blank samples.[103] The standard and background samples provide quality control and are used in the calculation of results.

Replicate determinations may be made on all standards and samples in order to calculate uncertainties in the $^{14}C/^{12}C$ ratio, but some laboratories base their quoted uncertainties on aggregated historical data. Between-run uncertainties are generally higher than uncertainties based on replicate determinations within the same run.

5.6 BACKGROUND SAMPLES: MAGNITUDE AND ORIGIN

Metrology requires that the background sample be of the same matrix type as the sample to be analyzed. Table 5.4 lists background data published by three laboratories for wood and bone matrices.[104]

Table 5.4 Background measurements and calculated *LODs* from several laboratories						
		Published Data (a)			Calculated *LODs* (b)	
Laboratory	Sample Type	Background *pMC*	sd		*LOD* BP	*LOD pMC*
Waikato/ Keck (c)	Charcoal	0.186	0.029		48300	0.24
	Ancient wood (ABA)	0.157	0.061		47200	0.28
	Ancient wood (α-cellulose)	0.146	0.053		48100	0.25

Centre takes 134 samples; the Keck Carbon Cycle AMS instrument at the University of California (Irvine) takes 60.

103. A standard sample can be obtained from large batches of material held and provided by testing authorities. These samples have been analyzed many times usually by many laboratories, and for which there is an agreed value and uncertainty. A series of standards should be available across the analytical range. Using standards is a check on the stability of the instrument and its reproducibility. The use of a modern standard allows the determination of the isotopic ratios required in the calculations.

104. Waikato University Radiocarbon Dating Laboratory, AMS Processing Technical Report (2017); Aerts-Bijma et al., "An independent Assessment," 11; St-Jean et al., "Semi-Automated Equipment for CO_2 Purification," 952.

Table 5.4 Background measurements and calculated *LODs* from several laboratories					
		Published Data (a)		Calculated *LODs* (b)	
Centre for Isotope Research (d)	Wood Kitzbuhel I (ABA)	0.23	0.035	46700	0.30
	Bone (collagen)	0.25	0.034	46100	0.32
A E Lalonde AMS Laboratory (e)	Wood (AVR-07-PAL-37)	0.12	0.01	52800	0.14
	Mammoth bone	0.19	0.01	49500	0.21

Notes to Table 5.4

a. The published data are listed in the shaded section and from it *LODs* have been calculated in both radiocarbon years BP and *pMC*.
b. Calculated *LODs* are based on background + 2sd when expressed as *pMC*. Calculated BP results have been rounded to the nearest 100 years.
c. The Waikato Laboratory performs its own sample preparation. The AMS radiocarbon determination is performed at the Keck Radiocarbon Dating Laboratory, University of California (Irvine).
d. The Centre for Isotope Research is at Groningen University.
e. The A. E. Lalonde AMS laboratory is associated with the University of Ottawa.

Preferred background samples are those that have minimal contamination. Criteria used to assess low contamination include:

- the nature of the specimen's depositional environment and preservation status.
- the specimen's physical appearance. For example, discoloration is evidence of contamination.
- whether the background result is low and whether it is similar when different pre-treatments are used. Note the similar results on ancient wood obtained in the Waikato laboratory for ABA and α-cellulose extractions.

These criteria for purity also apply to finite age samples, except that in these cases, the measured radiocarbon content is expected to be age dependent. The uncalibrated *LODs* based on the background results are in the range of the high 40,000s of years BP to the low 50,000s of years BP and correspond to ^{14}C levels of up to several tenths pMC. It is not unusual for different laboratories to find different values for a background sample, which is indicative of the different methodologies employed or the differing performance of the instruments used. The main difference between *LOD*s in these data sets derived not so much from the background results themselves but from the smaller uncertainties associated with the ^{14}C measurements quoted by the Lalonde laboratory. This resulted in the highest *LOD*s for radiocarbon ages. Given that one of this laboratory's special research interests is the measurement of old carbon samples, it is very likely that both the instrument and the procedures used are designed with particular care to minimize uncertainty.

The apparent presence of small amounts of ^{14}C in measurements on blank samples is seen by proponents as a technical problem in the analysis which is to be understood and minimized in order to extend the temporal range of radiocarbon dating. Critics, on the other hand, interpret non-zero blanks as evidence of a flaw in the assumption of dead carbon and cite this as evidence that this dating method and the geological timescale are unreliable.

The analytical issue is to understand why a small, finite reading was obtained for a sample that was expected to be carbon dead. The following discussion reviews experimental data relevant to the origin of ^{14}C in background samples. Potential sources of contamination are examined. These include environments the specimens have experienced, sampling and target preparation procedures, and processes that occur in the AMS. We also discuss an experiment that was designed to amplify the presence of ^{14}C, if any, in a presumed dead carbon sample of methane and consider the implications.

Both the development of better instrumentation and the interpretation of results require an understanding of all possible components of the background signal in AMS analysis. In discussing this matter, Taylor et al. have listed possible sources of ^{14}C that might contribute to the background in AMS determinations of ^{14}C.[105] These may be grouped as follows, and some examples are provided.

---

105. Taylor et al., "Misunderstandings Concerning the Significance of AMS."

5.6.1 Contributions to the Background Count from Specimen Contamination

Contamination of a specimen can occur in-situ or during handling and storage at any point prior to processing for analysis. It should not be assumed that pre-treatment necessarily removes 100 percent of the contamination from the sample.[106] Taylor also observed that it is relatively easy to remove contaminants from wood and charcoal, but difficult in the case of bones. This caution is illustrated by the results (discussed above) that showed older dates were obtained as pre-treatment methods were made more rigorous for charcoal, wood, and bone specimen analysis. They show that there has been contamination removal. However, comparison experiments such as this cannot demonstrate whether the most successful extraction (the one which has removed the most modern carbon) has in fact removed all the contaminants. Therefore, it must be possible that some contamination might remain even after complex extraction processes.

5.6.2 Contributions to the Background Count Due to Target Preparation

The reagents (CuO and Fe) used for converting the sample to CO_2 and then reducing the CO_2 to graphite have been shown to contribute ^{14}C to the target.[107] Zhao et al. report experiments on a graphite sample measured directly as the target, compared with taking graphite from the same batch through their standard combustion and (re) graphitization process.[108] The difference in reported ages showed that approximately 0.09 *pMC* was added during sample conversion to graphite. Wood et al. provide data that suggest about 0.06 *pMC* is added during the combustion step. Such amounts may vary from laboratory to laboratory.[109]

Crossover of ^{14}C between samples during graphitization batch processing has been measured separately at 0.025 percent[110] and 0.035 per-

---

106. Taylor et al., "Misunderstandings Concerning the Significance of AMS," 733.

107. Vandeputte and van der Plicht, "Study of the ^{14}C -Contamination Potential of C-Impurities in CuO and Fe."

108. Zhao et al., "Preliminary Ion Source Background Study," 1101.

109. Wood et al., "Refining Background Corrections," 604.

110. St-Jean et al., "Semi-Automated Equipment for CO_2 Purification," 953.

cent[111] of the previous sample content. This is the reason that laboratories ask for an estimate of the age of a submitted sample. If samples of similar age are processed in sequence the effect of this crossover can be minimized.

CO_2 adsorbed onto the inner surfaces of reaction vessels and the tubing of the vacuum system used to transfer the CO_2 during sample preparation can be incorporated into samples during processing.[112] CO_2 is also adsorbed onto the graphite when targets are exposed to the atmosphere when they are being pressed into sample holders, while in storage, and during placement into the sample wheel of the AMS. Some molecules are loosely adsorbed, while others are more tightly bound. The loosely adsorbed CO_2 is rapidly desorbed by the cesium sputtering, but the effect of the more tightly bound molecules has been observed for up to fifteen minutes of measurements, which may be significant for background sample results.[113]

Indirect evidence for target preparation contamination during processing also comes from the fact that very small (less than 0.3 mg) samples return higher ^{14}C results than larger samples.[114] This is consistent with what would be observed if a constant mass of contamination from the process is shared over increasingly larger quantities of target.

5.6.3 Instrumental Contributions to the Background Count

Instrumental noise from the electronics of an instrument is an unavoidable signal source that most likely makes only a minor contribution. Zhao and others have identified the ion source as a significant contributor to the blank sample radiocarbon value. They estimated that during a 200-sample run up to 10 mg of carbon (a mixture of carbon from all the targets analyzed) is progressively sputtered onto the surrounding surface of the ion source and portions of this mixture are re-sputtered into the beamline with the carbon from whichever sample is under analysis. The energy of the sputtered carbon is sufficiently large to be incorporated into (as well as onto) the ion source surrounds. This means that complete cleaning of the

---

111. Southon, quoted in St-Jean et al., "Semi-Automated Equipment for CO_2 Purification."

112. Taylor et al., "Misunderstandings Concerning the Significance of AMS," 741.

113. Zhao et al., "Preliminary Ion Source Background Study," 1092.

114. Alderliesten et al., "Contamination and Fractionation Effects in AMS-Measured $^{14}C/^{12}C$"; Taylor et al., "Misunderstandings Concerning the Significance of AMS, Fig 6, 744."

ion source is extremely difficult. They report that "(t)he above tests with ... ^{14}C blanks all suggest that the background counts, resulting from the ion source memory effects, could contribute significantly in addition to the contamination introduced during sample preparation steps." This is another example of sample memory effects. They concluded that "the ion-source memory effects *may at times exceed sample processing contamination* [our emphasis] to become the final barrier to the measurement of very-low level samples."[115] They had already found that one step in the process contributed 0.09 *pMC*, implying that ion-source memory effects may be greater than this. Effects such as these that occur during processing also add to the overall measurement uncertainty.

5.6.4 Contributions to the Background Count Inherent to the Sample

We have shown that there are sources of modern carbon contamination that can occur during processing and analysis and that these can account for the few tenths of a percent of modern carbon that are observed in background counts. However, the question remains as to whether there may be any intrinsic ^{14}C in the background samples themselves. In other words, is dead carbon really "dead"?

That question was of interest to the Borexino project established during the 1990s to detect solar neutrinos that had been predicted by theoretical physics. Such neutrinos could be detected by scintillation detectors. The proposed scintillator solvent, 1,2,4-trimethylbenzene (TMB) was to be made from presumed carbon-dead petrochemicals. At that time the radiocarbon content of commercial CO_2 derived from natural gas was measured by the Isotrace Laboratory (the forerunner of the Lalonde Laboratory) at around 0.08 *pMC*.[116] Additional data suggested that this was a consequence of the graphitization process.

However, if this signal (or a significant part of it) came from the natural gas then the proposed neutrino detector would not work. The ^{14}C decay radiation in the TMB would interfere with its performance.[117] The Borexino project sought stronger evidence than their assumption that fossil

    115. Zhao et al., "Preliminary Ion Source Background Study," 1105.
    116. Beukens, "Radiocarbon Accelerator Mass Spectrometry," 622.
    117. Alimonti et al., "Measurement of the ^{14}C Abundance in a Low-background Liquid Scintillator," 350.

Radiocarbon Dating of Once-living Specimens

carbon was "dead" before embarking on the expensive task of constructing a prototype detector that required about four tons of TMB. They devised an experiment to test how much of the measured 0.08 *pMC* background might be attributed to the methane. The results of this experiment are directly relevant to the analytical assumption that very old samples intrinsically contain only dead carbon.

Carbon isotope enrichment was at the time used to greatly increase the ^{13}C content of natural carbon for stable isotope studies of biochemical pathways. This process enriched the ^{13}C approximately one hundred times. Diffusion characteristics implied that any ^{14}C present would have been enriched approximately 200 times. This was done *prior to the graphitization step that was considered responsible for the measured ^{14}C*. The experimental design is shown in Figure 5.4.

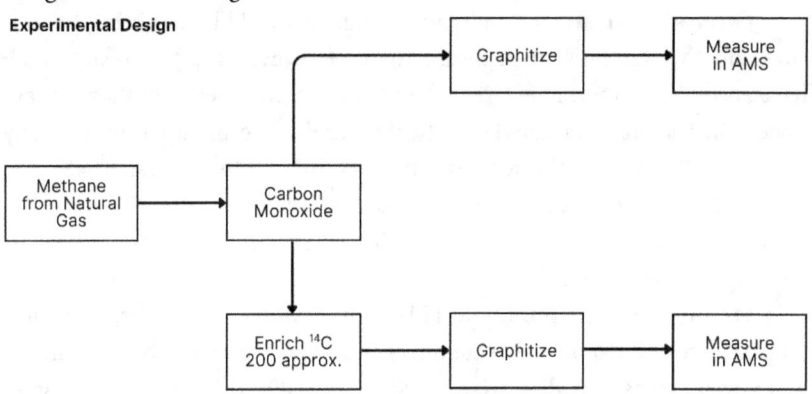

Figure 5.4 Experimental design for isotopic enrichment.

The upper branch is the path of the unenriched sample, while the lower is that of the enriched sample. The only difference between the two branches in the experimental design is the box in the lower branch where any ^{14}C in the original methane (or introduced in the conversion to carbon monoxide) would be enriched 200 times.

The results have been discussed in three publications[118] and there is a discrepancy in reporting the enrichment factor which is almost certain to be typographical.[119] The reported ^{14}C value is consistent with the

---

118. Beukens, "Radiocarbon Accelerator"; Alimonti et al., "Measurement of the ^{14}C Abundance"; Litherland et al., "Low-level ^{14}C Measurements and Accelerator Mass Spectrometry."

119. Beukens gives the enrichment factor as 20,000 and Litherland (with Beukens as

lower reported enrichment factor of two hundred. This is also the more conservative interpretation because it results in a higher value for any ^{14}C found, which is intrinsic to the methane.

The experiment was performed with extra care taken to remove adsorbed CO_2 from the equipment and to minimize vacuum leaks. The methane was converted to carbon monoxide, part of which was analyzed for ^{14}C by the standard procedure, giving a radiocarbon content of 0.049 ± 0.012 *pMC*. If even 1 percent of the ^{14}C detected in this unenriched sample had been intrinsic to the methane, then the expected result after enrichment would have been about 0.15 *pMC*. If all the ^{14}C detected in the unenriched sample had been intrinsic to the methane, then the expected result after enrichment would have been about 10 *pMC*. The ^{14}C enriched sample was measured in the same way, giving a result of 0.048 ± 0.003 *pMC*.[120]

Given that there is virtually no change, it would be tempting to conclude no ^{14}C was present in the methane. However, the two results each have an uncertainty that is larger than the difference between them. These uncertainties must be treated statistically to calculate an upper limit for any excess ^{14}C that was in the second sample compared to the first. That value divided by two hundred will give a *maximum* value for the ^{14}C content of the original methane consistent with the experimental results. The calculated figure was 0.00014 *pMC*.[121]

On this basis, the prototype TMB scintillation counter was constructed underground (to provide shielding) and the trace amounts of ^{14}C in the TMB were measured directly as 0.00017 ± 0.00001 *pMC*.[122] This figure should also be considered as an upper limit for the radiocarbon content of the petrochemicals used because some contamination by modern carbon was also a possibility during synthesis of the TMB. This is an independent confirmation because the enriched sample was measured by AMS and the

---

one of the co-authors) as 200. The relationship to ^{13}C enrichment heavily suggests 200. The derived conclusions reported by Alimonti are consistent with 200 being the factor. It is assumed that 20,000 should have been reported as 20,000 percent. In addition, if the factor was 20,000 and the background was intrinsic to the methane the expected result would have been ten times that of modern carbon, a ^{14}C level that a radiocarbon dating laboratory would not willingly place in its instrument.

120. Beukens, "Radiocarbon Accelerator."

121. While insufficient information is provided to redo the statistics, calculations made with reasonable assumptions indicate that this value is quoted at the 95 percent confidence level.

122. Some of the Borexino experimental results were reported as $^{14}C/^{12}C$ ratios. They have been converted to *pMC* for comparison; Alimonti et al., 353.

TMB was measured using scintillation counting. It would make a stronger case if more experiments of this nature could be cited confirming the observation. However, the lack of additional experiments is understandable given that the Borexino results confirmed what was already considered by science to be the case. It also strengthened the assumption that the graphitization step was a source of contamination.

5.6.5 Conclusions about Background Samples

Evidence has been provided that modern carbon is introduced during sample preparation and in the AMS itself, particularly from the combustion/graphitization steps and from the ion-source. The quantities identified are sufficiently high to be plausible explanations of the background signals that are observed experimentally for specimens expected to be carbon dead. There is also the possibility that pre-treatment has not removed all the contamination from the sample.

Using the Boreximo data we can conclude that, at most, only 0.35 percent of the measured methane background of 0.049 pMC could be attributed to the methane. The rest must come from other parts of the analytical pathway. It is reasonable to extend this conclusion to the intrinsic radiocarbon content of specimens of high geological age used as background samples. The small, measured finite background counts are compatible with the assumption that there is no intrinsic ^{14}C in background specimens.

Understanding the origin of the background signal enables steps to be taken in design and practice to minimize sources of ^{14}C and ^{14}C-like signals. We anticipate that improvements in pre-treatment methods and instrument design will reduce background levels and increase the range of radiocarbon dating. However, both theoretical and practical considerations preclude background-level measurements ever reaching zero.

5.6.6 Evaluating Published Radiocarbon Results

The primary issue in the evaluation of radiocarbon dates is the reliability of the ^{14}C content analysis. Unfortunately, the information required to make this evaluation is often absent in the publication of results. Results obtained using XAD and HYP isolation pretreatments of bones have reinforced Higham's assertion that a large proportion of results published prior to 2011 reported dates that were too young.

Wood lamented that "Radiocarbon's long history means a range of methods and approaches exist, *but the scant details published alongside the majority of dates means assessment of their quality is impossible* (our emphasis), either in terms of association with archaeology or accuracy of the number. Whether this is due to a lack of education, inadequate journal guidelines, or poor laboratory reporting, work must focus on improving the situation. If we cannot improve publication, many of the thousands of dates produced every year will be unusable in the future. This would be a terrible waste of what is a valuable resource of increasingly high-quality chronological information." [123]

Herrando-Perez published the results of a survey of scientists from disciplines that used radiocarbon dating of bones regularly for their data and found many of them left the choice of pretreatment in the hands of the radiocarbon laboratory (not necessarily a bad thing) but this often meant that the authors were not in a position to discuss their data in terms of sample quality.[124] The precision of the result is often presented in terms of the physics of AMS, but we have seen that the accuracy of the result is more dependent on the chemistry of the contamination removal. This information is still not regularly discussed by end-users in their publications.

If the quality assessment of published results is impossible for experts in the field because of insufficient data, it is even more fraught for interested nonscientists and for scientists from other disciplines, particularly when the data they see has been extracted from the original literature setting and published in secondary sources such as books and magazine articles. Some knowledge of chemistry and the dating process is required to apply the quality criteria for collagen dating. These include C:N ratios and the carbon and nitrogen content of both the collagen and the whole bone. We have attempted to provide an introduction so readers at least can understand whether suitable quality criteria have been provided. As pre-treatment chemistry has improved radiocarbon dates on bones have generally become older and more consistent with stratigraphy and other dating techniques. This coherence provides a good case for their acceptance. Conversely, results obtained earlier in the history of radiocarbon dating should be viewed with caution.

---

123. Wood, "From Revolution to Convention: The Past, Present and Future of Radiocarbon Dating," 61.

124. Herrando-Perez, "Bone Need Not Remain an Elephant in the Room."

Radiocarbon Dating of Once-living Specimens

The reader interested in radiocarbon dating and the age of the earth most likely will have encountered reports of radiocarbon dates obtained on dinosaur bones. These can be traced back to three publications.[125] The majority of these results were obtained using the method of Cherkinsky on bone apatite and consist of values in the range 0.61 to 7.46 *pMC* (approximate *CRA* range 41,000 to 21,000 years BP). The range of the modern carbon content of these bones is very similar to the range of contamination found by Zazzo to account for the difference between bioapatite ages and the reference ages in his study discussed above. Therefore, in the absence of any evidence to the contrary, contamination of the apatite fraction should be the default explanation for these results.

In a few cases, there was an attempt to extract collagen. However, no data were presented in conjunction with the radiocarbon results to show the collagen yield, C:N ratios for either the whole bone or the collagen fraction, or any other quality criteria that might be used to support the reported collagen dates. None of the newer pretreatments (ultrafiltration or either of the XAD or HYP extractions) was attempted. Therefore, there is no data on which to build a scientific case for the reliability of these results.

In the paper by Lindgren et al. not only was no evidence provided for the quality of the extracted collagen fraction used to obtain a radiocarbon age, but their own discussion of the spectroscopic data used to identify the presence of collagen in the bone required them to conclude that the collagen present in the bone was degraded.[126]

As discussed in Paul Cameron's chapter regarding the discoveries of soft tissue in old bones, any work that seeks to call an existing paradigm into question must be able to demonstrate the highest quality for its results. This has not yet been done for dinosaur radiocarbon ages.[127]

5.7 ARE NUCLIDE DECAY RATES CONSTANTS OF NATURE?

This question has been discussed with varying degrees of intensity ever since the discovery of radioactivity by Becquerel in 1896. Rutherford raised

---

125. Miller et al., "Search for Solutions to Mysterious Anomalies in the Geologic Column"; Thomas and Nelson, "Radiocarbon in Dinosaur and Other Fossils"; Lindgren et al., "Microspectroscopic Evidence of Cretaceous Bone Proteins."
126. Lindgren et al., "Microspectroscopic Evidence."
127. Cameron, this publication, Chapter 10.

the possibility of varying decay rates in a 1913 study investigating gamma-ray emission from radon gas in a high-pressure bomb.[128] Some seventy years later, Alburger et al. reported a small annual variation in measurements of the $^{32}Si/^{36}Cl$ ratio taken over a four-year period.[129] It was suggested that temperature and relative humidity variations might be responsible, but unfortunately, these data were not recorded. In 2009, Jenkins et al. stirred the debate by claiming very small (at the 10^{-3} level) seasonal variations in the decay rate measurements of $^{32}Si/^{36}Cl$ and ^{226}Ra.[130] This report, along with some other studies conducted between 1990 and 2007 (see Table 1 of Fischbach et al.), suggested that the varying Sun-Earth distance might produce small variations in nuclide half-life.[131] However, no variation from the expected exponential radioactive curve was observed for the ^{238}Pu that powered the Cassini spacecraft, and certainly no Sun-distance dependence.[132] If there is any solar influence at all on nuclide half-life (and the Cassini data suggest there is not), then any plausible mechanism emerging would promise insights into solar processes deep in the Sun's core, which might affect nuclear dynamics on Earth and perhaps even suggest a new "force" in nature. These discoveries would clearly be of great interest to science. In order to understand the discussion and appreciate whether a solar-related variation in nuclide half-life is reasonable, some understanding of the internal processes of atoms and beta decay is useful.

As noted at the start of this chapter, the present set of rules that successfully predicts nuclear reactions and particle physics is the Standard Model, the accepted quantum theory of matter. The theory identifies twelve fundamental particles (six quarks and six leptons) governed by fundamental interactions and the exchange of interaction carrier particles (bosons). The interactions are often called "forces." These are the strong and weak nuclear forces, the electromagnetic force, and gravity. Einstein insisted that gravity is not a force but rather a manifestation of warped space-time. Either way, gravitational interactions are excluded from the Standard Model. A combined theory of Quantum Gravity is at present being actively pursued (e.g., String theory and Emergence theory).

---

128. Rutherford, *Radioactive Substances and Their Radiations.*

129. Alburger et al., "Half-life of ^{32}Si."

130. Jenkins et al., "Evidence of Correlations Between Nuclear Decay Rates and Earth–Sun Distance."

131. Fischbach et al., "Time-dependent Nuclear Decay Parameters."

132. Cooper, "Searching for Modifications to the Exponential Radioactive Decay Law."

Recall that ^{14}C transmutation is a β- decay process. The weak interaction of β- decay is carried by W bosons and is well understood and described by the Standard Model and Quantum Electrodynamics (QED). The development of our present understanding of the weak nuclear force began with Fermi in the 1930s. The explanation of the continuum energy spectra of the emitted β- within a quantum view of matter, the identification of the neutron, and the prediction and subsequent identification of W bosons are now all matters of historical record. The Feynman diagram of the underlying quark process of β- decay is shown in Figure 5.5.

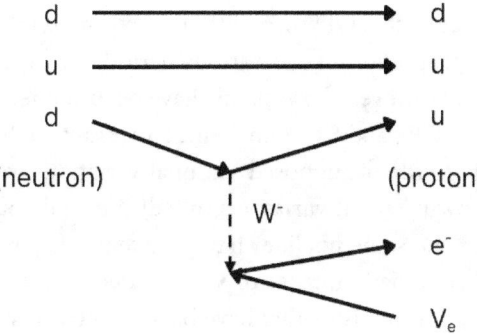

Figure 5.5 The quark process of β^- decay where one down-quark (d) changes into an up-quark (u) mediated by the W⁻ boson with the emission of an electron (e^-) and anti-electron neutrino. The other up- and down-quarks (at the top) remain unaffected. This transmutes a neutron into a proton.

Since the weak interaction is responsible for β decay it follows that neutrinos must only "feel" the weak "force." Fischbach et al. reported tiny changes in count rates of ^{54}Mn and suggested that these may be caused by changes in the flux of solar neutrinos during a solar flare interval.[133] However, it is unclear how these flux changes might interact with the mechanism shown in Figure 5.5 and possibly modify nuclide half-life for conditions on Earth.

Since neutrinos only interact through the weak force, they are very difficult to detect. This has presented a significant challenge in metrology and sub-atomic particle detection technology. Briefly, solar neutrinos are signatures of the fusion energy source in the core of the Sun. Over 90 percent of solar neutrinos have maximum energies around 400 keV (low energy) and arise from a proton-proton nuclear process. Other processes

133. Fischbach et al., "Time-dependent Nuclear Decay Parameters."

involving boron and beryllium produce neutrinos with larger energies. A summary of neutrino research was given by Nakahata, who is associated with the Super-Kamiokande.[134] This neutrino detector incorporates a 50,000 ton water tank located one kilometer underground in the Mozumi mine in Japan and has returned data on solar neutrino flux for over twenty years, covering two solar cycles. A summary of recent results was presented by Nakano et al.[135] Importantly, the data are consistent with a constant solar neutrino flux and show no significant correlation with sunspot number. These data constitute a clear rebuttal of the earlier claim by Fischback et al., mentioned above.

Jenkins, Fischbach, and Sturrock[136] have reported small variations in decay rates and proposed links to various periodic fluctuations in the solar neutrino flux. However, these claims have been refuted by Kossert and Nähle, Bergeson et al., and S. Pommé and co-workers.[137] The inconsistent phasing and amplitude of supposed seasonal variations, reports of alpha-emitters also showing slight variations in half-life, and counter reports of no variations for the same nuclides have weakened arguments for a solar neutrino or other radiation cause of varying decay rates. Recent reports list the suggested mechanisms that have been proposed, such as solar and cosmic neutrinos, gravity waves, and space weather (e.g., x-ray flares).[138] Pomme et al. state, "Most of these claims of new physics have been convincingly invalidated by high-quality experiments showing invariability of the decay constants, such that the discussion is largely settled." They attribute the small oscillations in the decay-rate data reported in the literature to

---

134. Nakahata, "History of Solar Neutrino Observations."

135. Nakano for the Super-Kamiokande Collaboration, "Recent Solar Neutrino Results from Super-Kamiokande."

136. Jenkins et al., "Evidence of Correlations Between Nuclear Decay Rates and Earth–Sun Distance"; Fischbach et al., Time-dependent Nuclear Decay Parameters"; Sturrock et al., "Comparative Analysis of Super-Kamiokande Solar Neutrino Measurements."

137. Kossert and Nähle, "Disproof of Solar Influence on the Decay Rates of $^{90}Sr/^{90}Y$; Bergeson et al., "Precision Long-term Measurements of Beta-decay-rate Ratios in a Controlled Environment; Pommé and Pelczar, "Role of Ambient Humidity Underestimated in Research on Correlation Between Radioactive Decay Rates and Space Weather"; Pommé et al., "On the Decay Constants and Orbital Distance to the Sun – part 1: Alpha Decay"; Pommé et al., "Is Decay Constant?"; Pomme and Pelczar, "On the Recent Claim of Correlation Between Radioactive Decay Rates and Space Weather"; Pommé et al., "On the Interpretation of Annual Oscillations in ^{32}Si and ^{36}Cl Decay Rate Measurements."

138. Such as Pommé et al., "Role of Ambient Humidity"; Pommé et al., "On the Interpretation of Annual Oscillations."

temperature and humidity changes to which the measuring instruments are sensitive.[139]

Even if the variations in half-life do arise from some mechanism that alters the decay parameter, λ (and Pommé et al. argue this is false), the effect on ^{14}C dates is very small for two reasons. Firstly, the variations reported are of the order 10^{-3}, which would have little effect on derived dates. Secondly, for the same reason that it does not matter if the Libby or the presently accepted value for the ^{14}C half-life is used, the calibration curves discussed in Section 3 align ^{14}C derived times with calendar dates using additional cross-checked non-radioactive data such as tree rings, marine varves, and ice-core layers.

Perhaps a more fundamental aspect concerns the constants of nature, and whether they are in fact, constant. The advances in our understanding of cosmology since the 1920s, a growing appreciation of just how large the universe is, and relativistic insights into the relationship between space and time have pushed age estimates of past events in the universe into the billions of years. Can any quantity, such as the speed of light in a vacuum, really remain the same over such vast periods of time? One combination of physical constants that is known to have a constant value even for distant galaxies is the fine structure (Sommerfeld) constant,

$$\alpha = \frac{1}{4\pi\varepsilon_0}\frac{e^2}{\hbar c} \approx \frac{1}{137} \qquad (12)$$

Where c is the speed of light, e the electron charge, ε_0 the permittivity of free space, and $\hbar$ a version of Plank's constant. Yes, this ratio has been observed to change with scattering energy (e.g., at TeV energies, α~1/127) but not with time. There is a weak interaction coupling constant, e_w, and a corresponding ε_w, so for the weak nuclear interaction equation (12) becomes,

$$\alpha_w = \frac{1}{4\pi\varepsilon_w}\frac{e_w^2}{\hbar c} \approx 10^{-6} \qquad (13)$$

Any proposed temporal variation in physical constants, whether the speed of light, the electron charge, or Planck's constant, would show a variation of α_w with distance. Distant astrophysical observations repeatedly show no such variations.[140]

139. Pommé et al., "On the Interpretation of Annual Oscillations."
140. See, for example, Nakamura et al., "Precise Measurement of the μ+ Lifetime."

Perhaps one reason why the possibility of time (or distance) varying physical constants is so regularly proposed is that while the Standard Model proposes these fundamental constants it does not explain why they have the values that they do. The only method of obtaining these values is via experiment. Strong evidence suggests that in order for the natural world to exist as we observe it a very fine tuning of these constants is required, a point often repeated by those who argue for design in nature.[141] Given that these parameters are instrumental at the fundamental level of natural interactions there would be clear and obvious consequences if they had altered. Any proposal for such change must then recognize this reality and account for the absence of supporting data in comparisons between astrophysical observations of past processes and those taking place today.

5.8 CONCLUSION

The use of radiometric nuclides as clocks into the past has developed into a highly technical discipline involving over forty different radioactive elements. The use of ^{14}C has attracted particular attention, as estimates of age for once-living organisms consistently yield values much greater than 10,000 years, which is problematic for some Christians. In Equation 6, there are only three parameters used in the estimation of dates. These are N, N_0, and λ (respectively, the number of ^{14}C atoms present at the time of measurement, the number of ^{14}C atoms present initially, and the decay constant). Each of these has attracted scrutiny over the accuracy of measurement, underlying assumptions, and the development of technology. The method requires meticulous sample preparation, sophisticated sensing equipment, research experience, and knowledge of the sample context, in addition to fastidious cross-checking protocols and careful calibration of ^{14}C-derived dates with those obtained from non-radioactive methods. Variations of ^{14}C in the environment are known and accounted for in the calibration curves.

It is important to recognize that metrology techniques and alternative sources of data for cross-checking with ^{14}C measurements have improved and developed over time, which results in complications when comparing results obtained recently with those given in older publications. Rightly dividing and interpreting the research literature requires a careful, balanced,

---

141. See, for example, Dembski, *Intelligent Design, The Bridge Between Science and Theology*.

and honest appraisal of the improvements in dating once-living specimens using ^{14}C. Some of the earlier results have stood the test of scientific scrutiny over time, while others have not. The reader should be suspicious of out-of-context quotes from older scientific results and should be aware of the strengths and weaknesses of different measurement hardware and techniques that have been used. Sensational descriptions of preliminary results should also be questioned.

Radiometric dating is based on nuclear processes that operate at the sub-atomic scale of the interchange of matter and energy. Nature is a wonderful, complex, and interconnected dynamic system. While human endeavors tend to categorize disciplines of knowledge, these are artificial compartments. For example, radiometric phenomena are linked to research areas in space and solar science, astrophysical emissions and cosmology, particle physics, and the fundamental nature of matter. The scientific models that explain and enable accurate predictions of these processes critically depend on the value of physical constants. The reader should be wary of imprecise and oversimplified explanations that do not take into account their consequences in other areas of nature.

The authors submit that subject to the caveats presented and discussed in this chapter, the ^{14}C dating method is consistent with honest and competent scientific practice and, accordingly, should be taken seriously.

BIBLIOGRAPHY

Adolphi, Florian, et al. "Persistent Link Between Solar Activity and Greenland Climate During the Last Glacial Maximum." *Nature Geoscience* 7:9 (2014) 662–66. https//www.nature.com/articles/ngeo2225.

Aerts-Bijma, Anita T., et al. "An Independent Assessment of Uncertainty for Radiocarbon Analysis with the New Generation High-yield Accelerator Mass Spectrometers." *Radiocarbon* 63:1 (2021) 1–22.

Airey, Peter, et al. "The Scientific Basis." In *Radioactivity in the Environment*, 18, edited by John R. Twining, 1–57. Amsterdam, Netherlands: Elsevier, 2012. https://www.sciencedirect.com/science/article/abs/pii/B9780080450162000011?via%3Dihub.

Aitken, Martin J. *Science-Based Dating in Archaeology*. London: Routledge, 1990. https://www.taylorfrancis.com/books/mono/10.4324/9781315836645/science-based-dating-archaeology-aitken.

Alburger, David E., et al. "Half-life of ^{32}Si." *Earth and Planetary Science Letters* 78: 2–3 (1986) 168–76.

Alderliesten, Cees, et al. "Contamination and Fractionation Effects in AMS-Measured ^{14}C/^{12}C and ^{13}C/^{12}C Ratios of Small Samples." *Radiocarbon* 40:1 (1997) 215–21. https://doi.org/10.1017/S0033822200018075.

Alimonti, Gianluca, et al. "Measurement of the ^{14}C Abundance in a Low-background Liquid Scintillator." *Physics Letters B* 422 (1998) 349–58.

Bao, Rui, et al. "Dimensions of Radiocarbon Variability Within Sedimentary Organic Matter." *Radiocarbon* 60 (2018) 775–90.

Bard, Edouard, et al. "Calibration of the ^{14}C Timescale Over the Past 30,000 Years Using Mass Spectrometric U-Th Ages from Barbados Corals." *Nature* 345 (1990) 405–10.

BenZvi, Segev, et al. "Obtaining a History of the Flux of Cosmic Rays Using In Situ Cosmogenic ^{14}C Trapped in Polar Ice." Presented at the International Cosmic Ray Conference. Madison, WI: Cornell University, 2019. https://doi.org/10.48550/arXiv.1909.07994.

Bergeson, Scott D., et al. "Precision Long-term Measurements of Beta-decay-rate Ratios in a Controlled Environment." *Physic Letters B* 767 (2017) 171–76. https://doi.org/10.1016/j.physletb.2017.01.030.

Bertsch, George F., et al. "Atom." In *The New Encyclopaedia Britannica*, 15th ed., 32 vols. Encyclopaedia Britannica, 2010.

Beta Analytic. *Introduction to Radiocarbon Determination by the Accelerator Mass Spectrometry Method*, (undated). https://www.radiocarbon.com/PDF/AMS-Methodology.pdf.

Beukens, Roelf P. "Radiocarbon Accelerator Mass Spectrometry: Background and Contamination." *Nuclear Instruments and Methods in Physics Research* B79 (1993) 620–23.

Bird, Michael I. et al. "Radiocarbon Dating of 'Old' Charcoal Using a Wet Oxidation, Stepped-Combustion Procedure." *Radiocarbon* 41:2 (1999) 127–40.

Brock, Fiona, et al. "Analysis of Bone 'Collagen' Extraction Products for Radiocarbon Dating." *Radiocarbon* 55:2 (2013) 445–63.

Brock, Fiona, et al. "Current Pre-treatment Methods for AMS Radiocarbon Dating at the Oxford Radiocarbon Accelerator Unit (ORAU)." *Radiocarbon* 52:1 (2010) 103–12.

Brock, Fiona, et al. "Quality Assurance of Ultrafiltered Bone Dating." *Radiocarbon* 49:2 (2007) 187–92.

Brock, Fiona, et al. "Reliability of Nitrogen Content (%N) and Carbon: Nitrogen Atomic Ratios (C:N) as Indicators of Collagen Preservation Suitable for Radiocarbon Dating." *Radiocarbon*, 54:3, 4 (2012) 879–86.

Budzikiewicz, Herbert, and Ronald D. Grigsby. "Mass spectrometry and Isotopes: A Century of Research and Discussion." *Mass Spectrometry Reviews* 25 (2006) 146–57. https://doi.org/10.1002/mas.20061.

Bureau International des Poids et Mesures. https://www.bipm.org/en/committees/cg/cgpm.

Cercatillo, Silvia, et al. "Exploring Different Methods of Cellulose Extraction for ^{14}C dating." *New Journal of Chemistry* 45 (2021) 8936–41.

Cherkinsky, Alexander, and Christine Chataigner. "^{14}C Ages of Bone Fractions from Armenian Prehistoric Sites." *Radiocarbon* 52:2, 3 (2010) 569–77.

Cherkinsky, Alexander. "Can We Get a Good Radiocarbon Age from 'Bad Bone'? Determining the Reliability of Radiocarbon Age from Bioapatite." *Radiocarbon* 51:2 (2009) 647–55.

Choppin, Gregory R., et al. "Radionuclides in Nature." In *Radiochemistry and Nuclear Chemistry*. 3rd ed. Woburn, MA: Butterworth-Heineman, 2002. https://doi.org/10.1016/B978-0-7506-7463-8.X5000-6.

Cooper, Peter. S. "Searching for Modifications to the Exponential Radioactive Decay Law with the Cassini Spacecraft." *Astroparticle Physics* 31 (2009) 267–69. https://doi.org/10.1016/j.astropartphys.2009.02.005.

Dee, Michael W., et al. "Radiocarbon Dating at Groningen: New and Updated Chemical Pretreatment Procedures." *Radiocarbon* 62:1 (2020) 63–74.

Dembski, William A. *Intelligent Design, The Bridge Between Science and Theology.* Downers Grove, IL: InterVarsity, 1999.

Devièse, Thibaut D., et al. "Increasing Accuracy for the Radiocarbon Dating of Sites Occupied by the First Americans." *Quaternary Science Reviews* 198 (2018b) 171–80. https://hal-amu.archives-ouvertes.fr/hal-03207790/file/Paper_HYP_North_America_QSR_180901.pdf.

Devièse, Thibaut D., et al. "New Protocol for Compound-specific Radiocarbon Analysis of Archaeological Bones." *Rapid Communications in Mass Spectrometry* 32 (2018a) 373–79. https://analyticalsciencejournals.onlinelibrary.wiley.com/doi/epdf/10.1002/rcm.8047.

Dobberstein, Reimer C., et al. "Archaeological Collagen: Why Worry about Collagen Diagenesis?" *Archaeological and Anthropological Sciences* 1 (2009) 38. https://doi.org/10.1007/s12520-009-0002-7.

Engelkemeir, Antoinette. G., et al. "The Half-life of Radiocarbon." *Physical Review* 75 (1949) 1825. https://doi.org/10.1103/PhysRev.75.1825.

Fewlass, Helen, et al. "Pretreatment and Gaseous Radiocarbon Dating of 40–100 mg Archaeological Bone." *Scientific Reports* 9:5342 (2019). https://doi.org/10.1038/s41598-019-41557-8.

Fischbach, Ephraim, et al. "Time-dependent Nuclear Decay Parameters: New Evidence for New Forces?" *Space Science Reviews* 145 (2009) 285–335. https://doi.org/10.1007/s11214-009-9518-5.

Garnier-Laplace, Jacqueline, and Sylvie Roussel-Debet. "Carbon-14 and the Environment." *Institute de Radioprotection et de Surete Nucleaire* (2012). https://inis.iaea.org/records/9snf2-tsz06. The English version is document:55096293.pdf.

Hans-Arno, Synal. "Developments in Accelerator Mass Spectrometry." *International Journal of Mass Spectrometry* 349–350 (2013) 192–202. https://doi.org/10.1016/j.ijms.2013.05.008.

Herrando-Pérez, Salvador. "Bone Need Not Remain an Elephant in the Room for Radiocarbon Dating." *Royal Society Open Science* 8:1 (2021). https://doi.org/10.1098/rsos.201351.

Higham, Thomas F. G. "European Middle and Upper Palaeolithic Radiocarbon Dates are Often Older Than They Look: Problems with Previous Dates and Some Remedies." *Antiquity* 85:327 (2011) 235–49.

Jenkins, Jere H., et al. "Evidence of Correlations Between Nuclear Decay Rates and Earth-Sun Distance." *Astroparticle Physics* 32:1 (2009) 42–46.

Kennett, James P., et al. "Bayesian Chronological Analyses Consistent with Synchronous Age of 12,835–12,735 Cal B.P. for Younger Dryas Boundary on Four Continents." *Proceedings of the National Academy of Sciences of the United States of America (PNAS)* (2015). https://doi.org/10.1073/pnas.1507146112.

Kossert, Karsten, and O. J. Nähle. "Disproof of Solar Influence on the Decay Rates of $^{90}Sr/^{90}Y$." *Astroparticle Physics* 69 (2015) 18–23. https://doi.org/10.1016/j.astropartphys.2015.03.003.

Krane, Kenneth S. *Introductory Nuclear Physics.* Hoboken, NJ: Wiley, 1988.

Kutschera, Walter. "Accelerator Mass Spectrometry: State of the Art and Perspectives," *Advances in Physics: X* 1:4 (2016) 570–95. https://doi.org/10.1080/23746149.2016.1224603.

Kutschera, Walter. "Applications of Accelerator Mass Spectrometry." *International Journal of Mass Spectrometry* 349–50 (2013) 203–218. https://doi.org/10.1016/j.ijms.2013.05.023.

Libby, Willard F. "Radiocarbon Dating." *Science* 133 (1961) 621–29.

Libby, Willard F., et al. "Age Determination by Radiocarbon Content: World-Wide Assay of Natural Radiocarbon." *Science* 109 (1949) 227–28. https://doi.org/10.1126/science.109.2827.227.

Lindgren, Johan, et al. "Microspectroscopic Evidence of Cretaceous Bone Proteins." *Public Library of Science (PLOS) One* 6:4 (2011). https://doi.org/10.1371/journal.pone.0019445.

Litherland, Albert, et al. "Low-level ^{14}C Measurements and Accelerator Mass Spectrometry." *AIP Conference Proceedings* 785:48-56 (2005). https://www.researchgate.net/publication/234873380_Low-level_14C_measurements_and_Accelerator_Mass_Spectrometry.

Marcillac, Pierre, et al. "Experimental Detection of α-particles From the Radioactive Decay of Natural Bismuth." *Nature* 422 (2003) 876–78. https://doi.org/10.1038/nature01541.

Marom, Anat, et al. "Single Amino Acid Radiocarbon Dating of Upper Paleolithic Modern Humans." *Proceedings of the National Academy of Sciences of the United States of America (PNAS)* 109:18 (2012) 6878–81. www.pnas.org/cgi/doi/10.1073/pnas.1116328109.

Marsh, Eric J., et al. "IntCal, ShCal, or a Mixed Curve? Choosing a ^{14}C Calibration Curve for Archaeological and Paleoenvironmental Records from Tropical South America," *Radiocarbon* 60 (2018) 925–40.

McCormac, F. Gerry, et al. "Calibration of the Radiocarbon Time Scale for the Southern Hemisphere: AD 1850–1950." *Radiocarbon* 44:3 (2002) 641–51.

Millard, Andrew R. "Conventions for Reporting Radiocarbon Determinations." *Radiocarbon* 56:2 (2014) 555–59. https://doi.org/10.2458/56.17455.

Miller, Hugh, et al. "The Search for Solutions to Mysterious Anomalies in the Geologic Column." *Research Open: Geology, Earth and Marine Sciences* 1:1 (2019) 1–15. https://researchopenworld.com/wp-content/uploads/2020/01/Gems-19-104_Hugh-Miller.pdf.

Mook, Willem G., and Johannes Plicht. "Reporting ^{14}C Activities and Concentrations." *Radiocarbon* 14:3 (1999) 227–39.

Nadeau, Marie-Josée, et al. "Carbonate ^{14}C Background: Does it Have Multiple Personalities?" *Radiocarbon* 43:2A (2001).

Nakahata, Masayuki. "History of Solar Neutrino Observations," *Progress of Theoretical and Experimental Physics* 2022:12 (2022). https://doi.org/10.1093/ptep/ptac039.

Nakamura, Satoshi N., et al. "The Precise Measurement of the μ+ Lifetime." *Hyperfine Interactions* 138 (2001) 445–50. https://doi.org/10.1023/A:1020818411395.

Nakano, Yuuki, for the Super-Kamiokande Collaboration. "Recent Solar Neutrino Results from Super-Kamiokande." *Journal of Physics: Conference Series* 1342 (2020). https://doi.org/10.1088/1742-6596/1342/1/012037.

NATA (National Association of Testing Authorities, Australia) Technical Circular. *General Accreditation Guidance – Validation and Verification of Quantitative and Qualitative*

Test Methods. 2018. https//dastmardi.ir/wp-content/uploads/2018/08/Validation-and-Verification-of-Quantitative-and-Qualitative-Test-Methods.pdf.

New World Encyclopedia. *Dendrochronology*. 2020. https://www.newworldencyclopedia.org/entry/Dendrochronology.

Nuclear Data. http//www.lnhb.fr/home/nuclear-data/nuclear-data-table/; http://www.lnhb.fr/nuclides/C-14_tables.pdphone.

Oxford Radiocarbon Accelerator Unit. "Reporting Radiocarbon Dates." (1980). https://c14.arch.ox.ac.uk/calibration.html#conventions.

"Periodic Table." https://www.nndc.bnl.gov/nudat2/.

Pommé Stefaan, and K. Pelczar. "On the Recent Claim of Correlation Between Radioactive Decay Rates and Space Weather." *European Physical Journal* 80:1093 (2020). https://doi.org/10.1140/epjc/s10052-020-08667-4.

Pommé, Stefaan, and K. Pelczar. "Role of Ambient Humidity Underestimated in Research on Correlation Between Radioactive Decay Rates and Space Weather." *Nature Scientific Reports* (2022). https://doi.org/10.1038/s41598-022-06171-1.

Pommé, Stefaan, H., et al. "On the Decay Constants and Orbital Distance to the Sun – part 1: Alpha Decay." *Metrologia* 54 (2017) 1–18. https://doi.org/10.1088/1681-7575/54/1/1.

Pommé, Stefaan, H., et al., "Is Decay Constant?" *Applied Radiation Isotopes* 134:4 (2018) 6–12. https://doi.org/10.1016/j.apradiso.2017.09.002.

Pommé, Stefaan H., et al. "On the Interpretation of Annual Oscillations in ^{32}Si and ^{36}Cl Decay Rate Measurements." *Nature Scientific Reports* (2021). https://www.nature.com/articles/s41598-021-95600-8

Radiocarbon Calibration. *Wikipedia* (2024). https://en.wikipedia.org/wiki/Radiocarbon_calibration.

Reimer, Paula J., et al. "The INTCAL20 Northern Hemisphere Radiocarbon Age Calibration Curve, (0–55 Cal kBP)." *Radiocarbon* 62 (2020) 725–57. https://doi.org/10.1017/RDC.2020.41.

Reimer, Paula J., et al. "Selection and Treatment of Data for Radiocarbon Calibration: An Update to the International Calibration (INTCAL) Criteria." *Radiocarbon* 55:4 (2013) 1923–45.

Rutherford, Ernest. *Radioactive Substances and Their Radiations*. New York: Cambridge University Press, 1913.

Rutherford, Ernest, et al. *Radiations from Radioactive Substances*. Cambridge: Cambridge University Press, 1930.

Sealy, Judith, et al. "Comparison of Two Methods of Extracting Bone Collagen for Stable Carbon and Nitrogen Isotope Analysis: Comparing Whole Bone Demineralization with Gelatinization and Ultrafiltration." *Journal of Archaeological Science* 47 (2014) 64–69. https://doi.org/10.1016/j.jas.2014.04.011.

Sitek, Arkadiusz, and A. M. Celler. "Limitations of Poisson Statistics in Describing Radioactive Decay." *Physica Medica* 31:8 (2015) 1105–07. https://doi.org/10.1016/j.ejmp.2015.08.015.

Southon, John R., 2007, quoted in Gilles St-Jean et al., "Semi-Automated Equipment for CO_2 Purification and Graphitization at the A. E. Lalonde AMS Laboratory (Ottawa, Canada)." *Radiocarbon* 59:3 (2017) 952.

Southon, John R., and Alexandra L. Magana., "A Comparison of Cellulose Extraction and ABA Pretreatment Methods for AMS ^{14}C Dating of Ancient Wood." *Radiocarbon* 52:3 (2010) 1371–79. https://doi:10.1017/S0033822200046452.

Steinhilber, Friedhelm, et al. "9,400 Years of Cosmic Radiation and Solar Activity from Ice Cores and Tree Rings." *Proceedings of the National Academy of Sciences of the United States of America (PNAS)* 109 (2012) 5967–71.

Stenström, Kristina E., et al. *A Guide to Radiocarbon Units and Calculations*. Lund University, Internal Report LUNFD6(NFFR-3111)/1-17/ (2011), 11. https://www.hic.ch.ntu.edu.tw/AMS/A%20guide%20to%20radiocarbon%20units%20and%20calculations.pdf.

St-Jean, Gilles, et al. "Semi-automated Equipment for CO_2 Purification and Graphitization at the A. E. Lalonde AMS Laboratory (Ottawa, Canada)." *Radiocarbon* 59:3 (2017) 952.

Stuiver, Minze. "Workshop on ^{14}C Data Reporting." *Radiocarbon* 22:3 (1980) 944–66.

Sturrock, Peter A., et al. "Comparative Analysis of Super-Kamiokande Solar Neutrino Measurements and Geological Survey of Israel Radon Decay Measurements." *Frontiers In Physics* (2021). https://doi.org/10.3389/fphy.2021.718306.

Synal, Hans-Arno. "Developments in Accelerator Mass Spectrometry." *International Journal of Mass Spectrometry* 349–350 (2013) 192–202,. https://doi.org/10.1016/j.ijms.2013.05.008.

Talamo, Sandra, et al. "'Here We Go Again': the Inspection of Collagen Extraction Protocols for ^{14}C Dating and Palaeodietary Analysis." *STAR: Science & Technology of Archaeological Research* 7:1 (2021) 62–77. https://doi.org/10.1080/20548923.2021.1944479.

Taylor, R. Ervin, et al. "Misunderstandings Concerning the Significance of AMS Background ^{14}C Measurements." *Radiocarbon* 60:3 (2018) 727–49.

Thomas, Brian, and Vance Nelson. "Radiocarbon in Dinosaur and Other Fossils." *Creation Research Society Quarterly* 51 (2015) 299–311.

Tomizuka, Akira. "Is a Box Model Effective for Understanding the Carbon Cycle." *American Journal of Physics* 77 (2009) 156–63. https://doi.org/10.1119/1.3013196.

United Nations Scientific Committee on the Effects of Atomic Radiation (UNSCEAR). *Sources and Effects of Ionizing Radiation*, Report vol. I. New York: United Nations, 2008.

Vandeputte, Kurt, and Johannes van der Plicht. "Study of the ^{14}C -Contamination Potential of C-Impurities in CuO and Fe." *Radiocarbon* 40:1 (1998) 103–10.

Waikato University Radiocarbon Dating Laboratory. *AMS Processing Technical Report*, 2017. https://www.waikato.ac.nz/assets/Uploads/Research/Services-and-facilities/Radiocarbon-dating/Waikato-Radiocarbon-Dating-Laboratory-AMS-Processing-Technical-Report-2017.pdf.

Wiens, Roger C. "Radiometric Dating: A Christian Perspective." *American Scientific Affiliation* (2002). https://www.asa3.org/ASA/resources/Wiens2002.pdf.

Wood, Rachel. "From Revolution to Convention: The Past, Present and Future of Radiocarbon Dating." *Journal of Archaeological Science* 56 (2015) 61.

Wood, Rachel, et al. "Refining Background Corrections for Radiocarbon Dating of Bone Collagen at ORAU." *Radiocarbon* 52:2, 3 (2010) 600–11.

Zazzo, Antoine. "Bone and Enamel Carbonate Diagenesis: A Radiocarbon Prospective." *Palaeogeography, Palaeoclimatology, Palaeoecology* 416 (2014) 168–78.

Zhao, Xiao-Lei, et al. "A Preliminary Ion Source Background Study at Lalonde." *Radiocarbon* 61:4 (2019) 1101.

6

How Far Can a Kangaroo Jump?
Plate Tectonics and the Biogeography of Marsupials

HOWARD J. FISHER

6.1 INTRODUCTION

PLATE TECTONICS IS THE theory (in the scientific sense of the word) that deals with the dynamics of Earth's outer, rigid shell. The shell is termed the lithosphere and is broken up into pieces, termed plates, of which seven are large in area and a dozen or more are medium to small. The theory has been widely accepted by geoscientists since the 1960s, following the discovery of paleomagnetic evidence that validated the notion that the seafloor is spreading. The theory of plate tectonics has provided a framework by which to understand several phenomena of Earth's physical environment, including the past geography of continents and oceans. Among other things, plate tectonics theory provides a mechanism for the lateral movement of continents, popularly known as "continental drift," which is of special relevance to this chapter. The acceptance of plate tectonics has been described as a paradigm shift and a scientific revolution.

Biogeography is the study of the distribution of living organisms. Biogeographers look for patterns in the distribution of life and attempt to develop explanations for those patterns. Such explanations usually depend on contemporary data obtained from many disciplines, including geography, climatology, ecology, physiology, genetics, geology, and paleoclimatology. In this chapter, the historical and contemporary distributions of marsupials will be examined from the perspective of current understanding within the geological and biological sciences.

6.2 MARSUPIALS

Defining precisely what constitutes a marsupial is especially important for establishing and understanding the historical distribution of marsupials. Marsupials are mammals. Mammals are grouped together in the Class Mammalia. Characteristics possessed by all mammals include having three bones in the middle ear, a lower jaw made up of a single pair of bones that articulates in a unique way with the skull, and mammary glands that produce milk to suckle the young. Among living mammals, biologists recognize three distinct groups, popularly known as monotremes, marsupials, and placentals, respectively.

In technical terms, monotremes belong to the Order Monotremata, within the *Subclass Prototheria*. Monotremes lay eggs. They are represented today by the platypus and four species of echidna. Echidnas also have pouches in which they incubate the egg after it has passed from the body, although they are anatomically different from the pouches of marsupials. There are many extinct monotreme species known, including a Patagonian platypus and a toothed platypus, *Obduron*, that left fossils near Lake Eyre in South Australia and at Riversleigh in north Queensland.

Marsupials and placentals are placed together in the *Subclass Theria*. Therian mammals produce live young without shelled eggs. Subclass Theria is split into two infraclasses, Metatheria and Eutheria.

Infraclass Metatheria includes mammals in which the placenta is short-lived. Metatherians are now represented only by marsupials, although many extinct metatherian species are known that differ from marsupials in some details and are believed to be related to them.

Marsupials give birth to poorly developed young (altricial) that in most species are nurtured inside a pouch (marsupium) where they attach to a teat. Modern and ancient marsupials have an extra pair of bones, the epipubic bones, that project forward from pelvic bones and support the pouch in females. Epipubic bones occur in modern marsupials and in most non-placental fossil mammals, including multituberculates, monotremes, and the ancestors of eutherian mammals.[1] The fact that these bones occurred in some non-marsupials suggests that they served a different function in those groups, possibly to assist locomotion by supporting some of

---

1. Novacek et al., "Epipubic Bones in Eutherian Mammals."

the muscles that flex the thigh.[2] In addition to epipubic bones, which occur in both sexes, there are consistent differences between marsupials and the eutherians in the anatomy of the skull and in dentition.

Infraclass Eutheria includes the so-called placental mammals, ranging from the bumblebee bat of Thailand, which weighs in at two grams, to the blue whale, which can weigh 150 million grams (i.e., 150 tons) or more. Placental mammals give birth to well-developed (precocial) young.

The determination of when and where marsupials first appeared on Earth depends to a considerable degree on what are regarded as the defining characteristics of a marsupial. Today it is easy to categorise a living mammal species as a marsupial or some other kind of mammal. For many fossils, however, some of the features that distinguish between contemporary mammal groups are absent or ambiguous. It may be difficult to determine whether some fossils represent an early eutherian or an early metatherian. Sometimes there may be a change of opinion about the status of a fossil, as with *Sinodelphys szalayi*, discovered in China in 2003.[3] It was believed originally to be the earliest known metatherian, but outside Marsupialia (true marsupials). However, subsequent examination has led to the reassessment of this fossil as an early *eutherian*.[4] This kind of difficulty is to be expected if all mammals stem from a common ancestral population—paleontologists have almost as many arguments as theologians do.

Some of the features that distinguish marsupials from eutherians are not preserved in fossils; for example, the marsupium (pouch), differences in the anatomy of genitalia and reproductive system, differences in the placenta (marsupials have a short-lived, relatively simple placenta, except for bandicoots, which have two, one more complex than the other). However, skeletal features and teeth *are* preserved in fossils. Teeth are as useful to a paleontologist as fingerprints are to a forensic scientist.

Sometimes, especially when more data become available, specialists tighten definitions of certain groups so that species that were once placed within a certain group may be excluded subsequently and transferred to another group. This has happened with respect to marsupials. Over the last twenty years or so some fossils that were regarded as marsupials when discovered in the late twentieth century are no longer regarded as such because the criteria have been refined. These fossils are still classed as metatherians, but not as marsupials (see, for example, the report of a marsupial fossil

2. Reilly and White, "Hypaxial Motor Patterns."
3. Luo et al., "Early Cretaceous Tribosphenic Mammal."
4. Bi et al., "Early Cretaceous Eutherian."

from the Late Cretaceous of southeastern Utah, now regarded as metatherian in the sub-clade Marsupialiformes but not a true marsupial)[5] and some are no longer interpreted as metatherians at all (as with *Sinodelphys*, already mentioned).[6]

As Feldhamer et al. stated, "There is not a consensus on the classification of the Marsupialiformes, including the boundaries of the Marsupialia."[7] Table 6.1 provides an overview of the main metatherian groups as delineated by Eldridge et al.,[8] with some additions.

Williamson et al. summarised past and present metatherian biogeography as follows (remembering that all extant metatherians are marsupials): "Today, metatherians are abundant and taxonomically and morphologically diverse in Central America, South America, and Australia, and are the dominant mammals on only one continent, Australia. However, during the Late Cretaceous, they were a diverse group on the northern continents of Laurasia. In North America, metatherians were far more numerous and taxonomically diverse than were eutherian mammals, the stem placental mammalian group that is dominant across most of the world today."[9]

6.3 CONTINENTAL MOVEMENTS

Fossils of metatherians are known from all continents except Zealandia.[10] As a prelude to tracing the historical migrations of metatherians, this section provides a brief description of the changing historical arrangement of the continents since the Triassic, the oldest Period within the Mesozoic Era. Figure 6.1 provides two snapshots of the positions of the continents, one in the Oligocene and one in the present (Holocene).

---

5. Cifelli and Eaton, "Marsupial from the Earliest Late Cretaceous."

6. For other examples of subsequent change of taxonomic status from marsupial to non-marsupial metatherian see Benton, "First Marsupial Fossil from Asia," 313 (Kazakhstan); Woodburne and Zinsmeister, "First Land Mammal from Antarctica," 913–48 (Antarctic Peninsula); Bown and Simons, "First Record of marsupials (Metatheria: Polyprotodonta," 447–49 (Egypt); Tsofimov and Szalay, "New Cretaceous Marsupial from Mongolia," 12569–73; Storch and Qiu, "First Neogene Marsupial from China."

7. Feldhamer et al., *Mammalogy: Adaptation, Diversity, Ecology*. 5th ed. 238. For more on metatherian taxonomy see Weisbecker and Beck, "Marsupial and Monotreme Evolution and Biogeography"; Eldridge et al., "An Emerging Consensus in the Evolution."

8. Eldridge et al., "Emerging Consensus," 8.

9. Williamson et al., "Origin and Early Evolution of Metatherian Mammals," 1.

10. For more on Zealandia, see Mortimer et al., "Zealandia: Earth's Hidden Continent."

Table 6.1 Main Metatherian Groups	
Group[11]	Comment
Deltatheroidea*	Carnivorous. Cretaceous North America and Asia
Marsupialiformes incertae sedis*	Incertae sedis = uncertain placement. Group proposed by Vullo et al.[12] Late Cretaceous to Pliocene. Twelve families.
Polydolopimorphia*	Paleocene to early Oligocene. South America and Antarctica.
Sparassodonta*	Early Eocene to early Pliocene. South America
Marsupialia (includes all groups below)	True Marsupials
Argyrolagoidea*	Some place this group in Polydolopimorphia
Didelphimorphia	Opossums. South America, Central America, and North America (1 species)
Paucituberculata	Shrew Opossums
Australidelphia	Australasian Marsupials
*Djarthia murgonensis**	The oldest known definitive crown marsupials are the stem australidelphian *Djarthia murgonensis* and an isolated "ameridelphian" marsupial calcaneus, both from the Eocene Tingamarra Fauna, Murgon, Queensland.[13]
Dasyurimorphia	Australian carnivorous marsupials
Diprotodontia	Kangaroos, wallabies, possums, koala, wombats, and many others (Australasian group)
Microbiotheria	One extant species (monito del monte, Argentina, Chile) and fossils from South America, West Antarctica, and Australia)
Notoryctemorphia	Marsupial Moles
Paramelemorphia	Bandicoots and bilbies
Yalkaparadontidae *	New order proposed by Archer et al.[14]

* signifies an extinct group.

11. Most of these groups have the taxonomic status of Order. Black et al. included Deltatheroidea, Polydolopimorphia and Sparassodonta in Marsupialia. See Black et al., "Rise of Australian Marsupials," 990.
12. Vullo et al., "Oldest Modern Therian Mammal from Europe."
13. Beck, "'Amerindian' Marsupial."
14. Archer et al., "New Order of Tertiary Zalambdodont Marsupials."

The Age of Life on Earth

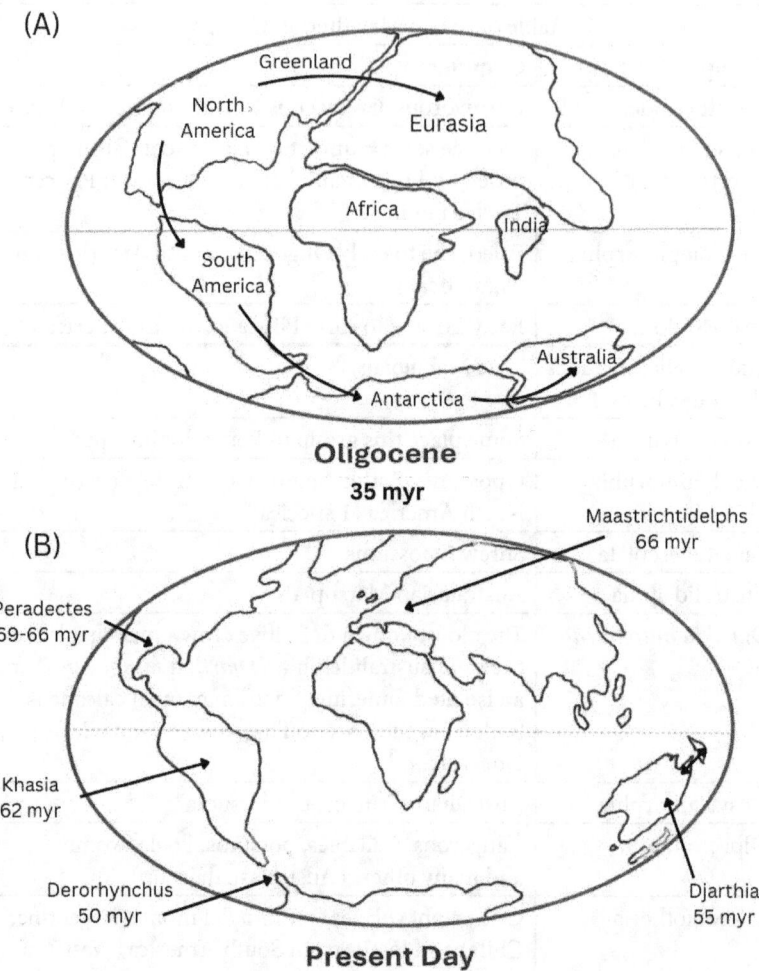

Figure 6.1 Relative positions of the continents in the Oligocene (A) and the Present (B). The continents are shown in approximate outline. The relative levels of land and sea have changed progressively and at various times parts of the continents were submerged. On Map A (Oligocene) arrows show likely routes of migration of marsupials out of North America (see Section 6.4). Map B (Present) shows the location and approximate age of some significant fossils. The presence of a fossil at any location does not preclude the existence of the species in the area earlier or later than the date of the fossil. Most Indonesian islands are not shown, although marsupials have spread westwards from New Guinea as far as Sulawesi (see Section 6.4) (drawn by H. Fisher and L. Rogers).

How Far Can a Kangaroo Jump?

There are many excellent maps showing the past arrangements of the continents available online.[15] Table 6.2 provides some details of the upper geological timescale.

Table 6.2 Upper Geological Timescale[16]			
Era	Period	Epoch	Age at base (Myr)
Cenozoic	Quaternary	Holocene	0.012
		Pleistocene	2.6
	Neogene	Pliocene	5
		Miocene	23
	Paleogene	Oligocene	37
		Eocene	58
		Paleocene	66
Mesozoic	Cretaceous	Upper	100
		Lower	145
	Jurassic		201
	Triassic		251

The Triassic is the last time in Earth's history when all the continents were contiguous, joined in a supercontinent known as Pangaea. Centered on the Equator, this supercontinent stretched from the southern polar region to high latitudes in the Northern Hemisphere. The outlines of some of the continents, especially Asia, were very different from those with which we are familiar today.

By the end of the Triassic, Pangaea had almost separated into two large continents: a northern continent, Laurasia, consisting of North America, Europe, and northern Asia, and a southern continent, Gondwana, which included Africa, Antarctica, Australia, India, South America, Zealandia, and various fragments that later formed south-east Asia.

By the Late Jurassic Gondwana had effectively separated from Laurasia. The gap between North America/Greenland and Europe was not large and peninsulas extended south from North America on the west (Mexico) and on the east (from Florida to the Caribbean Ridge). The Tethys Ocean was filling a widening gap between Eurasia and Gondwana.

---

15. For example, Scotese, *Paleomap Project*.
16. Cohen et al, "ICS International Chronostratigraphic Chart."

In the Mid-Cretaceous South America and Africa separated. By the Late Cretaceous, there was still potential for "island-hopping" between North and South America. Beck suggested that there may have been up to three independent dispersals of marsupials from North to South America in the Late Cretaceous-Early Paleocene.[17] North America/Greenland were still relatively close to Europe. North America was close to Asia in the region now known as Beringia and migration between the two continents was feasible.[18] India/Madagascar had separated from Africa and Zealandia separated from Antarctica.

In the Eocene, there was a connection between South America and Australia. These two continents were located on opposite sides of Antarctica, which had much milder climates than at present and there was a potential for migration of both plants and animal species either way between South America and Australia. In the mid-Eocene India collided with Asia, generating the uplift of the Himalayas. In the latter Eocene, climates became colder and the formation of the Antarctic ice sheet began. By the mid-Oligocene, both Australia and South America had separated from Antarctica and the circumpolar current was established in the Southern Hemisphere. Australia began a northward drift towards south-east Asia, elevating the island of New Guinea in the process. By the mid-Miocene, all the continents were close to their current positions.

6.4 THE ORIGIN AND SPREAD OF METATHERIANS

"Metatherians appear to have been confined to Laurasia until at least the latest Cretaceous, before dispersing into Gondwana, presumably from North America to South America."[19] Williamson et al. advocated a North American origin for metatherians and concluded that "Disregarding *Sinodelphys* [see earlier] the oldest certain metatherians are the deltatheroidans *Oklatheidium szalayi* and *Atokatheridium boreni* from the Lower Cretaceous (Albian ca 104–108 million years old) Antlers Formation of Oklahoma . . . and of an indeterminate genus and species from the Lower Cretaceous (Albian) Cloverly Formation of Montana."[20] Fossils referable to the Mar-

---

17. Beck, "Dated Phylogeny of Marsupials."

18. Davies et al., "Late Cretaceous Seasonal Ocean Variability from the Arctic," Fig. 1; Florillo et al., "Hard Structure in Late Cretaceous Polar Dinosaurs."

19. Eldridge et al., "Emerging Consensus," 803.

20. Williamson et al., "Origin and Early Evolution," 37.

supialiformes first appear in North America near the Albian-Cenomanian boundary in the Early–Late Cretaceous.[21] Cohen et al. claimed the oldest pediomyoid marsupialiforms from the Turonian of Utah (Late Cretaceous, ca 90–94 Myr),[22] while Carneiro contended that his "results demonstrate that Metatheria originates in North America during the late Early Cretaceous, with Gondwanan lineages evolving in the Northern Hemisphere during the Late Cretaceous prior to their dispersal to South America."[23] The greatest diversity of Cretaceous metatherians occurs in North America.[24] According to this interpretation, in the Late Cretaceous metatherians moved east out of North America to Europe[25] and on to Afro-Arabia[26] and Asia, where Late Cretaceous deltatheroidan fossils in Uzbekistan have been confirmed.[27] At about the same time, metatherians moved south to South America, possibly via the . . . Greater Antilles or Aves Ridge, a volcanic arc that was subaerially exposed between the Campanian [Late Cretaceous] and Eocene. Owing to continual fluctuations in tectonism, magmatic activity, and sea level, this created an intermittent land connection between North and South America."[28] Nonetheless, there remains a much less likely possibility that Metatheria originated in China and spread from there to both North America and Europe.

Many Laurasian metatherian taxa were lost in the major extinction that occurred at the Cretaceous/Paleogene boundary, with a sharp decrease in diversity evident in North America, Europe, and Asia. However, Gondwanan metatherians diversified greatly during the Cenozoic. There is general agreement that metatherians arrived in South America from North America in the Late Cretaceous.[29]

---

21. Cifelli, "Marsupial Mammals from the Albian-Cenomanian"; Williamson et al., "Origin and Early Evolution"; Bi et al., "Early Cretaceous Eutherian."
22. Cohen et al., "Geologically Oldest Pediomyoidea."
23. Carneiro, "New Species of *Varalphadon*," 88.
24. Bennett et al., "Deep Time Diversity of Metatherian Mammals."
25. Martin et al., "New European Marsupial Indicates a Late Cretaceous."
26. Hooker et al., "Origin of Afro-Arabian 'Didelphimorph' Marsupials."
27. Averianov et al., "New Material of the Late Cretaceous Deltatheroidan."
28. Bennett et al., "Deep Time Diversity," 186.
29. See, for example, Judd, "'South American' Marsupials from the Late Cretaceous"; Ladavèze and de Muizon, "Evidence of Early Evolution of Australidelphia"; Goin et al., "Dispersal of Vertebrates Between the Americas"; Carneiro and Oliveira, "Systematic Affinities of the Extinct Metatherian"; Carneiro, "New Species of *Varalphodon*."

Determining the place of origin of true marsupials (Marsupialia) may depend on where the taxonomic line is drawn between marsupials and non-marsupial metatherians. Whether the metatherians that arrived in South America included true marsupials or were all non-marsupial metatherians is still unsettled. South American metatherians are known from the early Paleocene (64.5–63.0 Myr) Tiupampa Fauna of Bolivia.[30] Wilson et al. argued that five major marsupialiform lineages, including Marsupialia, appeared in North America by the Late Santonian of the Cretaceous (86.3–83.6 Myr), claiming a North American origin for marsupials and dispersal to South America during the Late Cretaceous or Early Paleocene.[31] However, the genera that Wilson et al. place in Marsupialia are relegated to Marsupialiformes in recent classifications.[32] Hence Beck could concede, "It is entirely possible that the origin and early evolution of Marsupialia was restricted to the "Austral Kingdom" (southern South America, Antarctica, and Australia)."[33] Marsupials in South America diversified into many species, but eutherian mammals were also diverse on that continent. South American marsupials were and are small animals.

The early to middle Paleocene is the most likely time for mammalian dispersal from South America to Australia.[34] At that time there was a land connection between these two continents through Antarctica. Mid-Eocene metatherian and marsupial fossils, including a microbiotheriid, are known from the Antarctic Peninsula region.[35] South America was isolated during the Oligocene and most of the Miocene. Antarctica did not have an ice cap until the Miocene and fossil evidence indicates the presence of cool-temperate forests, including araucarians, on the Antarctic Peninsula in the Paleocene.[36] Meanwhile, metatherians became extinct in the Northern Hemisphere during the Miocene. The progenitors of Australasian marsupials spread across Antarctica to reach the Australian continent. The earliest

30. Black et al., "Rise of Australian Marsupials," 987.
31. Wilson et al., "Large Carnivorous Mammal."
32. For example, Eldridge et al., "Emerging Consensus."
33. Beck, "Skull of *Epidolops ameghinoi*," 373.
34. Goin et al., "Dispersal of Vertebrates," 116.

35. Goin and Carlini, "Early Tertiary Microbiotheriid Marsupial"; Woodburne and Zinsmeister, "First Land Mammal"; Goin et al., "New Discoveries of 'Opossum-like' Marsupials"; Goin et al., "New Marsupial (Mammalia) from the Eocene."; Gelfo et al., "Fossil Record of Antarctic Land Mammals" Goin et al., "New Metatherian Mammal."

36. Pujana et al., "Fossil Woods from the Cross Valley Formation"; Tosolini et al., "Paleocene High-latitude Leaf Flora of Antarctica Part 1."

known marsupial fossil in Australia (*Djarthia murgonensis*) comes from the Eocene Tingamarra Fauna at Murgon in Queensland.[37] "The presence of a suite of otherwise Australian groups, such as lungfish in the genus *Ceratodus*, myobatrachid frogs, chelid turtles and ornithorhynchids in the early Paleocene (~63 Myr) of at least southern Argentina, demonstrates that by at least the earliest part of the Cenozoic, a biogeographic corridor linked the southern part of South America to Australia via Antarctica."[38] The final separation of Antarctica and Australia and the effective closure of this migration route occurred during the Oligocene. Fossils of the Australasian marsupial orders Dasyurimorphia, Diprotodontia, Notoryctemorphia, Paramelemorphia, and Yalkaparadontidae are not known outside of Australasia.

The relict genus, *Dromiciops*, the mouse-sized monito del monte, is native to southwestern South America and is the only extant genus of the order Microbiotheria. Regarded initially as one species (*Dromiciops gliroides* syn. *australis*), in 2016 two additional species were recognized: *D. mondaca* and *D. bozinovici*.[39] *Dromiciops* is regarded as a member of the Australidephids and related to *Djarthia*.[40] Microbiotherians like *Dromiciops* may have been the first marsupials to reach Australia.[41]

Marsupials spread north from Australia into New Guinea and thence to adjacent islands such as the Moluccas (cuscus, bandicoots, wallaby),[42] the Bismarck Archipelago, the Solomons (six species), Timor (one cuscus species, introduced from New Guinea), and Sulawesi (two species of cuscus). A famous biogeographical boundary, Wallace's Line, named after the nineteenth century biologist-explorer, Alfred Russel Wallace, runs between Sulawesi and Borneo and between Bali and Lombok. The line, noted by Wallace in 1859, delineates South-East Asian fauna from Australasian fauna. Marsupials have to date not penetrated west beyond this line, but macaques (seven endemic species) and tarsiers (nine endemic species) have migrated east and lived on Sulawesi and some surrounding islands.[43]

37. Beck et al., "Australia's Oldest Marsupial Fossils," e1858.
38. Black et al., "Rise of Australian Marsupials," 994.
39. D'Elía et al., "Alpha Taxonomy of *Dromiciops* (Microbiotheriidae)."
40. Nilsson et al., "Tracking Marsupial Evolution," e1000436.
41. Fontúrbel et al., "Ecology and Evolution of the Monito Del Monte."
42. Flannery et al., "Fossil Marsupials (Macropodidae,Peroryctidae)"; O'Connor et al., "Sailing the Deep Blue Sea."
43. Supriatna et al., "Primates of Sulawesi: An Update."

In the absence of eutherian mammals, the Australian/New Guinean marsupials occupied many ecological niches. There are some species in common between Cape York and New Guinea: Torres Strait is very shallow—only seven to fifteen m deep—and there has been a land connection between Australia and New Guinea until very recently. Bats are known as fossils in Australia from the late Oligocene[44] and there is one species known from the Eocene deposits at Murgon,[45] which raises the possibility that the first bats in Australia may have arrived via the Antarctic Gondwanan route rather than via Southeast Asia. Rodents (all in the Family Muridae) began to arrive, presumably by island-hopping from Southeast Asia, from the mid-Miocene, as Australasia gradually drifted closer to Asia—how far can a hopping-mouse hop?

The Virginia opossum of North America is a Pliocene migrant from South America (along with armadillos and porcupines). The approach of North and South America and the formation of the volcanic Panamanian Isthmus in the Pliocene facilitated this northward migration. Mexico has eight marsupial species (all opossums).

So why are there no kangaroos in Austria? Kangaroos appeared first in Australia—the iconic red kangaroo is a late arrival on the scene—Late Pliocene or Pleistocene. Kangaroos (and wallabies) cannot jump far enough to get beyond New Guinea or perhaps the Moluccas. If they had crossed Wallace's Line they would have encountered tigers! Australia's two species of tree kangaroo are believed to have migrated from New Guinea at a time of lower sea level.

6.5 CONCLUSION

Plate tectonics theory is the best explanation available for the behavior of the Earth's crust. Plate tectonics is a characteristic feature of the planet. This theory necessarily implies a great age for the continents and hence for the fossils embedded in them. The fossils are as old as the rocks that contain them. The marsupials came on the scene quite late. Most features of their present geographical distribution can be explained by means of plate tectonics theory and continental movement, in combination with other processes such as speciation, dispersal, and extinction. The geography of marsupials is difficult to explain by other means. The interpretation of the

---

44. Archer et al., "Fossil Mammals of Riversleigh, Northwestern Queensland."
45. Hand et al., "First Eocene Bat from Australia."

geological understanding and paleontological evidence presented here cannot be accommodated in a literal interpretation of Genesis. A scientific explanation of the planet and its life was never the purpose of those who wrote Genesis and hence an interpretation of Genesis as modern science is inappropriate.

BIBLIOGRAPHY

Archer, Michael, et al. "Fossil Mammals of Riversleigh, Northwestern Queensland: Preliminary Overview of Biostratigraphy, Correlation and Environmental Change." *Australian Zoologist* 25:2 (1989) 29–66.

Archer, Michael, et al. "A New Order of Tertiary Zalambdodont Marsupials." *Science* 239 (1988) 1528–31.

Averianov, Alexander O., et al. "New Material of the Late Cretaceous Deltatheroidan Mammal *Sulestes* from Uzbekistan and Phylogenetic Reassessment of the Metatherian-eutherian Dichotomy." *Journal of Systematic Palaeontology* 8:3 (2010) 301–30.

Beck, Robin M. D. "An 'Amerindian' Marsupial from the Early Eocene of Australia Supports a Complex Model of Southern Hemisphere Biogeography." *Naturwissenschaften* 99 (2019) 715–29.

———. "A Dated Phylogeny of Marsupials using a Molecular Supermatrix and Multiple Fossil Constraints." *Journal of Mammalogy* 89:1 (2008) 175–89.

———. "The Skull of *Epidolops ameghinoi* from the Early Eocene Itaborai Fauna, Southeastern Brazil, and the Affinities of the Extinct Marsupialiform Order Polydolopimorphia." *Journal of Mammalian Evolution* 24:4 (2017) 373–414.

Beck, Robin M. D., et al. "Australia's Oldest Marsupial Fossils and their Biogeographical Implications." *Public Library of Science (PLOS) One* 3:3 (2008). https://doi.org/10.1371/journal.pone.0001858.

Bennett, Verity, et al. "Deep Time Diversity of Metatherian Mammals: Implications for Evolutionary History and Fossil-record Quality." *Paleobiology* 44:2 (2018) 171–98.

Benton, M. J. "First Marsupial Fossil from Asia." *Nature* 318 (1985) 313.

Bi, Shudong, et al. "An Early Cretaceous Eutherian and the Placental–marsupial Dichotomy." *Nature* 558:7710 (2018) 390–95.

Black, Karen H., et al. "The Rise of Australian Marsupials: A Synopsis of Biostratigraphic, Phylogenetic, Palaeoecologic and Palaeobiogeographic Understanding." In *International Year of Planet Earth Sciences: Earth and Life*, edited by John A. Talent, 990. Dordrecht: Springer, 2012.

Bown, T. M., and E. L. Simons. "First Record of Marsupials (Metatheria: Polyprotodonta) from the Oligocene in Africa." *Nature* 308 (1984) 447–49.

Carneiro, Leonardo M. "A New Species of *Varalphadon* (Mammalia, Metatheria, Sparassodonta) from the Upper Cenomanian of Southern Utah, North America: Phylogenetic and Biogeographic Insights." *Cretaceous Research* 84 (April 2018) 88–96.

Carneiro, Leonardo M., and Édison V. Oliveira. "Systematic Affinities of the Extinct Metatherian *Eobrasilia coutoi* Simpson, 1947, a South American Early Eocene

Stagodontidae: Implications for 'Eobrasiliinae.'" *Revista Brasileira de Paleontologia* 20:3 (2017) 355-72.

Cifelli, Richard L. "Marsupial Mammals from the Albian-Cenomanian (Early-Late Cretaceous) Boundary, Utah." *Bulletin of the American Museum of Natural History* 285 (2004) 62-79.

Cifelli, Richard L., and Jeffrey G. Eaton. "Marsupial from the Earliest Late Cretaceous of the Western US." *Nature* 325 (1987) 520-22.

Cohen, Joshua E., et al. "Geologically Oldest Pediomyoidea (Mammalia, Marsupialiformes) from the Late Cretaceous of North America, with Implications for Taxonomy and Diet of Earliest Late Cretaceous Mammals." *Journal of Vertebrate Paleontology* 40:5 (2020) 1-13.

Cohen, Kim M., et al. "The ICS International Chronostratigraphic Chart." *Episodes* 36:3 (2013) 199-204 (updated 2022). https://stratigraphy.org/ICSchart/ChronostratChart2022-02.pdf.

D'Elía, Guillermo, et al. "Alpha Taxonomy of *Dromiciops* (Microbiotheriidae) with the Description of 2 New Species of Monito Del Monte." *Journal of Mammalogy* 97:4 (2016) 1136-52.

Davies, Andrew, et al. "Late Cretaceous Seasonal Ocean Variability from the Arctic." *Nature* 460:7252 (2009) 254-58.

Eldridge, Mark, et al. "An Emerging Consensus in the Evolution, Phylogeny and Systematics of Marsupials and their Fossil Relatives (Metatheria)." *Journal of Mammalogy* 100:3 (2019) 802-37.

Feldhamer, George A., et al. *Mammalogy: Adaptation, Diversity, Ecology.* 5th ed. Baltimore: Johns Hopkins University Press, 2020.

Flannery, T., et al. "Fossil Marsupials (Macropodidae, Peroryctidae) and Other Mammals of Holocene Age from Halmahera, North Moluccas, Indonesia." *Alcheringa* 19:1 (1995) 17-25.

Florillo, Anthony R., et al. "Hard Structure in Late Cretaceous Polar Dinosaurs: A Remarkable New Dinosaur Track Site, Denali National Park, Alaska, USA." *Geology* 42:8 (2014) 719-22.

Fontúrbel, Francisco E., et al. "The Ecology and Evolution of the Monito Del Monte, a Relict Species from the Southern South America Temperate Forests." *Ecology and Evolution* 12:3 (2022). https://doi.org/10.1002/ece3.8645.

Gelfo, Javier N., et al. "The Fossil Record of Antarctic Land Mammals: Commented Review and Hypotheses for Future Research." *Advances in Polar Science* 30:3 (2019) 274-92.

Goin, Francisco J., and Alfredo A. Carlini. "An Early Tertiary Microbiotheriid Marsupial from Antarctica." *Journal of Vertebrate Paleontology* 15:1 (1995) 205-07.

Goin, Francisco J., et al. "Dispersal of Vertebrates Between the Americas, Antarctica, and Australia in the Late Cretaceous and Early Cenozoic," chapter 3. In *A Brief History of South American Metatherians: Evolutionary Context and Intercontinental Dispersals,* 77-124. Dordrecht: Springer, 2016.

Goin, Francisco. J., et al. "New Discoveries of 'Opossum-like' Marsupials from Antarctica (Seymour Island, Medial Eocene)." *Journal of Mammalian Evolution* 6 (1999) 335-65.

Goin, Francisco J., et al. "New Marsupial (Mammalia) from the Eocene of Antarctica, and the Origin and Affinities of the Microbiotheria." *Revista de la Asociación Geológica Argentina* 62:4 (2007) 597-603.

Goin, Francisco J., et al. "New Metatherian Mammal from the Early Eocene of Antarctica." *Journal of Mammalian Evolution* 27:1 (2020) 17–36.

Hand, Suzanne J., et al. "First Eocene Bat from Australia," *Journal of Vertebrate Paleontology* 14 (1994) 375–81.

Hooker, Jerry J., et al. "The Origin of Afro-Arabian 'Didelphimorph' Marsupials." *Palaeontology* 51:3 (2008) 635–48.

Judd, A. "'South American' Marsupials from the Late Cretaceous of North America and the Origin of Marsupial Cohorts." *Journal of Mammalian Evolution* 11:3–4 (2005) 223–55.

Ladavèze, Sandrine, and Christian de Muizon. "Evidence of Early Evolution of Australidelphia (Metatheria, Mammalia) in South America: Phylogenetic Relationships of the Metatherians from the Late Palaeocene of Itaboraí (Brazil) Based on Teeth and Petrosal Bones." *Zoological Journal of the Linnean Society* 159:3 (2010) 746–84.

Luo, Zhe-Xi, et al. "An Early Cretaceous Tribosphenic Mammal and Metatherian Evolution." *Science* 302:5262 (2003) 1934–40.

Martin, James E., et al. "A New European Marsupial Indicates a Late Cretaceous High-latitude Transatlantic Dispersal Route." *Journal of Mammalian Evolution* 12:3/4 (2005) 495–511.

Mortimer, Nick, et al. "Zealandia: Earth's Hidden Continent." *Geological Society of America (GSA) Today* 27:3 (2017) 27–35.

Nilsson, Maria A., et al. "Tracking Marsupial Evolution Using Archaic Genomic Retroposon Inversions." *Public Library of Science (PLOS) Biology* 8:7 (2010). https://doi.org/10.1371/journal.pbio.1000436.

Novacek, Michael J., et al. "Epipubic Bones in Eutherian Mammals from the Late Cretaceous of Mongolia." *Nature* 389: 6650 (1997) 483–86.

O'Connor, Sue, et al. "Sailing the Deep Blue Sea: The Rock Art of Wetang Island, Maluku Barat Daya, Indonesia." *The Journal of Island and Coastal Archaeology* (2022). https://doi.org/10.1080/15564894.2021.1991056.

Pujana, Roberto R., et al. "Fossil Woods from the Cross Valley Formation (Paleocene of Western Antarctica): Araucariaceae-dominated Forests." *Review of Palaeobotany and Palynology* 222 (2015) 56–66.

Reilly, Stephen M., and Thomas D. White. "Hypaxial Motor Patterns and the Function of Epipubic Bones in Primitive Mammals." *Science* 299:5605 (2003) 400–402.

Scotese, Christopher E. *Paleomap Project*. http://www.scotese.com/earth.htm.

Storch, Gerhard, and Zhuding Qiu. "First Neogene Marsupial from China." *Journal of Vertebrate Paleontology* 22:1 (2002) 179–81.

Supriatna, Jatna, et al. "Primates of Sulawesi: An Update on Habitat, Distribution, Population and Conservation." *Taprobotanica* 7:3 (2015) 170–92.

Tosolini, Anne-Marie P., et al. "Paleocene High-latitude Leaf Flora of Antarctica Part 1: Entire-margined Angiosperms." *Review of Paleobotany and Palynology* 285 (2021) Article 104317.

Tsofimov, B. A., and Frederick S. Szalay. "New Cretaceous Marsupial from Mongolia and the Early Radiation of Metatheria." *Proceedings of the National Academy of Sciences of the United States of America (PNAS)* 91:26 (1995) 12569–73.

Vullo, Romain, et al. "The Oldest Modern Therian Mammal from Europe and its Bearing on Stem Marsupial Paleobiogeography." *Proceedings of the National Academy of Sciences of the United States of America (PNAS)* 106:47 (2009) 19910–15.

Weisbecker, Vera, and Robin M. D. Beck. "Marsupial and Monotreme Evolution and Biogeography." In *Marsupials and Monotremes - Nature's Enigmatic Mammals*, edited by Athol Klieve et al., 1–31. New York: Nova Science, 2015.

Williamson, Thomas E., et al. "The Origin and Early Evolution of Metatherian Mammals: The Cretaceous record." *Zookeys* 465 (2014) 1–76.

Wilson, Gregory P., et al. "A Large Carnivorous Mammal from the Late Cretaceous and the North American Origin of Marsupials." *Nature Communications* 7:13734 (2016).

Woodburne, Michael O., and William J. Zinsmeister. "First Land Mammal from Antarctica and its Biogeographic Implications." *Journal of Paleontology* 58:4 (1984) 913–48.

7

Ice Cores and What They Tell Us About Past Life

Terence Annable

7.1 INTRODUCTION

Permanent ice covers Earth's land surface in many places. The largest areas of ice are in Antarctica and Greenland, but smaller areas persist in high mountain areas, even in the tropics. Samples of this ice have been collected from many places, especially from the vast ice sheets of Antarctica and Greenland, but also from all other continents except Australia. Core samples of ice extending to depths of more than three kilometers have been extracted in both Antarctica and Greenland.

Undoubtedly, the major incentive for the worldwide scientific study of ice cores conducted over the last fifty years has been climate research. Climate scientists have been intensifying their research into paleoclimates to increase their understanding of the mechanisms of climate change, now a major world concern.[1] Ice-core science constitutes one of the most important components of paleoclimate research.[2] Jouzel provides a brief history of scientific activity in this area over the fifty years ending in 2013.[3]

---

1. Jansen et al., "Palaeoclimate."
2. Augustin et al., "Eight Glacial Cycles from an Antarctic Ice Core."
3. Jouzel, "Brief History of Ice Core Science Over the Last 50yr."

Ice core research is also important to long-term weather forecasting, so this endeavor attracts significant funding.[4]

Steinhilber et al. reported that the isotope studies of beryllium-10 (^{10}Be) in ice cores and carbon-14 (^{14}C) in tree rings also offered "the unique opportunity to reconstruct the history of cosmic radiation and solar activity over many millennia." They found that combining ice-core and tree-ring data had the potential to improve the quantification of the solar influence on climate.[5] It should be noted here that the ice-core data extend much longer into the past than tree-ring data.

There are several attributes of ice deposits that assist in the determination of the ages of ice at different depths.

1. The snow which is eventually compacted to form the ice cover is typically deposited according to a similar seasonal pattern, year by year. This gives rise to a series of annual layers, like tree rings, which can often be counted visually with a high degree of accuracy, enabling the age of any given layer to be determined. A range of other layer-counting techniques have been developed to support visual counting and to substitute for it in circumstances where visual counting is difficult or impossible.

2. The ice layers trap ejecta from volcanic eruptions, especially ash. The composition of the ejecta frequently enables the source eruption to be identified. Since the dates of eruption for ancient volcanoes can often be determined using historical records or techniques such as radiometric dating, volcanic inclusions can provide a cross-check of ages derived from ice cores.

3. The inclusion of radioactive trace elements in the ice can also be used to confirm dates of deposition, such as in the Steinhilber study mentioned above.

Many other inclusions are found in the layers of ice, such as air bubbles, non-radiogenic trace elements, dust, and sea salt.[6] The analysis of the

---

4. Armstrong et al., "Comparing Instrumental, Palaeoclimate, and Projected Rainfall Data."

5. Steinhilber et al., "9,400 Years of Cosmic Radiation and Solar Activity from Ice Cores and Tree Rings."

6. Röthlisberger et al., "Technique for Continuous High-resolution Analysis of Trace Substances in Firn."

air trapped in the ice cores gives important information about past climates, including temperatures,[7] carbon dioxide levels,[8] methane concentrations, and other atmospheric content parameters.[9] Such measurements provide primary information on paleoclimates, the detailed mapping and analysis of which provide data that help us to understand modern climate change, predict future climatic trends, and possibly mitigate the potentially catastrophic effects of rapid climate change.[10] Chemical analysis of trace elements also provides clues about past levels of air pollution. Dust inclusions speak of weather conditions, in that high dust content indicates both very dry conditions and high-speed winds that carry the dust over long distances. The concentration of sea salt in ice layers can indicate variations in ice cover of the oceans during the period preceding deposition.

Microorganisms, both living and dead, are found throughout the ice sheets. These can often be isolated, cultured, and identified, and while they offer an additional commentary on prevailing climatic conditions, they also speak to the age of life on Earth. Both eukaryotes and prokaryotes are represented, including amoeboids, bacteria, pollen grains, various spores including those from fungi, and also many virus species. Analyses of this biological content found in ice cores have provided evidence of old life.[11]

7.2 EARTH'S HIGH-LATITUDE ICE-COVERED REGIONS

Earth's axis of daily rotation is currently tilted at 23.5° from perpendicular to the ecliptic plane, (the plane on which Earth orbits the Sun). This angle is understood to fluctuate from 22.1° to 24.5° with a period of 41,000 years. This is one of the three variations in Earth-Sun geometry known as the Milankovitch Variations. The tilt or obliquity of the axis is primarily responsible for the annual alternations of summer and winter, opposite for each hemisphere, because the orientation of the respective hemispheres towards the Sun changes over the annual cycle of Earth's orbit around the

7. Yan et al., "Two-million-year-old Snapshots of Atmospheric Gases from Antarctic Ice."

8. Barnola et al., "Vostok Ice Core Provides 160,000 Year Record of Atmospheric CO2"; Hönisch et al., "Atmospheric Carbon Dioxide Concentration."

9. Mitchell et al., "Constraints on the Late Holocene Anthropogenic Contribution."

10. Alley, *Two-Mile Time Machine*, 191.

11. Knowlton, "Microbial Analyses of Ancient Ice Core Sections from Greenland and Antarctica."

Sun. A second variation is the direction in which the tilted axis is pointed. As Earth rotates, its axis of rotation wobbles like a child's toy spinning top. This is also cyclical—the full cycle, known as axial precession or the precession of the equinoxes, takes 27,551 years.

The relative severity of winter compared to summer generally increases with latitude, matching the increase in length of the period of winter darkness with increasing latitude, a result of the axial tilt. But the seasonal contrasts in the vicinity of each pole, including the amount of snow deposited, are not only a consequence of their high latitudes but of the very different geographical features of the extreme north and south. Earth's small orbital variations can also affect global temperatures and could theoretically alter precipitation rates and hence ice-layer thickness.[12]

The region of the North Pole has no emergent land surface. For much of the year, most of it is covered by sea ice (about two to three meters thick), floating and shifting on the ocean. The low average altitude and the surrounding warmer ocean currents give rise to a mean maximum summer temperature of about 0°C. Over the last few decades, this ice has been melted from above by warmer air and from below by warming oceans. This melting of polar ice means that the enormous latent heat of the melting/freezing cycle will be less available to help ameliorate the extremes of climate caused by global climate change.[13]

Greenland is located between latitudes 59°N and 83°N, mostly inside the Arctic Circle, and has emergent land surface giving it considerably higher altitude than the North Pole (Mt Gunnbjörn, the highest peak, reaches 3,694 m above sea level). This landmass has provided a stable environment for collecting annual layers of snow for thousands of years, and about 75 percent is covered permanently by snow and ice, with only coastal regions being suitable for habitation.[14] Conditions in central Greenland have led to the formation of very thick annual ice layers.[15] Although the maximum altitude is approximately 3,700 m, the ice is thicker than this, being so heavy that it has depressed the bedrock by up to 300 m below sea

---

12. Alley, *Two-Mile Time Machine*, 4. In fact, Alley is a late arrival! In the 19th century James Croll suggested that Earth's orbital variations influenced distribution patterns of solar radiation, and in the 1920s Milutin Milankovitch amplified this to relate orbital forcing to Earth's climate history.

13. Ban-Weiss et al., "Climate forcing."

14. *Times Atlas of the World, Comprehensive Edition*, Plate 48.

15. Alley, *Two-Mile Time Machine*, 35–36; Oard, *The Frozen Record*.

level. Because central Greenland receives about one meter of snow annually (and even more near the coast), the annual layers of ice are relatively easy to count, even when greatly compressed and then thinned by lateral ice flow.

The Greenland ice sheet, like the ice caps found in northern Canada and Siberia, is only being melted from above (melt being dependent on altitude, latitude, and proximity to the ocean). It has been estimated that if all the ice on Greenland melted, sea levels would be raised by about seven meters.[16]

The Antarctic continent contrasts in many respects to the northern polar regions, and the Australian Antarctic Division (AAD) news service documents some of these differences.[17] Antarctica has a higher average altitude than Greenland, despite the fact that, like the latter, large areas of bedrock have been depressed well below sea level. About 98 percent of Antarctica is covered by the ice sheet.

The South Pole has a mean maximum mid-summer temperature of just -12°C and, apart from being much colder than the North Pole, it has lower precipitation. These conditions appear to have been very uniform over a long period of time. In fact, because of its low precipitation, Antarctica is technically a desert and is the driest continent on Earth.[18] The southern polar region receives only about 160 mm of precipitation (as snow) each year, which results in only about 10–20 mm of ice being deposited each year. This ice does not melt, although a small amount sublimates because even solid ice has a vapor pressure which is significant at very low humidities.

Low rates of precipitation, together with the great depth of the Antarctic ice sheet (up to 4.8 km), suggest that it has built up over a very long time (assuming approximately constant rates of deposition, as discussed by Winski et al.).[19] Furthermore, the very high pressures at the base of the ice sheet (they can exceed four thousand tons per square meter) cause the ice layers to stretch out and become thinned as the ice deforms towards areas of lower pressure, which are usually downslope towards the coast. This causes a general movement of the ice towards the sea (a continental glacier) and

---

16. NASA, "If all of Earth's Ice Melts."
17. Australian Antarctic Division (AAD) Government News Website.
18. Australian Bureau of Meteorology, "Antarctica; Driest Continent on Earth."
19. Winski et al., *South Pole Ice Core (SPICEcore) Chronology and Supporting Data.*

means that the ice sheet may be even older than it first appears.[20] Antarctica and Greenland are the only landmasses that have continental glaciers at present.

According to a NASA report published in 2020, the Antarctic ice sheet is so thick and so large in area (it also extends out to sea around the coast as many ice shelves that cover thousands of square kilometers) that its collapse would raise the ocean level by many meters.[21] It is widely understood that if all the southern polar ice were to melt, sea levels would be raised by about sixty-six meters.

7.3 FORMATION OF ICE LAYERS

7.3.1 How the Ice Forms

In the Antarctic, there is no melting (except in the most northerly coastal regions), but there is some sublimation, as noted above. As the annual snow layers build up, pressures lower down in the ice increase, and air is either extruded near the surface or trapped in bubbles in the ice. The loose surface snow soon becomes firn—an intermediate between snow and solid glacial ice— in which the snow crystals are crushed together and recrystallized, but through which air can continue to diffuse and percolate (as in a snowball). At a depth of about seventy meters, the pressure caused by the overburden becomes so great that air channels are cut off and the firn becomes solid ice with trapped air bubbles.[22] These features are shown in Figure 7.1, which illustrates the typical structure of a deep ice column.

---

20. Alley, *Two-Mile Time Machine*, 31, 100.
21. NASA, "Sea Levels."
22. Bender et al., "Gases in Ice Cores"; Alley, *Two-Mile Time Machine*, 50.

Ice Cores and What They Tell Us About Past Life

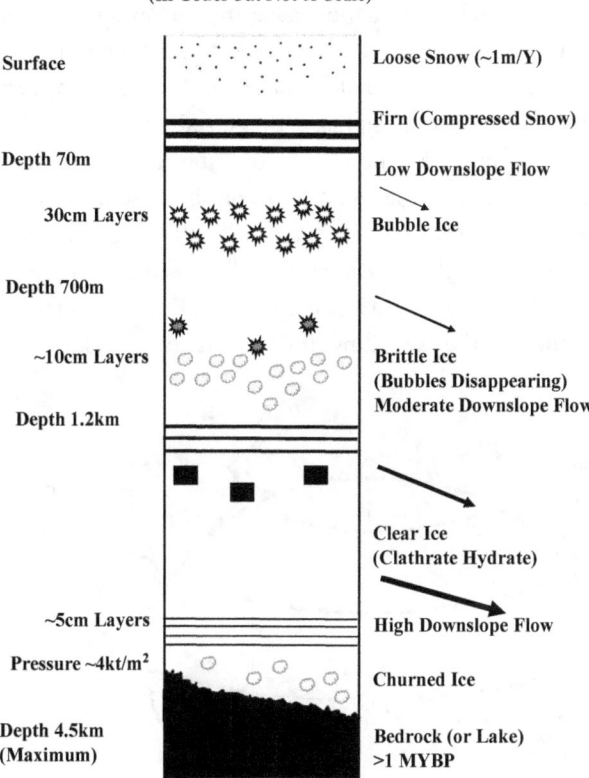

Figure 7.1 Schematic (and non-linear) diagram of the ice column, showing composition at various depths. The base of such an ice column could be on bedrock or soil/sediment (drawn by T. Annable).

At a depth of about 700 m, the ice tends to become brittle, as the extreme pressure causes the structure of the ice crystals to change from a hexagonal molecular arrangement to a pentagonal form. At a depth of about 1,200 m, the air bubbles disappear as the various gas molecules normally found in air (N_2, O_2, Ar, CO_2, CH_4, etc.) are forced within the ice-cage molecules to form clathrate hydrates.[23] Clathrate hydrates are crystalline, water-based solids that physically resemble ice. Small non-polar molecules (typically gases) or polar molecules with water-repellent properties are trapped inside cages of hydrogen-bonded, frozen water molecules.

---

23. Kipfstuhl et al., "Air Bubbles and Clathrate Hydrates in the Transition Zone."

7.3.2 How the Inclusions Get in the Ice

The global atmospheric circulation basically consists of convection cells with warm air rising and cool air descending, modified by Earth's daily rotation that causes apparent deflection of winds across the surface. While several other factors can complicate this circulation, including seasonal variations, jet streams, and the relative distribution of continents, mountain ranges, and oceans, the main convection currents spiral around in three toroidal cells in each hemisphere, each cell occupying approximately 30° of latitude. These cells are shown two-dimensionally in Figure 7.2. The descending limbs of the cells create high atmospheric pressure at the Earth's solid/liquid surface, the ascending limbs create low pressure.

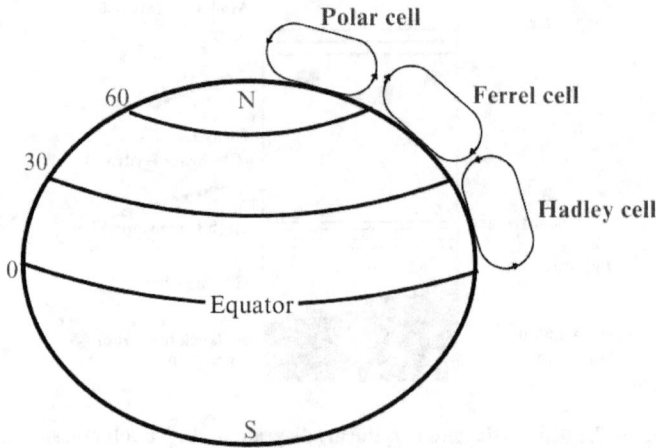

Figure 7.2 Two-dimensional representation of global air circulation patterns. (Vertical scale in atmosphere greatly exaggerated) (drawn by T. Annable).

As can be discerned from Figure 7.2, the northern Ferrel cell uplifts particles, such as dust, ash, spores, bacteria, and pollen from latitudes between approximately 30° and 60° N. Some of these are transferred to the Polar cell, which carries them at high altitudes towards the North Pole, where they may be deposited with the snow. Air uplifted from latitudes between approximately 30° and 60° N is likely to carry only particles from temperate or psychrophile species (cold-loving micro-organisms). As can be inferred from the figure, the Polar cell also transports particles from 60° to 90° N, but not so many species inhabit these colder regions. This atmospheric circulation pattern means that traces of tropical or warm temperate species are unlikely to end up in the polar ice. A similar pattern occurs with the southern Ferrel and Polar cells carrying particles towards the South Pole.[24] Arctic and Antarctic storms are also significant agents of particle transport, particularly dust and salt. These storms are somewhat erratic but tend to be more severe in winter.

7.3.3 The Survival of Living Organisms in Snow

Various psychrophiles can survive in surface snow, although many others will perish. Some cells of phototrophic algae, such as some *Chlamydomonas* spp., may survive and even thrive.[25] Provided that sufficient nutrients are present, they may actually color the snow reddish or orange, or green (depending on the species and density). Other motile microorganisms can move around in firn, but both non-motile and motile organisms get trapped *in situ* when the ice solidifies. Deeper down in the ice, no light penetrates, so only chemotrophic psychrophiles (those that can utilize environmental chemicals instead of light for their energy source) will survive. The living species found deep in the ice are also oligotrophs (i.e., they exist on extremely limited nutrient resources).[26]

7.4 ICE CORES

7.4.1 Extraction of Ice Cores

Ice cores are extracted for analysis by means of hollow drills. Each cylindrical segment, often one to three meters long and about twelve centimeters in diameter, must be extracted from the drill before the next segment of the core can be taken. Shallow cores can be extracted using a simple hand-operated ice-core drill. However, deeper cores require a mechanical drill. In some instances, ice cores are extracted with the aid of a heat-operated drill head that melts its way into the ice.

Drilling is usually only done in the summer, and it may take up to ten years to complete a deep ice core. The Parrenin team, working with the European Project for Ice Coring in Antarctica (EPICA), drilled one deep ice core (EDC3) at Dome C where a depth of 3,270 m was reached.[27] Barnola et

---

24. Global Atmospheric Circulation.
25. Williams et al., "Surface Gas Exchange Processes of Snow Algae."
26. Mosier et al., "Microbiota Within the Perennial Ice Cover of Lake Vida, Antarctica."
27. Parrenin et al., "EDC3 Chronology for the EPICA Dome Ice Core."

al. and Petit et al. report on the work of the Russian team which has drilled more than one of their cores at Vostok station right through the ice into Lake Vostok below.[28] Most ice cores are stopped before they get to bedrock because here the ice has been churned up by ice flow and ice layers cannot be counted or dated accurately. Also, if there is meltwater below or a lake beneath the ice, great care must be taken not to contaminate the water with impurities such as antifreeze, drill fluid, or alien organisms, because it is expected that this water might contain unique life forms that have existed in isolation for many years.

After extraction, each core segment is cataloged and labeled with the site, number, date, position, depth, and compass orientation. Each segment is then sealed in a stainless-steel tube until it can be analyzed. Care must be taken to prevent melting and contamination during transport, and special precautions might be required depending on the analyses proposed. Cores are packed and transported to various refrigerated warehouse stores and research laboratories around the world. Needless to say, this is very expensive ice! A typical view within a refrigerated ice storage facility is shown in Figure 7.3.

Figure 7.3 Ice core storage at approximately -36°C (photograph taken at the National Ice Core Laboratory, Denver, Colorado in 2002 by Lynden Rogers).

28. Barnola et al, "Vostok Ice Core Provides 160,000-year Record of Atmospheric CO_2"; Petit et al., "Climate and Atmospheric History of the Past 420,000 Years from the Vostok Ice Core."

7.4.2 The Location of Major Drilling Sites

The deepest ice cores have been extracted from the two ice sheets (Antarctica and Greenland), but shorter ice cores have been extracted from ice caps and glaciers elsewhere.

There have been six major deep-ice-core drilling projects conducted in Greenland (Camp Century, Dye-3, GRIP, GISP2, Renland, and North GRIP).[29] Not only are the results obtained from these sites very comparable, but they are also largely concordant with results obtained from Antarctica.

According to advice released by the AAD, there are now seventy bases in the Antarctic continent, representing twenty-nine countries, although not all of these involve ice-core extraction. Most of the deep-ice-core drill sites within the Antarctic are far inland, where there is a great depth of continuous layers of ice that have minimal disturbance and less lateral flow. The locations of these Greenland and Antarctic drilling sites can be obtained readily.[30]

7.5 METHODS OF ICE-CORE ANALYSIS AND DATING

Scientists who study ice cores usually try to use at least three different dating methods in order to improve the confidence levels of their results. In the Greenland Ice Sheet Project 2 (GISP2), at least six different counting and measuring methods were used down to a depth of 2.8 km, at which depth the age of the ice was estimated to be 110,000 years.[31] As earlier noted, the successive layers, particularly in recent ice, can usually be differentiated visually. Where this may not be possible, there are several additional techniques now used to establish accurate dates. These are particularly useful for deep ice-core samples. The dating techniques used involve visual stratigraphy, isotopic ratios (particularly oxygen), electrical conductivity, laser-light scattering, chemical analysis, radioactive isotopes, and paleomagnetism. These dating and analysis techniques are explained briefly below.

---

29. Johnsen et al., "Oxygen Isotope and Palaeotemperature Records from Six Greenland Ice-core Stations."

30. Drill Sites.

31. Meese et al., "Greenland Ice Sheet Project 2, Depth-age Scale: Methods and Results."

7.5.1 Dating and Analysis Techniques

Visual Stratigraphy

It is generally recognized that the annual layers within Greenland ice cores can be counted visually down to at least 60,000 years.[32] Automated instrumentation has also been used to enhance visual observation.[33] Figure 7.4 shows an ice-core sample exhibiting visual bands differentiating the annual layers.

Figure 7.4 Ice core with visual banding (photograph taken at the National Ice Core Laboratory, Denver, Colorado in 2002 by Lynden Rogers).

Inclusions, such as dust and volcanic reference horizons, assist visual stratigraphy. However, although the high winds that transport dust are more common during Greenland winters than in summers, they are not always sufficiently consistent to enable individual years to be distinguished by using dust inclusions alone. Despite this drawback, dust bands have been found to be useful in older, compressed layers and Shimohara and colleagues have used them to help date deep layers of ice from Greenland.[34]

Visual counting is usually more difficult for ice cores from Antarctica because the layers are so much thinner.[35] In Antarctica, there is less dust in the ice than found in Greenland. In addition, the Antarctic winds are quite consistently katabatic, blowing at any time downslope towards the coast at velocities often over 100 km/h, and therefore dating by dust bands is of

32. Svensson et al., "60,000-year Greenland Stratigraphic Ice Core Chronology."
33. Svensson, "Visual Stratigraphy of the North Greenland Ice Core Project."
34. Shimohara et al., "Cloudy Band Observations for Annual Layer Counting."
35. Alley et al., "Visual-stratigraphic Dating of the GISP2 Ice Core"; Svensson et al., "Visual Stratigraphy of the North Greenland Ice Core Project (NorthGRIP) Ice Core."

limited use there.[36] However, volcanic inclusions are common in the Antarctic ice and these help in dating. There are 251 well-dated, and visually detectable, volcanic reference horizons identified from the last fifty-four thousand years, most of them generated by the nearly 100 volcanoes known in the Antarctic region.[37] Typically, major volcanic eruptions lower global temperatures initially (a result of the blocking of sunlight) but then raise temperatures as increased CO_2 levels take effect after the ash has settled.

Isotopic Ratios

Most elements have a number of different isotopes. Each isotope of a given element has an identical atomic number but has a different mass number depending on how many neutrons are present in the nucleus. Molecules that contain heavier isotopes evaporate from liquid surfaces less readily than molecules of the same atomic composition, but which contain the lighter isotope. This means that as water evaporates, the concentrations of the heavier isotopes of hydrogen and oxygen relative to their lighter isotopes will increase in the remaining water. The converse is true for the snow that forms from the evaporated water and accumulates in ice cores, i.e., in the snow, the concentration of heavy isotopes relative to light isotopes is less than in the remaining body of water.

The rate of evaporation for all isotopes also increases with temperature. This means that it is possible to detect the different summer and winter concentrations in an ice-core segment and to estimate the summer and winter temperatures at the time of evaporation. The ratios of the stable isotopes of oxygen, ^{16}O, and the heavier, less abundant ^{18}O, are commonly used in this way to determine past temperatures.[38] Such isotopes are called temperature proxies. There is a whole range of heavy and light isotopes that can be used to determine past climatic conditions. The concentration of these isotopes can be measured very accurately by mass spectroscopy, and the systematic variations in their occurrence through the ice core can be used to differentiate annual layers.[39]

The ratio of deuterium (a stable, heavy isotope of hydrogen) to common hydrogen (D/H) in water molecules also varies with temperature and

36. Australian Antarctic Program. "From the Katabatic to the Polar Vortex."
37. Winski et al. "South Pole Ice Core."
38. Blunier et al., "Synchronization of Ice Core Records via Atmospheric Gases."
39. Bauska et al., "High Precision Dual-inlet IRMS Measurements."

hence can be used to determine past temperatures, especially when the water is preserved as ice.[40] The ratios of some noble gases (krypton, xenon, argon) to nitrogen in air bubbles within ice cores have also been used as indicators of global mean ocean temperatures. These noble gases are unlikely to interfere with other planned chemical analyses.[41]

Several other molecules can be used as temperature proxies because of their varying solubilities with temperature. These can provide confirmation of counts of annual layers and estimates of past atmospheric temperatures even when the deep ice cores do not show layers visible to the eye or to laser scans.

Electrical Conductivity

Salt spray is often deposited with summer snowfalls since the sea-ice cover is minimal in this season, whereas in winter the surrounding ocean has typically frozen over and sea spray is reduced accordingly. These variations in salt (a good electrolyte) levels produce regular fluctuations in the electrical conductivity of the ice in cores taken from drill sites nearer the coast. These variations can be measured easily with simple electrical equipment and used to differentiate annual layers and also to detect deposits caused by fallout from volcanic eruptions.[42]

Salt content may not be the only factor that produces higher conductivity in summer. There is evidence that dimethyl sulfide, which is thought to be produced in greater quantities during the warmer months of summer by marine algae and phytoplankton (and also by volcanoes), reacts in the atmosphere to produce a low concentration of sulfuric acid, which is then deposited with summer snow, also increasing conductivity.[43] Clearly, these two mechanisms are similarly linked to the summer/winter cycle.

Laser-light Scattering

Another method of complementing visual inspections involves passing the ice cores through a device that incorporates a narrow laser beam and

   40. Pol et al., "New MIS 19 EPICA Dome C High Resolution Deuterium Data"; Ritz et al., "Noble Gases as Proxies."
   41. Ritz et al., "Noble Gases as Proxies."
   42. Mulvaney, "Ice Core Methods, Conductivity Studies."
   43. NASA, "Ice Core Records; from Volcanos to Supernovas."

a reflected-light detector. This technique enables the detection of annual bands that may be too faint for detection by the eye. Such a scanner can also be used to detect and analyze dust bands, including those too faint for visual confirmation.[44]

Chemical Analysis

Chemical analyses may be undertaken for more than forty different contaminants of the ice cores. Various acids, salts, and compounds such as peroxides, nitrates, sulfates, and chlorides, together with various trace elements such as sodium, magnesium, and potassium are found. Gases such as nitrogen, oxygen, argon, carbon dioxide[45], and methane[46] may also be present. Although methane can be produced inorganically, it is mostly generated by organic decomposition, especially in warm swamps and lake sediments and changes in its atmospheric concentration can indicate variation in biological activity. Knowledge of the varying concentrations at different ice levels of these atmospheric gases is useful in synchronizing other aspects of ice-core dating.[47]

Hydrogen peroxide (H_2O_2) is produced in the atmosphere only during the summer and its analysis can be used to count annual layers in relatively young ice.[48] However, it gradually decomposes at great depths and so is less useful lower in the column.

Radioisotopes

Certain radioactive isotopes are found in the ice in very small concentrations, and these can be analyzed using a scintillation counter or a gamma counter, such as a germanium detector. An example is the isotope beryllium-10 (^{10}Be), which is continuously formed in the atmosphere by

44. Stolz and Ram, "Using Laser-light Scattering."
45. Barnola et al., "Vostok Ice Core Provides 160,000 Year Record of Atmospheric CO2"; Hönisch et al., "Atmospheric Carbon Dioxide Concentration Across the Mid Pleistocene Transition"; Röthlisberger et al., "Technique for Continuous High-resolution Analysis of Trace Substances in Firn."
46. Mitchell et al., "Constraints on the Late Holocene Anthropogenic Contribution to the Atmospheric Methane."
47. Blunier et al., "Synchronization of Ice Core Records via Atmospheric Gases."
48. Sigg and Neftel, "Seasonal Variations in Hydrogen Peroxide in Polar Ice Cores."

high-energy incoming cosmic radiation. The amount of ^{10}Be in the atmosphere is modulated by variations in the sun's magnetic field and can be used to confirm the eleven-year sunspot cycles in ice as well as longer Milankovitch cycles in ancient ice cores. ^{10}Be has a half-life of 1.4 million years and therefore can be used to confirm dates of given ice layers from a few thousand to millions of years.[49] Kyle Meyer et al. explain the radiogenic isotopic composition method used for dating the deepest ice.[50]

The analysis of radioactive isotopes with a very long half-life can be used in confirming dates, particularly for very ancient ice where visual or laser scanning methods are less reliable. For example, the potassium-argon dating method involves quantifying the radioactive potassium-40 (^{40}K) and one of its daughter products argon-40 (^{40}Ar) found trapped in the ice. Potassium-40 has a half-life of ~1.25 billion years and can be used to date objects from about twenty thousand up to billions of years. This method is also commonly used for dating rocks.[51]

Paleomagnetism

The last paleomagnetic reversal, i.e., when the North and South magnetic poles switched magnetic polarity, is dated at 780,000 years ago, which is older than most of the ice cores extracted. However, the orientation of magnetic material trapped in some old ice can indicate whether the snow from which it formed was deposited before or after this reversal.[52]

7.5.2 How Old is the Ice?

Numerous cores have been extracted from the central Greenland ice sheet, and these have produced continuous records for up to about 120,000 years.[53] Investigations by several research groups have reported continuous

---

49. Yiou et al., "Beryllium 10 in the Greenland Ice Core Project Ice Core at Summit, Greenland"; Schafer et al., "Cosmogenic Nuclide Techniques."

50. Meyer et al., "Radiogenic Isotopic Compositions of Low Concentration Dust and Aerosol."

51. McDougall and Harrison, *Geochronology and Thermochronology by the 40Ar/39Ar Method*; MacDougall, *Nature's Clocks*.

52. Singer et al. "Synchronizing Volcanic, Sedimentary and Ice Core Records."

53. Gkinis et al., "120,000-year long Climate Record."

sequences of deep Antarctic ice cores that yielded strata counts reaching back to 800,000 years BP.[54]

However, during the last decade or so, there have been surveys to find ancient ice nearer the surface. In 2017, estimates of the age of ice from the Allan Hills Blue Ice area of East Antarctica obtained by using the radiometric potassium-argon (^{40}K-^{40}Ar) dating method were announced. The age of some of the ice was estimated to be 2.7 (± 9 percent) million years.[55] In 2024, Ed Brook, leader of the US Center for Oldest Ice Exploration (COLDEX), announced a provisional age for ice from the Allan Hills Blue Ice Area of 4.6 million years, but this has not been confirmed.[56] It must be noted that this ancient ice was not extracted from deep core samples. Topographic irregularities below the ice in some places cause moving ice to rise and appear close to or at the surface.

7.5.3 Consistency and Reliability

As stated at the beginning of 7.5, Meese et al. obtained an age of 110,000 years for the 2,800 m level of the GISP2 ice core. A number of the independent methods presented in 7.5.1 were used. The uncertainty in the ages for layers down to 2,500 m was determined to be between 1 percent and 10 percent, with an average uncertainty of about 5 percent. The uncertainty for the last 300 m, where counting was much more difficult, was some 20 percent.[57] These levels of uncertainty are typical. Within this study, the group reported a comparison of four different counting methods for a five-meter section of Greenland ice from a depth of about 270 m.[58] In this section, visual techniques were used to count twenty-one layers, the oxygen isotope method gave a result of twenty layers, the count based on electrical conductivity was twenty-two layers, and that based on dust inclusions was twenty-three years. If the latter is discounted because of the more tentative

54. Jousel et al., "Orbital and Millennial Antarctic Climate Variability"; Lambert et al. "Dust Climate Couplings"; Lüthi et al., "High-resolution Carbon Dioxide Concentration Record."

55. Spaulding et al., "Climate Archives from 90 to 250 ka in Horizontal and Vertical Ice Cores"; Yan et al., "2.7-Million-year-old Ice from Allan Hills Blue Ice Area."

56. Brook et al., "Plio-Pleistocene Ice Cores from the Allan Hills Blue Ice Area."

57. Meese et al., "Greenland Ice Sheet Project 2, Depth-age Scale: Methods and Results"; Svensson et al., "60,000-yr Greenland Stratigraphic Ice Core."

58. Meese et al., "Greenland Ice Sheet Project 2, Depth-age Scale: Methods and Results."

nature of dust inclusions, as has been recognized, when combined, these measurements might be interpreted to represent a period of 21±1 years, i.e., about 5 percent uncertainty. This example was selected by Oard, an ice-core skeptic, in order to demonstrate divergence and hence the unreliability of ice-core dating methods generally.[59] However, even with this example, the broad agreement between methods is clearly demonstrated. Besides, differences of 5 percent, even 10 percent, will never collapse hundreds of thousands or millions of years into thousands.

In the Antarctic, where visual counting is usually less reliable, dating techniques are more sophisticated, frequently involving mathematical modeling. Even here, however, techniques can be combined and compared in order to enhance accuracy. Researchers at the Vostok core site used three different models, one involving comparisons with another site, to claim uncertainties of the order of two to ten thousand years for ages of hundreds of thousands of years.[60] It should be remembered that scientists attempting to claim greater accuracy for their dating than that achieved by similar teams, or as constrained by the quality of their age correlations within this broad field, would soon be caught out.

7.5.4 Concordance of Ice-core Dating and Other Dating Methods

This section presents some additional, commonly sourced results showing important atmospheric correlations that suggest the general reliability of ice-core dating methods.

It is now many decades since reports were published of lead inclusions in the Greenland ice which matched familiar history. Low levels of lead were found in layers of ice independently dated to the period of the Greek and Roman civilizations, which were known to have smelted this metal (known as plumbum, from which we obtain the chemical symbol for lead, "Pb," and the word "plumbing") in order to manufacture pipes for carrying water, and for use in coinage and other utilities. Much higher levels were noted in ice from the early 1750s and onwards, a consequence of the Industrial Revolution. Another significant rise was noted in ice dated to around the 1950s, corresponding to the increasing use of lead additives in petrol for internal combustion engines. Lead levels in the ice peaked in the 1970s, and thereafter sharply declined, following the widespread

---

59. Oard, *Frozen Record*.
60. Salamatin, "Vostok (Antarctica) Ice Core Time-scale."

introduction of unleaded petrol.[61] The close agreement of information and dates from historical records with ages derived from ice cores by the use of the dating methods described earlier strongly supports the reliability of claims made for these methods.

The Antarctic ice records a number of systematic fluctuations in the concentrations of methane and carbon dioxide, together with temperature changes, occurring over many hundreds of thousands of years. These have been measured using the techniques outlined earlier. The evidence shows at least eight complete cycles over a span of 740,000 years, each consisting of a glacial period enduring for tens of thousands of years and a comparatively brief and warm interglacial period.[62] The correlation between the dates of these transitions established by ice-core science and those obtained from independent techniques, such as those using marine sediment cores and terrestrial formations, means that these methods cannot be dismissed.[63]

7.6 LIFE IN AND UNDER THE ICE

Some samples from ice cores have been melted to extract the microscopic particles or inclusions that they contain. These have included live cells, which stain green with fluorography, and dead cells, which stain red. Theoretically, motile organisms (such as spirochaetes, ciliophorans, or *Chlamydomonas* spp.) could move through firn but not through solid ice, so organisms found below about 70 m must have been trapped there, at the latest, when the solid ice formed. A large variety of such cells has been extracted from ice, which is confidently dated to more than a hundred thousand years ago.[64]

Fossil plants and compacted remains of plants have also been taken from rock and soil cores taken from *beneath* the ice. These constitute additional evidence for ancient life since the species from which these formed must have lived during the period before the first ice was deposited. During

---

61. Boutron et al., "Decrease in Anthropgenic Lead"; Hong et al., Greenland Ice Evidence of Hemispheric Lead."

62. Lang and Wolff, "Interglacial and Glacial Variability"; Augustin, "Eight Glacial Cycles from an Antarctic Ice Core."

63. Lang and Wolff, "Interglacial and Glacial Variability"; York and Farquhar, *Earth's Age and Geochronology*, 186.

64. D'Elia et al., "Isolation of Microbes from Lake Vostok Accretion Ice"; Knowlton, "Microbial Analyses of Ancient Ice Core Sections from Greenland and Antarctica."

a three-year period from 1963 to 1966, an ice core was extracted at Camp Century, a US military and scientific research base situated 120 km from the coast in northwestern Greenland near the periphery of the ice sheet. After penetrating through 1,368 m of glacial ice and 14 m of silty ice, the core terminated in 3.44 m of frozen subglacial sediment. In 1966, the scientists were only really interested in the ice samples and did not investigate these last few meters of subglacial sediment beyond reporting "microfossils, including abundant freshwater diatoms and chrysophyte cysts, pollen, and scarce marine fossils (likely windblown), such as marine diatoms, sponge spicules, and dinoflagellates."[65]

In the 1970s, the sediment core was moved from a military freezer in the US to the University of Buffalo. Twenty years later, it was shipped to Copenhagen, Denmark, where it was labeled, stored, and largely forgotten. In 2018, two researchers at the University of Copenhagen rediscovered the subglacial samples stored in jars. The sediment contained well-preserved fossil plants and biomolecules. The investigators concluded that ". . . the Camp Century subglacial sediment preserves a unique, multimillion-year-old record of glaciation and vegetation . . . The unique subglacial record from Camp Century documents at least two episodes of ice-free, vegetated conditions, each followed by glaciation."[66] The sediment beneath the ice is much older than the ice itself. "Cosmogenic $^{26}Al/^{10}Be$ and luminescence data bracket the burial of the lower-most sediment between <3.2±0.4 Myr and >0.7 to 1.4 Myr. In the uppermost sediment, cosmogenic $^{26}Al/^{10}Be$ data require exposure within the last 1.0±0.1 Myr."[67]

In 2024, results were published of an analysis of ". . . glacial till collected in 1993 from below three kilometers of ice at Summit, Greenland. The till contained plant fragments, wood, insect parts, fungi, and cosmogenic nuclides showing that the bed of the GrIS (Greenland Ice Sheet) at Summit is a long-lived, stable land surface preserving a record of deposition, exposure, and interglacial ecosystems."[68]

Related to ice-core science and very relevant to ancient Antarctic life is the discovery of living organisms in subglacial Lake Vostok, lying four kilometers beneath the surface of the Antarctic ice. This lake, which is 250 km long, was outlined in 1993 by aerial radar from a European meteorological

65. Christ et al., "Multimillion-year-old Record of Greenland Vegetation."
66. Christ et al., "Multimillion-year-old Record of Greenland Vegetation."
67. Christ et al., "Multimillion-year-old Record of Greenland Vegetation."
68. Bierman et al., "Plant, Insect and Fungi Fossils."

Ice Cores and What They Tell Us About Past Life

satellite. This image, together with seismic data collected earlier, enabled the announcement of this lake to the world in 1994.[69] The presence of living organisms, including multicellular eukaryotes, in Lake Vostok was inferred during the first decade or so of the twenty-first century from samples of accretion ice taken from a short distance above the lake. Accretion ice is formed when water from the lake freezes onto the bottom of the ice sheet. In 2012, an ice core drilled by the Russian Antarctic team reached Lake Vostok after passing through more than 3.7 vertical kilometers of ice. Samples of the oxic water were extracted from the lake and analyzed for the presence of environmental DNA. These revealed the presence of psychrophiles, thermophiles, halophiles, fungi, worms, crustaceans, and toothfish, all of which live in total darkness and have been estimated to have lived there in isolation for at least fifteen million years.[70] Figure 7.5 shows a not-to-scale vertical section of the Lake Vostok drilling site in East Antarctica.

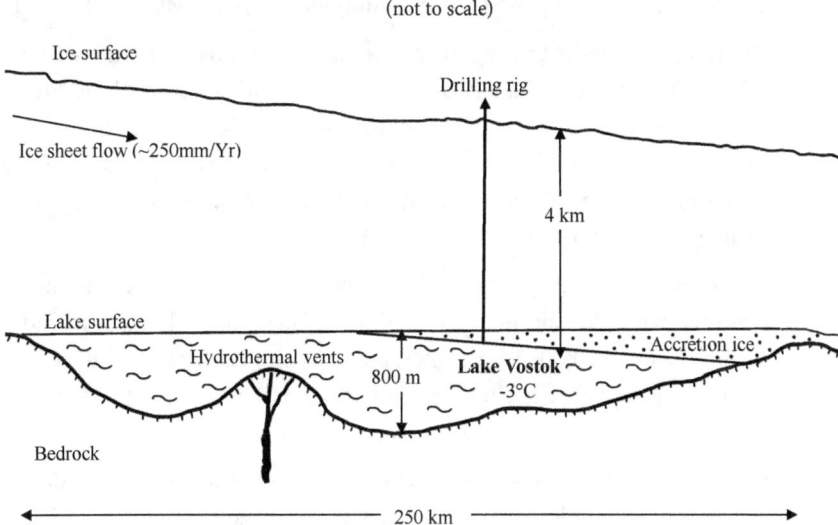

Figure 7.5 Lake Vostok Russian drill site section, age of accretion ice at base dated at several Myr. (drawn by T. Annable).

69. Kapitsa et al., "Large Deep Freshwater Lake Beneath the Ice."

70. Bulat et al., "Thermophile's Microbe Signatures in Lake Vostok, Antarctica"; D'Elia et al., "Isolation of Microbes from Lake Vostok Accretion Ice"; Bulat et al., "DNA Signature of Thermophilic Bacteria"; Shtarkman et al., "Subglacial Lake Vostok (Antarctica) Accretion Ice."

Also of relevance to age-of-life studies is the presence of living organisms and numerous plant and animal fossils which have been found in rocks beneath the ice,[71] and in uplifted Antarctic cliffs.[72] It may also be noted in passing that at least sixteen species of living microbes have been found in basalt crevices at 220 m below the seabed.[73]

7.7 IMPORTANT RESULTS FROM ICE-CORE RESEARCH

Several significant facts emerge from studies of ice cores. Some of these are listed below.

1. The accumulations of ice on Earth contain ice that is unequivocally ancient. Antarctic ice has existed throughout the Pleistocene (from 2.6 Myr) and the Holocene (from 11,700 years ago to the present). Yan et al. found ice dated at about 2.7 Myr.[74] So far, the oldest age claimed for ice found in a trapped (non-flowing) glacier is 4.6 Myr.[75]

2. The temperature in the region of the South Pole has remained well below 0°C for more than two million years and consistently within the average range -53° to -65°C within the last 420 thousand years.[76] Consequently, there is no evidence of any melting near the South Pole. However, the coastal regions of Antarctica have experienced greater temperature variations and some melting.

3. While Holocene temperatures have been relatively stable, evidence suggests that eight successive glacial periods (ice ages) have occurred within the last 800,000 years, interrupted by shorter, warmer interglacial periods and abrupt climate changes.[77] Earth is believed by climate scientists to be currently in an interglacial period.

4. Levels of carbon dioxide, methane, and most atmospheric pollutants, apart from volcanic ash and dust, have varied little over a period

71. Klages et al., "Temperate Rainforests Near the South Pole During Peak Cretaceous Warmth."
72. Francis and Poole, "Cretaceous and Early Tertiary Climates of Antarctica."
73. Suzuki et al., "Deep Microbial Proliferation at the Basalt Interface."
74. Yan et al., "2.7-Million-year-old Ice from the Allan Hills Blue Ice Areas."
75. Brook et al., "Plio-Pleistocene Ice Cores from the Allan Hills Blue Ice Area."
76. Petit et al., "Climate and Atmospheric History of the Past 420,000 Years."
77. Jouzel et al, "Orbital and Millennial Antarctic Climate Variability Over the Past 800,000 Years."

of at least 800,000 years, but have risen sharply with the Industrial Revolution.[78]

5. There has been a tight coupling between atmospheric carbon dioxide and global temperatures for at least 400,000 years.[79]

6. The sun was shining 50,000 years ago in a similar manner to today, producing eleven-year sunspot cycles.[80]

7. Only very small particles, such as pollen, bacteria, spores, dust, ash, etc., that can be carried in high-altitude jet streams are likely to reach the polar ice.[81]

8. Living microorganisms have been found in the surface snow and throughout the ice column in 83 percent of core samples taken from Greenland and Antarctica.[82]

9. Recent research shows that a range of psychrotolerant organisms can survive in and below the polar ice at -60°C, the mean July temperature at the South Pole. Living oligotrophs, which can exist on limited trace elements, dust, etc., are also found in the ice.[83] Pollen grains prove the existence of seed-producing plants (such as conifers and flowering plants) at the time of deposition; fungal spores show the existence of various fungi, and numerous bacterial species have been found at depths equivalent to more than one million years ago.

10. Ages for ice at the base of the two major ice sheets have been derived from ice-core data. The evidence for past life beneath the ice sheets suggests that it is significantly older than the ice sheets.

11. There is no evidence of water having covered the polar regions in the last 2.7 million years.

---

78. Barnola et al, "Vostok Ice Core Provides 160,000 Year Record of Atmospheric CO2"; Mulhern, "Graphical History of Atmospheric CO2 Levels Over Time."

79. Petit et al., "Climate and Atmospheric History over the Past 420,000 Years."

80. Yiou et al, "Beryllium 10 in the Greenland Ice Core Project Ice Core at Summit, Greenland"; Steinhilber et al., "9,400 Years of Cosmic Radiation and Solar Activity."

81. Knowlton et al, "Microbial Analyses of Ancient Ice Core Sections from Greenland and Antarctica."

82. D'Elia et al, "Isolation of Microbes from Lake Vostok Accretion Ice."

83. Knowlton et al, "Microbial Analyses of Ancient Ice Core Sections from Greenland and Antarctica."

7.8 CONCLUSION

Young-Earth-Creationists typically assert that there has been just one ice inundation.[84] They also insist that it must have occurred after Noah's Flood and that it could have lasted only about a thousand years. In order to explain the present massive depths of ice, it is proposed that there must have been vastly increased annual snowfalls. However, the ice cores show there was no such increase (only a decrease in annual layer thickness with depth, as expected). The ice cores show that there has been no glacial period during the whole of the Holocene (the last 11,700 years). The so-called "Little Ice Age," which began in the sixteenth century and persisted with fluctuations into the nineteenth century, was a relatively minor cool period during which mean temperatures in some places dropped by about 2°C, nothing like any one of the last eight glacial/interglacial cycles when global temperatures dropped about 8°C.[85]

In order to account for the hundreds of thousands of annual snow and ice layers, Young-Earth-Creationists suggest that glaciologists must be counting sub-annual layers, possibly layers laid down by successive snow storms.[86] This would mean that such storms would have to have occurred at a rate of about one a day for 7,000 years, which is not consistent with any data we have. The fact that independent research teams, using multiple methodologies, have produced very similar results from numerous ice cores provides evidence for the integrity of ice-core science. Much of this evidence speaks to a long age of life on Earth. It should be remembered that ice-core dating of ages in the tens to hundreds of thousands of years is essentially independent of radiometric age determinations, although consistent with them.

Ice-core science also correlates closely with marine sediment cores and terrestrial glacial varve formations. These data provide cogent corroborating evidence, not only for long ages for rocks but also for the existence of ancient life on Earth.[87] This high level of concordance between the non-radiometric scientific measurements made on ice cores is powerful evidence for their validity.

---

84. Clark, "Was There an Ice Age?"; Oard, *The Frozen Record*.
85. Augustin et al, "Eight Glacial Cycles from an Antarctic Ice Core."
86. Oard, *Frozen Record*.
87. York and Farquhar, *Earth's Age and Geochronology*, 186; Lang and Wolff, "Interglacial and Glacial Variability from the Last 800 ka."

BIBLIOGRAPHY

Alley, Richard B. *The Two-Mile Time Machine*. Princeton: Princeton University Press, 2000.

Alley, Richard B., et al. "Visual-stratigraphic Dating of the GISP2 Ice Core: Basis, Reproducibility and Application." *Journal of Geophysical Research* 102:C12 (1997) 26,367–81.

Armstrong, M. S., et al. "Comparing Instrumental, Palaeoclimate, and Projected Rainfall Data: Implications for Water Resources Management and Hydrological Modelling." *Journal of Hydrology: Regional Studies* 31 (2020). https://doi.org/10.1016/j.ejrh.2020.100728.

Augustin, Laurent, et al. "Eight Glacial Cycles from an Antarctic Ice Core." *Nature* 429:6992 (2004) 623–28.

Australian Antarctic Division (AAD) Government News Website. (continuous updates). https://www.antarctica.gov.au/news/.

Australian Antarctic Program. "From the Katabatic to the Polar Vortex." https://www.antarctica.gov.au>atmosphere>from_the_katabatic.

Australian Bureau of Meteorology. "Antarctica: Driest Continent on Earth." http://www.bom.gov.au.

Ban-Weiss, George A., et al. "Climate Forcing and Response to Idealized Changes in Surface Latent and Sensible Heat." *Environmental Research Letters* 6:3 (2011). doi 10.1088/1748-9326/6/3/034032.

Barnola, Jean-Marc, et al. "Vostok Ice Core Provides 160,000 Year Record of Atmospheric CO2." *Nature* 329 (1987) 408–14.

Bauska, Thomas K., et al. "High Precision Dual-inlet IRMS Measurements of the Stable Isotopes of CO_2 and the $N_2O:CO_2$ Ratio from Polar Ice Core Samples." *Atmospheric Measurement Techniques* 7:11 (2014) 3825–37.

Bender, Michael, et al. "Gases in Ice Cores." *Proceedings of the National Academy of Sciences of the United States of America (PNAS)* 94:16 (1997) 8343–49.

Bereiter, Bernard, et al. "Diffusive Equilibration of N2, O2 and CO2 Mixing Ratios in a 1.5-million-years-old Ice Core." *Cryosphere* 8:1 (2014) 245–56.

Berger, Andre, et al. "Modelling Northern Hemisphere Ice Volume over the Last 3 Ma." *Quaternary Science Reviews* 18:1 (1999) 1–11.

Bierman, Paul R., et al. "Plant, Insect and Fungi Fossils Under the Centre of Greenland's Ice Sheet are Evidence of Ice-free Times." *Proceedings of the National Academy of Sciences of the United States of America (PNAS)* 121:33 (August, 2024) e2407465121. https://doi.org/10.1073/pnas.2407465121.

Blunier, Thomas, et al. "Synchronization of Ice Core Records via Atmospheric Gases." *Climate of the Past* 3:2 (2007) 325–30.

Boutron, C. F., et al. "Decrease in Anthropogenic Lead, Cadmium and Zinc in Greenland Snows Since the Late 1960s." *Science* 353 (1991) 153–56.

Bradford, M. "Dependence of the Duration of Geomagnetic Polarity Reversals on Site Latitude." *Nature* 428:6983 (2019) 637–40.

British Antarctic Survey. "How Antarctic Ice Cores Give Us Clues about Earth's Future climate." https://www.bas.ac.uk/media-post/how-antarctic-ice-cores-give-us-clues-about-earths-future-climate.

The Age of Life on Earth

Brook, Ed, et al. "Plio-Pleistocene Ice Cores from the Allan Hills Blue Ice Area, Antarctica: Recent Results and Prospects for Future Work." *European Geosciences Union General Assembly, Vienna Abstract EGU24–4997* (April 2014) 14–19.

Bulat, Sergey A., et al. "DNA Signature of Thermophilic Bacteria from the Aged Accretion Ice of Lake Vostok, Antarctica: Implications for Searching for Life in Extreme Icy Environments." *International Journal of Astrobiology* 3:01 (2024) 1–12.

Bulat, Sergey A., et al. "Thermophile's Microbe Signatures in Lake Vostok, Antarctica." *Eos Transactions* 83 (2002) B021–A09.

Christ, Andrew J., et al. "A Multimillion-year-old Record of Greenland Vegetation and Glacial History Preserved in Sediment Beneath 1.4 km of Ice at Camp Century." *Proceedings of the National Academy of Sciences of the United States of America (PNAS)* 118:13 (March 15, 2021) e2021442118. https://doi.org/10.1073/pnas.2021442118.

Clark, Harold W. "Was There an Ice Age?" *Adventist Review* (July 24, 1980) 4–6.

Craig, Harmon, et al. "Gravitational Separation of Gases and Isotopes in Polar Ice Caps." *Science* 242:4886 (1988) 1675–78.

D'Elia, Tom, et al. "Isolation of Microbes from Lake Vostok Accretion Ice." *Applied and Environmental Microbiology* 74:15 (2008) 4962–65.

Drill Sites. For Greenland, https://www.researchgate.net/figure/The-locations-of-five-deep-drilling-sites-on-the-Greenland-ice-sheet-NGRIP-751-8-N_fig1_227641205. For Antarctica, https://www.google.com/search?client=firefox-b-d&channel=entpr&q=Antarctic+drill+site+locations#vhid=zarIibPeVd_iIM&vssid=_WQ7qZ8H9KvLh2roPlZDQ-QQ_69.

Erdman, Jonathan. "Bizarre temperatures: North Pole Rises Above Freezing While Parts of Russia Plunge Below -40 Degrees." (2016). https://weather.com/news/climate/news/north-pole-above-freezing-siberia-cold-nov2016.

Francis, Jane E., and I. Poole. "Cretaceous and Early Tertiary Climates of Antarctica: Evidence from Fossil Wood." *Palaeogeography, Palaeoclimatology, Palaeoecology* 182:1–2 (2002) 47–64.

Gkinis, Vasileos, et al. "A 120,000-year Long Climate Record from a NW- Greenland Deep Ice Core at Ultra-high Resolution." *Scientific Data* 8:1 (2001) 141. https://doi.org/10.1038/s41597-021-00916-9.

Global Atmospheric Circulation. https://www.internetgeography.net/topics/what-is-global-atmospheric-circulation.

Hong, S., et al. "Greenland Ice Evidence of Hemispheric Lead Pollution Two Millenia Ago by Greek and Roman Civilizations." *Science* 265:5180 (1994) 1841–43.

Hönisch, Baerbel, et al. "Atmospheric Carbon Dioxide Concentration Across the Mid Pleistocene Transition." *Science* 324:5934 (2009) 1551–54.

Jansen, E., et al. "Palaeoclimate," in *Climate Change 2007: The Physical Science Basis*. Contribution of Working Group 1 to the Fourth Assessment Report of the Intergovernmental Panel on Climate Change. Cambridge: Cambridge University Press, 2007.

Johnsen, Sigfús J., et al. "Oxygen Isotope and Palaeotemperature Records from Six Greenland Ice-core Stations: Camp Century, Dye-3, GRIP, GISP2, Renland and NorthGRIP." *Journal of Quaternary Science* 16:4 (2001) 299–307.

Jouzel, Jean. "A Brief History of Ice Core Science Over the Last 50yr." *Climate of the Past* 9 (2013) 2,525–47.

Jouzel, Jean, et al. "Orbital and Millennial Antarctic Climate Variability Over the Past 800,000 Years." *Science* 317:5839 (2007) 793–96.

Ice Cores and What They Tell Us About Past Life

Kapitsa, Andrei, et al. "A Large Deep Freshwater Lake Beneath the Ice of Central East Antarctica." *Nature* 381 (1996) 684–86.

Kipfstuhl, Sepp, et al. "Air Bubbles and Clathrate Hydrates in the Transition Zone of the NGRIP Deep Ice Core." *Geophysical Research Letters* 28:4 (2001) 591–94.

Klages, Johann P., et al. "Temperate Rainforests Near the South Pole During Peak Cretaceous Warmth." *Nature* 580 (2020) 81–86.

Knowlton, Caitlin, et al. "Microbial Analyses of Ancient Ice Core Sections from Greenland and Antarctica." *Biology* (Basel) 2:1 (2013) 206–32.

Lambert, Fabrice, et al. "Dust-climate Couplings over the Past 800,000 Years from the EPICA Dome C Ice Core." *Nature* 452 (2008) 616–19.

Lang, N., and E. W. Wolff. "Interglacial and Glacial Variability from the Last 800 ka in Marine, Ice and Terrestrial Archives." *Climate of the Past* 7:2 (2011) 361–80.

Lüthi, Dieter, et al. "High Resolution Carbon Dioxide Concentration Record 650,000–800,000 Years Before Present." *Nature* 453 (2008) 379–82.

Masson-Delmonte, V., et al. "Orbital and Millennial Antarctic Climate Variability over the Past 800,000 Years." *Science* 317:5839 (2007) 793–96.

MacDougall, Doug. *Nature's Clocks*. Berkeley: University of California Press, 2008.

McDougall, Ian, and M. Harrison. *Geochronology and Thermochronology by the 40Ar/39Ar Method*. Oxford, UK: Oxford University Press, 1999.

Meese, Debra A., et al. "The Greenland Ice Sheet Project 2, Depth-age Scale: Methods and Results." *Journal of Geophysical Research* 102:C12 (1997) 26411–23.

Meyer, Kyle W., et al. "Radiogenic Isotopic Compositions of Low Concentration Dust and Aerosol from the GISP2 Ice Core." *Chemical Geology* 472 (2017) 31–43.

Mitchell, Logan, et al. "Constraints on the Late Holocene Anthropogenic Contribution to the Atmospheric Methane Budget." *Science* 342:6161 (2013) 964–66.

Mosier, Annika, et al. "Microbiota Within the Perennial Ice Cover of Lake Vida, Antarctica." *Federation of European Microbiological Societies: Microbiology Ecology* 59:2 (2007) 274–88.

Mulhern, Owen. "A Graphical History of Atmospheric CO_2 Levels Over Time." (2025). https://earth.org/data_visualization/a-brief-history-of-co2/.

Mulvaney, R. "Ice Core Methods: Conductivity Studies." *Encyclopedia of Quaternary Science*, Elsevier (2013) 319–25.

NASA. "Ice Core Records: from Volcanos to Supernovas." https://chandra.harvard.edu/edu/formal/icecore/sci_evidence.html.

NASA. "If all of Earth's Ice melts and Flows into the Ocean What Would Happen to the Planet's Rotation?" https://climate.nasa.gov/faq/30/if-all-of-earths-ice-melts-and-flows-into-the-ocean-what-would-happen-to-the-planets-rotation/.

NASA. "Sea Levels." https://sealevel.nasa.gov/understanding-sea-level/global-sea-level/ice-melt#:~:text=When%20this%20ice%20melts%20or,195%20feet%20(60%20meters).

Oard, Michael J. *The Frozen Record: ICR Technical Monograph*. Santee, CA: Institute for Creation Research, 2005.

Parrenin, Frédéric, et al. "The EDC3 Chronology for the EPICA Dome Ice Core." *Climate of the Past* 3:3 (2007) 485–97.

Petit, Jean R., et al. "Climate and Atmospheric History of the Past 420,000 Years from the Vostok Ice Core, Antarctica." *Nature* 399 (1999) 429–36.

Pol, Katy, et al. "New MIS 19 EPICA Dome C High Resolution Deuterium Data: Hints for a Problematic Preservation of Climate Variability at Sub-millennial Scale in the 'Oldest Ice.'" *Earth and Planetary Science Letters* 298:1–2 (2010) 95–103.

Ritz, Stefan P., et al. "Noble Gases as Proxies of Mean Ocean Temperature: Sensitivity Studies Using a Climate Model of Reduced Complexity." *Quaternary Science Reviews* 30:25–26 (2011) 3728–41.

Röthlisberger, Regine, et al. "Technique for Continuous High-resolution Analysis of Trace Substances in Firn and Ice Cores." *Environmental Science and Technology* 34:2 (2000) 338–42.

Salamatin, Andrey, et al. "Vostok (Antarctica) Ice Core Time-scale from Datings of Different Origins." *Annals of Glaciology* 39 (2004) 283–92. doi:10.3189/172756404781814023.

Schafer, Joerg M., et al. "Cosmogenic Nuclide Techniques." *Nature Reviews, Methods, Primers* 2:18 (2022). https:www.nature.com/articles/s43586-022-00096-9.

Shimohara, Kimiko, et al. "Cloudy Band Observations for Annual Layer Counting on the GRIP and NGRIP, Greenland, Deep Ice Core Samples." *Memoirs of the National Institute of Polar Research, Special Issue* 57 (2003) 161–67.

Shtarkman, Yuri M., et al. "Subglacial Lake Vostok (Antarctica) Accretion Ice Contains a Diverse Set of Sequences from Aquatic, Marine and Sediment-inhabiting Bacteria and Eukarya." *Public Library of Science (PLOS) One* 8:7 (2013). https://doi.org/10.1371/journal.pone.0067221.

Sig, Andreas, and Albrecht Neftel. "Seasonal Variations in Hydrogen Peroxide in Polar Ice Cores." *Annals of Glaciology* 10 (2017). https://www.cambridge.org/core/journals/annals-of-glaciology/article/seasonal-variations-in-hydrogen-peroxide-in-polar-ice-cores/2B824B387A565B45600FC8A402CCE67A.

Singer, Brad, et al. "Synchronizing Volcanic, Sedimentary and Ice Core Records of Earth's Last Magnetic Polarity Reversal." *Science Advances* 5:8 (2019). https/doi.org/10.1126/sciadv.aaw4621.

Spaulding, Nicole, et al. "Climate Archives from 90 to 250 ka in Horizontal and Vertical Ice Cores from the Allan Hills Blue Ice Area, Antarctica." *Quaternary Research* 80:3 (2013) 562–74.

Steinhilber, Friedhelm, et al. "9,400 Years of Cosmic Radiation and Solar Activity from Ice Cores and Tree Rings." *Proceedings of the National Academy of Sciences of the United States of America (PNAS)* 109:16 (2012) 5967–71.

Stolz, M. R., and M. Ram. "Using Laser-light Scattering to Measure Impurities, Bubbles, and Imperfections in Ice Cores. *Journal of Geophysical Research Atmospheres* 110:D11 (2005).

Suzuki, Yohey, et al. "Deep Microbial Proliferation at the Basalt Interface in 33.5–104 Million-year-old Oceanic Crust." *Communications Biology* 3:136 (2020).

Svensson, Anders. "Visual Stratigraphy of the North Greenland Ice Core Project (NorthGRIP) Ice Core During the Last Glacial Period." *Journal of Geophysical Research* 110:2 (2005) 1–11.

Svensson, Anders, et al. "A 60,000-year Greenland Stratigraphic Ice Core Chronology." *Climate of the Past* 4:1 (2008) 47–57.

The Times Atlas of the World, Comprehensive Edition. London: Times Newspapers, 2017.

Williams, William E., et al. "Surface Gas Exchange Processes of Snow Algae." *Proceedings of the National Academy of Sciences, United States of America (PNAS)* 100:2 (2003) 562–66.

Winski, Dominic A., et al. *The South Pole Ice Core (SPICEcore) Chronology and Supporting Data*. U.S. Antarctic Program (USAP) Data Center (2019). doi.org/10.15784/601206.

Yan, Yuzhen, et al. "2.7-Million-year-old Ice from Allan Hills Blue Ice Areas: East Antarctica Reveals Climate Snapshots Since Early Pleistocene." *Goldschmidt Conference* (2017). https://goldschmidt.info/2017/abstracts/abstractView?id=2017004920.

Yan, Yuzhen, et al. "Two-million-year-old Snapshots of Atmospheric Gases from Antarctic Ice," *Nature* 574 (2019) 663–66.

Yiou, Françoise, et al. "Beryllium 10 in the Greenland Ice Core Project Ice Core at Summit, Greenland." *Journal of Geophysical Research* 102:C12 (1997) 26783–94.

York, Derek, and Ronald M. Farquhar. *The Earth's Age and Geochronology*. New York: Pergamon, 2013.

8

Mary Schweitzer and Dinosaur Soft Tissues
Initial Reactions and Current Opinions

Paul U. Cameron

8.1 INTRODUCTION

The story of Mary Schweitzer's search for DNA, protein, and other biological material in ancient soft tissue is an example of how technical advances fuel biological research and of the importance of hypothesis-testing as the basis for science. It demonstrates how a scientific question is developed and shows the way in which theory and experiment interact to produce a progressively refined model of some aspect of nature. Schweitzer's story has an interesting added twist: she began her scientific career skeptical of the truth of the scientific consensus on old life and evolution. However, in offering her critique, she was prepared to subject her assumptions to the scrutiny of the scientific method. She engaged in observation and experiment, the fundamental processes and *sine qua non* of scientific research, and finally arrived at a position at which she accepted the standard dating schema but questioned some of the prevailing paradigms for the preservation of biomolecules during fossilization. After thoroughly testing her models and data, she was then prepared to defend her observations and claims against her critics.

Schweitzer's work shows the essentially tentative nature of science, that there are always questions remaining and that final answers are just beyond our grasp. This is often because the methods or the materials required to address the question are not currently available. The trajectory of her research started with the idea of testing for ancient DNA sequences in dinosaur fossils that contained the residue of soft tissue. There is no doubt that finding intact DNA in fossils that were 60 Myr old would constitute a major shakeup in biochemistry and paleontology, but such a discovery has never been claimed. However, what advances in the methods of biochemical analysis have shown is that there is definite evidence of much more residual biological material in ancient remains than had been suspected before Schweitzer's work. This includes proteins such as hemoglobin and the connective tissue proteins collagen, skin keratin, and melanin. Her work is now a driver for research in the field of the molecular biology of fossils and has firmly made obsolete the idea that all fossils are simply mineral casts of biological material that are now completely devoid of the molecules of life.

8.2 BASICS OF TAXONOMY

Life forms are classified according to their position within a nested hierarchy—domain, kingdom, phylum, class, order, family, genus, and species. This taxonomy, originally developed by Linnaeus (Carl von Linne, 1707–1778), was based almost entirely on relative similarities in appearance and features in common between species that indicated relatedness. Unlike post-1859 versions of Linnaeus' taxonomy, his system was not based on an evolutionary hypothesis. The model of common descent and its associated mechanisms championed by Darwin and Wallace in the mid-nineteenth century was accommodated in this taxonomy, although the idea of a tree of life and some commonality between species was certainly emergent before Darwin.[1] A classification system in the form of a nested hierarchy was thus well formed before the appearance in the mid-to-late twentieth century of the modern tools of molecular genetics that are now used forensically to trace kindred and common descent.

Over time, the classification of living species was extended to include fossil remains of extinct species that were assumed to be in some way ancestral to the extant species. One of the aims of paleontologists is to reconstruct the morphology of extinct species and to place them within the taxonomy. This has been attempted from fossil remains such as vertebrate

---

1. For example, one simplified representation of the "tree of life" (among many available) may be viewed at http://www.tolweb.org/tree/.

skeletons and teeth, which are very diagnostic. Of course, preconceived biases can affect the final construction and identification. This task is also complicated by the fact that, according to appearance, very different species may be assumed to be closely related when they are not. Thus, for example, certain marsupial species are quite similar in appearance to some placental mammals. Furthermore, they are found in similar ecological niches. Cats and Australian "native cats" (quolls) or mice and "marsupial mice" occupy corresponding roles in the placental mammalian world and the marsupial world, respectively, but are very different genetically.

Developments within the fields of genetics and, more recently, molecular biology and molecular genetics, have revolutionized the study of the relationships between living species. Modern iterations of the tree of life are based as much on molecular details as on outward morphology. These techniques have also been applied to the study of extinct species and fossils. However, this is a relatively new field, one in which progress and success depend on advances in specialized techniques such as amplification by polymerase chain reaction (PCR), a process that can amplify very tiny amounts of DNA.[2] Understandably, technical questions have been raised concerning the sensitivity and specificity of the methods that have been used in the molecular study of fossils. We shall examine some of these.

8.3 INFORMATION CONTENT OF DNA AND PROTEIN SEQUENCES

The DNA (deoxyribonucleic acid) molecule, referred to by Francis Collins as *the language of life*,[3] has the configuration of a double helix formed from two long molecular strands or chains. The "backbone" of each strand consists of molecules of a sugar and a phosphate. The nucleobases (thymine, adenosine, guanine, and cytosine) are arranged in pairs (termed base-pairs) along the double helix (T with A, G with C), linking the two strands of the double helix. The sequence of base-pairs forms the genetic "language" referred to by Collins and has sufficient specificity to code for the various proteins and regulators that give an individual organism its set of observable characteristics (i.e., its phenotype). For various reasons,

---

2. PCR involves the logarithmic amplification of DNA between two fixed points defined by short oligonucleotide primers. It allows very small amounts of DNA to be amplified and provides the platform for sequencing DNA.

3. Collins, *Language of Life*.

heritable changes (mutations) can occur at individual base-pairs, and these can provide a means of assigning a relationship within a phylogeny or lineage. This is simply an extension of the way that DNA-testing in a human family can provide evidence of paternity and ancestry.

Protein analysis can yield similar information, since some of the DNA in an organism codes for proteins, which constitute the direct substrates for the specific enzymatic and structural elements of which any life form consists. The proportion of DNA that codes for proteins varies between species: in humans, it is not more than 2 percent, while in some bacteria it is as much as 88 percent. Humans share most of their protein-coding genes with other mammals, it is the other 98 percent that produce the differences. Proteins are each composed of a string of α-amino acids, of which there are about twenty different types. While the amino acid sequence defines the specific proteins, it is frequently found to vary between species, providing signatures that define relationships between individuals and species. This variation in protein amino acids can therefore provide a useful additional way of following changes over time and, more importantly, assigning relationships beyond the phylogeny established by morphology or the location of fossils within the geological record.

8.4 DINOSAUR FOSSILS

8.4.1 Dinosaur Fossils: Age and Ancestry

While all dinosaur species are extinct, their lineages have been inferred and putative relationships with existing species, such as New Zealand's Tuatara, drawn from their morphological similarity to other fossil remains. A putative lineage for dinosaurs can be defined in the same way as for other species, both extant and extinct. In this manner, they have been placed within the framework of the Tree of Life. Several factors are useful in establishing these tentative relationships, including the structure or morphology of the fossils, their location, and their age. The relative time sequence of specific fossils can be inferred from their positions in the various geological layers. (It is true that layers are sometimes dated by means of the index fossils they contain, which can appear to be a somewhat circular process, as recent creationists have sometimes pointed out.[4] However, index fossils are those that occur within a very restricted period in the geological column.

---

4. Thomas, "Questionable Dating of Bloody Mosquito Fossil."

Hence, if they are found at a new site, the age of the undated stratum at which they occur can reasonably be assumed to be similar to that of sites already dated and which contain these same fossils. Furthermore, the use of supporting dating methods, such as radiometry, which are used to date quantitatively the surrounding rocks, provides additional justification for the dates assigned.)

Using these techniques, a widely accepted sequence has been developed, with specific ages assigned for the various dinosaur species.[5] According to this evidence, dinosaurs lived during the Triassic, Jurassic, and Cretaceous periods, from about 245 million to sixty-six million years ago. The latter ended with a global extinction event, the most likely cause of which was an asteroid impact, now designated the Chicxulub impactor, on the Yucatan peninsula in Mexico (the center of the crater is offshore). This resulted in the deposition of the iridium-rich layer at the K-Pg (Cretaceous-Paleogene) boundary, now considered to mark the end of the Cretaceous. It seems that non-avian dinosaurs became extinct within about 30,000 years following the asteroid impact. Birds are believed to have developed from a dinosaurian lineage from about 155 million years ago. They survived the mass extinction at the end of the Cretaceous (as did mammals). Hence, the distinction is made between avian and non-avian dinosaurs. The extinction of the non-avian dinosaurs led to the subsequent dominance of mammals, which filled the ecological niches vacated by the former.

8.4.2 Taphonomy: Fossil Formation

Taphonomy[6] is the field within paleontology that is dedicated to the study of the process of fossil formation. An associated area of research within this field that impacts the analysis of fossils is the study of diagenesis,[7] the process of formation of sedimentary rock. Most exposed corpses will rapidly lose soft tissue to scavengers and from microbial, worm, and insect depredation. This means that only a small proportion of the species that have lived have left fossil remains. It is thought that fossils form where

---

5. Here I offer no critique of the accepted stratigraphy and geological time scale. See https://stratigraphy.org/timescale.

6. Taphonomy is the sub-discipline of paleontology and archaeology that is concerned with characteristics and context of fossil remains.

7. Diagenesis is the process of conversion of sediment to sedimentary rock usually via processes including cementation and dissolution occurring at low temperatures.

preservation is more likely because of rapid burial by sediment (sub-aquatic and sub-aerial), by burial in ice, or in anaerobic environments, such as peat bogs. The nature of the preservation process is complex and depends on several factors.[8] Clearly, for the subject of this chapter, one key question concerns the rate at which soft tissues degrade in skeletal remains.

Although it has always been deemed unlikely, it was recognized that if there were any DNA or other biological materials left after these taphonomic processes, such material could provide important information about these species and their origin. The attraction of molecular methods as tools for genetic or molecular comparisons rests on the fact that they can yield very large amounts of information, even from very tiny samples. Moreover, this information is "digital" compared to the largely "analog" data provided by subjective comparisons of morphological features.

8.4.3 Early Studies of Fossil Bone Structures

The field of paleo-histology, or the study of fossil tissue, goes back to the mid-nineteenth century when scientists began to apply the newly developing methods of histological examination used in the study of bones taken from extant animals to fossil material. These studies and their observations have been recently summarized by Schweitzer and her colleagues.[9] Some milestones are of interest. In 1850, Mantell described the preservation of the "Haversian canals," "bone cells," and "decussating ossified fibers" in fossil *Pelorosaurus*.[10] He described "beautifully preserved bone cells and Haversian canals which were as distinct as those found in recent bones."

However, such observations were quite limited until the 1950s, when Enlow and Brown confirmed that the microscopic structure or histology of some fossil bones was well preserved and that these structures could be used to define the growth rate of the animal and make inferences about endothermy in dinosaurs.[11] In the 1950s, '60s, and '70s, there were several comparative studies published concerning the histology of a range of dinosaur bones. These were used in attempts to classify the various species.

8. Parry et al., "Soft-Bodied Fossils Are Not Simply Rotten Carcasses."

9. Bailleul et al., "Dinosaur Paleohistology."

10. Genus of titanosauriform sauropod dinosaur of estimated length 24 m and living 150.8–109 MYBP. Found in England and Portugal.

11. The ability to maintain constant body temperature independent of environmental temperatures. Mammals and birds are endothermic.

Later, the vascular channels in the fibrolamellar bone of the outer cortex were shown to be much more like those in endothermic birds than in the bones of slow-growing species such as crocodiles. The observation of lines of arrested growth led to the hypothesis that the dinosaurs were rapidly growing, active animals that had high metabolic rates. These data suggested that they were likely to have been endothermic. This conclusion has been largely confirmed in subsequent studies.[12]

8.5 MARY HIGBY SCHWEITZER

8.5.1 Background

Coming from a fundamentalist Christian background, Schweitzer was exposed to and accepted the dominant ideas of her religious culture. These included the idea that dinosaurs and their fossil remains were, in fact, of recent origin and hence the fossils could be expected to have within them preserved tissue, rather than being simply inert mineral remains of long-extinct life. The background behind Schweitzer's research has been published in the journal *Science*, where much of her subsequent, high-profile work has been published.[13]

> A third-generation Montanan, Schweitzer, 62, grew up outside of Helena and was the youngest of three children in a conservative Catholic family. Her father, with whom she was very close, died of a heart attack when she was 16, and Schweitzer turned to fundamentalist Christianity for solace, embedding herself deeply in her new community. She also rejected evolution and adopted the belief that Earth is only 6,000 years old. After earning an undergraduate degree in audiology, Schweitzer married and had three children. She went back to school at Montana State University in Bozeman for an education degree, planning to become a high school science teacher. But then she sat in on a dinosaur lecture given by Jack Horner, now retired from the university, who was the model for the paleontologist in the original *Jurassic Park* movie. After the talk, Schweitzer went up to Horner to ask whether she could audit his class.

---

12. Köhler et al., "Seasonal Bone Growth and Physiology in Endotherms."
13. Service, "I Don't Care What They Say About Me."

"Hi Jack, I'm Mary," Schweitzer recalls telling him. "I'm a young Earth creationist. I'm going to show you that you are wrong about evolution."

"Hi Mary, I'm Jack. I'm an atheist," he told her. Then he agreed to let her sit in on the course.

Over the next six months, Horner opened Schweitzer's eyes to the overwhelming evidence supporting evolution and Earth's antiquity. "He didn't try to convince me," Schweitzer says. "He just laid out the evidence."

She rejected her fundamentalist views, a painful conversion. "It cost me a lot: my friends, my church, my husband." But it didn't destroy her faith. She felt that she saw God's handiwork in setting evolution in motion. "It made God bigger," she says.[14]

As noted earlier, a critical question about the use of molecular techniques on fossil material concerns the effect of long periods of time and the processes of fossilization on these biological molecules. Could any of the soft tissue required for DNA or protein assessments have survived over thousands or even millions of years? At the time, the generally accepted answer to this question was "No"! But not all agreed. Finding DNA in dinosaur material had been seen as an important quest by a few researchers from early in the 1980s.[15]

It was in this endeavor that, as a graduate student, Schweitzer's observation of soft tissue in fossils first gained some prominence, as evidenced by a commentary of the time.[16] In 1990, she volunteered to work in Horner's lab, slicing pieces of *Tyrannosaurus rex*[17] bone into thin sections for analysis. This volunteer work with the Horner lab led to the publication of her observations and to a PhD from the University of Montana. The initial incentive to work on this problem was to determine whether there was any DNA in dinosaur fossils, according to the scenario of *Jurassic Park*. An additional reason for Schweitzer's interest in the use of modern molecular techniques as tools to reveal any remaining DNA structures was that such clues might provide evidence for or against the relationships between dinosaur species, which had been suggested by stratigraphic studies of these fossils.

---

14. Service, "I Don't Care What They Say About Me."
15. Jones, "Ancient DNA: a History of the Science Before Jurassic Park."
16. Morell, "Dino DNA: the Hunt and the Hype."
17. Dinosaur of the coelurosaurian theropod genus, Western North America cretaceous period.

While no DNA was revealed, Schweitzer was able to observe hopeful signs of soft tissue structures within the fossil material, which she suspected to be blood vessels. She then developed methods for demineralizing the bone to look specifically at these soft tissue structures. Removing the hard, calcified bone that had become mineralized left the soft tissue scaffold available for analysis.[18]

8.5.2 A Cautionary Tale

One of Schweitzer's first publications was an attempted re-analysis of the DNA sequences from the cytochrome B gene found in a bone fragment from a Cretaceous dinosaur having a nominal age of 80 million years.[19] In their study, Woodward, Weyman, and Bunnell used a neighborhood-joining phylogenetic analysis to compare the cytochrome B gene sequence obtained from the bone fragment with the published sequences from a number of different mammalian species.[20] Contrary to all expectations, the study showed the Cretaceous bone to be situated close to the human bone. This result made no sense according to any accepted scientific scenario or to recent life models.

The conclusion drawn by Hedges and Schweitzer from their re-analysis was that it was most likely that human DNA had contaminated the ancient material and had been preferentially amplified. Others also came to this conclusion, namely, that it was unlikely that the amplification was from dinosaur DNA.[21] This experience illustrates the primary limitation of the PCR methods when used to obtain DNA for sequences from ancient material. Because it is capable of amplifying trace amounts of *all* DNA present in the sample, the result can be affected by contamination with extant DNA.

8.5.3 Ongoing Research

However, some findings of genuine significance emerged. Schweitzer's work continued with the analysis of the long limb bones of *Tyrannosaurus rex* fossils. She took the trabecular material, the cavitated and porous material

    18. Service, "'Protein' in 80-Million-Year-Old Fossil Bolsters Controversial *T. rex* Claim."
    19. Hedges and Schweitzer, "Detecting Dinosaur DNA."
    20. Woodward et al., "DNA Sequence from Cretaceous Period Bone Fragments."
    21. Allard et al., "Detecting Dinosaur DNA"; Steven Henikoff, "Detecting Dinosaur DNA."

from the center of the bone and subjected it to a process of demineralization that removed the residual calcium and minerals. A technique of mass spectroscopy was then used to examine protein fragments. Such analysis allows the determination of protein sequences, and evidence emerged that some of these had been preserved. Fluorescent antibodies that bind to specific proteins were used to identify residual protein fragments that may be similar to proteins in modern reptiles or birds. The remaining soft tissue structures were examined by microscopy techniques, including high-resolution scanning electron microscopy to identify any fine structure.

The studies on soft tissue by Schweitzer that are most cited are her papers in *Science* in 2005[22] and 2007.[23] These studies went beyond the previous suggestions of preservation of some biological molecules and suggested that there was wholesale preservation of anatomical soft tissue structures. She used a destructive analysis of the fossil material that removed the mineral from bone to examine the structural proteins and the apparent blood vessels and structural components present in what remained. Several researchers, using a range of cutting-edge techniques, have since expanded on these initial methods of analyzing the material. Conventional visual-light microscopy, scanning electron microscopy (SEM), and energy-dispersive X-ray analyzer techniques (DEX) can examine the composition of the material in situ.[24] Mass spectroscopy has also been expanded to examine in-situ-imaging mass spectroscopy.

There is a hierarchy of tissue preservation, related to selective degradation of proteins into heterocyclic polymers. As well as with the techniques already noted, these polymers can be studied by a method called Raman micro-spectroscopy.[25] This method of analysis provides the ability to compare the composition of tissue residuals from various specimens. These compositions are sometimes used to assign a position for the species in the relevant phylogeny.

A selection of seminal publications by Schweitzer and others on these topics is shown in Table 8.1.

---

22. Schweitzer et al., "Soft-tissue Vessels and Cellular Preservation."

23. Schweitzer et al., "Analyses of Soft Tissue from *Tyrannosaurus rex*"; Mary H. Schweitzer et al., "Do Egg-laying Crocodilian"; Mary H. Schweitzer et al., "Soft Tissue and Cellular Preservation."

24. Schweitzer et al., "Soft-tissue Vessels and Cellular Preservation."

25. Wiemann et al., "Fossilization Transforms Vertebrate Hard Tissue Proteins."

Table 8.1 Timeline of critical research publications	
Note: The MOR and MRF codes are inventory numbers assigned to various specimens.	
Year	Observation
1995	Cretaceous Fossil DNA Contamination with Human DNA (*Hedges and Schweitzer, 1995*)
1997	**MOR 555** Heme Compounds in Dinosaur Trabecular Bone (*Schweitzer et al., 1997*)
2005	**MOR 1125** Soft-tissue Blood Vessel Proteins by Immunostaining (*Schweitzer et al., 2005a*)
2005	**MOR 1125** Gender-Specific Reproductive Tissue in Ratites and *Tyrannosaurus rex* (*Schweitzer et al., 2005b*)
2005	Molecular Preservation in Late Cretaceous Sauropod Dinosaur Eggshells (*Schweitzer et al., 2005c*)
2007	**MOR 1125** Analyses of Soft Tissue from *Tyrannosaurus rex* Suggest the Presence of Protein (*Schweitzer et al., 2007a*)
2007	**MOR 1125** Protein Sequences from Mastodon and *Tyrannosaurus rex* Revealed by Mass Spectrometry (*Asara et al., 2007a*)
2007	Interpreting Sequences from Mastodon and *T. rex* (*Asara et al., 2007b*)
2008	Weighing the Mass Spectrometric Evidence for Authentic *Tyrannosaurus rex* Collagen (*Buckley et al., 2008*)
2008	Comment on "Protein Sequences from Mastodon and *Tyrannosaurus rex* Revealed by Mass Spectrometry" Re-analysis of *Tyrannosaurus rex* Mass Spectra (*Pevzner et al., 2008*)
2009	Reanalysis of *Tyrannosaurus rex* Mass Spectra (*Bern et al., 2009*)
2009	**MOR 2598** Biomolecular Characterization and Protein Sequences of the Campanian Hadrosaur *Brachylophosaurus canadensis*. (*Schweitzer et al., 2009*)
2009	**MRF-03** Mineralized Soft-tissue Structure and Chemistry in a Mummified Hadrosaur from the Hell Creek Formation, North Dakota (*Manning et al., 2009*)
2010	Influence of Microbial Biofilms on the Preservation of Primary Soft Tissue in Fossil and Extant Archosaurs. (*Peterson et al., 2010*)
2015	Mass Spectrometry and Antibody-based Characterization of Blood Vessels from *Brachylophosaurus canadensis*. (*Cleland et al., 2015*)
2016	**MOR 1125, MOR 2598** Testing the Hypothesis of Biofilm as a Source for Soft Tissue and Cell-Like Structures Preserved in Dinosaur Bone (*Schweitzer et al., 2016*)

2017	**MOR 2598** Expansion of the *Brachylophosaurus canadensis* Collagen I Sequence and Additional Evidence for the Preservation of Cretaceous Protein (*Schroeter et al., 2017*)
2017	A Fossil Protein Chimera; Difficulties in Discriminating Dinosaur Peptide Sequences from Modern Cross-contamination (*Buckley et al., 2017*)
2018	**MH 432** Soft-tissue Evidence for Homeothermy and Crypsis in a Jurassic Ichthyosaur (*Lindgren et al., 2018*)
2018	**YELL 147421** Preservation Potential of Keratin in Deep Time (*Schweitzer et al., 2018*)
2019	Cretaceous Dinosaur Bone Contains Recent Organic Material and Provides an Environment Conducive to Microbial Communities (*Saitta et al., 2019*)
2020	**MOR 548** Evidence of Proteins, Chromosomes, and Chemical Markers of DNA in Exceptionally Preserved Dinosaur Cartilage (*Bailleul et al., 2020*)
2020	Taphonomic Experiments Resolve Controls on the Preservation of Melanosomes and Keratinous Tissues in Feathers (*Slater et al., 2020*)

8.5.4 Initial Reactions

The publication of evidence supporting the idea of some soft tissue preservation from the iconic dinosaur, *T. rex.* significantly disrupted and invigorated the quiet world of fossil research.[26] Not surprisingly, this claim was quickly picked up by paleontologists, nearly all of whom considered it highly unlikely that any soft tissue structures could remain recognizable after millions of years and during the processes understood to occur during fossilization.[27] It also came quickly to the notice of recent-creationists who, understandably, welcomed it as evidence for a young age for life on Earth.[28]

8.6 PRESERVATION AND DETECTION OF ANCIENT BIOLOGICAL MATERIAL

This lengthy section presents a summary of work reported over the last two decades on the fossil preservation of a range of biological materials. The

---

26. Schweitzer et al., "Soft-tissue Vessels and Cellular Preservation."
27. Eglinton et al., "Molecular Preservation."
28. Catchpole and Sarfati, "Schweitzer's Dangerous Discovery"; Standish, "Is There Biological Evidence of Life's Recent Creation?"

work of Schweitzer and other early leaders has led to a persistent search for other biomolecules in fossils with ages of 70 to 80 million years. Consequently, a number of biomolecules have been found in ancient material from dinosaurs.[29] This preserved biological material has been expanded to include ancient peptides,[30] as well as ancient biomolecules such as sterols,[31] melanin,[32] and amino acids.[33] Some additional studies involve fossil ages much less than those supposed by paleontologists for dinosaurs, but they are of interest in the general context of Schweitzer's work. Much of the work reported in this section is rather technical in nature and, if desired, may be scanned for a general impression rather than for detailed understanding.

8.6.1 DNA

Although, as stated above, samples with ages of 70 million years appear to be far too ancient to allow DNA amplification techniques to detect intact or semi-intact DNA,[34] researchers were interested in determining the practical and theoretical age limits for detectable DNA. One estimate of the decay rate of DNA in fossils was determined by Allentoft and colleagues in a study of 158 fossil moa from three sites in New Zealand.[35] Clear evidence of exponential decay in the amount of intact DNA was found in these dated fossils. Allentoft's group showed that 6,000–8,000 years appears to be the maximum age over which such determinations can be made in these fossils.

These investigators went on to develop models for the rates of decay of the individual bases of both nuclear and the more abundant mitochondrial DNA. They also obtained estimates of the probability that small, intact sequences remain. They concluded:

> Factors such as bone thickness, burial depth, surrounding pH and water saturation can be tested and modeled in future research, whereas information on season of death, speed of cadaver incorporation into sediment and climatic fluctuations will probably be less accessible. It is tempting to suggest that we can now predict

---

29. Saitta et al., "Cretaceous Dinosaur Bone Contains Recent Organic Material."
30. Buckley, "Ancient Collagen Reveals Evolutionary History."
31. Melendez et al., "Exceptional Preservation of Palaeozoic Steroids."
32. Vinther et al., "Colour of Fossil Feathers."
33. Curry et al., "Biogeochemistry of Brachiopod Ontracrystalline Molecules."
34. Allentoft et al., "Half-life of DNA in Bone."
35. Allentoft et al., "Half-life of DNA in Bone."

the temporal limits of DNA survival, and finally refute the claims of authentic DNA from Cretaceous and Miocene specimens. This is, however, not straightforward. One needs information on the number of template molecules in living tissues, and estimates of post-mortem DNA decay rates for each tissue type. However, the half-life predictions . . . display the extreme improbability that an authentic 174 bp long mtDNA fragment of an 80–85 Myr old bone could have been amplified . . .

In other studies, ancient DNA from Denisovan man[36] and from horses[37] have been examined. These have been used to make phylogenetic comparisons with existing species. The milestones in ancient DNA studies of humans and some other species are shown in Table 8.2.

Table 8.2 Milestones in the analysis of ancient DNA (data from Morozova et al.)[38] DNA Res 2016) Note: The directions to the publications corresponding to the numbers shown in this table are listed in footnote #38

Milestone	Species	Year	Observation
45,000 to 7,000-yr-old Eurasians[29]	human	2016	first ancient genome population study focused on the Paleolithic period

36. Orlando et al., "Recalibrating Equus Evolution Using the Genome Sequence."

37. Orlando et al., "Recalibrating Equus Evolution Using the Genome Sequence."

38. 1 – Green et al., "Draft Sequence of the Neanderthal Genome"; 2 – Rasmussen et al., "Ancient Human Genome Sequence of an Extinct Palaeo-Eskimo"; 5 – Orlando et al., "Recalibrating Equus Evolution Using the Genome Sequence of an Early Middle Pleistocene Horse"; 11 – Allentoft et al., "Population Genomics of Bronze Age Eurasia"; 12 – Haak et al., "Massive Migration from the Steppe was a Source for Indo-European Languages in Europe"; 15 – Higuchi et al., "DNA Sequences from the Quagga, an Extinct Member of the Horse Family"; 17 – Hagelberg et al., "Isolation and Characterization of DNA from Archaeological Bone"; 18 – Stone et al., "Sex Determination of Ancient Human Skeletons Using DNA"; 19 – Taubenberger et al., "Initial Genetic Characterization of the 1918 'Spanish' Influenza Virus"; 20 – Poinar et al., "Metagenomics to Paleoge-nomics: Large-scale Sequencing of Mammoth DNA"; 21 – Lalueza-Fox et al., "Melanocortin 1 Receptor allele Suggests Varying Pigmentation Among Neanderthals"; 22 – Krause et al., "Derived FOXP2 Variant of Modern Humans was Shared with Neandertals"; 23 – Green et al., "Complete Neanderthal Mitochondrial Genome Sequence Determined by High-throughput Sequencing"; 24 – Gilbert et al., "Paleo-Eskimo mtDNA Genome Reveals Matrilineal Discontinuity in Greenland"; 25 – Pedersen et al., "Genome-wide Nucleosome Map and Cytosine Methylation Levels of an Ancient Human Genome"; 27 – Meyer et al., "Nuclear DNA Sequences from the Middle Pleistocene Sima de los Huesos Hominins"; 28 – Fu et al., "Genetic History of Ice Age Europe"; 29 – Pääbo et al., "Mitochondrial DNA Sequences from a 7000-year old Brain"; 30 – Pickrell et al., "Toward a New History and Geography of Human Genes Informed by Ancient DNA."

Table 8.2 Milestones in the analysis of ancient DNA (data from Morozova et al.)[38] DNA Res 2016) Note: The directions to the publications corresponding to the numbers shown in this table are listed in footnote #38

Milestone	Species	Year	Observation
430,000-yr-old hominin[28]	human	2016	oldest *Homo* genome sequenced to date
Bronze Age Eurasian population[11,12]	human	2015	first ancient human whole genome population data
45,000-yr-old Ethiopian[27]	human	2015	first ancient genome from Africa
3,400–4,500 yr-old paleo Eskimo[25]	human	2014	first ancient human epigenome
560,000–780,000-yr-old ancient horse[5]	horse	2013	oldest whole genome sequenced to date
38,000-yr-old Neanderthal[2] 3,400–4,500 yr-old paleo Eskimo[1]	human	2010	first *Homo* whole genome using NGS (Next generation sequencing)
38,000-yr-old Neanderthal[23] 3,400–4,500 yr-old paleo Eskimo[24]	human	2008	first ancient *Homo* complete mitochondrial genome
43,000 and 50,000-yr-old Neanderthals; MC1R[21], FOX2P[22]	human	2007	first ancient Homo nuclear gene analysis
28,000-yr-old woolly mammoth[20]	mammoth	2006	first aDNA (ancient DNA) analysis by NGS
1918 Spanish influenza virus; formalin-fixed, paraffin-embedded, lung tissue sample[19]	virus	1997	first analysis of historical RNA
skeletal samples, 1,300 CE, amelogenin gene[18]	human	1996	first human sex determination on aDNA
human and pig bones, from thirteenth century to present[17]	human/pig	1991	first successful aDNA extraction from bones
7,000-yr-old human brain[30]	human	1988	first aDNA analysis using PCR amplification
approx. 140-yr-old *Equus quagga*, dried muscle; bacterial cloning[15]	horse	1984	first successful aDNA extraction and analysis

Before leaving the DNA discussion, it should be pointed out that, according to the moa study cited above, if dinosaur fossils did indeed date back only some 4,000 years, according to recent creationist flood scenarios, then we should expect to find some intact DNA remaining, whereas studies have found none.

8.6.2 Amino Acids

Amino acid racemization had been developed as a dating technique in the 1970s by a Seventh-day Adventist scientist, Peter Hare. He and his colleagues studied the rates of change of amino acids that constitute proteins from left-hand into right-hand versions after the death of an organism. This methodology was initially developed to critique Libbey's carbon-dating technique by an independent process of dating ancient proteins.[39] Rather than debunking Libbey, Hare, and his colleagues showed that the quantitation of amino acid racemization was in broad agreement with carbon-dating results and, in fact, could be effective as an alternative dating method for samples of ages up to 200 thousand years. The longevity of protein has been demonstrated by analysis of different non-collagenous protein profiles in bovine bones ranging from four thousand to 1.5 million years of age.[40]

8.6.3 Blood Proteins in Trabecular Bone

One of the most convincing explanations initially posed for the unexpectedly high levels of preservation of blood vessels in soft tissue was based on the discovery of hemoglobin components in fossil bones. Schweitzer's first paper on dinosaur trabecular bone was published in 1997, in which she described the isolation of trabecular bone from a very well-preserved and complete *T. rex* (MOR 555) from the Hell Creek Formation (67–65 Myr) in Montana.[41] In follow-up research Schweitzer used another well-preserved *T. rex* specimen (MOR1125).[42] Subsequent work by others has provided corroborating evidence. Blood proteins and the heme molecule from hemoglobin have been identified in several fossils using techniques based on those used by Schweitzer. Similar observations were found for several additional species, including *Tarbosaurus bataar*,[43] *Brachylophosau-*

---

39. Brooks et al., "Dating Pleistocene Archeological Sites by Protein Diagenesis"; King and Hare, "Amino Acid Composition of Planktonic Foraminifera."

40. Wadsworth and Buckley, "Proteome Degradation in Fossils."

41. Schweitzer et al., "Heme Compounds in Dinosaur Trabecular Bone."

42. Schweitzer and Horner, "Intravascular Microstructures in Trabecular Bone Tissues."

43. Dinosaur of the tyrannosaurid theropod genus in Asia about 70 million years ago in late Cretaceous. See https://australian.museum/learn/dinosaurs/fact-sheets/tarbosaurus-bataar/; Pawlicki, "Morphological Differentiation of the Fossil Dinosaur Bone Cells";

rus canadensis,[44] and *Triceratops horridus*.[45] Each was examined for preservation of bone structure and soft tissue.

The main observation has been the finding of biological molecules that were consistent with hemoglobin. The use of techniques such as nuclear magnetic resonance (NMR) and electron-spin-resonance, two methods for the study of molecular structure, suggested the presence of a paramagnetic compound consistent with heme, the oxygen-binding core of hemoglobin. The presence of the globulin protein component of hemoglobin was tested by using soft tissue extracted for protein, which was then used to immunize rats by raising antibodies against the peptide fragments of the biological materials. When the antiserum generated by this vaccination was then tested against turkey hemoglobin, it was found to bind at a level not seen using sera from animals not immunized with the protein material. This discovery led to the conclusion that hemoglobin was present in these tissues at a level sufficient to generate an antibody response. Schweitzer and her colleagues suggested that the extraordinary protein preservation may have been due to the protective presence of iron and heme, which had guarded these proteins over millions of years.

This theme has been expanded in subsequent publications on dinosaurs[46] and by others investigating fossil insects from the middle Eocene period (35 million years).[47] The study of blood-sucking insects fossilized in shale rock is particularly robust and informative. It has remarkable internal controls in that the fossils of blood-sucking females and of non-blood-sucking males could be separately identified and compared, even to the differentiation of their thoraxes and abdomens. No scanning spectroscopy profile for heme was found in the thoraxes or abdomens of the males or in the thoraxes of the females. However, there was a clear profile found for the abdomens of the females. The specificity of this result would seem to provide internal validation, with the evidence for blood being found exactly where it would be expected, were any to have remained!

Pawlicki and Nowogrodzka-Zagórska, "Blood Vessels and Red Blood Cells Preserved in Dinosaur Bones."

44. Schweitzer et al., "Soft Tissue and Cellular Preservation in Vertebrate Skeletal Elements."

45. Zylberberg and Laurin, "Analysis of Fossil Bone Organic Matrix."

46. Schweitzer et al., "Role for Iron and Oxygen Chemistry."

47. Briggs, "Mosquito's Last Supper"; Greenwalt et al., "Hemoglobin-derived Porphyrins."

8.6.4 Blood-Vessel Structures in Fibrous Tissue

Quite apart from the signatures of blood itself, there was evidence of blood vessels. After demineralization of a *T. rex* bone fragment (MOR 1125), Schweitzer found structures resembling transparent, hollow blood vessels within the collagen scaffolding of the bone, as well as other soft tissues. Surprisingly, these exhibited elasticity, extensibility, and resilience.[48] This indicated that the soft tissue had retained some of the mechanical properties found in fresh tissue.

Furthermore, microscopy of this tissue revealed that within the blood vessels, there were smaller structures that had the appearance of red blood cells. This evidence of blood provided confirmation that these structures had been correctly identified. The structure of these supposed blood vessels was analyzed by the technique of scanning electron microscopy (SEM), which can examine surface structures at high resolution. They were compared to similarly processed material from a modern ostrich. The internal surface of the putative blood vessels showed a paved structure with structures resembling nuclei. This was similar to that found in the ostrich blood vessels.

8.6.5 Preservation of Cells and Bone Matrix Within the Bone

The preservation of cellular structures from ancient bone has been reported, with visual-light microscopic images being obtained of what appeared to be isolated bone cells (osteocytes) within the demineralized bone. These osteocytes appeared to be embedded within the bone's fibrous matrix, and they were similar to those in modern ostriches.[49]

8.6.6 Protein Sequences in Trabecular Bone

In the earlier-mentioned report, Schweitzer suggested that the presence of fossil bone tissue and blood vessels showing similar flexibility and mechanical properties to tissue from ostrich bone indicated the preservation of the proteins that controlled these properties. Biochemical techniques

---

48. Schweitzer et al., "Soft-tissue Vessels and Cellular Preservation."

49. Schweitzer et al., Gender-specific Reproductive Tissue in Ratites and *Tyrannosaurus rex*."

used to characterize components of the soft tissue were discussed in two subsequent publications by Schweitzer and colleagues.[50]

Schweitzer and colleagues extended the initial observation of relatively preserved soft tissue, examining this tissue biochemically to identify protein fragments.[51] This analysis was performed on bone samples from different species. The morphology of these bone tissues was initially established by atomic force microscopy (AFM), a method producing high-resolution of surfaces, as well as transmission and scanning electron microscopy.[52] It was found that there was a periodicity to the surface of bone which was consistent with the presence of a collagen matrix. Demineralized soft tissue was then tested for reactivity to antibody, again chicken type 1 collagen, using fluorescence microscopy. Reactivity was detected, but at a much lower intensity than was found with material from extant species. This could be interpreted as differences in the collagen itself, or what is much more likely, as indicating that there were low levels of intact collagen protein present in the ancient material. The specificity of the reaction, however, was further supported by the loss of the antibody binding signal after treatment of the tissue with collagenase, an enzyme that specifically degrades collagen.

Any peptide fragments in the tissue were discerned by mass spectroscopy using a method called time-of-flight-secondary-ion-mass-spectroscopy (TOF-SIMS). This method allows the identification of peptide fragments. In turn, this allows the assignment of sequence to the protein. The most abundant protein in bone and tissue is collagen and sequence data were published with this additional tissue analysis. These sequence data, like DNA analysis on ancient samples, were subject to robust criticism in the journal where they were published.

The difficulty in the assignment of sequence is that the original protein material would be expected to be degraded significantly, and indeed, such was found to be the case. The isolation of a pure protein is much more difficult where there is such degradation, since size and mass will be different from the intact protein. In addition, it is difficult to isolate a single, uniform molecular series by means of mass spectroscopy. Despite these difficulties,

50. Schweitzer et al., "Analyses of Soft Tissue from *Tyrannosaurus rex*"; Asara et al., "Protein Sequences from Mastodon and *Tyrannosaurus rex*."

51. Schweitzer et al., "Analyses of Soft Tissue from *Tyrannosaurus rex*."

52. AFM is a microscope that scans the surface of tissue at very close proximity. Electron microscopy uses an electron beam to image at high resolution and can either look at electrons penetrating thin sections or scan the reflected electrons from the surface of tissue that have been spray-coated with a fine layer of metal ions.

some sequencing of collagen protein from both *T. rex* and mastodon was performed. Sequences were obtained from the 68-million-year-old fossil dinosaur MOR 1125, as well as from mastodon (160,000–600,000 years).[53] Both showed defective and incomplete sequences, although the degradation was less than expected. Only seven peptide sequences from the dinosaur could be isolated and compared to those from the mastodon.

8.6.7 Fossil Feathers

Ancient keratin proteins, common components of skin and feathers, have been found in some highly preserved specimens that have feathers. For example, material binding to antibodies specific for keratin, was found in the feather-like material of the fossil *Shuvuuia deserti*, which dates from the Late Cretaceous at 75 Myr.[54] Ancient keratin shows the characteristic change in amino acids consistent with old age, but different, slower rates have been found in feathers embedded in amber. Resins, such as amber, appear to offer an environment producing low rates of degradation. The extent of preservation in such media appears to vary with the source of the resin and with the temperature.[55]

8.6.8 Fossil Pigmentation

For some well-preserved fossils, the residual soft tissue material may be subjected to immunological assay after the removal of feather material. The fine structure of the preserved tissue sometimes includes melanosomes, a pigmentation material. In one criticism of this observation, it was claimed that these apparently ancient materials are products of more recent bacterial or microbial activity.[56] This is to some extent a moot point since it is the preservation of these prehistoric materials that is at issue, rather than their origin at a precise time in the deep past. However, the criticism is valid if the observations correspond to modern contamination, there being no

---

53. Asara et al., "Protein Sequences from Mastodon and *Tyrannosaurus rex*"; Asara et al., "Interpreting Sequences from Mastodon and *T. rex*"; Organ et al., "Molecular Phylogenetics of Mastodon and *Tyrannosaurus rex*."

54. Schweitzer et al., "Beta-keratin Specific Immunological Reactivity."

55. McCoy et al., "Ancient Amino Acids from Fossil Feathers in Amber."

56. Kaye et al., "Dinosaurian Soft Tissues Interpreted as Bacterial Biofilms"; Buckley et al., "A Fossil Protein Chimera."

preservation of ancient soft tissue. Recent studies, though, by Lindgren[57] and Volker[58] have suggested that this is not the case. Taphonic experiments on the preservation of fossil material have suggested that the presence of antioxidants may help the preservation of pigmentation in a similar manner to that in which iron and heme help to preserve proteins in bone.[59]

8.7 PEER CRITICISM AND SUBSEQUENT RESPONSE

8.7.1 Methodological Criticisms

Several methodological questions were raised in the initial critiques of Schweitzer's work, some of which were quite pointed, to say the least!

> Since the publication of their report (1), Asara et al. have reinterpreted (3) four out of seven of the *T. rex* peptides originally reported. The most likely outcome of further criticism is that Asara and colleagues will continue changing their original interpretations until the critics give up. So far, five out of six of the remaining significant *T. rex* peptides have already emerged as identical to chicken peptides. Maybe *T. rex* was a chicken after all? Recently, a group of 27 mass spectrometrists, bioinformaticians, and dinosaur experts published an insightful criticism of the *T. rex* protein analysis (7). Still, Asara and Schweitzer (8), refused to acknowledge the problems with their analysis. It is now the turn of the mass spectrometry community to question whether the monkey can actually spell. It is very easy to check; just ask the boy how many words (e.g., spectra) the monkey has generated and what tests of statistical significance were used to compute FPR (False Positive Rate). With this information in hand, the scientists can finally match all dinosaur proteins against Webster's dictionary to see whether mass spectrometers can spell and whether *T. rex* was a chicken.
>
> Schweitzer et al. previously reported multiple lines of evidence, including immunological reactions, for hemoglobin-derived compounds in *T. rex* bone, and collagen from younger fossil bones is well-known. Contamination remains a tricky and possibly unresolvable issue for this particular sample. Perhaps a bird died

---

57. Lindgren et al., "Skin Pigmentation Provides Evidence of Convergent Melanism"; Lindgren, "Interpreting Melanin-based Coloration Through Deep Time"; Lindgren et al., "Biochemistry and Adaptive Colouration of an Exceptionally Preserved Juvenile Fossil."

58. Lindgren et al., "Soft-tissue Evidence for Homeothermy."

59. Slater et al., "Taphonomic Experiments Resolve Controls."

on top of the *T. rex* excavation in the field; perhaps ostrich bone lingered in the mass spectrometry facility for a year; or perhaps avian collagen from a cosmetic or medical product found its way into the *T. rex* sample. Complete sequencing of ostrich collagen would help dispel one contamination scenario. In just-published work on an 80-million-year-old hadrosaur fossil, Schweitzer et al. took extra precautions against contamination, including excavation with sterilized tools and analysis of the fossil extracts by more than one mass spectrometry laboratory. So far, this new study has met with much less skepticism. It is fair to say that the scientific community is still working out standards for sample handling and data analysis of fossil protein.[60]

Such critiques are normal in scientific research. The first analysis of the integrity of any work is during peer review of the manuscript before its publication. Other criticism comes later in letters of response to the original publication and in further original research that seeks to replicate the original report or to test specific hypotheses arising from the work.

The main criticism questioned Schweitzer's sequence data. It was argued that the publications of 2007 did not adequately establish the sequence data claimed.[61] The other significant criticism concerned the source of the biomolecules. One critic was Tom Kaye from Bourke Museum in Seattle, who suggested in his critique that the material and biological molecules were derived from microbial contamination.[62]

The Possibility of Biofilms

The initial skepticism about these findings was that the blood vessels under study may not have been original blood vessels at all but instead may be biofilms or layers of organic material formed by microbes within the canals present in the trabecular bone of the original tissue during the process of degradation. This possibility of contamination by biofilm was also advanced by York University researchers, Matthew Collins and associates,

---

60. Bern et al., "Reanalysis of *Tyrannosaurus rex* Mass Spectra."

61. Pevzner et al., Comment on "Protein Sequences from Mastodon and *Tyrannosaurus rex* Revealed by Mass Spectrometry"; Buckley et al., Comment on "Protein Sequences from Mastodon and *Tyrannosaurus rex* Revealed by Mass Spectrometry," author reply, 33; Buckley et al., "Fossil Protein Chimera."

62. Kaye et al., "Dinosaurian Soft Tissues Interpreted as Bacterial Biofilms."

particularly in the context of the authenticity of the reported protein sequences.[63]

It has been claimed that dinosaur bones differ from surrounding tissue, comprising an environment that is rich in nutrients and which may become preferential sites for microorganism growth and the formation of biofilms, explaining the amino acid compositions obtained.[64] Schweitzer has subsequently addressed this criticism directly with experiments on the colonization of MOR 1125 (*T. rex*) samples and analysis of contaminated bones isolated using sterile techniques, as well as by further analysis of additional dinosaur samples.[65] Using these samples, additional sequences of collagen have been obtained, and a phylogeny constructed that places dinosaurs with basal birds. Another approach used by Schweitzer has been to analyze soft tissue from other species, including the bony carapace of fossil turtles.[66] Subsequent work has shown that microbes are indeed associated with bone, but the consensus has emerged that these may preserve soft tissues as much as degrade them.[67] These studies appear to have reduced the impact and significance of this specific criticism.

Listening to the Critics

In November 2008, Schweitzer invited many of her critics, including Tom Kaye, Matthew Collins, William Stetler-Stevenson (biochemists studying bone proteins), and Martin McIntosh (biostatistician at the Fred Hutchinson Cancer Research Centre, Seattle) to a meeting in Raleigh to examine the latest data.[68] The consensus of the meeting was that there should be more control studies, independent verification, and better mass spectroscopy analysis. In response to the critiques of these scientists, Schweitzer, along with fifteen others in her team, published a paper in *Science* in which

---

63. Buckley et al., Comment on "Protein Sequences from Mastodon and *Tyrannosaurus rex* by Mass Spectrometry," 33.

64. Saitta et al., "Cretaceous Dinosaur Bone Contains Recent Organic Material."

65. Schroeter et al., "Expansion for the Brachylophosaurus Canadensis Collagen I Sequence"; Schroeter et al., "Proteomic Method to Extract, Concentrate"; Schweitzer et al., "Testing the Hypothesis of Biofilm as a Source for Soft Tissue."

66. Cadena and Schweitzer, "Variation in Osteocytes Morphology."

67. Buckley, "Ancient Collagen Reveals Evolutionary History."

68. Service, "'Protein' in 80-Million-Year-Old Fossil."

there was an attempt to address many of the issues raised in these meetings and by the other published criticisms.[69]

8.7.2 Confirmatory Work from Schweitzer's Critics

Recent work from Collins and others has now confirmed the presence of protein in ancient material, including an ostrich egg dated at 3.8 Myr[70] and a large hominin dated at 42,000 yr,[71] and has studied the decay of protein associated with minerals.[72] (However, Collins remains skeptical that there is preservation of protein for tens of millions of years.)[73] Nonetheless, Reisz and colleagues have now described collagen in a 195 Myr fossil rib from a large herbivorous Jurassic dinosaur, *Lufengosaurus*.[74] They used Raman spectroscopy and synchrotron radiation Fourier transformation infrared micro-spectroscopy (SR-FTIR) to show the presence of putative collagen *in situ*.

8.7.3 A More-Recent Visit to DNA in Ancient Fossils

In 2019, a team, including Schweitzer published their study in which they had returned to the issue of DNA preservation in chondrocytes by looking at DNA staining using intercalating dyes.[75] Both propidium iodine, which binds to DNA independent of sequence, and DAPI fluorescent stain, which binds double-stranded DNA having at least 3 AT base-pairs, were found to stain chondrocyte cells in cartilage in well-preserved dinosaur fossils from the Campanian age (c 80 Myr), suggesting there is at least some preservation of 6-base-pair sequences of DNA.

---

69. Schweitzer et al., "Biomolecular Characterization and Protein Sequences."
70. McCoy et al., "Ancient Amino Acids from Fossil Feathers."
71. Lanigan et al., "Multi-protease Analysis of Pleistocene Bone Proteomes."
72. Demarchi et al., "Protein Sequences Bound to Mineral Surfaces."
73. Service, "Researchers Close in on Ancient Dinosaur Proteins."
74. Lee et al., "Evidence of Preserved Collagen in an Early Jurassic Sauropodomorph."
75. Bailleul et al., "Evidence of Proteins, Chromosomes and Chemical Markers."

8.8 WHAT DINOSAUR SOFT TISSUE DISCOVERIES REVEAL CONCERNING THE SCIENTIFIC PROCESS

The observation of soft tissue in dinosaur fossils was widely reported in popular literature and scientific journals. These results were clearly unexpected by most scientists. The process of fundamentally changing a deeply embedded idea in science inevitably and properly involves resistance and requires experimental observations sufficiently compelling to force a change. This process has been described by Kuhn.[76] Scientists do their observations and experiments within interpretive frameworks or paradigms. Sometimes data emerge that appear out of harmony with these structures. These anomalies are often resolved by the recognition of observational or experimental error: in other instances, they result in minor changes to the paradigm. However, as time passes, unresolved discrepancies between data and paradigm may accumulate to the point where scientists begin to question the paradigm itself. This creates a crisis in the discipline, which is resolved when the old paradigm is replaced with a new one that provides a better fit to the data and enables better predictions.

The shift from a view of very old fossils as being just rocky remains of a long-dead organism to their being possible repositories of vestiges of ancient, once-living material constitutes such a paradigm shift. While it had begun earlier, it was certainly Schweitzer who brought it to the popular imagination. Schweitzer has described the challenges inherent in this process of dramatic change.

> Any time you turn over a theory that has taken a lot of work to establish, of *course* challenging that theory should be hard. That's why when we were preparing to publish, we did these things again and again and again. Even so, people criticized me saying we should have had more data, but there was no way to get more data without more funding and no way to get more funding without publishing our initial results. The scientific response was exactly what it should be: a "wait and see" response. I have a lot of respect for the people who wouldn't just immediately accept our results.

Quoted from Ruppel, 2014[77]

In this statement, Schweitzer has described a functional framework for research, the reality of which is known by all those who practice the

---

76. Kuhn, *Structure of Scientific Revolutions*.
77. Ruppel and Schweitzer, "Not So Dry Bones: An Interview with Mary Schweitzer."

discipline of modern science. Science is inherently and appropriately a conservative process. Hypothesis and experimental testing are its core activities. Hypothesis generation requires only a creative mind and an ability to examine the available data. However, performing experiments to test these hypotheses increasingly requires equipment that is expensive to buy and operate. This is certainly the case in the biological and paleontological sciences. This experimental work must be funded, usually through grants.

If the endeavor has low risk but is interesting and topical, it will likely find funding. However, if the project is more incremental and less impactful, then obtaining funding will be much more difficult. Sometimes, as in Schweitzer's case, the hypothesis is both disruptive, i.e., high-risk and unorthodox, which certainly implies high levels of excitement, but may also induce hesitation among funding authorities. Besides, one will only get funding if one represents a good investment. Those researchers who have done previous experiments and published, thereby establishing their *bona fides* as a worthwhile investment, then have a much higher chance of being funded for further work. This circularity is a research reality!

This need to publish is also useful in that it both encourages the timely publication of work and promotes the collaborative and communal nature of science. New proposals or hypotheses that are advanced can then be subjected to critique and independent testing. In this case, as we have seen, Schweitzer's work was certainly critiqued, which led to advancement and progress.

The transition between the initial, disruptive, high-impact publication of 2005 and the current understanding of the nature of biomolecules in fossils, which has resulted from this process, is reflected in the papers listed in Table 8.1.

8.9 CONCLUSION

This story is really one about the importance of data in changing ideas and paradigms in science. For data to be persuasive, they obviously need to be accurate. But data also need to be accessible and available to all who would question the observations. Schweitzer appears to have largely converted the skeptics, particularly with the better quality of data that resulted from the application of newer and more rigorous methods in her later experiments. These data have given rise to definite refinements in the understanding of the extent of preservation. The current scholarly consensus seems to be that no intact, sequenceable DNA has yet been found in ancient dinosaur fossils. However, most skeptics are now persuaded that the data do demonstrate the occurrence of proteins, including collagen in bone, and melanin and keratin in skin and feathers. Schweitzer has not realized her early Jurassic-Park-style hopes of discovering dinosaur DNA in the fossils, but she has changed the field significantly with her convincing data and her evidence-based arguments with her critics. It is a salient lesson for those who would critique the current understanding of the evolution of dinosaurs. Where is your evidence?

BIBLIOGRAPHY

Allard, Marc W., et al. "Detecting Dinosaur DNA." *Science* 268:5214 (1995) 1192. https://doi.org/10.1126/science.7761840.

Allentoft, Moreton, et al. "Population Genomics of Bronze Age Eurasia." *Nature* 522 (2015) 167–72. https://pubmed.ncbi.nlm.nih.gov/26062507/.

Allentoft, Morton E., et al. "The Half-life of DNA in Bone: Measuring Decay Kinetics in 158 Dated Fossils." *Proceedings of the Royal Society B Biological Sciences* (2012). https://royalsocietypublishing.org/doi/10.1098/rspb.2012.1745.

Asara, John M., et al. "Interpreting Sequences from Mastodon and *T. rex*." *Science* 317:5843 (2007) 1324–25. https://www.science.org/doi/10.1126/science.317.5843.1324.

Asara, John M., et al. "Protein Sequences from Mastodon and *Tyrannosaurus rex* Revealed by Mass Spectrometry." *Science* 316:5822 (2007) 280–85. https://www.science.org/doi/10.1126/science.1137614.

Bailleul, Alida M., et al. "Dinosaur Paleohistology: Review, Trends and New Avenues of Investigation." *Peer J Life & Environment* 7:e7764 (2019). https://peerj.com/articles/7764.

Bailleul, Alida M., et al. "Evidence of Proteins, Chromosomes and Chemical Markers of DNA in Exceptionally Preserved Dinosaur Cartilage." *National Science Review* 7:4 (2020) 815–22. https://academic.oup.com/nsr/article/7/4/815/5762999.

Bern, Marshall, et al. "Reanalysis of *Tyrannosaurus rex* Mass Spectra." *Journal of Proteome Research* 8:9 (2009) 4328–32. https://pubs.acs.org/doi/10.1021/pr900349r.

Briggs, Derek E. G. "A Mosquito's Last Supper Reminds Us Not to Underestimate the Fossil Record." *Proceedings of the National Academy of Sciences of the United States of America (PNAS)* 110:46 (2013) 18353–54. https://www.pnas.org/doi/full/10.1073/pnas.1319306110.

Brooks, Andrew S., et al. "Dating Pleistocene Archeological Sites by Protein Diagenesis in Ostrich Eggshell." *Science* 248:4951 (1990) 60–64. https://www.science.org/doi/10.1126/science.248.4951.60.

Buckley, Michael. "Ancient Collagen Reveals Evolutionary History of the Endemic South American 'ungulates.'" *Proceedings of the Royal Society B Biological Sciences* 282:1806 (2015). https://royalsocietypublishing.org/doi/10.1098/rspb.2014.2671.

Buckley, Michael, et al. "A Fossil Protein Chimera: Difficulties in Discriminating Dinosaur Peptide Sequences from Modern Cross-contamination." *Proceedings of the Royal*

Society B Biological Sciences 284:1855 (2017). https://royalsocietypublishing.org/doi/10.1098/rspb.2017.0544.

Buckley, Michael, et al. Comment on "Protein Sequences from Mastodon and Tyrannosaurus rex Revealed by Mass Spectrometry." *Science* 319:5859 (2008) 33. https://www.science.org/doi/10.1126/science.1147046.

Cadena, Edwin A., and Mary H. Schweitzer. "Variation in Osteocytes Morphology vs Bone Type in Turtle Shell and their Exceptional Preservation from the Jurassic to the Present." *Bone* 51:3 (2012) 614–20. https://doi.org/10.1016/j.bone.2012.05.002.

Catchpole, David, and Jonathon Sarfati. "Schweitzer's Dangerous Discovery." *Creation.com*. (2006). http://creation.com/schweitzers-dangerous-discovery.

Collins, Francis S. *The Language of Life: DNA and the Revolution in Personalized Medicine*, Illustrated edition. New York: Harper Perennial, 2011.

Curry, Gordon. B., et al. "Biogeochemistry of Brachiopod Ontracrystalline Molecules." *Philosophical Transactions of the Royal Society B Biological Sciences* 333:1268 (1991) 359–66. https://royalsocietypublishing.org/doi/10.1098/rstb.1991.0085.

Demarchi, Beatrice, et al. "Protein Sequences Bound to Mineral Surfaces Persist into Deep Time." *eLife* 5 (2016). https://doi.org/10.7554/eLife.17092.

Eglinton, Geoffrey, et al. "Molecular Preservation." *Philosophical Transactions of the Royal Society B Biological Sciences* 333:1268 (1991) 315–28. https://royalsocietypublishing.org/doi/10.1098/rstb.1991.0081.

Fu, Qiaomei, et al. "The Genetic History of Ice Age Europe." *Nature* 534:7606 (2016) 200–05. https://doi.org/10.1038/nature17993.

Gilbert, M. Thomas P., et al. "Paleo-Eskimo mtDNA Genome Reveals Matrilineal Discontinuity in Greenland." *Science* 320:5884 (2008) 1781. https://doi.org/10.1126/science.1159750.

Green, Richard E., et al. "A Complete Neanderthal Mitochondrial Genome Sequence Determined by High-throughput Sequencing." *Cell* 134:3 (2008) 416. https://doi.org/10.1016/j.cell.2008.06.021.

Green, Richard E., et al. "A Draft Sequence of the Neanderthal Genome." *Science* 328:5979 (2010) 710–22. https://doi.org/10.1126/science.1188021.

Greenwalt, Dale E., et al. "Hemoglobin-derived Porphyrins Preserved in a Middle Eocene Blood-engorged Mosquito." *Proceedings of the National Academy of Sciences of the United States of America (PNAS)* 110:46 (2013) 18496–500. https://www.pnas.org/doi/full/10.1073/pnas.1310885110.

Haak, Wolfgang, et al. "Massive Migration from the Steppe was a Source for Indo-European Languages in Europe. *Nature* 522 (2015). 207–11. https://doi.org/10.1038/nature14317.

Hagelberg, Erika, et al. "Isolation and Characterization of DNA from Archaeological Bone." *Proceedings of the Royal Society B Biological Sciences* 244 (1991) 45. https://doi.org/10.1098/rspb.1991.0049.

Hedges, S. Blair, and Mary H. Schweitzer. "Detecting Dinosaur DNA." *Science* 268:5214 (1995) 1191–92; author reply 1194. https://www.science.org/doi/10.1126/science.7761839.

Henikoff, Steven. "Detecting Dinosaur DNA." *Science* 268:5214 (1995) 1192, author reply 1194. https://www.science.org/doi/10.1126/science.7761841.

Higuchi, Russell, et al. "DNA Sequences from the Quagga, an Extinct Member of the Horse Family." *Nature* 312 (1984) 282–84. https://doi.org/10.1038/312282a0.

Jones, Elizabeth D. "Ancient DNA: A History of the Science Before Jurassic Park." *Studies in History and Philosophy of Biological and Biomedical Sciences* (2018) 1–14.

Kaye, Thomas G., et al. "Dinosaurian Soft Tissues Interpreted as Bacterial Biofilms." *Public Library of Science (PLOS) One* 3:7 (2008). https://doi.org/10.1371/journal.pone.0002808.

King, Kenneth, and Peter E. Hare. "Amino Acid Composition of Planktonic Foraminifera: A Paleobiochemical Approach to Evolution." *Science* 175:4029 (1972) 1461–63. https://www.science.org/doi/10.1126/science.175.4029.1461.

Köhler, Meike, et al. "Seasonal Bone Growth and Physiology in Endotherms Shed Light on Dinosaur Physiology." *Nature* 487:7407 (2012) 358–61. https://www.nature.com/articles/nature11264.

Krause, Johannes, et al. "The Derived FOXP2 Variant of Modern Humans was Shared with Neandertals." *Current Biology* 17 (2007) 1908. https://doi.org/10.1016/j.cub.2007.10.008.

Kuhn, Thomas H. *The Structure of Scientific Revolutions: 50th Anniversary Edition*. 4th ed. Chicago: University of Chicago Press, 2012.

Lalueza-Fox, Carles, et al. "A Melanocortin 1 Receptor allele Suggests Varying Pigmentation Among Neanderthals." *Science* 318 (2007) 1453. https://www.science.org/doi/10.1126/science.1147417.

Lanigan, Liam T., et al. "Multi-protease Analysis of Pleistocene Bone Proteomes." *Journal of Proteomics* (2020). https://doi.org/10.1016/j.jprot.2020.103889.

Lee, Yao-Cheng, et al. "Evidence of Preserved Collagen in an Early Jurassic Sauropodomorph Dinosaur Revealed by Synchrotron FTIR Microspectroscopy." *Nature Communications* 8:1 (2017) 14220. https://www.nature.com/articles/ncomms14220.

Lindgren, Johan, et al. "Biochemistry and Adaptive Colouration of an Exceptionally Preserved Juvenile Fossil Sea Turtle." *Scientific Reports* 7:1 (2017) 1–13. https://www.nature.com/articles/s41598-017-13187-5.

Lindgren, Johan, et al. "Interpreting Melanin-based Coloration Through Deep Time: A Critical Review." *Proceedings of the Royal Society B Biological Sciences* 282:1813 (2015). https://royalsocietypublishing.org/doi/10.1098/rspb.2015.0614.

Lindgren, Johan, et al. "Skin Pigmentation Provides Evidence of Convergent Melanism in Extinct Marine Reptiles." *Nature* 506:7489 (2014) 484–88. https://www.nature.com/articles/nature12899.

Lindgren, Johan, et al. "Soft-tissue Evidence for Homeothermy and Crypsis in a Jurassic Ichthyosaur." *Nature* 564:7736 (2018) 359–65. https://www.nature.com/articles/s41586-018-0775-x.

McCoy, Victoria E., et al. "Ancient Amino Acids from Fossil Feathers in Amber." *Scientific Reports* 9:1 (2019) 6420. https://www.nature.com/articles/s41598-019-42938-9.

Melendez, Ines, et al. "Exceptional Preservation of Palaeozoic Steroids in a Diagenetic Continuum." *Scientific Reports* 3:1 (2013) 2768. https://www.nature.com/articles/srep02768.

Meyer, Matthias, et al. "Nuclear DNA Sequences from the Middle Pleistocene Sima de los Huesos Hominins." *Nature* 531 (2016) 504. https://doi.org/10.1038/nature17405.

Morell, Virginia. "Dino DNA: the Hunt and the Hype." *Science* 261:5118 (1993) 160–62. https://www.science.org/doi/10.1126/science.8327889.

Organ, Chris L., et al. "Molecular Phylogenetics of Mastodon and *Tyrannosaurus rex*." *Science* 320:5875 (2008) 499. https://www.science.org/doi/10.1126/science.1154284.

Orlando, Ludovic, et al. "Recalibrating Equus Evolution Using the Genome Sequence of an Early Middle Pleistocene Horse." *Nature* 499:7456 (2013) 74–78. https://www.nature.com/articles/nature12323.

Pääbo, Svante, et al. "Mitochondrial DNA Sequences from a 7000-year old Brain." *Nucleic Acids Research* 16 (1988) 9775. https://doi.org/10.1093/nar/16.20.9775.

Parry, Luke A., et al. "Soft-Bodied Fossils Are Not Simply Rotten Carcasses – Toward a Holistic Understanding of Exceptional Fossil Preservation." *BioEssays* 40:1 (2018) 1700167. https://doi.org/10.1002/bies.201700167.

Pawlicki, Roman. "Morphological Differentiation of the Fossil Dinosaur Bone Cells: Light, Transmission Electron - and Scanning Electron-microscopic Studies." *Acta Anat (Basel)* 100:4 (1978) 411–18. https://doi.org/10.1159/000144925.

Pawlicki, Roman, and Maria Nowogrodzka-Zagórska. "Blood Vessels and Red Blood Cells Preserved in Dinosaur Bones." *Annals of Anatomy* 180:1 (1998) 73–77. https://doi.org/10.1016/S0940-9602(98)80140-4.

Pedersen, Jacob S., et al. "Genome-wide Nucleosome Map and Cytosine Methylation Levels of an Ancient Human Genome." *Genome Research* 24 (2014) 454–66. https://doi.org/10.1101/gr.163592.113.

Pevzner, Pavel A., et al. Comment on "Protein Sequences from Mastodon and *Tyrannosaurus rex* Revealed by Mass Spectrometry." *Science* 321:5892 (2008) 1040. https://www.science.org/doi/10.1126/science.1155006.

Pickrell, Joseph K., et al. "Toward a New History and Geography of Human Genes Informed by Ancient DNA." *Trends in Genetics* 30:9 (2014) 377–89. https://doi.org/10.1016/j.tig.2014.07.007.

Poinar, Hendrick N., et al. "Metagenomics to Paleoge-nomics: Large-scale Sequencing of Mammoth DNA." *Science* 311 (2006) 392. https://doi.org/10.1126/science.1123360.

Rasmussen, Moreton, et al. "Ancient Human Genome Sequence of an Extinct Palaeo-Eskimo." *Nature* 463 (2010) 757. https://doi.org/10.1038/nature08835.

Ruppel, Emily, and Mary Schweitzer. "Not So Dry Bones: An Interview with Mary Schweitzer." *BioLogos* (2014). https://biologos.org/articles/not-so-dry-bones-an-interview-with-mary-schweitzer/.

Saitta, Evan T., et al. "Cretaceous Dinosaur Bone Contains Recent Organic Material and Provides an Environment Conducive to Microbial Communities." *eLife* 8:e46205 (2019). https://elifesciences.org/articles/46205.

Schroeter, Elena R., et al. "Expansion for the Brachylophosaurus Canadensis Collagen I Sequence and Additional Evidence of the Preservation of Cretaceous Protein." *Journal of Proteome Research* 16:2 (2017) 920–32. https://pubs.acs.org/doi/10.1021/acs.jproteome.6b00873.

Schroeter, Elena R., et al. "Proteomic Method to Extract, Concentrate, Digest and Enrich Peptides from Fossils with Coloured (humic) Substances for Mass Spectrometry Analyses." *Royal Society Open Science* 6:8 (2019). https://royalsocietypublishing.org/doi/10.1098/rsos.181433.

Schweitzer, Mary H., and Jack R. Horner. "Intravascular Microstructures in Trabecular Bone Tissues of *Tyrannosaurus rex*." *Annales de Paléontologie* 85:3 (1999) 179–92. https://doi.org/10.1016/S0753-3969(99)80013-5.

Schweitzer, Mary H., et al. "Analyses of Soft Tissue from *Tyrannosaurus rex* Suggest the Presence of Protein." *Science* 316:5822 (2007) 277–80. https://www.science.org/doi/10.1126/science.1138709.

Schweitzer, Mary H., et al. "Beta-keratin Specific Immunological Reactivity in Feather-like Structures of the Cretaceous Alvarezsaurid, *Shuvuuia deserti*." *Journal of Experimental Zoology - A(JEZ-A)* 285:2 (1999) 146–57. https://doi.org/10.1002/(SICI)1097-010X(19990815)285:2%3C146::AID-JEZ7%3E3.0.CO;2-A.

Schweitzer, Mary H., et al. "Biomolecular Characterization and Protein Sequences of the Campanian Hadrosaur *B. canadensis*." *Science* 324:5927 (2009) 626–31. https://www.science.org/doi/10.1126/science.1165069.

Schweitzer, Mary H., et al. "Do Egg-laying Crocodilian (*Alligator mississippiensis*) Archosaurs Form Medullary Bone?" *Bone* 40:4 (2007) 1152–58. https://doi.org/10.1016/j.bone.2006.10.029.

Schweitzer, Mary H., et al. "Gender-specific reproductive tissue in ratites and Tyrannosaurus rex." *Science* 308:5727 (2005) 1456–60. https://doi.org/10.1126/science.1112158.

Schweitzer, Mary H., et al. "Heme Compounds in Dinosaur Trabecular Bone." *Proceedings of the National Academy of Sciences of the United States of America (PNAS)* 94:12 (1997) 6291–96. https://www.pnas.org/doi/full/10.1073/pnas.94.12.6291.

Schweitzer, Mary H., et al. "A Role for Iron and Oxygen Chemistry in Preserving Soft Tissues, Cells and Molecules from Deep Time." *Proceedings of the Royal Society B Biological Sciences* 281:1775 (2014). https://royalsocietypublishing.org/doi/10.1098/rspb.2013.2741.

Schweitzer, Mary H., et al. "Soft Tissue and Cellular Preservation in Vertebrate Skeletal Elements from the Cretaceous to the Present." *Proceedings of the Royal Society B Biological Sciences* 274:1607 (2007) 183–97. https://royalsocietypublishing.org/doi/10.1098/rspb.2006.3705.

Schweitzer, Mary H., et al. "Soft-tissue Vessels and Cellular Preservation in *Tyrannosaurus rex*." *Science* 307:5717 (2005) 1952–55. https://www.science.org/doi/10.1126/science.1108397.

Schweitzer, Mary H., et al. "Testing the Hypothesis of Biofilm as a Source for Soft Tissue and Cell-Like Structures Preserved in Dinosaur Bone." *Public Library of Science (PLOS) One* 11:2 (2016). https://doi.org/10.1371/journal.pone.0150238.

Service, Robert F. "'I Don't Care What They Say About Me': Paleontologist Stares Down Critics in Her Hunt for Dinosaur Proteins." *Science* (2017). https://doi.org/10.1126/science.aap9404.

———. "'Protein' in 80-Million-Year-Old Fossil Bolsters Controversial *T. rex* Claim." *Science* 324:5927 (2009) 578. https://www.science.org/doi/10.1126/science.324_578.

———. "Researchers Close in on Ancient Dinosaur Proteins." *Science* 355:6324 (2017) 441–42. https://www.science.org/doi/10.1126/science.355.6324.441.

Slater, Tiffany S., et al. "Taphonomic Experiments Resolve Controls on the Preservation of Melanosomes and Keratinous Tissues in Feathers." *Palaeontology* 63:1 (2020) 103–15. https://doi.org/10.5061/dryad.7290t40.

Standish, Timothy. "Is There Biological Evidence of Life's Recent Creation?" *Geoscience Research Institute* (2018). https://www.grisda.org/is-there-biological-evidence-of-lifes-recent-creation-1.

Stone, Anne C., et al. "Sex Determination of Ancient Human Skeletons Using DNA." *American Journal of Biological Anthropology* 99:2 (1996) 231–38. https://doi.org/10.1002/(sici)1096-8644(199602)99:2%3C231::aid-ajpa1%3E3.0.co;2-1.

Taubenberger, Jeffery, et al. "Initial Genetic Characterization of the 1918 'Spanish' Influenza Virus." *Science* 275 (1997) 1793. https://doi.org/10.1126/science.275.5307.1793.

Thomas, Brian. "Questionable Dating of Bloody Mosquito Fossil." *Institute for Creation Research* (2013). https://www.icr.org/article/7848.

Vinther, Jakob., et al. "The Colour of Fossil Feathers." *Biology Letters* 4:5 (2008) 522–25. https://royalsocietypublishing.org/doi/10.1098/rsbl.2008.0302.

Wadsworth, Caroline, and Mike Buckley. "Proteome Degradation in Fossils: Investigating the Longevity of Protein Survival in Ancient Bone." *Rapid Communications in Mass Spectrometry* 28 (2014) 605–15. https://doi.org/10.1002/rcm.6821.

Wiemann, Jasmina, et al. "Fossilization Transforms Vertebrate Hard Tissue Proteins into N-heterocyclic Polymers." *Nature Communications* 9:1 (2018) 4741. https://doi.org/10.1038/s41467-018-07013-3.

Woodward, Scott R., et al. "DNA Sequence from Cretaceous Period Bone Fragments." *Science* 266:5188 (1994) 1229–32. https://doi.org/10.1126/science.7973705.

Zylberberg, Louise, and Michel Laurin. "Analysis of Fossil Bone Organic Matrix by Transmission Electron Microscopy." *Comptes Rendus Palevol* 10:5 (2011) 357–66. https://doi.org/10.1016/j.crpv.2011.04.004.

9

Theological Problems with Old-Age Models for Life

David Thiele

9.1 INTRODUCTION

THE TRADITIONAL CHRISTIAN UNDERSTANDING of the origin of the world is that around 6,000 years ago it was created by God over a period of seven days—literally one week. This process, described in Genesis 1, reached a high point with the creation of "man" in the divine image (Gen 1:26–27). The Creation is further elaborated in Genesis 2 where the tree of life and the forbidden tree of the knowledge of good and evil are introduced (Gen 2:9). Adam and Eve live together in this Edenic paradise until Eve is tempted by the serpent to eat the forbidden fruit which she shares with Adam (Gen 3:6). At this point the earth is cursed and nature thrown into disarray (Gen 3:17–18). Adam and Eve are driven from the Garden of Eden with its Tree of Life (Gen 3:22–24). Consequently, death reigns supreme throughout the creation (Gen 3:19b).

In modern times, this traditional view has been subject to sustained critique, often but not always due to scientific discoveries. Some Christians have responded by doubling down on the traditional position, arguing in a variety of ways that Young-Earth-Creationism (which obviously includes the recent origin of life on Earth) is either scientifically valid or because it is rooted in Scripture, is simply to be accepted in the place of scientific views.[1] Others have tried to accommodate the emerging scientific data in a variety of ways, including theistic evolution, satanic evolution, and progressive creationism. They have also used a number of interpretative strategies in order to reconcile these views with Scripture.[2] All of these models for convenience will be referred to here as "old-life creationism."[3]

The scientific issues involved in this controversy have been widely canvassed, but what theological issues are involved? What are the theological implications of the various positions taken? There are two basic groupings of arguments to be investigated in turn. First, those to which Young-Earth-Creationists point as the theological reasons why old-life models are untenable and why Young-Earth-Creationism must be accepted and defended; and secondly, those proffered by old-life believers as ways of harmonizing the Bible and old-life positions. The intention is that these arguments will be presented as accurately, fairly, and sympathetically as possible. A critique will then be offered on their validity and strength. Ultimately, the reader must evaluate what is presented.

9.2 THEOLOGICAL PROBLEMS WITH OLD-LIFE POSITIONS IDENTIFIED BY YOUNG-EARTH ADHERENTS

9.2.1 Authority of Scripture

For Young-Earth-Creationists, the fundamental issue is the inspiration and authority of the Bible. The Bible is viewed as the inspired, authoritative, infallible word of God. As such, it cannot be in error in its teaching, and this includes the teachings about the origins of the world and humanity, the Fall of humanity into sin, and the worldwide destruction wrought by Noah's flood. If scientific theories challenge any of these views, they must be wrong. After all, scientists are fallible; God's word alone is infallible.

Numerous issues are conflated here. The Bible nowhere declares its "inerrancy." That is a theological construct imposed upon it—and it is fair

---

1. See, for example, Goldstein, *Baptizing the Devil*. See also Baldwin, "Revelation 14:7," 19–39, and Zinke, "Theistic Evolution," 159–71.

2. The whole spectrum of views is conveniently outlined by Scott, "Creation/Evolution Continuum." See also Pennock, *Tower of Babel*, 1–42.

3. The more usual term "Old World Creationism" is avoided here, where the focus is on how recent or ancient life is. Old World Creationism can encompass views that suggest that while the world is old, life on it is recent.

The Age of Life on Earth

to say that numerically, at least, it is a "fringe" position. The vast majority of Christian theologians would dissent—some quite radically.[4] Even if an absolute inerrantist position is adopted, the question of Origins is not automatically closed. Serious hermeneutical questions remain. Are the "days" of Genesis 1 to be understood literally?[5] What is the scope of the phrase "heaven and earth" (Gen 1:1)? Does creation take in just the earth and its immediate environment, or does it involve the totality of the universe? Should the opening line of the chapter be understood as "In the beginning, God created . . . ," or as "When God began to create . . ."?[6] Does the spirit—or wind, or breath—of God moving "over the face of the waters" in Gen 1:2 signal the beginning of the creation, or further describe the pre-creation chaos, the being "without form and void"? Is it actually possible for a modern to accept a literal view of Gen 1:6–8, which envisages a solid dome separating the waters above from the waters below and having the sun, moon, and stars embedded in it, given that modern astronomy tells us that the moon is 384,000 kilometers away from the earth, the sun some 150 million kilometers away, and the nearest star, Proxima Centauri 40,208,000,000,000 kilometers away?[7] Is it possible to harmonize the Creation narrative in Gen 1:1–2:3 with that found in Gen 2:4–31?[8]

More serious than any of these questions is that regarding the genre of Genesis 1 and 2. Are these chapters to be understood as straightforward scientific and/or historical prose or are they poetic, metaphorical, or parabolic in nature? Meredith Kline concludes,

---

4. Pennock, *Tower of Babel*, 9.

5. For a comprehensive survey of opinions on this question see Booth, "Days of Genesis 1," 101–20.

6. See the extensive discussion in Copan and Craig, *Creation out of Nothing*, 29–70.

7. Turner, "Rainbow," 120. At this point, it should be pointed out that modern "flat earthers" do exactly this. See, for example, Schadewald, "Flat-Earth Bible." They often have a view of Scripture that is similar to young-earth creationists—inerrancy, and validity of scientific data contained therein and a hermeneutic of literalism. Given that they accept the plain reading of Gen 1:6–8, it may fairly be said that they are more consistent than young-earth creationists who deny a flat earth. Typically, young-earth creationists deny that the Bible contains any representation of the firmament as a solid dome. See, for example, Younker and Davidson, "Solid Heavenly Dome," 31–56.

8. In an early seminal work Meredith Kline finds the impossibility of harmonizing the chronology of Gen 2:4–7 with a literal creation week to be the major reason for rejection of the literalness of the "days" of Gen 1:1–2:3. See Kline, "Because it had not Rained," 146–157. When he later revisited this topic he integrated this problem into a "two register" understanding of the first creation narrative. See Kline, "Space and Time,"

This passage is not, of course, full-fledged Semitic poetry. But neither is it ordinary prose. Its structure is strophic and throughout the strophes many refrains echo and re-echo. Instances occur of other poetic features like parallelism (1:27; 2:2) and alliteration (1:1). In general then the literary treatment of the creation in Genesis 1 is in the epic tradition.[9]

If they are more poetic in nature, should the categories of scientific accuracy and scientific error enter into their interpretation? After all, should Robert Burns' metaphorical description, "My love is a red, red rose," be considered to be in error because it is not literally true? "Error" is a category that must be correlated to the purpose and genre of a statement.

Clifford Goldstein has argued that the Genesis Creation accounts cannot be considered to be parabolic because effective parables have a fundamentally parallel relationship with the meaning they are intended to teach.[10] This works well enough with the parable of the Sower (Matt 13:1–9, 18–23) or the wheat and the tares (Mat 13:24–30, 36–43), but it is surely not the case in the parable of the trees choosing a king to rule over them (Judg 9:7–15) or the rich man and Lazarus (Luke 16:19–31).

When attention moves from the broad focus of the inspiration and authority of Scripture, it inevitably focuses on the issues relating to the historicity of Adam and Eve and the Garden of Eden narrative. Again, there are several distinct aspects of this issue to be considered.

It is undeniable that a considerable section of Old Testament ethics *is* grounded in the theology of Creation.[11] The prohibition against murder is explicitly grounded in the fact that humans are made in the image of God (Gen 9:6; cf. 1:26–28). Similarly, much of the Old Testament's sexual ethic is grounded in the sacred nature of marriage which has its origins in the Creation story. In modern times, the slogan sometimes heard from those supporting historic views on homosexuality, "God made Adam and Eve, not Adam and Steve," is reflective of this.[12] Traditionalists often link the

---

9. Kline, "Because it had not Rained," 155.

10. Goldstein, *Baptizing the Devil*, 225–26.

11. Dumbrell affirms that the wisdom literature, a section of the Bible dedicated primarily to ethics, "reflected a theology based upon the fact of creation." See Dumbrell, *Creation and Covenant*, 205.

12. The slogan, of course, provokes the wit to respond, "Well who created Steve, then?" The witticism conceals a serious truth: even if the Bible grounds its ethics in creation, it is impossible—in a fallen world, at least—to construct any sort of comprehensive ethic on the creation narrative. What would such an ethic say about the *existence* of homosexuality, the validity of private property or self-defense and a myriad of other issues?

diminished status of marriage to the dominance of evolutionary theory. Indeed, the question of how an ethical foundation can be achieved without Creation is often posed. Why should people not behave like animals if that is all they are? However, it should be noted that if the early narratives of Genesis are taken literally, the first murderer—Cain—would undoubtedly have been a "creationist"!

9.2.2 The Need for an Historical Adam and the Doctrines of the Fall and Original Sin

It can be very plausibly argued that without an historical Adam in a literal perfect paradise, there is no room for a "Fall," and without a Fall, there is no need for Redemption, and without Redemption, there is no basis for expecting a restored paradise in the end. Without a biblical protology, biblical soteriology falls, and with it, biblical eschatology. If the foundations are removed, the entire edifice collapses. Or so the argument goes.[13]

In my opinion, this is the strongest theological argument presented by traditionalists. However, it faces some serious objections. It is not a new argument, and more liberal theologians who accept scientific data on Origins and incorporate these into their theology have long responded to it, implicitly or explicitly. An example is found in the case of Swiss theologian, Emil Brunner (1889–1966). The fact that the second volume of his *Church Dogmatics*—first published in German in 1950—is titled *The Christian Doctrine of Creation and Redemption* attests the importance he places on the doctrine of creation.[14] He declares, "In his revelation the Lord meets me, my Lord, as the Creator, as My Creator and the Creator of all things."[15] He further affirms that the "doctrine of Man is of particular, indeed, we might also say incomparable, importance . . . as the basis of social ethics."[16] In a similar way, he strongly asserts the reality of the Fall.[17]

However, Brunner is equally insistent on the fact of evolution and regards the accounts in Genesis 1–3 as mythological.[18] The overall position

---

13. Clifford Goldstein, *Baptizing the Devil*, 232–39; Zinke, "Theistic Evolution," 159–71.
14. Brunner, *Creation and Redemption*.
15. Brunner, *Creation and Redemption*, 35.
16. Brunner, *Creation and Redemption*, 46.
17. Brunner, *Creation and Redemption*, 100.
18. Brunner, *Creation and Redemption*, 7–8, 17–19, 39–41, 100–101.

Theological Problems with Old-Age Models for Life

he takes can be summarized as: God is our creator, but the Bible provides nothing more than a mythological account of *how* this occurred. Since we live in a post-mythical world, we cannot accept this, but must rely on science for any knowledge—however limited—of what God did. Similarly, wherever we look in the world today and as far back in history as we can go, humanity is sinful and the world is dominated by sin. Since a good God would not have made a world like this, we can deduce that our world is "fallen" but how and when this happened, we are not told—except in mythological terms. For Brunner, the acceptance of the doctrine of the Creatorship of God is separate from a literal reading of Genesis. He strongly affirms the first and equally strongly rejects the second.[19] But if this is the case, the argument that denying the literal understanding of Genesis inevitably undermines the entire structure of Christian theology, leading inexorably to its complete collapse, is clearly false. It may seem logical to think that if the historicity of Adam is denied, then the Fall—of Adam!—must also be denied, and with that, the entire structure of Christian theology is undermined. However, the evidence shows that this "logical consequence" of denying a literal seven-day Creation some six thousand years ago does not necessarily follow from denying the premise if the theological essence of the doctrine of creation is retained.

The issue of the "Fall" is particularly acute, for two reasons. First, the Fall represents a downward step, a degeneration in contrast to the evolutionary picture, which posits improvement and advancement. However, this conflict is surely more apparent than real: evolution is concerned with physical development—fitness for survival; the Fall is concerned with morality. There is no logical reason why physical development might not happen coincidentally with moral decline. By analogy, Christians have had little difficulty bemoaning modern society's moral decline despite its technological development.[20] Would it really be difficult to construct an argument that suggests that moral decline has an evolutionary advantage? Is this not close to what some evolutionary ethics seem to posit, when they argue for the evolutionary benefits of adultery and promiscuity?[21] Beyond all question, there are times when morality and ethics can put personal survival at risk.

---

19. We should not think that Brunner is either alone in this position, or that his position is considered antiquated by more recent theologians. See, for example, Moltmann, *God in Creation*, 185–214.

20. See, for example, Weber, *Millenimania*, 5–20.

21. See, for example, Diamond, *Why is Sex Fun?* 51–52.

The second issue concerning the Fall relates to the fact that the Bible appears to clearly teach the Fall in a way that presupposes the literal existence of an individual Adam—as literal as Jesus himself. The story as told in Genesis 3 might be dismissed as myth, but it is also presupposed by Paul in Romans 5:

> Therefore, just as sin came into the world through one man and death through sin, and so death spread to all men because all sinned—for sin indeed was in the world before the law was given, but sin is not counted where there is no law. Yet death reigned from Adam to Moses, even over those whose sinning was not like the transgression of Adam, who was a type of the one who was to come" (Rom 5:12–14).[22]

In this foundational biblical text on the topic of Original Sin, Paul seems to clearly presuppose the historicity of both Adam and the Fall.

It should be noted, however, that Paul, having no knowledge of later scientific views on Origins or of scientific questions at all, would have been speaking to more immediate issues. Karl Giberson comments:

> Paul's engagement with Adam, however, is far from straightforward. His tradition read their scriptures with the assumption that Adam and Eve were historical figures, as real as Moses and David. But precisely because they assumed this history uncritically, it is hard to tell how important it was to them. Our historical questions are not theirs.[23]

So, Paul's comment needs to be treated with a degree of caution when it is introduced to a discussion of that topic. Paul accepted the view of the Bible common to the Jews of his day. He could scarcely have communicated with them had he not. It should also be noted that the "simple reading" of Romans 5 accepted without question by fundamentalists is actually a reading through Augustinian glasses.[24] The church's understanding of Original Sin had a quite different emphasis before St Augustine weaponized Romans 5 in his struggle against Pelagius. Can the biblical doctrine of the Fall and

---

22. On the broader question of whether Paul's exegesis of Genesis 3 coheres with the actual teaching of Genesis 1–3, and especially whether or not humans are thought to be non-mortal before the fall, see Foster, *Selfless Gene*, 160–61; Barr, *Garden of Eden*.

23. Giberson, *Original Sinner*, 30.

24. This is a key thesis of Giberson's *Original Sinner*. For a treatment of a pre-Augustinian view of the Fall see, Lane, "Irenaeus on the Fall," 130–48. For a general survey of the development of the doctrine in the patristic period see, Rondet, *Original Sin*.

Original Sin survive a non-literal reading of Genesis? Bruce Vawter concludes that

> ... the message of the Fall, as of original sin, is that a sinful world is not of God's design, that it has come to be through human failing, and that through this fact all human beings are born into a sinful world and, failing the grace of God, themselves become sinners.[25]

None of these affirmations requires a literal reading of Genesis 3 as history.

9.2.3 The Descent of All Humans from the Edenic Pair

Closely related to the issue of the Fall is the question of the descent of all the human race from an original pair of ancestors—Adam and Eve. This is certainly implied, not only in the usual reading of the Creation and Fall narratives of Genesis 1–3 but also by the direct connection of Adam's Fall with "all men" in Rom 5:12, and other texts such as Acts 17:26, "And he made from one man every nation of mankind to live on all the face of the earth." This is certainly an important issue. Denial of common human ancestry leaves the door open to the most serious of racial speculations. Any theory that allows for some section of humanity to be designated on genetic grounds as somehow sub-human has potentially catastrophic consequences, as history has shown. However, from a biblical perspective, the issue is not as completely straightforward as it might first seem. One issue that raises questions is the narrative of Cain and Abel (Genesis 4). The biblical narrative to this point mentions only four people living on the earth—Adam, Eve, Cain and Abel. Yet after the murder of Abel, Cain expresses the fear that anyone who meets him will kill him (Gen 4:14). He proceeds to the land of Nod (Gen 4:16), where he finds a wife (Gen 4:17).[26] The population base of Nod is sufficient that Cain is able to found a city (Gen 4:17) and see urban civilization flourish (4:18–24). These various features of the story can easily be read as indicating that the Adamites were only one

---

25. Vawter, "Fall," 209.

26. This is admittedly an extrapolation of the text. It is not completely clear from the narrative that he was not married before his exile. In that case, his wife would have been (one of) his hitherto unmentioned sister(s). However, the fact that his wife is not mentioned until after his arrival in Nod and the fact that no mention is made of him taking his family into exile with him make it more likely that his wife was, in fact, a native of Nod.

grouping in humanity—one that, however imperfectly, acknowledged God, in contrast to the Nodians who did not.[27]

9.2.4 Death Before the Fall

Acceptance of some form of ancient life involves Christians with other related difficulties as well. The most important of these is the inevitable fact of death before the Fall.[28] Four biblical passages are generally adduced to support the view that human sin introduced death into the world and that prior to the Fall, there was neither animal death nor predatory behavior by any animal.[29]

1. Genesis 1:29–30 cf. 9:1–4. These passages are similar in many ways and reflect the role of Noah as a "new Adam" after the world's return to its original chaos in the flood.[30] However, in Genesis 1:29–30 Adam is given "every plant yielding seed that is on the face of all the earth, and every tree with seed in its fruit" for food, whereas in Gen 9:3, Noah is also given "every moving thing that lives." Obviously, when animals form part of the diet, animal death is a reality; if animals were part of the Edenic diet there was death before the Fall. Generally, the implication drawn from the contrast between Gen 1:29–30 and 9:1–4, is that prior to the flood, animals were not killed for food. This implication is denied by some who suggest that Gen 1:29 needs to be understood in the literary context of the prohibition against eating the fruit of the tree of knowledge of good and evil, rather than a comprehensive statement of Adam's diet.[31] This suggestion gains plausibility from the fact that the parallel text, Gen 9:3, is explicitly set in the literary context of the prohibition against eating blood (Gen 9:4). The emphasis in both cases may fall on what is forbidden rather than on what is permitted. Thus, to refer to these texts as evidence of a strictly vegetarian diet in Eden is to focus on something other than what the texts were intended

---

27. Coffen, "Whom did Cain Marry?" 6–9.

28. Irons, "Animal Death."

29. It is worth noting that although such views are extremely common in conservative Christianity today, they have not been universally held by Christians in the past. Neither St Augustine nor St Thomas Aquinas denied the existence of animal death before the fall. See Bimson, "Cosmic Fall," 71.

30. Dumbrell, *Covenant and Creation*, 26–27; Gage, *Gospel in Genesis*, 10–12.

31. Irons, "Animal Death."

to draw to the readers' attention. Furthermore, Genesis 1 is explicit in teaching man's dominion over the animals—an idea given expression again in a later context where human exploitation of the animal kingdom for food and raw material is evident (Ps 8:6–7).[32] Lastly, it should be remembered that the question of animals as *human* food before the Fall, is not the focus when more progressive views of Origins are proposed. Animal death could certainly have been a feature of the world, without animals being food for humans. Surely, much more germane to the topic is the question of animals eating other animals—although even that is not necessary for animal death to have been a reality. The crucial issue of debate is animal *death*, not animals as *food*.

2. Isa 11:6–9; 65:25. These passages are often taken as an eschatological vision of the new earth (Rev 22:1), where animals live at complete peace with one another. However, there are problems with this reading. John Bimson notes,

> A non-predatory, herbivorous lion would need a different digestive system, different teeth, a different kind of jaw structure, a different musculature and overall anatomy—in short, it would cease to be a lion in any meaningful sense. Taken literally, the passage would indicate the abolition, rather than the redemptive transformation of lions![33]

The passage is, in fact, a highly poetic and figurative picture of the restored Israel after the Babylonian captivity, when human death would still be a reality (Isa 65:19–20).[34] We should not think that dust will

---

32. The connection of Psalm 8 to the creation narratives, and especially to Gen 1:26–28, is generally acknowledged. See Anderson, *Psalms (1–72)*, 103; Anderson, "Psalms," 40; Kselman and Barré; "Psalms," 528; Kraus, *Psalm 1–59*, 180; Taylor and McCullough, "Psalms," 4: 50–52; Weiser, *Psalms*, 144–45. In the Psalms man's dominion over nature is asserted with a particular emphasis on herd animals and other animals used for food. Kraus' comment on Ps 8:6 is insightful: "The shepherding and the slaughtering of animals, the hunting and catching of wild game and fish is a sovereign right emanating from God by which the superiority of the human being over all created things—even more the אלהים-status ["a little less than *God*"]—is revealed" (Kraus, *Psalms 1–59*, 183.)

33. Bimson, "Cosmic Fall," 69.

34. This is less evident in Isa 11:6–9 than in Isa 65:19–25. However, Isa 65 has been correctly described as "a condensed version of 11:6–9." See Whybray, *Isaiah 40–66*, 278. Westermann's observations are also pertinent: "In the Old Testament life is fulfilled life. But only if it is not cut off prematurely is it such. Thus long life, life lived to the end, is to be everyone's in the era of salvation . . . There is to be no more work that is vain and pointless . . . This work was just of the kind with which the speaker's own circumstances

literally be the food of serpents in the new earth (Isa 65:25), any more than it is in this world (Gen 3:14). We should also note that Isaiah in another eschatological picture portrays feasting on "marrow" in celebration of Yahweh's victory over death—which suggests the eating of flesh food.[35] A metaphorical reading referring to the safety and security of the restored Israel is highlighted by the fact that the animals that are not harmed are all domesticated animals. The lion does not lay down with the gazelle.[36] In any case, it is not correct "to assume that the eschatological state will be merely a return to the pre-Fall conditions of paradise."[37] It is a return to paradise with an "overplus."[38] After all, the biblical narrative begins with a garden (Genesis 2) but ends with a city (Rev 22).

3. Rom 8:18–21. This passage declares that at the Fall, Creation was subjected to "futility" (v. 20) from which it hopes with "eager longing" (v. 19) to be released at the eschaton. The implication drawn from this is that the non-human Creation was thrown into chaos along with humanity at the Fall. This, it is suggested, involved animal death and animal predation.[39] This is certainly possible. However, it is certainly not the only way to read the text. For example, Meredith Kline argues, drawing support from Isa 24:4–6, 19–21, that it is the role of the earth as a mass graveyard that constitutes the futility from which the earth longs to be delivered.[40] He notes that even if one wishes to see the

---

had made him familiar, building houses, sowing fields and planting vineyards, and tending these. The only difference now is that the worker is assured of the fruits of his labor. This is the voice of experience, of the ordinary man living in a land constantly overrun by enemies, the bitter experience of men living under enemy occupation." See Westermann, *Isaiah 40–66*, 409–10. However, we should take note of Dumbrell's (*Covenant and Creation*, 174) suggestion that the picture of the returned Israel is an "ideal" picture, and even if the ideal was realized in the restoration it will still ultimately be realized.

35. Faro, "Animal Death," 13 fn 45.

36. Bimson, "Cosmic Fall," 69–70. Bimson does not draw attention to Jer 50:17. The text obviously could not have been in Isaiah's mind when he wrote, but the reverse may not be the case. The situation envisaged by Jeremiah is the opposite of that presented by Isaiah, but the metaphorical nature of his language needs no comment at all: "Israel is a hunted sheep driven away by lions. First, the king of Assyria devoured him, and now at last Nebuchadnezzar king of Babylon has gnawed his bones."

37. Irons, "Animal Death."

38. Dumbrell, *Creation and Covenant*, 184.

39. Lacey, "Animal Death?"; Turpin, "Death of Any Kind," 112–13.

40. Kline, "Leviathan, and Martyrs."

"groaning" of Creation in Romans 8 more specifically in terms of the general curse of Gen 3:17, a significant part of that curse is that the earth is no longer to be subservient to humanity's dominion, but will overcome humans who will be reduced again to dust (Gen 3:19).[41] Alternatively, J. Ramsay Michaels has argued that the "creation" referred to in Romans 8 is not the non-human natural world, but specifically the human bodies of the redeemed.[42] Michaels acknowledges that, in this argument, he is departing from an "almost universal agreement."[43] However, no one can deny that the resurrection of the body is a prominent and explicit theme in this section of Romans 8. Reading this passage as precluding animal death and predation before the Fall is thus not as straightforward as it is often assumed to be.

4. Rom 5:12–14. This verse clearly links Adam's sin and the entrance of death into the world. However, it is clearly human death to which it is referring. Paul is quite explicit: ". . . so death spread to all men because all sinned . . . death reigned from Adam to Moses, even over those whose sinning was not like the transgression of Adam . . ." No direct reference to animal death is found in this passage at all. Furthermore, Rom 5:12 echoes Gen 2:17, where Adam is warned that if he eats of the fruit of the forbidden tree (sin), *he* will die. Again, there is no mention of animal death at all.

Beyond the weakness of any argument based on these four texts, note must also be taken of the fact that there are texts that at least suggest animal death and predation before the Fall. The most important of these is Ps 104:19–28. Richard Davidson observes that the Psalm "from beginning to end, has as its subject God's creation of the world."[44] That there are references to Creation in verse nineteen is beyond question.[45] The next verse

---

41. Kline, "Leviathan, and Martyrs," fn 30.

42. Michaels, "Redemption of our Body," 92–114. For the difference between "person" and "body" and the complexities of the relationship between the two see Baker, *Persons and Bodies*.

43. Michaels, "Redemption of our Body," 92.

44. Davidson, "Psalm 104," 149–88.

45. The verse opens with the affirmation that "he made," pointing to the time when things were "made." The Hebrew word used here is עָשָׂה, ('*āśāh*, to make) rather than בָּרָא (*bā rā'*, to create) in Gen 1:1. However the use of the more general word in Gen 3:1 in a summary of God's creative work shows that little should be made of the difference in vocabulary here. What specifically was "made" in this verse was the moon which marked the seasons (cf. Gen 1:14). The sun and its setting introduces the night (cf. the "evening"

refers to "young lions roar[ing] for their prey" and "seeking their food from God." Reflecting on this, verse twenty-four declares, "O Lord, how manifold are your works! In wisdom have you made them all; the earth is full of your creatures." The clear implication is that God created the lions as hunters and provides food for them! Ps 145:16 declares that God "satisfy[ies] the desire of every living thing" and in so doing is nevertheless "righteous in all his ways" (Ps 145:17). The nature poem of Job 38–39 points in the same direction.[46]

Ingrid Faro's conclusion must be accepted as valid: "The Bible says surprisingly little theologically about animal death, and nothing specifically about animal death before human existence."[47] The cumulative exegetical case for there being neither animal death nor animal predation before the Fall is very weak. So conservative a scholar as Wayne Grudem concludes, "From the information we have in Scripture, we cannot now know whether God created animals subject to aging and death from the beginning, but it remains a real possibility."[48]

Perhaps the strongest argument against the existence of animal death before the Fall is the theological one: such a state of affairs is contradictory to the love of God; God simply would not have created a world like that! [49] This is, in fact, a version of an argument against God having used evolution as a means of creation. Goldstein declares

> If death were part of how God created life on earth, and if God declared the finished creation "very good" (Gen 1:31), then death must also be good, because it's among the means God used to create life to begin with. And though death-as-the-means-of-life might not be an issue in an atheistic model of origins, for a theistic evolutionary model—especially when the *Theos* is the Lord depicted in Scripture—this view of death becomes difficult to harmonize with the Bible, because the Bible uniformly depicts death as bad, as something opposed to life. Far from death being among the means to general life, Scripture portrays death as an enemy, an intruder, an unwanted factor to one day be eradicated.[50]

---

and "morning" of Gen 1:5, 8, 13, 19, 23, 31). This is followed in verse 20 by specific references to "darkness," "beasts" and "forests," again recalling the language of the creation narrative (Gen 1:4–5; 11–12; 24–25).

46. For a more detailed discussion of these texts see Bimson, "Cosmic Fall," 72–73.
47. Faro, "Animal Death," 2.
48. Grudem, *Systematic Theology*, 293.
49. Turpin, "Death of Any Kind?" 106–07; Batten et. al., *Answer Book*, 31–34.
50. Goldstein, *Baptizing the Devil*, 2017, 196.

However, this is a dangerous argument that assumes implicitly that fallen humans are qualified to determine how the love of God must be manifested. It is akin to the argument based on the existence of suffering in the world, that there is no God of love—which, of course, Christians reject. Theology must be firmly grounded in Scripture, or it is suspect.

9.2.5 The Sabbath

A final critical issue arises for Sabbatarian Christians: If the Creation story is not taken literally, what remains as a basis of Sabbath keeping? There is no doubt that the Bible directly and explicitly links the Sabbath to the creatorship of God (Exod 20:7-11; 31:17; Mark 2:29; John 5:17; Heb 4:4). Seventh-day Adventists note that the three angels' messages of Rev 14—the self-perceived *raison d'etre* of the church—begins with a clarion call to "worship him who made heaven and earth, the sea and the springs of water" (Rev 14:7)—words that echo the command to keep the Sabbath in Exodus 20:8-11.[51] John Baldwin argues from this connection with Exodus 20 that the New Testament "endorsed a six-day creation worldview" and "implies a six-day creation cosmogony/worldview."[52] Others have suggested that the rise of a Sabbatarian movement at the same time as evolution was coming to prominence was providential.[53] Does not any accommodation to ancient life mean that the teaching of the Sabbath inevitably falls? Again, several issues are involved that must be dealt with separately.

Baldwin's argument is encapsulated in a diagram he presents, which highlights the connections between Rev 14:7 and Exod 20:11:[54]

Exod 20:11a "For in six days the LORD (1) made (2) heaven and (3) earth, the (4) sea, and all that is in them."
Rev 14:7 "worship him who [in six days] (1) made (2) heaven and (3) earth, the (4) sea and the springs of water."

---

51. Stefanovic, *Revelation of Jesus Christ*, 445; Baldwin, "Revelation 14:7: An Angel's Worldview," 2000, 19-20.

52. Baldwin, "Revelation 14:7," 20-21.

53. See, for example, Nichol, "Increasing Timeliness," 1: 565-73, 616-18.

54. Baldwin, "Revelation 14:7," 21. I have reproduced the textual substance of Baldwin's diagram, rather than the entire diagram. I have also retained the use of the ESV here although Baldwin seems to use the NKV. These changes have no impact on the point Baldwin is attempting to make.

Baldwin argues that Rev "implicitly" endorses a six-day creation, and argues on that basis that we should accept it also.[55] However, surely it is just as valid logically to argue that the fact that Rev 14:7 contains so many explicit verbal parallels with Exod 20:11a and yet does not mention the six days indicates that this feature is, in fact, being de-emphasized by Revelation, even if it were "implicitly" accepted. This suggestion gains further weight from the fact that there is another parallel New Testament text—Acts 14:15—which does exactly the same thing: "that you should turn from these vain things to a living God, who (1) made the (2) heaven and the (3) earth and the (4) sea and all that is in them."[56]

But even apart from Baldwin's argument, should any move from the literalistic reading of Genesis threaten the doctrine of the Sabbath? From a literary point of view, the Sabbath is the focus of the first Creation narrative.[57] Each of the first three days finds a corresponding echo in the next three days, as the following chart makes clear:

The Days of Creation (Gen 1:1–2:3)	
Day 1 Light	**Day 4** Sun, Moon, Stars
Day 2 Heaven and Ocean	**Day 5** Birds, Sea Creatures
Day 3 Dry Earth and Ocean	**Day 6** Land Animals, Humans
Day 7 Sabbath: Rest, Worship	

The focus of this literary pattern suggests that the Sabbath is the point of the story. Theologically, it indicates that the Sabbath was God's gift and intention for humanity *from the beginning*. The story stresses the universality of the Sabbath's obligation. Cuthbert A. Simpson, viewing the passage

---

55. Baldwin, "Revelation 14:7," 21–22.

56. Several commentators refer to Acts 14:15 rather than Exod 20 in their discussion of the background of Rev 14:7. See, for example, Mounce, *Revelation*, 273; Caird, *Revelation*, 183; Beale, *Revelation*, 753; Aune, *Revelation*, 2: 828.

57. The question of whether the seventh day of creation is correctly represented as the Sabbath is much discussed. Among those who regard it as a Sabbath are Hasel, "Sabbath in the Pentateuch," 22; Tonstad, *Lost Meaning*, 24–26; Cole, "Sabbath and Genesis 2:1–3," 5–12; Lee, *Covenantal Sabbath*, 65–70. Among those who deny a reference to an actual Sabbath in Gen 2:1–3 are Dressler, "Sabbath in the Old Testament," 23; Westermann, *Genesis 1–11*, 237; von Rad, *Genesis*, 60.

through the lens of the documentary hypothesis of the Pentateuchal origins, notes:

> The verse [Gen 2:3], together with vs. 2b, is an etiological myth accounting for the sabbath. It invests the sabbath with all the reality of creation itself, and represents its observance as a fundamental law of the world order ... The fact that P thus connects the origins of the sabbath not with some event in the life of one of the patriarchs—as he connected circumcision in chapter 19—or in the history of Israel, but with Creation itself, is of some significance. For the implication of this passage is that observance of the day—actually a peculiarly Jewish institution—is really binding upon all mankind.[58]

This theological point is in no way dependent on a specific understanding of "creation." The point may still be valid regardless of whether humanity was created by divine fiat, some 6,000 years ago, or has its origins much earlier.

It should also be noted that rich theologies of the Sabbath have been developed by modern scholars who are certainly not Young-Earth-Creationists. Karl Barth's treatment of the topic is extensive and profound.[59] Jürgen Moltmann's treatment is briefer but no less profound. Note his comment:

> The completion of creation through the peace of the sabbath distinguishes the view of the world as creation from the view of the world as nature; for nature is unremittingly fruitful and, though it has seasons and rhythms, knows no sabbath. It is the sabbath which blesses, sanctifies and reveals the world as God's creation.[60]

This scarcely exhausts the list of scholars who might be cited. Walter Brueggemann provides another and even more recent example.[61] Admittedly, those who believe in the binding obligation of the seventh-day Sabbath cannot follow such scholars in all they say on the topic. However, the theologies of Barth and Moltmann, and others, are enough to show that rejection of Young-Earth-Creationism does not automatically consign the Sabbath to irrelevance.

---

58. Simpson, "Genesis," 1:489.

59. Barth *Church Dogmatics*, III.1, 47–72. Brown, "Barth's Doctrine of the Sabbath," 409–25; Brown, "Doctrine of the Sabbath," 1–25.

60. Moltmann, *God in Creation*, 6.

61. Brueggemann, *Sabbath as Resistance*.

9.3 THEOLOGICAL RATIONALES FOR OLD-LIFE VIEWS

But what of other ways of reading the Genesis creation and Fall narratives than the often wooden literalness of Young-Earth-Creationism? There are, in fact, a number of alternative ways of understanding the texts, some involving more radical interpretations than others. Two attempts to harmonize Genesis 1 with modern science go back to the nineteenth century. These are the gap theory and the day-age theory.

9.3.1 Gap Theory

The gap theory suggests that two creations are referred to in Genesis 1. The first appears in verse one—the subsequent history of which is passed over in silence, except that it evidently ended in total destruction by a deluge alluded to in verse 2; the second, beginning with verse 2b (or 3),[62] is the Creation in six literal days about six thousand years ago of the world we now know. With an exegetical stroke, all the difficulties created by the fossil record, geology, and the age of the earth are swept away, consigned to that previous Creation, or at least that is the claim! However, this view suffers from the fatal flaw that it is entirely hypothetical. There is no supporting evidence for it at all—unless the truth of the theory is accepted *a priori*. Unless Genesis is accepted as a scientific view, the "water" in Gen 1:2 does not even need to be accounted for. If the chapter is viewed in literary, rather than scientific terms, the water is readily viewed as a symbol of chaos or, more radically, as a fragment of an underlying myth.[63]

---

62. The difference here hinges on whether or "Spirit of God hovering over the face of the waters" represents the beginning of God's creative activity or represents a further statement of the "chaos" of the prevailing flood of v. 2a. Note the different perspectives of von Rad, *Genesis*, 50–51 and Speiser, *Genesis*, 5.

63. Thus, Gerhard von Rad, referring to Genesis 1:2 says, "The declaration, then belongs completely to the description of chaos and does not yet lead into the creative activity . . . Thus this second verse speaks not only of a reality that once existed in a pre-primeval period but also of a possibility that always exists. Man has always suspected that behind all creation lies the abyss of formlessness; that all creation is always ready to sink into the abyss of the formless; that the chaos, therefore, signified simply the threat to everything created." See von Rad, *Genesis*, 49–51. Simpson notes, "The Hebrew word $t^ehôm$, rendered the deep, is the philological equivalent of Tiamat, the name borne by the personified chaos monster in the Babylonian creation myth (Simpson, "Genesis," 1:467). For a nuanced treatment of the relationship of the Genesis creation accounts to the ancient Near Eastern myths see Enns, *Inspiration and Incarnation*, 25–27, 39–41, 49–56.

9.3.2 Day-Age Theory

The day-age theory is likewise completely hypothetical, and even worse, does not lead to a coherent *literal* picture of Creation, despite the radical expediency it employs. The days of Creation are divided into "evening and morning" (day and night).[64] Are we to suppose that these are also long ages? It is difficult to imagine any *literal* reading whereby the plant life could be created long ages before the insects that were to pollinate it. Furthermore, the only biblical option for the length of the ages symbolized by these "days" is "a thousand years" (2 Pet 3:8), but that gets nowhere near the time periods suggested by science.[65] Virtually all that is left of the Genesis story on this account is that the order of Creation of the world and its various life forms is broadly similar to that postulated by science.[66] In fact, though, this parallel order is far from exact. A strictly literal reading of Genesis 1 would indicate that the sun, moon, and stars are younger than the earth (Gen 1:14–19); modern scientific cosmology would indicate the exact opposite.[67] The difficulties seem too insurmountable; the gains too meagre, for this option to be considered genuinely viable.

9.3.3 Days of Revelation

More recently, it has been suggested that the "days" of Genesis 1 are not "days of creation" but "days of revelation (about creation)."[68] Here, a key

---

64. Booth, "Days of Genesis 1," 104.

65. It should also be noted that although "day" can refer to an ill-defined era in Hebrew, as it can in English, there are no examples of this being the case in the Old Testament when that word is preceded by an ordinal number, as they are in Genesis 1. See Hasel, "'Days' of Creation," 40–68; Davidson, "Genesis Account of Origins," 78–79.

66. A good example of this type of outcome is found in Parker, *Genesis Enigma*.

67. Kline, "Space and Time."

68. Wiseman, *Creation Revealed*, 124–25; Ramm, *Science and Scripture*, 151–54. Such a view does not necessarily entail an old age for life on earth. It should be noted that the view espoused by Adventist apologist Frank L. Marsh is closely related to this position. Marsh argued that descriptions of the natural world in the Bible are given from the perspective of appearance on earth. Thus, the creation of light on the first day of creation indicates that light was first manifest on earth due presumably to the thinning of the dense cloud cover. (The cloud cover thinned sufficiently by day five for the source of that light to be seen. None of this suggested, for Marsh that the creation took longer than a literal week, some six thousand years ago. See Marsh, *Studies in Creationism*, 209–36, 127–54, 190–96.

issue is whether or not the Hebrew verb 'āśāh, usually translated "do" or "make" can be translated "show" in Exod 20:11, giving the reading "For in six days the Lord revealed..." Such a meaning is peripheral at best. It is true that the King James Versions renders 'āśāh as "shew" forty-four times. In the English Standard Version, the number of these verses translated in an explicitly visual and revelatory way reduces to twenty-five.[69] Even if it could be established that "show" was well within the semantic range of 'āśāh, it would still have to be shown that it was the most appropriate meaning to assign the word in Exod 20:11.[70]

9.3.4 A Sanctuary Parallel

Another non-literal reading of the Creation narratives sees them in terms of the Old Testament sanctuary—a view which Richard Davidson describes as "an emerging consensus among biblical scholars."[71] Kline refers to the earth as being much like the Mosaic tabernacle, which was "the earthly reproduction of the heavenly reality" (cf. Exod 25:40).[72] It may be instructive to note that in Rabbinic tradition, Exodus 35 begins with a prohibition of working on the Sabbath. This is followed by the directions for building and furnishing the tabernacle, which use the same word for "work." From the "work" mentioned in connection with the sanctuary, the Rabbis derived the thirty-nine categories of work prohibited on the Sabbath.[73] This binds the Sabbath, which culminates and celebrates the creation, closely with the sanctuary, and in effect brings the creation and the sanctuary close together.

On a "sanctuary" reading of the Creation account, the narratives are more symbolic than literal. The seven days may be understood as paralleling the seven speeches of Exod 25–31—each with its own introductory formula (Exod 25:1; 30:11; 30:17; 30:22; 30:34; 31:1; 31:12—giving

---

69. Gen 19:19; 24:12, 14; 32:10; Exod 20:6; Deut 5:10; Jud 6:17; 8:35; 1 Sam 15:6; 20:14; 2 Sam 2:5–6; 3:8; 9:1, 3, 7; 22:51; 1 Kgs 3:6; 16:27; 22:45; Ps 18:50; 86:17; 109:16; Jer 32:18; Zech 7:9. Even a casual reading of these verses makes it obvious that in many cases the "showing" is achieved by "doing."

70. Booth, "Days of Genesis 1," 113–14.

71. Davidson, "Earth's First Sanctuary," 65. Of course, seeing sanctuary allusions in the creation/fall account does not commit a person to a long life on earth position. (Davidson, himself, favors an old earth, young life creationist view). However, a non-literal reading of the account makes a long life on earth position much more tenable.

72. Kline, "Space and Time," 1996.

73. Jewett, *Lord's Day*, 19.

Theological Problems with Old-Age Models for Life

instructions for the building of the sanctuary and the establishment of the cult.[74] One of the strengths of this approach is that it is clear from the Old Testament itself that the language of the Creation narratives could certainly be used metaphorically. One example is found in Jer 4:23–26:

> [23] I looked on the earth, and behold, it was without form and void;
>   and to the heavens, and they had no light.
> [24] I looked on the mountains, and behold, they were quaking,
>   and all the hills moved to and fro.
> [25] I looked, and behold, there was no man,
>   and all the birds of the air had fled.
> [26] I looked, and behold, the fruitful land was a desert,
>   and all its cities were laid in ruins
> before the Lord, before his fierce anger.

The context here is the destruction of Judah and Jerusalem at the hands of the "foe from the north." This is clearly described in the language of "uncreation"—a return to a time when the land is formless and void, without light, human presence, or birds, or plants. This is certainly not to be understood literally, but metaphorically.[75] It should be noted that in certain inter-testamental Jewish writing, the children of Adam are sometimes identified specifically as the Israelites, who in this age are oppressed by the wild animals—the pagan nations—even though it was God's intention that Adam should rule over them (Gen 1:26–28; Ps 8:3–8), as Israel will in the future age.[76] Of course, this metaphorical use of language does not prove that the Creation narratives are also metaphorical, but it does demonstrate the possibility that they are.

The Genesis Creation narratives are admittedly not explicitly presented in temple cult language. Adam is not explicitly described as a priest, for example. However, unlike the gap and day-age theories, this approach is not entirely hypothetical. That there are parallels between these narratives and the Israelite temple/cultus is hard to deny. One of the clearest is found in the account of the Fall (Genesis 3), which cannot be separated from the

---

74. Kearney, "Creation and Liturgy," 119. See also Doukhan, "Creation," 58–59.

75. Another example might be found in Rev 9:2. Jon Paulien notes the certain verbal parallels in this verse to both Exod 19:18 and Gen 1:2. See Paulien "Revelation's Symbolism," 1: 88–89. If this is so, it is certainly not a literal, but rather a metaphorical meaning of the text that is intended.

76. Hooker, *Son of Man in Mark*, 11–71. Hooker provides data from books such as Daniel, 1 Enoch, 2 Esdras, Ecclesiasticus, Wisdom of Solomon, Jubilees and the Testaments of the Twelve Patriarchs.

second Creation account of Gen 2:4–31. The Fall narrative concludes by declaring, "He drove out the man, and at the east of the garden of Eden he placed the cherubim and a flaming sword that turned every way to guard the way to the tree of life" (Gen 3:24). Evidently there was only one point of access to the garden: from the east. This access was blocked by cherubim, beyond whom was the tree of life. Similarly, the Israelite tabernacle could only be entered from the east—with the worshipper's back to the rising sun (Exod 25:9–14; cf. Ez 47:1). The way into the Most Holy Place was blocked by a veil, in which were woven representations of cherubim (Exod 26:35). Indeed, "[t]he majority of OT passages mentioning cherubim refer to representations associated with the cult of the tabernacle or temple."[77] Inside the veil were Aaron's rod, which had budded, and a sample of the manna which had sustained Israel in the wilderness (Exod 16:32–4; Num 17:10–11; cf. Heb 9:4), both potent symbols of life.

9.3.5 Fall Upwards

Another approach that has been advanced towards the Creation/Fall narratives does not necessarily entail an old-life perspective but harmonizes with it easily. Charles Foster focuses attention on some antimonies in the narrative. He points, for example, to the fact that Adam is warned not to eat of the fruit of the tree of knowledge of good and evil, "for in the day you eat of it you shall surely die" (Gen 2:17). This did not, in fact, happen. They did not die on that day.[78] The serpent denies that death will ensue (Gen 3:4) and posits an alternative consequence: "you will be like God" (Gen 3:5). This was evidently the outcome: "Then the Lord God said, "Behold, the man has become like one of us in knowing good and evil" (Gen 3:22). Throughout the Fall narrative one recurring theme is the knowledge that Adam and Eve have in fact acquired by their action (Gen 3:5–7, 11, 22). Foster asks how this can be considered a "Fall" unless it is a "fall upwards"?[79]

---

77. Freedman and O'Connor, " כְּרוּב k^{e}rûb cherub," 7: 313.

78. Attempts have been made to reinterpret "die" in terms of "spiritual death" or in terms of "beginning the process" which inevitably leads to death. On the inadequacy of these attempts see LaRondelle, *Perfection and Perfectionism*, 92–98.

79. Foster, *Selfless Gene*, 209–18. In a way somewhat analogous to Foster, Bechtel describes Genesis 2 and 3 as a myth of human—both individual and societal—maturation. According to here, Gen 3:1–15 corresponds to adolescence with its burgeoning sexuality before the onset of human responsibilities of child bearing (Gen 3:16) and the physical labor entailed in providing for a family (Gen 3:17b–19). The human story, of course ends in death (Gen 3:19b). See Bechtel, "Gen 2:4b–3:34," 3–26.

There is no question that Foster's comments have some validity. Adam and Eve do acquire knowledge, and that knowledge ultimately flowers into the development of civilization outside the garden (Gen 4:17–27). The idea of a Fall upwards fits naturally with the idea of evolutionary development— a progression to "higher" forms. However, it is a view that grows out of a reading of a very narrow selection of texts. In the overall context of Genesis 3 and 4, the Fall is clearly a negative development. Death, unmentioned in the Creation narratives (except as a warning), becomes a pervasive theme (Gen 3:19, 22–24; 4:8; 15, 23, 25). This culminates in a situation where "the wickedness of man was great in the earth, and that every intention of the thoughts of his heart was only evil continually" (Gen 6:5). There is a clear emphasis on the "curse" that follows from the Fall. The serpent is cursed (Gen 3:14); the ground is cursed (Gen 3:17), so that although Adam is to continue to "subdue" the earth (Gen 1:28) this is now to be characterized by pain, thorns, thistles, and sweat (Gen 3:17–19), none of which had previously been mentioned. The mandate to "multiply and fill the earth" (Gen 1:28) remains but is now characterized by "pain in childbearing" (Gen 3:16).[80]

Thus, when viewing the entire context of the Fall narrative (and indeed the entire primeval history of Gen 1–11), Foster's views are less than compelling. The evidence to which he points in support of his position actually fits better with a model of "technological advance concurrent with moral decline." This accords well with a downward moral Fall, as it is traditionally understood, rather than suggesting a "Fall upwards."

9.3.6 Kenosis

A final theological model of Creation needs to be considered. Again, this does not necessarily entail an old Earth or a lengthy development of life on Earth, but it lends itself to such scenarios and has often been utilized by adherents to these views.[81] John Polkinghorne and others, extrapolating from Paul's comment on the incarnation, Christ "emptied" (Gr: κενόω; kenoō) himself (Phil 2:7), suggests that such a self-emptying (kenosis) is

---

80. Foster (*Selfless Gene*, 161) notes that such pain is due to the disproportionately large head of human babies. He suggests that this is directly related to the need for increased capacity to handle the vastly increased volume of knowledge humans were dealing with after the fall.

81. Peacocke strongly links biological evolution and a kenotic model of creation. See Peacocke, "Cost of New Life," 22–39.

characteristic of the entirety of God's dealing with the world.[82] The universe ("the heavens and the earth," Gen 1:1) was created *ex nihilo,* out of nothing. But since God was all that there was before the Creation of the universe, he occupied all "space."[83] Given this, he would have had to "empty himself" to create a "nothing" in which to create the universe.[84]

This suggestion has the virtue of binding Creation and Redemption—two great works of God—closely together.[85] However, it has been pointed out that this model fits more closely with a pantheistic understanding of God than it does with a monotheistic or trinitarian model. Indeed, Foster—who is not overly impressed with the value of the kenotic model—declares that it may be "very useful for anyone trying to build bridges between Western Christian thought and the wisdom of the East."[86] These objections may well be true, but the model does not require a pantheistic theology, and Moltmann explicitly repudiates "a pantheistic dissolution of Creation into God."[87]

The kenotic model of Creation lends itself naturally to an understanding of God as not dominating nature and superseding natural laws and processes in creation. God has emptied himself in order to "create" a nothing in which natural laws and processes can operate rather than his supernatural power. As Moltmann puts it:

> It is only a withdrawal by God into himself that can free the space into which God can act creatively. The *nihil* for his *creatio ex nihilo* only comes into being because—and in as far as—the omnipotent and omnipresent God withdraws his presence and restricts his power."[88]

This freely chosen self-limiting of God in relation to nature means that God granted "freedom" to nature and respected its processes. From here, it is a small, perhaps inevitable step to an old earth and evolutionary processes.

---

82. A helpful selection of material from a range of authors utilizing this perspective is found in the book, *The Work of Love: Creation as Kenosis,* edited by John Polkinghorne.

83. Finding adequate language to describe the state of affairs then existing is difficult. Our language, including "time," "space" and even "state of affairs," presupposes the situation of a universe existing in time and space.

84. Moltmann, *God in Creation,* 87–88.

85. Barbour, "God's Power," 8–9.

86. Foster, *Selfless Gene,* 176.

87. Moltmann, *God in Creation,* 89.

88. Moltmann, *God in Creation,* 86–87.

Theological Problems with Old-Age Models for Life

One might counter that this sounds more like deism than orthodox theism. Indeed, Thomas Oord's summary of Moltmann's view has a distinctly deist flavor: "According to him, God is literally not omnipotent, not omnipresent, and not omniscient. This God distances himself from the world. In short, the God that Moltmann envisions runs half-throttle and from afar so that creatures can find the space to exist."[89] Such criticism certainly has validity, but more needs to be said. Christians have always acknowledged a certain "hands off-ness" on the part of God in relation to the world. This is particularly evident in the free will apology concerning the existence of evil and pain in the world. This "is not usually criticized for implying that God is not involved with humanity. Likewise, 'the free-process defense' need not imply God's non-involvement with the rest of creation."[90] Christians have increasingly come to recognize that looking for the activity of God solely in the supernatural is misguided. This leads inexorably to a "God of the gaps," whose domain shrinks with each new scientific advance.[91] This is true whether one thinks of miracles, providence, history, or the question of Origins. God works *within* nature and not just *above* it.[92] This realization is not confined to "deists" but is found among orthodox theists also.[93]

---

89. Oord, "Creation and Kenotic Love."

90. Bimson, "Cosmic Fall," 78.

91. Robinson, *New Reformation?* 107; Huxley, *Religion without Revelation*, 47–64.

92. Bull and Guy, "Then a Miracle Occurs," 67. This is a principle that can be and has been applied in a wide variety of areas beyond science. Christian historians may point to God acting in the realm of history, by which they mean the normal ebb and flow of historical events. Would the plagues on Egypt (Exod 7:14–12:32) necessarily be any less the work of God on behalf of Israel if they were susceptible to natural explanation? See Anderson, *Living World of the Old Testament*, 59–62. Or would the defeat of Sennacherib's army at Jerusalem (2 Kgs 19:35; 2 Chr 32:21; Isa 37:36) necessarily be any less the work of God if it was brought about by an outbreak of mouse-borne disease, or other historical occurrence? See Gray, *I & II Kings*, 630; Clement, *Deliverance of Jerusalem*, 9–27; and Childs, *Isaiah and the Assyrian Crisis*, 11–19. Lewis suggests that even the experience of God occurs within the normal experiences of life rather than being radically separated from them. He declares that ". . . it is in the human experience as it normally occurs, in the ups and downs of life, in moral struggle and failure, in art and intellectual pursuits, in personal and social relationship, in all that normally makes up human life and history, that religious experience usually forms itself and takes a course of its own." See Lewis, *Our Experience of God*, 213. Of course, none of this should suggest that God can never work beyond the normal and the natural, only that the usual realm of his activity is the normal and natural.

93. Of course, it may be that in the process, theism has commandeered some of the strengths of deism. This ought not to surprise us, as any encounter with opposing ideas always leaves an ideas-based movement marked and changed by the encounter.

A further objection to this suggestion is concerned with eschatology. If God created using natural processes because he respected the integrity of those processes, and as a result took millions of years of evolutionary time, does the same process take place in regard to the eschatological "new heavens and new earth" (Rev 22:1)? Does this not push the eschatological hope into the almost inconceivable future?

This view appears to have a certain plausibility. But several things can be said in response. First, it must be recognized that "time" functions differently for God than it does for us. The Bible is clear that for God, a thousand years is as a day and a day as a thousand years (2 Pet 3:8). We might think that even 6,000 years of sin on earth is more than could possibly be needed to resolve issues of the great controversy. Surely there doesn't need to be more than 2,000 years between the cross and the eschaton? Evidently, God disagrees.

Secondly, why does the fact that God created in one way with the current cosmos mean that the new heavens and new earth must be created the same way? The new earth is a restored paradise—but it is not exactly the same. The Bible starts with a garden and ends with a city! Adam and Eve are commanded to "be fruitful and multiply," but after the resurrection, the redeemed are said to be like the angels, neither marrying nor giving in marriage (Matt 22:30). Even in the current creation, God's love of diversity is evident. There are myriads of species of plants, animals, birds, and insects, exhibiting a tremendous diversity of colors, structures, and life cycles. Humans are differentiated from other animals as uniquely made in the image of God (Gen 1:26–27). If God created this world in such a way as to produce such diversity, on what basis can it be insisted that he will certainly create the next world in exactly the same way? Does not the sovereignty of God mean that he is free to create the new world in a different way, and a different time frame if he so chooses?

Lastly, even if the new heavens and new earth are created with the same respect for natural processes, would that really push the eschaton to the distant future? The best basis for thinking so is to understand John 14:1 as pointing to the beginning of the process. However, this is an unwarranted assumption. The "going away" of Jesus and the "preparation" he undertakes refers primarily to his death on the cross.[94] Since the redeemed are written in the Lamb's book of life from the foundation of the world (Rev 17:8), there is no logical or scriptural reason why the preparation of the new earth could not have begun when the creation of the natural world

---

94. Dodd, *Interpretation of the Fourth Gospel*, 403–9.

occurred. Indeed, some of the major differences between the natural world and the new world appear to be derived from the fact that the heavenly city descends on this world and God will then dwell with his people on the new earth. This means that much of the new earth could be as ancient as our current world.

9.4. CONCLUSION

Issues associated with the age of life on Earth have generated considerable heat in theological circles. Young-Earth-Creationists rail against those more sympathetic to old-life perspectives, either evolutionary or ancient Creationist, and vice versa. But all positions and arguments on both sides of the debate have ragged edges and loose threads. No stance has all the answers, and attempts to force thinking into too neat a rational system, devoid of sufficient humility, are bound to be inadequate. It is also worth remembering in closing that despite the heat sometimes generated, there are still tremendous amounts of agreement between the two perspectives. It is worth reiterating these commonalities.

It is true that some Christians, like Michael Dowd, whose "creatheism" is more pantheistic than orthodox Christian theistic, have no interest in reconciling the Creation narrative with science.[95] Indeed, Dowd makes it clear that his starting point is science rather than Scripture.[96] However, for those more interested in being authentically "biblical" in their views, there are major points on which consensus could be built. Consider some of the most important of these:

1. God is the creator of heaven and earth. This doctrine is native to the Judaeo-Christian traditions. It is so important in those traditions that one cannot claim to be an orthodox Christian without affirming it.
2. This world is the world God created.
3. The world we experience is badly broken. That brokenness is comprehensive, regardless of whether we view the world horizontally (i.e., wherever we look in the world today), or historically (i.e., regardless of how far we are able to go back in history). The brokenness of the world entails more than individuals. It encompasses social, political, and economic structures as well.

---

95. Dowd, *Thank God for Evolution*, 131.
96. Dowd, *Thank God for Evolution*, 142.

4. A good God would not have created a world as broken as this world now is. The world we live in has "fallen" from the state it was in when it was created by God.

5. The creator God has not left the world to its own fate but sent Christ to effect salvation.

6. God's will for salvation will ultimately come to fruition.

7. The position of the Sabbath in the Creation narrative suggests its universality of application as well as foreshadowing the final redemption of humanity on a renewed earth.

BIBLIOGRAPHY

Anderson, Arnold A. *Psalms (1-72)*. Grand Rapids: Eerdmans, 1972.
Anderson, Bernard W. *The Living World of the Old Testament*. 3rd ed. Harrow: Longman, 1978.
Anderson, George W. "The Psalms." In *Peake's Commentary on the Bible*. Revised ed., edited by Matthew Black and H. H. Rowley, 409-43. London: Thomas Nelson, 1962.
Aune, David E. *Revelation*. Dallas: Word, 1988.
Baker, Lynne Rudder. *Persons and Bodies: A Constitution View*. Cambridge: Cambridge University Press, 2000.
Baldwin, John T. "Revelation 14:7: An Angel's Worldview." In *Creation, Catastrophe and Calvary: Why a Global Flood is Vital to the Doctrine of the Atonement*, edited by John T. Baldwin, 19-39. Silver Springs, MD: Review and Herald, 2000.
Barbour, Ian G. "God's Power: A Process View." In *The Work of Love: Creation as Kenosis*, edited by John Polkinghorne, 1-20. Grand Rapids: Eerdmans, 2001.
Barr, James. *The Garden of Eden and the Hope of Immortality*. Minneapolis: Fortress, 1992.
Barth, Karl. *Church Dogmatics*. Edinburgh: T & T Clarke, 1932-67.
Batten, Don, et al. *The Answer Book*. Updated and Expanded. Acacia Ridge: Answers in Genesis, 2003.
Beale, Greg K. *The Book of Revelation*. Grand Rapids: Eerdmans, 1999.
Bechtel, Lyn M. "Gen 2:4b-3:34: A Myth about Human Maturation." *Journal for the Study of the Old Testament* 67 (1995) 3-26.
Bimson, John J. "Reconsidering a 'Cosmic Fall.'" *Science and Christian Belief* 18 (2006) 63-81.
Booth, Walter M. "Days of Genesis 1: Literal or Nonliteral?" *Journal of the Adventist Theological Society* 14 (2003) 101-20.
Brown, James. "The Doctrine of the Sabbath in Karl Barth's *Church Dogmatics*," *Scottish Journal of Theology* 20 (1967) 1-25.
———. "Karl Barth's Doctrine of the Sabbath." *Scottish Journal of Theology* 19 (1966) 409-25.
Brueggemann, Walter. *Sabbath as Resistance: Saying NO to the Culture of NOW*. Louisville: Westminster/John Knox, 2014.

Brunner, Emil. *The Christian Doctrine of Creation and Redemption.* Philadelphia: Westminster, 1952.

Bull, Brian S., and Fritz Guy, "Then a Miracle Occurs." In *Understanding Genesis: Contemporary Adventist Perspectives,* edited by Brian Bull, et al., 53–69. Riverside, CA: Adventist Today Foundation, 2006.

Caird, George B. *The Revelation of St. John the Divine.* New York: Harper and Row, 1966.

Childs, Brevard S. *Isaiah and the Assyrian Crisis.* Naperville, IL: Alec C. Allenson, 1967.

Clement, R. E. *Isaiah and the Deliverance of Jerusalem: A Study of the Interpretation of Prophecy in the Old Testament.* Sheffield: JSOT, 1980.

Coffen, Richard W. "Whom did Cain Marry?" *Adventist Today* (Winter, 2011) 6–9.

Cole, H. Ross. "The Sabbath and Genesis 2:1–3." *Andrews University Seminary Studies* 41 (2003) 5–12.

Copan, Paul, and William Lane Craig. *Creation out of Nothing: A Biblical, Philosophical and Scientific Exploration.* Grand Rapids: Baker, 2004.

Davidson, Richard M. "The Creation Theme in Psalm 104." In *The Genesis Creation Account and its Reverberations in the Old Testament,* edited by Gerald A. Klingbeil, 149–88. Berrien Springs, MI: Andrews University Press, 2015.

———. "Earth's First Sanctuary: Genesis 1–3 and Parallel Creation Accounts." *Andrews University Seminary Studies* 53 (2015) 65–89.

———. "The Genesis Account of Origins." In *The Genesis Creation Account and its Reverberations in the Old Testament,* edited by Gerald A. Klingbeil, 59–129. Berrien Springs, MI: Andrews University Press, 2015.

Diamond, Jared. *Why is Sex Fun? The Evolution of Human Sexuality.* London: Phoenix, 1997.

Dodd, Charles H. *The Interpretation of the Fourth Gospel.* Cambridge: Cambridge University Press, 1953.

Doukhan, Jacques. "Creation." In *The Future of Adventism: Theology, Society, Experience,* edited by Gary Chartier, 49–66. Ann Arbor, MI: Griffin & Lash, 2015.

Dowd, Michael. *Thank God for Evolution.* New York: Penguin, 2007.

Dressler, Harold P. "The Sabbath in the Old Testament." In *From Sabbath to Lord's Day,* edited by Donald A. Carson, 21–41. Grand Rapids: Zondervan, 1982.

Dumbrell, William J. *Creation and Covenant: A Theology of Old Testament Covenants.* Carlisle: Paternoster, 1984.

Enns, Peter. *Inspiration and Incarnation: Evangelicals and the Problem of the Old Testament.* Grand Rapids: Baker, 2005.

Faro, Ingrid. "The Question of Evil and Animal Death Before the Fall." *Trinity Journal* n.s. 36 (2015) 1–21.

Foster, Charles. *The Selfless Gene: Living with God and Darwin.* London: Hodder and Stoughton, 2009.

Freedman, David Noel, and Michael P. O'Connor. " כְּרוּב kerûb cherub." In *Theological Dictionary of the Old Testament,* edited by G. Johannes Botterweck, et al., 7: 307–19. Grand Rapids: Eerdmans, 1995.

Gage, Warren Austin. *The Gospel in Genesis: Studies in Protology and Eschatology.* Eugene, OR: Wipf and Stock, 2001.

Giberson, Karl. *Saving the Original Sinner: How Christians have Used the Bible's First Man to Oppress, Inspire and Make Sense of the World.* Boston: Beacon, 2015.

Goldstein, Clifford. *Baptizing the Devil: Evolution and the Seduction of Christianity.* Nampa, ID: Pacific, 2017.

Gray, John. *I & II Kings*. London: SCM, 1964.
Grudem, Wayne. *Systematic Theology: An Introduction to Biblical Doctrine*. Leicester: Inter-Varsity, 1994.
Hasel, Gerhard F. "The 'Days' of Creation in Genesis 1: Literal 'Days' or Figurative 'Periods/Epochs' of Time?" In *Creation, Catastrophe and Calvary*, edited by John T. Baldwin, 40–68. Hagerstown, MD: Review and Herald, 2000.
———. "The Sabbath in the Pentateuch." In *The Sabbath in Scripture and History*, edited by Kenneth A. Strand, 21–45. Washington, DC: Review and Herald, 1982.
Hooker, Morna D. *The Son of Man in Mark: A Study of the Background of the Term "Son of Man" and its Use in St Mark's Gospel*. Montreal: McGill University Press, 1967.
Huxley, Julian. *Religion without Revelation*. London: Max Parrish, 1957.
Irons, Lee. "Animal Death Before the Fall: What Does the Bible Say?" *Reasons to Believe*. https://reasons.org/explore/publications/articles/animal-death-before-the-fall-what-does-the-bible-say.
Jewett, Paul King. *The Lord's Day: A Theological Guide to the Christian Day of Worship*. Grand Rapids: Eerdmans, 1971.
Kearney, Peter J. "Creation and Liturgy: The P Redaction of Ex 25–40." In *Cult and Cosmos: Tilting Towards a Temple-Centred Theology*, edited by L. Michael Morales, 119–32. Leuven: Peeters, 2014. Original *Zeitschrift für die alttestamentliche Wissenschaft (ZAW)* 89 (1977) 375–86.
Kline, Meredith G. "Because it Had Not Rained." *Westminster Theological Journal* 20 (1958) 146–57.
———. "Death, Leviathan, and Martyrs: Isaiah 24:1–27:1." In *A Tribute to Gleason Archer*, edited by Walter C. Kaiser Jr and Ronald R. Youngblood, 229–49. https://meredithkline.com/klines-articles-and-essays/death-leviathan-and-martyrs-Isaiah24.
———. "Space and Time in the Genesis Cosmogony." *Perspectives on Science and Christian Faith* 48 (1996) 2–15. https:// meredithkline.com/klines-works/articles-and-essays/space-and-time-in-the-genesis-cosmogony.
Kraus, Hans-Joachim. *Psalm 1–59: A Commentary*. Minneapolis: Augsburg, 1988.
Kselman John S., and Michael L. Barré. "Psalms." In *Jerome Biblical Commentary*, edited by Raymond E. Brown, et al., 523–52. Englewood Cliffs, NJ: Prentice Hall, 1968.
Lacey, Troy. "Animal Death Before the Fall?" *Answers in Genesis* (2020). https://answersingenesis.org/death-before-sin/animal-death-before-the-fall/.
Lane, Anthony N. S. "Irenaeus on the Fall and Original Sin." In *Darwin, Creation and the Fall: Theological Challenges*, edited by Robert J. (Sam) Berry and Thomas A. Noble, 130–48. Nottingham: Apollos, 2009.
LaRondelle, Hans K. *Perfection and Perfectionism*. Berrien Springs, MI: Andrews University Press, 1971.
Lee, Francis N. *The Covenantal Sabbath: The Weekly Sabbath Scripturally and Historically Considered*. London: Lord's Day Observance Society, n.d.
Lewis, Hywel D. *Our Experience of God*. London: George Allen & Unwin, 1959.
Marsh, Frank L. *Studies in Creationism*. Washington, DC: Review and Herald, 1950.
Michaels, J. Ramsay. "The Redemption of our Body: The Riddle of Romans 8:19–22." In *Romans and the People of God: Essays in Honor of Gordon D. Fee on the Occasion of his 65th Birthday*, edited by Sven K. Soderlund and N. T. Wright, 92–114. Grand Rapids: Eerdmans, 1999.

Moltmann, Jürgen. *God in Creation: A New Theology of Creation and the Spirit of God*. San Francisco, CA: Harper and Row, 1985.

Mounce, Robert H. *The Book of Revelation*. Grand Rapids: Eerdmans, 1977.

Nichol, Francis D. "The Increasing Timeliness of the Threefold Message." In *Our Firm Foundation*, 1: 565-73, 616-18. Washington, DC: Review and Herald, 1953.

Oord, Thomas. "Creation and Kenotic Love: A Descriptive and Critical Review." Metanexus (2002). https://www.metanesus.net/creation-and-kenotic-love-descriptive-and-critcal-review/.

Parker, Andrew. *The Genesis Enigma: Why the Bible is Scientifically Accurate*. London: Black Swan, 2009.

Paulien, Jon. "Interpreting Revelation's Symbolism." In *Symposium on Revelation*, edited by Frank B. Holbrook, 1: 73-97. Silver Springs, MD: Biblical Research Institute, 1992.

Peacocke, Arthur. "The Cost of New Life." In *The Work of Love: Creation as Kenosis*, edited by John Polkinghorne, 22-39. Grand Rapids: Eerdmans, 2001.

Pennock, Robert T. *The Tower of Babel: The Evidence against the New Creationism*. Cambridge: MIT Press, 2000.

Polkinghorne, John, ed. *The Work of Love: Creation as Kenosis*. Grand Rapids: Eerdmans, 2001.

Ramm, Bernard. *The Christian View of Science and Scripture*. Grand Rapids: Eerdmans, 1954.

Robinson, John A. T. *A New Reformation?* London: SCM, 1965.

Rondet, Henri. *Original Sin: The Patristic and Theological Background*. Shannon: Ecclesia, 1972.

Schadewald, Robert J. "The Flat-Earth Bible." *Bulletin of the Tychonian Society* 44 (1985). www.ic.uincampt.br/~stolfi/misc/misc/FlatEarth/FlatEarthAndBible.htiml.

Scott, Eugenie C. "The Creation/Evolution Continuum." *National Center for Science Education* (2016). https://ncse.ngo/creationevolution-continuum.

Simpson, Cuthbert A. "Genesis: Introduction and Exegesis." In *The Interpreter's Bible*, edited by George A. Buttrick, 1: 436-829. Nashville: Abingdon, 1952.

Speiser, E. A. *Genesis*. 3rd ed. Garden City, NY: Doubleday, 1982.

Stefanovic, Ranko. *Revelation of Jesus Christ: Commentary on the Book of Revelation*. Berrien Springs, MI: Andrews University Press, 2002.

Taylor, William A., and W. Steward McCullough. "The Psalms: Exegesis." In *Interpreter's Bible*, edited by George A. Buttrick, 4:17-763. Nashville: Abingdon, 1955.

Tonstad, Sigve K. *The Lost Meaning of the Seventh Day*. Berrien Springs, MI: Andrews University Press, 2009.

Turner, Laurence. "The Rainbow as the Sign of the Covenant in Genesis IX 11-13." *Vetus Testamentum* 43 (1993) 119-24.

Turpin, Simon. "Did Death of Any Kind exist before the Fall? What the Bible Says about the Origins of Death and Suffering." *Answers Research Journal* 6 (2013) 99-116.

Vawter, Bruce. "The Fall." In *A New Dictionary of Christian Theology*, edited by Alan Richardson and John Bowden, 209. London: SCM, 1983.

von Rad, Gerhard. *Genesis*. Revised ed. London: SCM, 1972.

Weber, Martin. *Millenimania*. Silver Spring, MD: Ministerial Association of the General Conference, 1998.

Weiser, Artur. *Psalms*. Philadelphia: Westminster, 1962.

Westermann, Claus. *Genesis 1-11*. London: SPCK, 1984.

———. *Isaiah 40–66*. London: SCM, 1969.
Whybray, R. Norman. *Isaiah 40–66*. Grand Rapids: Eerdmans, 1981.
Wiseman, P. J. *Creation Revealed in Six Days*. London: Marshall, Morgan and Scott, 1956.
Younker, Randall W., and Richard M. Davidson, "The Myth of the Solid Heavenly Dome: Another Look at the Hebrew רָקִיעַ (rāqîaʿ [set ayin])." In *The Genesis Creation Account and its Reverberations in the Old Testament*, edited by Gerald A. Klingbeil, 31–56. Berrien Springs, MI: Andrews University Press, 2015. Reprinted from *Andrews University Seminary Studies* 49 (2011) 125–47.
Zinke, Ed. "Theistic Evolution: Implications for the Role of Creation in Seventh-day Adventist Theology." In *Creation, Catastrophe and Calvary: Why a Global Food is Vital to the Doctrine of the Atonement*, edited by John T. Baldwin, 159–71. Silver Springs, MD: Review and Herald, 2000.

10

Can a Seventh-day Adventist Hold Non-Traditional Views of Origins?

David Thiele

10.1 INTRODUCTION

In addressing the topic of whether or not a Seventh-day Adventist can hold non-traditional views of Origins, there are some preliminary matters that must be addressed briefly. There are two fairly obvious and rather silly approaches that need to be dismissed.

First, it may be said that since there are Seventh-day Adventists who hold non-traditional views of Origins, it must be possible to do so. This is akin to the response of some when Donald Trump was accused of being unpresidential: "He's the president and if he is doing something, it must, by definition, be presidential." End of argument. This reduces the topic at hand to a tautology.

The second view is the polar opposite of the first. It says in effect, "Since a Seventh-day Adventist is defined by the statement of twenty-eight Fundamental Beliefs, and since one of those beliefs specifies a traditional view of Origins, then by definition an Adventist cannot hold to non-traditional views on Origins." This elevates the Fundamentals to the level of a creed when, in fact, they are meant to be descriptive, not prescriptive.[1] This

---

1. The fuller statement of the Adventist baptismal vow includes the question "Knowing and understanding the fundamental Bible principles as taught in the Scriptures, is it your purpose, by the grace of God, to order your life in harmony with these principles?"

view also ignores the fact that the statements of Fundamentals are voted on after sometimes vigorous debate at General Conference sessions. Almost inevitably, according to the nature of this process, there are some who vote no—sometimes a sizeable minority.

Neither of these approaches is a serious answer to the question posed here. So, what is intended? Is it logically possible to retain a coherent system of beliefs that is recognizably Adventist, if one holds to non-traditional views of Origins? This way of putting the issue may be somewhat imprecise, but I think it is serviceable enough.

10.2 A SPECTRUM OF POSITIONS

There is another issue to consider before proceeding. It is customary to express the alternatives to non-traditional views of Origins in starkly dualistic terms—creation or evolution. But, in reality, it is much more complex than that. Modifying a diagram provided by Eugenie Scott gives the following spectrum of views on Origins (relevant to the age of life issue), and this could probably be made more comprehensive.[2] This is shown in Figure 10.1. Scott divided her chart into those views that assume a young Earth and those that assume an old Earth. (She saw a clear progression in the degree of biblical literalism involved: maximal for Flat Earthism to effectively non-existent for naturalistic evolution). I have added a position on the borderline of this division: that common Adventist view of an old Earth/universe, but a recent creation of life on Earth. (The only other change of substance was to divide Scott's rather unfortunately named category of "Atheistic Evolution" into "Punctuated Equilibrium" and "Neo-Darwinism").

The alternative baptismal vow introduced in 2005 has as one of its three questions, "Do you accept the teachings of the Bible as expressed in the Statement of Fundamental Beliefs of the Seventh-day Adventist Church and do you pledge by God's grace to live your life in harmony with these teachings?" This would appear to move the Fundamental Beliefs to a more credal position, despite the church's long-established antipathy to creeds. Whether or not it is, in fact, credal depends on precisely how strictly it is read and understood.

2. Scott, "Creation/Evolution Continuum."

Seventh-Day Adventist, Non-Traditional Views?

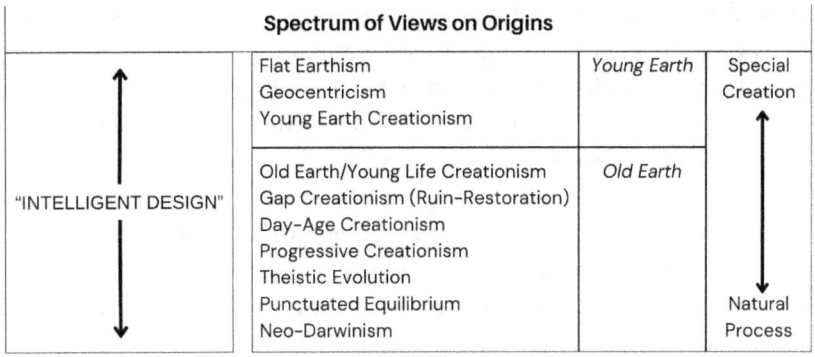

Figure 10.1 Spectrum of views on Origins.

The key designations in this chart require at least brief explanations. *The Flat Earth* view, as its name suggests, argues that the world is a flat disc, rather than a sphere.[3] Some, at least, accept that this earth is covered by a dome (firmament) into which the heavenly bodies are embedded. This view was common in the Ancient Near East. However, ancient Greek thinkers argued convincingly that the world was a globe. Edward Grant notes that "The earth's sphericity was a basic truth of Aristotle's system of the world... So reasonable were Aristotle's arguments that a spherical earth was readily accepted."[4] Indeed, another Greek, Eratosthenes of Cyrene, calculated the diameter of the Earth with startling accuracy.[5] Contrary to popular myth, the vast majority of people in the Middle Ages did not believe the earth was flat.[6] However, flat-Earth views are experiencing something of a resurgence today, even if they are still well outside the mainstream of modern thought.

Geocentrists insist that the earth, whether conceived of as a disc or a sphere, was created by fiat as the immovable center of the universe (or at least of the solar system). For them, the sun literally moves across the sky in the course of a day. Although they accepted a recent creation of the universe, it was this arrangement of the earth and sun that Copernicus and Galileo challenged.

Young-Earth-Creationism, in its purest form, insists on a recent creation of the universe, including Earth and life upon it, in a period of six

---

3. Variants include concave or convex surfaces, as well as squares instead of discs (accounting for the "four corners" of the earth).
4. Grant, *Foundations of Modern Science,* 57–58.
5. Goldstein, "'Measurement' of the Earth," 411–16.
6. Alexander, *Rebuilding the Matrix,* 24.

literal days.[7] This is generally thought of as having taken place six thousand years ago, although that chronology is often extended to ten or twenty thousand years, but rarely longer than that. Certainly, a period of hundreds of thousands, or millions, of years is absolutely rejected. A more moderate variation of this model moves the focus from the universe to the earth and its environs, perhaps to as much as the solar system, which is then seen as having been created *in toto* about six thousand years ago in six literal days.

A further variant is old Earth/young life creationism ("soft gap" creationism), which holds that the material universe, including Earth, was created in the long-distant past, but life on Earth in all its forms was created in a six-day period in the recent past, conveniently designated as "six thousand years" but often thought of as being somewhat longer.[8] In recent decades, this view has become relatively common among Adventists but is rare outside that church. It is, in effect, a version of the older gap theory mentioned below, but places the gap between Gen 1:2 and 1:3 rather than between Gen 1:1 and 1:2. It is important to note that only these first three options subscribe to a young age for earthly life.

The Gap Theory (in classical form, the ruin-restoration theory), dating back to the early nineteenth century, suggests that the world as we know it and the life forms with which we are familiar today were created in the relatively recent past in a six-day period. However, Gen 1:1—"In the beginning God created the heavens and the earth"—refers to the creation of the universe in the long distant past. The fact that Gen 1:2 indicates that at the time of the creation of our world, it was formless and void and covered with water is taken to indicate that this world had had a previous iteration that had been destroyed by a worldwide flood. It is to this previous iteration of the world that the fossils testify. There is, in short, a world history from creation to destruction to be located in the gap between Gen 1:1 and

---

7. Östring, "Miraculous Planet Earth," 6–10.

8. Lynden Rogers has outlined some of the conceptual and scientific inconsistencies with this approach (Rogers, "Old Universe but Young Life?" 6–22). Young-earth creationist, Don Batten, criticized Rogers' view, claiming that "The soft gap, like the older gap idea, does not solve anything anyway." ("'Soft' Gap Sophistry," 44–47.)

Gen 1:2.[9] Some versions of the gap theory allow for more than one cycle of ruin-restoration.[10]

Day-age Creationism, also dating back to the nineteenth century, attempts to harmonize science and the creation narrative by suggesting that each of the days of creation represents a long period of time. Adherents of this approach utilize varying degrees of literalness in their reading of the creation event on each of the days.

Progressive Creationism attributes the creation to God's intervention but suggests that God did not complete this in a single week. Rather, the creation was accomplished in stages over vast eras of time.

Theistic Evolution argues that life forms developed on Earth over a long period through a process of evolution, as science has suggested—with the qualification that God guided this process, perhaps by building this inevitability into natural law at a deep and previously unsuspected level and/or by intervening in it at various crucial points.

Punctuated Equilibrium, an hypothesis developed by Niles Eldredge and Stephen Jay Gould, accepts a long history of life on Earth.[11] However, unlike classical Darwinian theory, it does not accept that life forms developed through an incremental process of micro-changes which, when accumulated, amount to macro-changes. The history of life forms on Earth is seen to have a pattern of long periods of stability (equilibrium), interrupted ("punctuated") by periods of rapid change.[12] However, it should be noted that by "rapid change," Gould means rapid in terms of the geological time scale rather than the ecological one.[13]

Neo-Darwinism, represented ably today by Richard Dawkins, represents a modern restatement of Darwin's original theory that the diversity of life comes about through gradual change in response to changes in the

---

9. Ruin-restoration proponents cite Isa 45:18 (God originally created good, not chaos); Eze 28:13 (God created Satan as the most noble of his creatures and placed him in Eden); Jer. 4:23–26 (describing a time when the earth was formless and void after life on earth had been destroyed); 2 Pet 3:5–7 (interpreted by some gap theorists as describing the destruction of the original created earth by flood, not the Noachian flood, as the passage is interpreted by young-earth creationists).

10. See, for example, Galusha, *Fossils and the Word of God*, cited in McIver, "Formless and Void," 1–24.

11. The initial publication on this topic was Eldredge and Gould, "Punctuated Equilibria," 82–115.

12. See, for example, Gould, *Wonderful Life*.

13. Sterelny, *Darwin vs. Gould*, 75.

environment.[14] The "fittest," that is, those most able to cope with and thrive in the environment, have a survival and reproduction advantage. Adjustments to the environment may be gradual but accumulate over time to the extent that this results in the diversification of species and ultimately the vast variety of life forms seen both today and in the world of the past.[15]

The final term to be noted is "*Intelligent Design*," which, in its most general form, insists that the universe shows unmistakable signs of design. The "argument from design" has a long history in philosophy. However, the great diversity of meaning that can be encompassed by the term "Intelligent Design" limits its usefulness. Traditionally, the argument from design pointed to the complexity of what was known of the world and/or universe. More recently, it has been used to highlight what is, as yet, inexplicable in the world/universe. As a purportedly scientific theory, the modern version of "Intelligent Design" does not speak of a Creator and is capable of covering a considerable range of ideas. Many, but not all, adherents are fundamentalist Christians. Most, but again, not all, believe in a recent creation. Thus, it has been dismissed by some as "creationism in a cheap tuxedo."[16] Indeed, as Robert Pennock points out, the very concept of "design" is so amorphous that "natural selection" could theoretically be accepted as the design mechanism.[17] It follows that in theory at least, "Intelligent Design"—in some form or another—could be fitted in at any point on the chart.

10.3 LIMITATIONS OF KNOWLEDGE

Undoubtedly, there is biblical evidence that can be adduced for geocentrism. (For that matter, there are texts in the Bible that can be read to support a flat-Earth position. The earth is described in Isa 11:12 and Rev

---

14. This restatement takes note of and makes use of advances in genetics made since Darwin's time, and as such is distinct from Darwin's original theory. See "Neo-Darwinism."

15. See, for example, Dawkins and Wong, *Ancestor's Tale*.

16. Melott, "Intelligent Design," 48–50. A more positive evaluation of modern argument from "intelligent design" by an author who in other regards holds to a somewhat similar position to that expressed in this paper can be found in Hoehn, "Greater Controversy," 14–21.

17. Pennock, "Creationism and Intelligent Design," 154. Note also this comment from another author: "With fundamental elements, we can conceive of the world as being *constructed*, whether the Constructor be an active God or the more passive Laws of Nature. A constructed world implies order and design. And the faint suggestion of an intelligence behind that order." Lightman, *Searching for Stars*, 56.

7:1 as having four corners and in Isa 40:22 as having a tent-like canopy spread over it). The earth is declared to be unmovable (Ps 93:1), and the sun "stands still" only by divine intervention (Josh 10:12–13). Adventists have generally found ways to read Scripture that justify non-literal conclusions from such texts without our faith or theology unraveling. But prior to Copernicus (1473–1543) and Galileo (1564–1642) geocentrism was the standard view held by Christians. Luther is widely reputed to have said of Copernicus, "This fool wants to turn the whole art of astronomy upside down."[18] Had Adventism been born in the sixteenth century instead of the nineteenth century, we could have been discussing a different topic: "Can a Seventh-day Adventist hold heliocentric views"? But this denomination was born in the shadow of Darwin's scientific revolution, not that of Copernicus, and so has struggled to deal with the implications of this instead. Such is still the case.

The entire spectrum of views on Origins is theoretically open for Christians to endeavor to incorporate into their theology. Obviously, all the "Young-Earth" views, along with "old earth/young life" and "gap creationism" (ruin-restoration), may be immediately seen as compatible with Christian theology because they all purport to entail a literal reading of Scripture. Similarly, the next three views, which incorporate the words "creationism" or "theistic" into their name, despite their unpalatability for some, are also obviously options for incorporation into a theological schema. The last two options, however, are less obviously available. Both punctuated equilibrium and neo-Darwinism purport to be purely naturalistic theories. However, it is at least theoretically conceivable that God created the universe and the life forms in it, by creating natural laws and processes and allowing them to work as designed without further intervention. This would mean that God created by a process of evolution that worked as intended, rather than, as in the case of theistic evolution, creation by a process of evolution which he guided and in which he intervened at key points.

This state of affairs entails an obvious caveat: the form and characteristics of Christian theological systems that incorporate a non-traditional

---

18. Redd, "Nicolaus Copernicus Biography: Facts & Discoveries," para 14. Redd attributes the statement to Luther's associate, Andreas Osiander. Andreas Kleinert suggests the entire story is false and has its origins in Anti-Lutheran Catholic polemic. Kleinert, "Tangible Historical Lie," Ultimately it is impossible to improve on the judgment of Sheila Rabin: While noting "there are differing accounts of what Luther said," Rabin concluded that "Martin Luther may have made negative comments about Copernicus." Rabin, "Nicolaus Copernicus," sect. 2.6.

view of Origins will vary depending on which particular non-traditional view of Origins is being incorporated. A Christian theology incorporating a flat-Earth or geocentric worldview will differ significantly from one incorporating theistic evolution, and both will differ from one incorporating punctuated equilibrium.

This leads to another important point: the limits of our knowledge on both the scientific and biblical/theological sides of the discussion. On the science side, the criticism that events like the Big Bang had no witnesses and we simply cannot be certain what happened is valid as far as they go (which may not be very far). The events are unique and unrepeatable, so how do we know the laws of nature as we experience them today applied then? None of this should be taken as an attempt to disparage science or dismiss its conclusions as "mere" theories. In science, a theory is not a "guess," but a conclusion reached after careful scrutiny of the available data using the best means available.[19] Science endeavors to account for all the data available in the most satisfactory way. However, certainty is not attainable. Various issues—some of them of profound importance—remain hotly disputed. How much teleology is there in the evolutionary process? The answers range from "none at all" to "a considerable amount." Science endeavors to provide answers, but certainty is unattainable.

The very differentiation between punctuated equilibrium and neo-Darwinism points to this lack of certainty. Kim Sterelny suggests that the difference arises, at least in part, from the different perspectives of the key opposing proponents. Neo-Darwinist, Richard Dawkins, is a zoologist and evolutionary biologist whose fundamental questions arise from the diversity of life in the world today, whereas Stephen Jay Gould, a leading proponent of punctuated equilibrium, was a paleontologist whose leading questions arose from the problems of the mass extinction of species in the past.[20]

We should not think the limits to knowledge are all on the side of science, however. Creationism is able to furnish no more witnesses to the event than science! It may be objected that God, himself, provides witness in Genesis 1–2. However, this is to assume precisely that which is being

---

19. The American Museum of Natural History website makes this observation: "In everyday use, the word 'theory' often means an untested hunch, or a guess without supporting evidence. But for scientists, a theory has nearly the opposite meaning. A theory is a well-substantiated explanation of an aspect of the natural world that can incorporate laws, hypotheses and facts." "What is a theory," paras. 1–2.

20. Sterelny, *Dawkins vs. Gould*, 3–14.

challenged by non-traditional views of Origins. The point is that if Genesis 1–2 is taken to be a non-literal, non-scientific presentation of creation—whether pictorial, metaphoric, symbolic, theological, or mythical—there is no alternative presentation of the *process* of creation elsewhere in Scripture.[21] Creation is mentioned and alluded to elsewhere, but there is nothing that could be called a witness to the process.[22] This means that anything that an adherent of a non-traditional view of Origins says in religious or theological terms about creation must be hypothetical and to some extent speculative. Such speculative reasoning is most problematic when one is doing exegesis and attempting to explain the meaning of a text. The reading of the text should arise from evidence within the text and from its context. Thus, allegory is inappropriate as a method of exegesis.[23] Similarly, the day-age and gap theories of creation, which attempt a point-by-point harmonization of Genesis 1 and modern science, are suspect because they are built on nothing in the text (Genesis 1) that they purport to explain.[24] However, on broader theological questions, such speculation is to some extent inevitable. The results obviously can never attain certainty. The words of Albert C. Sundberg Jr., although originally addressed to a different problem, are apt here as well: "Admittedly, much in the area must be conjecture. But in an area where information is almost at a minimum, reasonable conjecture that is consistent with available evidence is not without some value."[25]

---

21. Although the point is subject to dispute, it is not difficult to regard Genesis 2 as being an account of the creation of the Garden of Eden rather than an account of a creation of the world. Beyond all doubt, Genesis 3—which belongs with and depends upon Genesis 2—indicates that there was more to the world than the garden paradise.

22. Tremper Longman III lists the most important passages dealing with creation in the Old Testament as Ps 8, 19, 24, 33, 74, 104, 136; Prov 3:19–20; 8:22–31; and Job 38:4–11. See Longman III, "What Genesis 1 and 2 Teaches," 112–19. However, although these passages are clearly paeons of praise to God as creator, it is equally clear that they are poetic reflections rather than a description of the process. Indeed, the striking differences between Psalm 104 and Genesis 1 have been used to argue that Genesis 1 should be read literally rather than poetically. See Beall, "Reading Genesis 1–2," 48. Beall could easily have extended this observation to all the other passages as well.

23. Bultmann, "Exegesis," 342–52.

24. This is one of few points of agreement I find with Michael Dowd. He eschews any "interest in a passage-by-passage *reconciliation* of the ancient story with today's cosmology." See Dowd, *Thank God for Evolution*, 142.

25. Sundberg, *Old Testament Canon*, 131.

10.4 THE BIG BANG AND THE IDEA OF PROCESS

In discussing attitudes to Origins that might be permissible within Adventism, it is necessary to start at the beginning. A consensus of scientists today is that the universe began around 13.8 billion years ago with the Big Bang. So pervasive is this consensus that it is easy to forget that it is relatively recent in origin and that the Big Bang is far from a logical necessity. It is logically possible that the universe is self-existent. Indeed, before the Big Bang theory gained general acceptance, the prevailing scientific cosmology was the steady state theory, which entailed an essentially eternal universe.

Can an Adventist believe in the Big Bang? To talk of "the Big Bang" as if it were a discrete event is actually misleading. It is rather the starting point of the ongoing process of the formation of the entire universe.[26] Some have argued that this is contrary to Gen 1:1 and 2:1. However, it is contextually quite clear that Gen 2:1 (and 2:4a) refers specifically to the creation of this world (and its environs) as being finished. Of course, the exact meaning of "finished" in this context is open to interpretation. Should the preservation of the world be regarded as an ongoing process of creation, or should the two be kept completely separate? In what sense was the creation of this world "finished" when obviously there were territories outside of the paradisical Garden of Eden that were not as "complete" as the garden itself? These and similar questions need not detain us now. It is sufficient to say that Genesis 1–2:3a refers to the completed creation of this world, in whatever sense the author intended.

It is highly likely that "the heavens and earth" in Gen 1:1 have the same referent as in Gen 2:1; 4a (i.e., this world and immediate environs), giving the beginning and end of the first creation narrative a conceptual balance.[27] This supposition is supported by the reference to the creation of a new heavens and new earth in Rev 21:1, where the phrase again refers quite clearly to this world, rather than the entire universe.[28] (The final

---

26. Rogers, "Old Universe," 14–15.

27. The fact that there are two creation accounts—one focusing on activity over six days and rest on the seventh, the other concentrating attention on the activities of a single day—is incontrovertible, whether or not one concludes that they derive from two separate sources. The literary question of two accounts should not be automatically conflated with the historical-critical question of the number of sources utilized.

28. Of course, the author of Genesis did not have the book of Revelation to refer to as we do. The point is rather that the author of Revelation appears to have understood the phrase in Gen 1:1 in the same way that we have suggested it should be understood on contextual grounds.

three chapters of Revelation give numerous conceptual parallels to the first three chapters of Genesis).[29] Even if the author of Gen 1:1 did intend to refer to the universe, his understanding of the scope of that term would have been radically different from ours. Without the aid of telescopes, only about five thousand stars can be seen from Earth. Now, in the age of the Hubble telescope, we know that the visible universe contains two hundred billion trillion stars! The universe we speak of is incomprehensibly vaster than was thought even fifty years ago, let alone in antiquity. To the ancients, "the universe" was far closer in scope to our solar system than it was to the universe we know.

Exactly what Gen 1:1 means by "in the beginning" is subject to dispute, but the answer that most harmonizes with the rest of Genesis 1 is that it refers to the time of the creation of this world.[30] None of this suggests in any way that God is not the creator of the entire universe and all matter within it; simply that this is not the author's concern in Genesis 1. If this is true, then there are no impediments to an Adventist believing the Big Bang theory.[31]

Some scientists have argued the feasibility of the Big Bang occurring without any external cause.[32] Be that as it may, it is at least equally possible that the Big Bang is the way in which God created the universe. Thus, Robert Jastrow, in considering the Big Bang, concludes:

> Now we would like to pursue that inquiry farther back in time, but the barrier to further progress seems insurmountable. It is not a matter of another year, another decade of work, another measurement, or another theory; at this moment it seems as though science will never be able to raise the curtain on the mystery of creation.

---

29. For example, the state of Earth during the millennium parallels the pre-creation chaos (Rev 20:2; Gen 1:2); the designation of Satan as "that ancient serpent" (Gen 20:2) directly echoes the fall account (Gen 3:1–5); the absence of death (Rev 21:4) corresponds to the intention for humanity in Eden (Gen 2:9; 3:22); the presence of God with his people (Rev 21:3) correlated to YHWH walking in Eden calling for Adam (Gen 3:8–9); the river of life parallels the four rivers that flowed out of Eden and nurtured life throughout the world (Gen 2:10–14); and the presence of the tree of life is explicitly mentioned in both settings (Rev 22: 2; Gen 2:9).

30. For a survey of the options on this topic see Copan and Craig, *Creation out of Nothing*, 36–49.

31. Rogers ("Old Universe," 10) points out that even the denominationally funded Geoscience Research Institute has given "outright support to the old-universe position" in its journal, *Origins*.

32. Davies, *Goldilocks Enigma*, 56–98; Hawking, *Brief History of Time*, 121–50.

> For the scientist who has lived by his faith in the power of reason, the story ends like a bad dream. He has scaled the mountains of ignorance; he is about to conquer the highest peak, as he pulls himself over the final rock, he is greeted by a band of theologians who have been sitting there for centuries.[33]

More recently, Stephen Hawking makes a similar point, although he avoided overtly religious language (and does not, himself, draw such a religious conclusion as Jastrow did). In concluding his survey of the development of views of space and time from Aristotle to Einstein, he declares,

> The idea of an unchanging universe that could have existed, and could continue to exist, forever, was replaced by the notion of a dynamic, expanding universe that seemed to have begun a finite time ago, and that might end at a finite time in the future.[34]

(It should not be thought the "Big Bang" is in any sense the final scientific word on the topic of the universe. Hawking, himself, suggests a model in which the universe is unbounded—having neither a beginning nor an end).[35]

A key element in any non-traditional view of creation revolves around the emergence of the world as we know it today in stages. Thus, evolutionary theory speaks of "development," "evolution" and "change." Of course, it should be noted that the Genesis account also speaks of stages in the development of the world—specifically those associated with the first six of seven days, on each of which the world is radically changed. This element of creation in stages has long been a subject of discussion. St Augustine of Hippo, probably the dominant figure in Western theological reflection after the writers of the New Testament, considered it in the fifth century. In "The Literal Meaning of Genesis," completed in 415 CE, he argues that God created the world in an instant and only presents creation as taking six or seven days as a concession to our inability to comprehend his greatness. He declares,

> In this narrative of creation Holy Scripture has said of the Creator that He completed His works in six days; and elsewhere, where, without contradicting this, it has been written of the same Creator that He created all things together. It follows, therefore, that He,

33. Jastrow, *God and the Astronomers*, 115–16.
34. Hawking, *Brief History of Time*, 36.
35. Hawking, *Brief History of Time*, 122.

who created all things together, simultaneously created these six days, or seven, or rather the one day six or seven times repeated. Why, then, was there any need for six distinct days to be set forth in the narrative one after the other? The reason is that those who cannot understand the meaning of the text, He created all things together, cannot arrive at the meaning of Scripture unless the narrative proceeds slowly step by step.[36]

Thus, Augustine finds the stages of creation in Genesis 1 to be too long to fit into his worldview; many modern Christians find them too short to fit into theirs. But it is evident that to the question sometimes asked of progressives by Young-Earth-Creationists, "Don't you believe God is powerful enough to have made the world in a week"? Augustine would have answered, "Don't you believe God was powerful enough to have made it in an instant"? Of course, both questions are misleading: the issue at hand is not whether God has the power to do either of those things, but whether the evidence indicates that he actually did them.

10.5 SPECIFIC THEOLOGICAL ISSUES FOR ADVENTISTS

Once the cosmological question proper has been dealt with, the issue of whether an Adventist can hold to non-traditional views of Origins tends to revolve around a series of questions that are more or less invariable: "Does acceptance of non-traditional views of Origins not exclude the Great Controversy"? "Can the biblical picture of God really be harmonized with non-traditional views of Origins"? "Did Jesus die for Neanderthals"? "How can an understanding of the Fall or original sin fit into non-traditional views"? "How can doctrines like the atonement and salvation survive if Creation and the Fall are not accepted literally"? "What is left of the Sabbath, if creation did not happen in seven literal days"? "What about eschatology? Is the understanding of the end not going to have to be reinterpreted just as radically as the understanding of the beginning"? Many of these same concerns are shared by other Christian groups.

It is important to acknowledge that these questions are neither foolish nor trivial, especially when the full implications of the doctrine of Creation are recognized. Notice, for example, the extent of the overlap between these questions and the breadth of the doctrine of creation as outlined by the noted theologian, Wolfhart Pannenberg:

36. Augustine, *Literal Meaning of Genesis*, 4.33.52.

The idea of God necessarily implies the comprehension of anything else. If there is one God—and only one God—then everything else is to be regarded as finite and as comprised within his presence. The doctrine of creation explicates this relationship... In traditional theological terminology, the doctrine of creation does not relate only to creation but also to conservation, redemption, and eschatology; in other words, to the entire economy of God's action.[37]

10.5.1 The Great Controversy and Death Before the Fall

So, we ask, can non-traditional views of Origins accommodate the Great Controversy, or are the two ideas mutually exclusive? This question is inextricably linked with the problem of death before the Fall, which is unavoidable in any non-traditional view of Origins. Two presuppositions incline conservative thinkers to a negative response to this question. First, the Bible teaches that there was no death before the Fall, and secondly, "demonic" involvement on the earth comes only with the temptation and fall of Adam and Eve recorded in Genesis 3, and thus after the creation is complete. But these are both precisely presuppositions and not facts based on evidence.

Having discussed the first point in some detail elsewhere, it is sufficient to say here that the Bible simply does not clearly teach that either animal death or animal predation exists only as a consequence of sin.[38] It is difficult to improve upon the words of conservative scholar Wayne A. Grudem: "From the information we have in Scripture, we cannot now know whether God created animals subject to aging and death from the beginning, but it remains a real possibility."[39]

What the Bible teaches, in fact, is that *human* death is a consequence of human sin (Rom 5:12). Death is an intruder, and enemy (1 Cor 15:26)—specifically an enemy of humanity, overcome in the end by resurrection. But the Bible does not teach the resurrection of animals, only of humans.

The second point requires more attention. The creation narrative is presented neither in terms of divine sexual activity nor divine victory in battle, as it is in the creation myths of the Ancient Near East. God speaks; it is done. The theological message here is profound and must have been quite

---

37. Pannenberg, *Introduction*, 39–40.
38. See the discussion in Chapter 9, "Theological Problems with the Old Age for Life."
39. Grudem, *Systematic Theology*, 293.

revolutionary in the ancient world. There is no question that from a literary as opposed to historical viewpoint, a "demonic" element is first explicitly introduced into primordial history with the appearance of the serpent in Genesis 3. But it must be remembered that a great deal here hinges on an argument from silence: no demonic resistance is mentioned in Genesis 1 and 2; therefore, there was no demonic resistance. But are there other plausible options?

Consider this possibility. The Luciferian revolt in heaven happens before or at the time of the creation of the earth. Satanic rage is directed towards God's creation of the entire earth, not simply against the humans on the earth. God creates the world in stages, over time. He does so by his sheer creative power. However, after each stage of creation, Satan attacks, distorting and marring God's creation. A battle ensures, not to enable creation, but to preserve it. It must be remembered that for the Great Controversy to have gained any sort of traction, Satan must have been "at least somewhere near the same league [as God]" and a "universe-class contender."[40] Ultimately, God is still able to declare the result of each day's creation "good" (Hebrew: *tôv*). This Hebrew word has a considerable semantic range. It can indicate moral goodness, aesthetic beauty, or even utility—fitness for purpose.[41] The outcome of each day of creation is that what God had created was "fit for purpose"—was able to fulfill the purpose God had intended for his creative act.[42]

The Genesis narration only describes—and that only in poetic, metaphorical, and pictorial language—the last attack of Satan on the final stage of God's creation. Thus, Genesis 3 focuses on the humans, who, created intentionally by God to be in his image (Gen 1:26–28), are seduced by the

---

40. Provonsha, "Creation/Evolution Debate," 305, 310.

41. Brown et al., *Lexicon*, s.v. "טוֹב"; Höver-Johag, "טוֹב," 5:296–317; Bowling, "טוֹב (*tôb*)," 1: 345–46.

42. Provonsha's essay ("Creation/Evolution Debate," 303–11), Hoehn's essay ("The Greater Controversy," 14–21) and this paper represent variants on a single essential theme. Rather than seeing Satanic attacks on God's creation as being in the creation process, Provonsha suggests that God allowed Satan to do his best to bring his alternative vision of reality to fruition. Thus, he is responsible for the development of the species up to, but not including, the image of God. At this point, God steps in and the battle is transposed to a different key. Similarly, Hoehn argues that Satan and his fallen angelic followers were present on Earth before the creation of Adam and Eve. He sees in the creation a series of battles between the "intelligent designer" and an "intelligent destroyer." These two papers are the only other attempts to integrate more-scientific views of origins with the Great Controversy of which I am aware.

prospect of having the power of God and determining for themselves what is good and what is evil in independence from God. The history of the world since has been the history both of Satan's continued marring of the image of God and God's response to undo the Fall and its subsequent results.

What might previous attacks by Satan on the creation have entailed? Environmental catastrophes (storms, floods, etc.)? Meteorite strikes? Sudden changes in temperature? It is impossible to say with any certainty. However, such things have been posited by scientists as major stimuli for evolutionary change.[43] Is there anything at all in the biblical narrative that might suggest the plausibility of any of this? In fact, yes. Adam and Eve were warned that they would die if they ate of the fruit of the Tree of Knowledge of Good and Evil. It is difficult to see how this could be meaningful unless they had seen death and already knew what it was. Their warning would then mean, "Do not let this act mar your fitness for purpose. If you do, you will share the fate of so much of the creation around you." It is perhaps also worth noting that in the Bible, "darkness," like "water," is a frequent symbol of chaos and opposition to God and of death.[44] In the creation narrative, each "day" of creation is followed by a "night" of darkness. Of course, it would be easy to read far too much historical significance into a literary feature of the narrative! However, on the first day of creation, God said, "Let there be light," not "Let there be light and darkness" (Gen 1:3). Might it not

---

43. Of course, as Dawkins (*Ancestor's Tale*, 646) points out, the nature of DNA and sexual reproduction means that some sort of developmental change was inevitable. (To be strictly correct, Dawkins refers to "the first replicators," which he doubts were formed with DNA. I have opted to refer to DNA in making the same point, for simplicity's sake.) From a Christian perspective, the developmental process in its entirety cannot simply be dismissed as a Satanic innovation. To so do would be to give Satan far too much credit. Rather, the evidence in the fossil record that life has changed through time is better seen as a Satanic distortion of God's creative intent.

44. The wicked are directly said to be "like the troubled sea" (Isa 57:20) and to "walk in the ways of darkness" (Pro 2:13). Darkness becomes a metaphor for the abode of the dead (Isa 47:5; Lam 3:16) and divine abandonment (Jer 23:12; Mat 22:13, 30). Similarly, the "deep"—the word used in Gen 1:2 for the watery chaos enshrouded in darkness—becomes a poetic synonym for the abode of the dead (Ps 69:15; 88:6). The Greek word used to translate "deep" in Gen 1:2 later comes to be used for the place of origin of demonic torments (Rev 9:1-12) and the millennial punishment of Satan (Rev 20:1-3). Often the opposition of the darkness and water to God are historicized to specific events in the past or future: the crossing of the Red Sea (Exod 14:20-29), the historical fall of Babylon (Jer 51:13), and the eschatological drying up of the Euphrates (Rev 16:12). By contrast, Jesus is called the "light of the world" (John 8:12). He walks on water (Mat 14:25) and stills a life-threatening storm (Mark 4:39)—both of which incidents happened in the darkness of night. The new earth is described as having neither sea nor night (Rev 21:1; 22:5).

be that forces in revolt against the creator God responded by attempting to bring back the darkness? Before this is dismissed as too fanciful, it should be noted that one of the features of the world, when the controversy is over, is that "there will be no night there (Rev 21:25). Before you say, "But that is symbolic," consider that this is precisely the point I am suggesting with Gen 1:3.

The scenario here outlined, far from precluding the Great Controversy, has it supercharged—on steroids, as it were. If this scenario were accepted, one last point comes into focus. Scripture makes it clear that God frequently thwarts the plans and intentions of Satan and evil human agencies, incorporating those plans and intentions into the schema for the revelation of his glory and greatness.[45] It would be in perfect harmony with this for God to use Satan's attacks on his creation as the basis for the next stage of his creation. The creation of this world may not have happened as God originally intended, but rather as it happened in the context of the Great Controversy.

The most telling weakness in this construction is that it appears to involve a considerable reinterpretation of Genesis 1. It is true that the biblical creation narrative is devoid of explicit mention of any conflict in the creation process. God spoke, and it was done. However, in order to give the correct weight to this fact, a number of other points also need to be considered. The Old Testament, to a large extent, de-emphasizes the "Satanic." Not even the fall narrative (Genesis 3) identifies the serpent with Satan.[46] Jewish tradition does not always make that association, although the New Testament does (Rev 12:9; 20:2).[47] The name (or more correctly,

---

45. God's sovereignty in the face of opposition is clearly implied in both the Old and New Testaments. Joseph speaks of God's overruling the intention of his brothers and bringing good out of their plan to harm him (Gen 45:5). A similar implication is found in Paul's confident assertion that "for those who love God all things work together for good" (Rom 8:28).

46. According to Sarna (*Genesis*, 24) this identification is first found in the apocryphal Wisdom of Solomon 2:24, written in the first century BCE.

47. Jewish tradition tends to see the serpent as human "evil inclination," which was externalized and embodied in the serpent before the sin of Adam and Eve, but is now seen as an internal component of human nature. See Moore, *Judaism*, 1: 492. Furthermore, as Sarna (*Genesis*, 24) points out, Genesis 3 actually downgrades the serpent's status as compared with that given it in the Ancient Near East more generally. The serpent was widely "endowed with divine or semidivine qualities; it was venerated as an emblem of health, fertility, immortality, occult wisdom and chaotic evil; and it was often worshipped." But in Gen 3, it alone is sentenced without interrogation; it alone of the three parties involved does not speak at all. Sarna concludes that in this chapter the serpent

title) "Satan" is used in only three contexts in the Old Testament—two of them (1 Chronicles 21; Zechariah 3) are unambiguously late and the other (Job 1–2) undated, but generally also regarded as late.[48] The Israelite nation was born in the context of Egyptian polytheism and matured until the time of the exile in the context of Canaanite polytheism. It seems that the Old Testament writers focused on the one great truth—"Hear, O Israel, the Lord our God is one" (Deut 6:4)—without confusing the people by introducing a non-divine malevolent power who acted like a god and could easily be mistaken for a god. Only after the temptation to idolatry and polytheism had been decisively defeated in the Babylonian exile did the person of Satan begin to be introduced.[49] With this as the background of the creation story—which has a polemic against idolatry as a sub-text—it is hardly surprising that the emphasis falls on the creatorship of God, and his unrivaled power, and that elements of the Great Controversy theme are omitted.[50]

This Great Controversy scenario has the effect of answering some of the objections raised to a more evolutionary understanding of creation: Some ask, "How can this sort of wasteful death-oriented approach to creation be reconciled with what the Bible reveals about the character of God"? The fact is that we have no difficulty attempting such a reconciliation of natural evil and the character of God in the period after the Fall. We assert that God created nature "good," but Satan has perverted this goodness, and the world we see today is an ambiguous blending of the original good and the perverted Satanic evil. If the Great Controversy is understood as starting on Earth before the Fall of humanity, the same principle applies. Jack Provonsha correctly notes that

---

"possesses no occult powers. It is not demonic . . . [It] is not the personification of evil."

48. The books of 1 Chronicles and Zechariah are clearly post-exilic (given that they relate events in the late exilic period or early post-exilic period). The book of Job is undated but its theology is usually seen as reflecting a post-exilic, or at least, late pre-exilic situation, regardless of when Job himself may have lived. It may be significant that while the reader (and the writer!) knows about the dialogue between (the) Satan and God as the root of Job's woes, neither Job nor his "comforters" take Satan into consideration when discussing his plight. On the date of Job see Eissfeldt, *The Old Testament*, 470; La Sor et al., *Old Testament Survey*, 561–62; Crenshaw, "Job, Book of," 3: 863.

49. Thompson, *Inspiration*, 173–86.

50. Hasel, "Polemical Nature." 81–102. The suggestion by Clifford Goldstein that any attempt to reinterpret the Genesis creation story reduces it to the level of any ancient creation myth is, at best, unfair. See Goldstein, *Baptizing the Devil*, 206. The account in Genesis is a rich deposit of biblical theology, teaching as it does profound truths about both God and humanity.

> The evolutionist's picture looks more like a painting of the devil than it does a portrait of God... In the light of the Great Controversy, the one thing we cannot allow is the confusion regarding God's character that is resulting from attempts to make God the author of the evolutionary process.[51]

This would mean that God would (presumably) not have created the world via such a death-oriented way if the rebellion had not occurred and marred his work.

This approach also eases some of the difficulties inherent in other attempts to produce a Christian evolutionary understanding of Origins. For example, the view of Nancey Murphy and others is that it is God's respect for the integrity of nature that leads him to create in a developmental and non-interventionist way.[52] This suggestion provokes Clifford Goldstein to ask,

> Will this new heaven and new earth be created by divine fiat—God speaks and it is—something similar to what was unambiguously depicted in Genesis 1 and 2? Or will life have to endure, again, the rigor and joy of natural selection and survival of the fittest for billions of years until a new world, one "in which righteousness dwells" (2 Pet 3:13), finally appears. If God used billions of years to create the world the first time—with the vicious and violent process of evolution as the means—is that how He is going to do it the second time too? If not, why not?[53]

But if a more evolutionary creation is a result of the Great Controversy, this question becomes mute. God did not create the way he did because of some abstract respect for nature (over which he is LORD), but in order that the Great Controversy might be seen in its full developmental process from beginning to end. Once that controversy is over, God can create in an instant if he so desires.

10.5.2 The Image of God

But all of this inevitably leads to another cluster of questions: "What about the Neanderthals (*Homo neanderthalensis*)? Did Jesus die for them? Will

---

51. Provonsha, "Creation/Evolution Debate," 2000, 311.

52. Murphy, "Problem of Evil," 135; Clayton and Knapp, "Divine Action." 183; Edwards, "Why is God doing This?" 264.

53. Goldstein, *Baptizing the Devil*, 235.

they be saved"? In some ways, this is a very natural question; in other ways, it is a very strange question. What is it about the Neanderthals that provokes such concern? Presumably, it is the fact that they are such close relatives of humans. Indeed, it is generally regarded that all humans except those African groups south of the Sahara have a small amount of DNA that originated in Neanderthals, suggesting that the Neanderthals did not so much become extinct as much as they interbred with and were absorbed into the *Homo sapiens* community.[54] So, we ask, were Neanderthals in the image of God? Did they have moral responsibility? Were their lives meaningful?[55] Were they candidates for salvation? (From a biblical perspective, being in the image of God, having moral responsibility, and being an object of God's saving activity are directly correlated.[56] A meaningful life seems to be a natural corollary.)

The underlying issue is the separation of humans from animals as a species alone made in the image of God. In what does this separation consist, or, to put the question differently, what is the image of God? For some Christians, the problem is solved easily: the image is constituted by the immortal soul in those creatures who are given such by God. Then the question becomes: Did the Neanderthals have immortal souls? Presumably not, but if they did, the image of God, and therefore the provision of salvation, includes them also. A sharply drawn criterion of differentiation exists; it is merely a matter of where the line is to be drawn. Clearly, this solution does not work for Christian wholists, like Seventh-day Adventists,

---

54. Slatkin and Racimo, "Ancient DNA and Human History," 6380–87. This view is challenged by some who suggest that commonality of Neanderthal and *Homo sapiens* DNA is a result of common ancestry rather than later interbreeding. See Eriksson and Manica, "Effect of Ancient Population Structure," 13956–60.

55. Lightman (*Searching for Stars*, 71–72) seems to suggest that the dividing line between animals and humans is the quest for meaning: "Unless there exists an infinite and permanent observer such as God—some absolute authority or scaffold by which to judge and preserve meaning—then the situation seems hopeless to me. On the other hand, *perhaps my starting assumption, that meaning requires permanence, is erroneous. Or perhaps meaning itself is an illusion. After all, why should I insist on meaning? Fish and squirrels get by quite well without it* [emphasis added]."

56. Note Provonsha's comment ("Creation/Evolution Debate," 305): "Only persons commit evil in the sense of SIN, for only they can be responsible through choosing." Interestingly, philosopher Lynne Rudder Baker—to whom further reference will shortly be made—states quite categorically that only "persons" can be moral agents and that "moral sentiments like guilt and regret" depend on personhood. Animals as such are not moral agents and do not experience such things. See Baker, *Persons and Bodies*, 148, 157. The importance of Baker for the position being argued here will become evident below.

who reject the notion of any being "having" a soul. Rather, it is argued that humans are souls, and since the same Hebrew word (*nephesh*) can be used for animals (e.g., Gen 1:20, 21, 24, 30) as well as humans (e.g., Gen 2:7; 12:5; 14:21), this criterion of differentiation vanishes.

However, that is not the end of the matter. Neanderthals and modern humans are physically similar and have compatible DNA, but it is highly doubtful that the "image of God" should be conceived of in physical terms. Both male and female are created in the image of God (Gen 1: 27), which immediately highlights physical difference within the image of God. Furthermore, human and chimpanzee coding DNA differs by less than 5 percent, but no one seems to ask, "What about the chimpanzees"?[57] Despite the closeness in coding DNA between humans and chimpanzees, Genesis 1 makes a sharp distinction between humans and even the highest animals, precisely at the point where humans are defined as the image of God.[58] Indeed, the sharpness of this distinction is regarded by modern animal liberationists, such as Peter Singer, as being one of the weaknesses of the biblical view.[59] But—and the point needs reiteration—this distinction cannot be substantiated on the basis of a vast physical difference between humans and the highest animals.[60]

In all likelihood, the symbol of the image of God derives from the ancient custom of the emperor erecting an image of himself in conquered territories to signify his rulership of that territory.[61] The data of Genesis suggests that the meaning of the image of God consists not in human physicality, but rather in human roles and functions—all performed in imitation of God, as his representative, and as a demonstration of his rulership of

---

57. Singer, *Rethinking Life and Death*, 177. Dawkins (*Ancestor's Tale*, 124–26) suggests caution in making such comparisons. He prefers the analogy of two editions of the same book which can have a very different look and feel about them. In any case, as Dawkins himself (*Ancestor's Tale*, 127) admits, humans and chimpanzees are "far more similar at the molecular level than expected."

58. It should be noted that despite the high similarity between the coding DNA of chimps and humans a much smaller percentage of our proteins is exactly identical. The much-touted high percentage of gene similarity faded from about 2005 with increased understanding of the function of the rest of the genome which had sometimes been called "junk" DNA in popularizing publications.

59. Singer, *Rethinking Life and Death*, 169–74.

60. If one regards the phrase "the highest animals" as too question-begging, evolutionary in tone, it can simply be replaced by the more cumbersome, "those animals that are closest to humans in their DNA."

61. von Rad, *Genesis*, 60.

the world. Specifically, the image involved the capacity for ruling creation, subduing it (as God has earlier limited the chaos symbolized in the primeval waters and the darkness), and (pro-)creating new life. The creation of the image is the immediate precursor of the seventh-day rest of God, which humanity enters into by worship, for the seventh day is sanctified and blessed. This suggests that worship is also at the heart of what being in the image of God means.

All of this suggests that the image of God should be understood in fundamentally relational terms. Humanity is presented in the creation narrative as beings who are intended to be in relationship with God—not another divinity, for that is impossible in a monotheistic context—but as close to God as a creature can be. Humans are to do as God does, in a worshipful relationship, within the broad parameters God sets. (There is only one prohibition: not to eat of the fruit of the tree of knowledge of good and evil.) How is the basis of this relationship to be understood? In physical terms? Surely not! Does it require an "immortal soul"? No.

Here, the work of philosopher Lynne Rudder Baker on the nature of personhood may provide a useful guide.[62] In her work, Baker explores what it is that makes a person. She is concerned with issues such as the continuity of personhood and how that can be understood in the light of beliefs in death and resurrection. She immediately rules out the suggestion that the "body" and the "person" are to be identified with one another. She is just as adamant that it is not a matter of a "ghost in the machine": personhood does not consist of a "soul" that inhabits a body like a letter in an envelope. Rather, Baker argues the body is a constituent necessity for personhood—there can be no personhood without a body—but personhood resides in the development of a "first-person perspective." This means that a person has the capacity to think of oneself in the first person. Such a capacity is expressed directly in such questions as "I wonder if I will be happy tomorrow"?[63] Pannenberg speaks in a similar way, although he refers to self-awareness, rather than a first-person perspective:

62. Baker, *Persons and Bodies*. Key elements of her position are presented more succinctly in Baker, "Metaphysics of Resurrection," 333–48.

63. Coincidently, if the Bible locates the difference between animals and humans in the "image of God," Baker (*Persons and Bodies*, 4) locates the difference between animals and human persons precisely in "first-person perspective." She declares, "What marks persons off from everything else in the world, I shall argue is that a person has a complex mental property: a first-person perspective that enables one to conceive of one's body and mental state as one's own. We human persons are animals in that we are constituted

> Thus, because the human being is the self-consciously discerning animal, it is also the religious animal. While all creatures are in fact related to God the creator, and the young lions seek their prey from God, they do not do so self-consciously. It is only in human beings that the relationship of creature to God becomes an explicit issue. This, however, is intimately connected with the human capacity for self-conscious discernment . . . It is how the human being is described in the Genesis story as created in the image of God.[64]

Baker allows the existence of such a thing as "proximate personhood": there are times and places where a fully-formed first-person perspective has not developed or no longer exists. To do justice to Baker's work would require us to enter into a great deal of discussion, but this is not the place for that. Nor is it necessary for our purpose, which is simply to suggest that if Baker's constituent view of personhood has validity, then might not a similar constituent view also provide a key to the understanding of the image of God? A certain physicality, a certain DNA, a certain degree of intelligence, or some such thing is a prerequisite for the image of God, but is not identical to that image itself. Rather, the image is found in a capacity for "God-awareness," a capacity for worship that goes beyond the physical constituents. This need not reside in a "soul" separate from the body, any more than personhood does. How then, does it manifest itself? Presumably, God at some point revealed himself to his creation in such a way as to create awareness that there is a God with whom one can have fellowship.[65] This "God-awareness" might be expressed in being able to ask the so-called "great questions": Why am I here? What is the meaning of life? Is there anything more than this life? What happens after death?[66]

---

by animals, but, having first-person perspectives, we are not 'just animals.' We are persons." It is obvious that a dog cannot aspire to be a guard dog or to be less bad tempered; a person, however, knows that they exist as an entity and can conceive of that entity playing a different role of being "better" than they are. Further highlighting this difference Stuart Babbage cites G. K. Chesterton: "If I wish to dissuade a man from drinking his tenth whisky and soda, I slap him on the back and say, 'Be a man!' No one who wished to dissuade a crocodile from eating its tenth explorer would slap it on the back and say, 'Be a crocodile!'" See Babbage, *Man in Nature and Grace*, 9.

64. Pannenberg, *Introduction*, 51.

65. If any of this were true it might be more correct to speak of the image of God being created in humans, rather than humans being created in the image of God.

66. Baker, in *Persons and Bodies*, 160 provides her own similar list of questions that only a person can ask: "What am I? Who am I? What kind of life ought I to live?" She

Do we need to assume that such God-awareness appeared fully formed in an instant? Not necessarily. If there is "proximate personhood," might there not also be, as it were, "proximate God-awareness"? We all know of cases where a pet is "almost a part of the family," and yet we would generally not think of such an animal as fully equal to humans. It is also important to recognize that each new life, beginning with a single fertilized cell, gradually develops into a fully formed personhood. The fetus does not begin with a fully-formed self-awareness or, for that matter, a fully-formed capacity to know God. This is something that develops, even as the body develops physically. Is it not possible that, similarly, Neanderthals reflect a "proximate," not fully-formed God awareness? Did the Neanderthals have the capacity to ask the big questions? Only God knows. If not, then they would be placed over the line with the brute creation rather than on this side, having the "image of God."

There are features of the fall narrative that suggest a non-literal reading. A talking snake? A "magic" tree that conferred immortality on anyone who ate its fruit, possibly even once?[67] (If so, why had Adam and Eve not already eaten of it?) A garden with a single eastern entrance? The fact that the stories of the creation and Fall have numerous points of contact with the Hebrew sanctuary likewise suggests a non-literal meaning. The greater the perceived *literary* reason for writing a text in a certain way, the less the likelihood that the text reflects *historical* facts.

This all has a further possible connection with modern scientific views. The general consensus among scientists is that *Homo sapiens*

---

immediately follows this list with the comment: "Such questions could not even be understood, much less seriously asked, by a being without a first-person perspective."

67. It is impossible to be certain whether Gen 3:22—"lest he reach out his hand and take also of the tree of life and eat, and live forever" expresses a concern over a single or repeated eating from the tree. See Sarna, *Genesis*, 18. On the one hand, the language used—"take" and "eat"—echoes the language of the single act of succumbing to temptation in Gen 3:6. See Matthews, *Genesis 1–11:26*, 256. Furthermore, James Barr is insistent that the text cannot mean that although they have eaten of the tree already, they might continue to do so. See Barr, *Garden of Eden*, 58. Gordon Wenham also sees this as the implication of the text. See Wenham, *Genesis 1–15*, 85. Hermann Gunkel highlights an urgency in the text—God has to act "before it is too late," suggesting a single eating is in mind. See Gunkel *Genesis*, 24. John Skinner is explicit "that a single partaking of the fruit would have conferred eternal life." See Skinner, *Genesis*, 89. On the other hand, the *Seventh-day Adventist Bible Commentary* appears to reject all such views. See "Genesis," 1:236. Furthermore, Rev 22:2 would seem to suggest a monthly eating of the tree on the new earth. It seems most commentaries ignore this particular issue, making no comment on it.

emerged through the evolutionary process some 300,000 years ago. That is to say that the humans who roamed the earth 300,000 years ago were physically and biologically indistinguishable from us (within the limits of normal human variations of height, skin color, etc.). However, something extraordinary happened 50,000 years ago, when suddenly, these humans made what has been called a "Great Leap Forward" and became culturally modern as well as physically modern.[68] Notice Richard Dawkins' comment:

> As far as we can tell, [before the Great Leap Forward] there were no paintings, no carvings, no figurines, no grave goods, no ornamentation. After the Leap, all these things suddenly appear in the archaeological record, together with musical instruments such as bone flutes and it wasn't long before stunning creations like the Lascaux Cave murals were created by Cro-Magnon people . . . Some authorities are so impressed by the Great Leap Forward that they think it coincided with the origin of language. What else, they ask, could account for such a sudden change?[69]

Could this correlate with the emergence of God-consciousness? Is this when humans were first in the image of God and first began to ask the "big questions"?

10.5.3 The Fall Narrative

What then is the meaning of the fall narrative? Humanity develops / is given / has revealed to it "God-awareness." The goal of this is that humans will enter into and remain in a worshipful relationship with God. The fall narrative tells us that humans either refused to enter this relationship or refused to remain in it. The real temptation was not to eat a piece of fruit, but to "be like God"—and thus, in their self-seized autonomy, to make their creator redundant and surplus to requirement. Rather than allow God to inform them of what was [morally] "good" and "evil," the humans chose to define these qualities for themselves. The underlying reality behind the fall narrative is seen all around us in our non-ideal world and all throughout history. Particularly telling is the fact that the most decent and morally sensitive people are very much possessed of a sense of falling short of

---

68. Dawkins (*Ancestor's Tale*, 48) attributes the title to Jared Diamond, but does not provide a reference. In fact, the reference is to *The Third Chimpanzee: The Evolution and Future of the Human Animal* (1991).

69. Dawkins, *Ancestor's Tale*, 48–49.

their ideals—of knowing that they should do better than they do; that they fall short. When and how did the Fall take place if not literally as Genesis describes it? I do not know. Nor do I need to know. The fact is that both experience and history tell us that we live in a fallen world.[70]

It is interesting to notice that modern theologians looking at the situation of the contemporary world, completely independent of reference to the creation and fall of humanity, highlight the same sort of issues: being fully human entails a relationship with God; a break in that relationship sees humanity become less than it ought to be—less than it could be—having more in common with beasts. Thus, Emil Brunner, writing in the immediate aftermath of the horrors of the Second World War, declares:

> We men, and quite specially we modern men, are constantly inclined to think that by our own intrinsic virtue we can be good, upright and human men; if only we are left to ourselves then all will be well. We do not at all, in fact, believe that without God we cannot be truly human. We suppose on the contrary that within ourselves we have the resources of true humanism. In reality, however, the fact is that the more we delude ourselves into thinking that we are independent of God, the more certainly we degenerate and sink to a sub-human level. It is that, of course, which today we are experiencing in a greater measure than ever before. In those states where human society and especially its rulers have emancipated themselves completely from the authority of God, as whole people and states have done to an unprecedented extent, then there emerges a dehumanization to which there is no parallel in previous history. With every step which separates man from God there springs up inhumanity, and the truly human element disappears from life. . . This destructive severance of our communion with God the Bible calls sin. And this latter reality lurks in us all like a malignant growth which, unless the transcendent One intervenes, consumes our vitality and health increasingly.[71]

When the question of the image of God has been resolved, all the other questions regarding salvation are also solved in principle. How can there be a fall in this evolutionary model? Well, the Fall does not depend on creation happening in seven days. Rather, it depends on humanity's being in the image of God. Obviously, if the creation narrative is understood in

---

70. Brunner, *Creation and Redemption*, 95–100.
71. Brunner, "Election," 47–48. This sermon was originally preached on February 20, 1949.

a non-literal way, the fall narrative must also be so understood; the two narratives cannot be separated.

The question of the atonement and salvation are likewise not dependent on the fact of a seven-day creation but rather have as an essential prerequisite the fact that God is the creator and that humans were intended to be in his image. If these two theological pillars are affirmed (as I have done throughout), non-traditional views of Origins present no insurmountable challenge to accepting the atonement or a belief in salvation. At this point, the traditionalist and the non-traditionalist stand on the same ground. No traditionalist actually bases belief in the atonement and salvation on creation *in seven days*. Rather, it is based on the reality of human sinfulness and rebellion against God, rooted in the Fall. But the Fall is still the Fall even if it is understood to have taken place in ways other than a literal reading of Genesis 3 suggests.

10.5.4 The Sabbath

Two last issues remain, specifically for Seventh-day Adventists. First, what is left of the Sabbath if the world was not created in seven days as Genesis 1 says? There is no question that the Bible writers directly link the Sabbath with a seven-day creation (Exod 20:8–11; 31:17). However, it must be asked whether the "seven-day" aspect is the important part of this formulation. Certainly, there are many instances in Scripture where the God of Israel is presented as creator—in contradistinction to the idols—with absolutely no reference to the seven days of creation (e.g., Isa 40:28; Rom 1:25). The key issue is that God is the creator.

Surely, the situation is similar within contemporary Adventism: "creation" is often spoken of with the often unexpressed presupposition that this means a literal seven-day creation some thousands of years ago. Similarly, the Sabbath is often mentioned but not necessarily in connection with the issue of Origins. But the key issue is not the "how" of creation, but the "fact" that God is the creator. The implications of creation are of staggering significance: life is not meaningless, the physical world is not the only—or even the main—reality, but neither is it to be abused; rather, it is to be cared for by us as faithful stewards. The meaningful beginning of the earth points to its meaningful end as well. None of this depends on creation taking place in a particular way, at a particular time; it depends on the fact that God is the creator. God's creatorship is easily forgotten as we live in the secular world, and for this reason alone, the Sabbath retains significance even if non-traditional views of Origins are adopted.

But even in the Old Testament, the Sabbath's meaning is not limited to its role as a memorial of creation. Rather, the Sabbath is also seen as a memorial of redemption (Deut 5:12–15). Those texts—much cherished by Adventists—which refer to the Sabbath as "seal" are, in fact, set in the context of the covenant made with the redeemed Israel (Exod 31:13–17). As such they point more to redemption than to creation—although the two themes are not strictly separated in the Bible. Again, the implications are staggering: the Sabbath levels the strata of society; master and slave are alike, equally redeemed. The redemption Sabbath points to the social responsibility of the redeemed for the poor, the needy, the weak, and the defenseless. How could this not continue to be relevant in our world?

The New Testament builds on these themes, likening the Sabbath to salvation in Christ (Heb 4:1–3) and to the coming eschatological Sabbath where the battle with sin will be over. The Sabbath of hope is as important today as it has ever been. Again, none of this depends on a literal seven-day creation.

One of the things the first creation narrative teaches is that the Sabbath was God's gift to humanity *from the beginning*. In a sinful world, that gift is reconceptualized as a beneficial command. The biblical story shows its observance and neglect. It outlines layers of interpretation and meaning that have accrued to it. None of these hinge on a literal seven-day creation and none of it is lost if belief in a literal seven-day creation is abandoned—unless the "seven-dayness" of creation has some intrinsic theological value. But it is difficult to see what that would be.

10.5.5 Eschatology

This brings us to the final issue that might confront Adventists considering non-traditional views of Origins: eschatology. If the initial chapters of the Bible are read non-literally, should the final chapters be similarly so read? We have already touched on some of the specific eschatological issues involved: if God created by means of a long evolutionary process, does that mean the new earth must be created similarly by a long, convoluted means? It has been argued that this does not follow if the process of creation was attacked and marred in the "Great Controversy." But what of the more general issue: if our views of creation change, can our views of eschatology remain the same?

The biblical picture of the future world is drawn in terms of the ancient cosmology of a three-tiered universe—in the middle a flat-Earth, above that the dome of the firmament, and below it the "great deep."[72] But much has changed. The Greeks discovered the world to be a globe. Modern cosmology has made this picture even more untenable as a literal, physical description. The Hubble Space Telescope allows us to see galaxies more than 10 billion light years away. This "almost unimaginably vast" universe is expanding at an incredible and accelerating speed and is thus "finite but unbounded."[73] Of the suggestion that the heaven where God dwells is "up there, beyond the stars," there is no evidence at all. Indeed, all the evidence that exists indicates that this is not so. So, has science overthrown Christian eschatology along with our understanding of Origins?

It hardly needs to be noted that if the Bible is taken strictly literally, it demands a vertical relationship between heaven and Earth. Jesus "goes up" into the clouds at the ascension (Acts 1:9); Jesus returns in the clouds of heaven (Matt 26:64) and the New Jerusalem descends to the earth (Rev 21:2). But rather than despair, a better strategy would be to ask, "what does this all mean"?

Clearly, the vertical language serves to emphasize that God and his dwelling place are wholly other than the world humans inhabit. The ascension of Jesus means that Jesus will no longer physically appear among his disciples.[74] The picture of the reward of the saints "in heaven" indicates that this reward is not part of this world. The descent of New Jerusalem, linked as it is with the creation of a new heavens and new earth, means that the heavenly reality and the reality of this world have been brought together.

What would be a meaningful way to express this in the twenty-first century, when the Bible's vertical language has lost its utility? One way is to

---

72. There are variations on this theme. Some have attempted to argue that biblical cosmology is actually two-tiered in distinction from the usual three-tiered cosmology more generally held in the ancient world. For the purposes of this discussion, this is a distinction that makes no difference. A two-tiered view has as many problems for the modern reader as a three-tiered view.

73. Davies, *Goldilocks Enigma*, 22, 44. The speed at which galaxies move away from each other is directly proportionate to how far away they are. Thus "a galaxy 20 million light years away is receding at twice the speed of a galaxy 10 million light years away" (Lightman, *Searching for Stars*, 166).

74. Moule, "Ascension—Acts 1:9," 54–63.

think of heaven as being a realm outside the space-time continuum experienced in this world—or as the Bible, itself, says "not of this creation" (Heb 9:11).[75] (This sort of language is not entirely novel in Adventism today.)[76] The words of N. T. Wright, with specific reference to Paul, are equally applicable to all biblical eschatology: "We should not make the mistake of supposing that Paul thought 'heaven' was literally 'up there,' a place within our time-space continuum. Ancient Jews were quite capable of using the language of a 'three-decker universe' without supposing it was to be taken literally. Heaven (we might say) is a different *dimension of* reality."[77] This could mean that heaven is right "here"—but currently inaccessible to us. After all, modern physics tells us that even in this world, there are billions of particles, neutrinos, which pass through us and all "solid" objects without anyone noticing and without leaving a trace behind.[78] If this is so, the possibility of an overlapping inaccessible reality beyond the reach of physics, outside the space-time continuum, is not far-fetched.

Such an understanding of the relationship of heaven to earth has several important implications that help to solve a number of exegetical puzzles. This approach literally brings heaven and earth into the closest proximity. Biblically, the time it takes to get from heaven to earth can be measured by the length of the prayer in Daniel 9. Gabriel arrives at the end of the prayer (Dan 9:20–21), announcing that he had been sent—presumably from heaven—when Daniel began to pray (Dan 9:22–23).[79] This would

---

75. N. T. Wright uses language that is less technical, but perhaps more accessible to make the same point: "... when the Bible speaks of 'heaven' and 'earth' it isn't talking about two localities related to each other within the same space-time continuum, nor yet about a 'non-physical' world on the one hand and a 'physical' one on the other, but about two different *kinds* of what we call 'space,' two different kinds of what we call 'matter,' and also, quite possibly (though this does not necessarily follow from the other two), two different kinds of what we call 'time.'" See Wright, *Surprised by Hope*, 126–27.

76. To note but one example: "He [the author of Hebrews] wants to assure us that 'the best is yet to be,' that beyond our space-time continuum lies the invisible, eternal order. That is the real; that is to be our goal," Johnsson, *In Absolute Confidence*, 157.

77. Wright, *Paul*, 220–21.

78. Davies, *Goldilocks Enigma*, 103.

79. More precisely, Gabriel is said to arrive before Daniel has finished his prayer which shortens the duration of the journey. There is also uncertainty regarding the "word" (*dabar*) which "went out." See the discussion in Ford, *Daniel*, 224. It is frequently taken, as here, as a command issued to Daniel. See, for example, Stefanovic, *Daniel*, 351. But it could also refer to the word of revelation outlined in vv. 24–27. See, for example, Montgomery, *Daniel*, 371–72. Perhaps the best option is that of Norman W. Porteous, who sees both meanings in this verse: "... a revelation was given for Daniel which

be inconceivable if Gabriel had to travel through the universe without completely negating the laws of physics. Yet it is perfectly congruent with the suggestion that heaven is simply on the other side of a spatial/temporal doorway. The fact that angelic beings are always present but only sometimes visible (e.g., 2 Kgs 16:17) also fits this model, as does the idea of a heavenly record being kept of events on Earth. In this model, "the new heavens and new earth" could already be in existence, but not revealed until the current spatial and temporal limitations are destroyed, or at least transcended.

10.6 CONCLUSION

Our exploration, which began with the origins of the universe, ends with a world cleansed of sin and made anew. What conclusions are to be drawn—and not drawn—from this survey? It does seem to me that it is possible to be a Seventh-day Adventist and yet hold to modern, science-informed understandings of creation. Has a proven model been presented? Far from it! Is this a model that everyone must adopt? Certainly not! But if this model is plausible and possible, it, at the very least, opens the door to the possibility of other, better models that are more convincing.

Some will feel that the very foundations of faith are being shaken by all of this. I would urge such people to turn their attention away from the question of Origins and consider the really important features of biblical revelation: the love of God; the saving death of Jesus; the victory over death at the resurrection: the certain hope of the return of Jesus and immortality in a world without sin: the practical responsibilities of a loving Christian life in the here-and-now (Mic 6:8). No-one should let anything in this presentation undermine their faith in the central biblical message. Turn away from the question of non-traditional models of Origins, if you need, but never turn away from the offer of salvation.

For myself, I cannot simply turn away from the issue of Origins for two reasons, or perhaps more correctly, for one reason viewed in two ways. First, there is the pastoral/evangelistic concern expressed by St Augustine of Hippo that a failure to accept scientific evidence risked the credibility of

---

Gabriel had been commissioned to bring to him as one specially favored by God . . ." See Porteous, *Daniel*, 139. Whichever meaning is adopted, there is a clear impression that Gabriel's journey from heaven to earth was as quick and simple as moving from one room into an adjacent one.

the gospel in the eyes of those the church was attempting to evangelize.[80] He declares,

> Usually, even a non-Christian knows something about the earth, the heavens, and the other elements of this world, about the motion and orbit of the stars and even their size and relative positions, about the predictable eclipses of the sun and moon, the cycles of the years and the seasons, about the kinds of animals, shrubs, stones, and so forth, and this knowledge he holds to as being certain from reason and experience. Now, it is a disgraceful and dangerous thing for an infidel to hear a Christian, presumably giving the meaning of Holy Scripture, talking nonsense on these topics; and we should take all means to prevent such an embarrassing situation, in which people show up vast ignorance in a Christian and laugh it to scorn. The shame is not so much that an ignorant individual is derided, but that people outside the household of the faith think our sacred writers held such opinions, and, to the great loss of those for whose salvation we toil, the writers of our Scripture are criticized and rejected as unlearned men. If they find a Christian mistaken in a field which they themselves know well and hear him maintaining his foolish opinions about our books, how are they going to believe those books in matters concerning the resurrection of the dead, the hope of eternal life, and the kingdom of heaven, when they think their pages are full of falsehoods on facts which they themselves have learnt from experience and the light of reason? Reckless and incompetent expounders of Holy Scripture bring untold trouble and sorrow on their wiser brethren when they are caught in one of their mischievous false opinions and are taken to task by those who are not bound by the authority of our sacred books. For then, to defend their utterly foolish and obviously untrue statements, they will try to call upon Holy Scripture for proof and even recite from memory many passages which they think support their position, although they understand neither what they say nor the things about which they make assertion.[81]

Second, there is the challenge given by Pannenberg to the thinkers and especially to the theologians of the church: if there is a God—and only one God—then all truth is God's truth. It follows that those who proclaim such a God have an obligation to try to present truth in a way that is consistent

---

80. The fact that Augustine's understanding of many "scientific facts" has been invalidated by modern research is irrelevant to the principle he is articulating.

81. Augustine, *Literal Meaning of Genesis*, 1.19.39.

with other truth, and thus "to present a coherent model of the world as God's creation." If such a model is to have the potential to be understood or considered seriously, it must not be based only on the authority, experience, or the consensus of Christian believers, but must also incorporate data and evidence—even data and evidence produced by non-Christians.[82]

Thus, this presentation is aimed at those for whom the traditional Adventist model of Origins and the associated difficulties in harmonizing it with modern science threaten to undermine their confidence in the Bible and the message of salvation it contains. To them, the message is that it may be possible to update the traditional Origins models without destroying faith in God!

BIBLIOGRAPHY

Alexander, Denis. *Rebuilding the Matrix: Science and Faith in the 21st Century*. Oxford: Lion, 2001.
American Museum of Natural History. "What is a Theory: A Scientific Definition." https://www.amnh.org/exhibitions/darwin/evolution-today/what-is-a-theory.
Augustine of Hippo. *The Literal Meaning of Genesis*. Translated by John Hammond Taylor. New York: Paulist, 1982.
Babbage, Stuart Barton. *Man in Nature and Grace*. Grand Rapids: Eerdmans, 1957.
Baker, Lynne Rudder. *Persons and Bodies: A Constitution View*. Cambridge: Cambridge University Press, 2000.
———. "Persons and the Metaphysics of Resurrection." *Religious Studies* 43 (2007) 333–48.
Barr, James. *The Garden of Eden and the Hope of Immortality*. Minneapolis: Fortress, 1992.
Batten, Don. "'Soft' Gap Sophistry." *Creation* 26:3 (June 2004) 44–47.
Beall, Todd. "Reading Genesis 1–2: A Literal Approach." In *Reading Genesis 1–2: An Evangelical Conversation*, edited by J. Daryl Charles, 45–59. Peabody, MA: Hendrickson, 2013.
Bowling, Andrew. "טוֹב (tôb)." In *Theological Wordbook of the Old Testament*, edited by R. Laird Harris et al., 1:345–46. Chicago: Moody, 1980.
Brown, Francis, et al. *A Hebrew and English Lexicon of the Old Testament*. Oxford: Clarendon, 1977.
Brunner, Emil. *The Christian Doctrine of Creation and Redemption*. Translated by Harold Knight. Philadelphia: Westminster, 1950.
———. "Election." In *The Great Invitation and Other Sermons*. Philadelphia: Westminster, 1955.
Bultmann, Rudolf. "Is Exegesis without Presupposition Possible?" In *Existence and Faith: Shorter Writings*, by Rudolf Bultmann, 342–52. London: Collins, 1961.

---

82. Pannenberg, *Introduction*, 6–10.

Clayton, Philip, and Steven Knapp. "Divine Action and the 'Argument from Neglect.'" In *Physics and Cosmology: Scientific Perspectives on the Problem of Natural Evil. Volume 1*, edited by Nancey Murphy, et al., 179–94. Vatican City: Vatican Observatory, 2007.

Copan, Paul, and William Lane Craig. *Creation out of Nothing: A Biblical Philosophical and Scientific Exploration*. Grand Rapids: Baker, 2004.

Crenshaw, James L. "Job, Book of." In *Anchor Yale Bible Dictionary*, edited by David Noel Freedman, 3:858–63. New York: Doubleday, 1992b.

Davies, Paul. *The Goldilocks Enigma: Why the Universe is Just Right for Life*. London: Allen Lane, 2006.

Dawkins, Richard, and Yan Wong. *The Ancestor's Tale: A Pilgrimage to the Dawn of Time*. London: Weidenfeld & Nicolson, 2004.

Dowd, Michael. *Thank God for Evolution*. New York: Penguin, 2007.

Edwards, Dennis. "Why is God doing This?" In *Physics and Cosmology: Scientific Perspectives on the Problem of Natural Evil. Volume 1*, edited by Nancey Murphy, et al., 247–66. Vatican City: Vatican Observatory, 2007.

Eissfeldt, Otto. *The Old Testament: An Introduction*. Oxford: Basil Blackwell, 1974.

Eldredge, Niles, and Stephen Jay Gould. "Punctuated Equilibria: An Alternative to Phyletic Gradualism." In *Models of Paleobiology*, edited by T. J. M. Schopf, 82–115. San Francisco: Freeman Cooper, 1972.

Eriksson, Anders, and Andrea Manica. "Effect of Ancient Population Structure on the Degree of Polymorphism Shared between Modern Human Populations and Ancient Hominins." *Proceedings of the National Academy of Sciences of the United States of America (PNAS)* 109 (2012) 13956–60.

Ford, Desmond. *Daniel*. Nashville: Southern, 1982.

Galusha, Walter. *Fossils and the Word of God*. New York: Exposition, 1964.

"Genesis." In *Seventh-day Adventist Bible Commentary*, edited by Francis D. Nichol, 1:199–487. Washington, DC: Review and Herald, 1979.

Goldstein, Bernard R. "Eratosthenes on the 'Measurement' of the Earth." *Historia Mathematica* 11 (1984) 411–16.

Goldstein, Clifford. *Baptizing the Devil: Evolution and the Seduction of Christianity*. Nampa, ID: Pacific, 2017.

Gould, Stephen Jay. *Wonderful Life: The Burgess Shale and the Nature of History*. London: Vintage, 2000.

Grant, Edward. *The Foundations of Modern Science in the Middle Ages: Their Religious Institutional and Intellectual Contexts*. Cambridge: Cambridge University Press, 1996.

Grudem, Wayne. *Systematic Theology: An Introduction to Biblical Doctrine*. Leicester: Inter-Varsity, 1994.

Gunkel, Hermann. *Genesis*. Macon, GA: Mercer University Press, 1997.

Hasel, Gerhard F. "The Polemical Nature of the Genesis Cosmology." *Evangelical Quarterly* 46 (1974) 81–102.

Hawking, Stephen. *A Brief History of Time: From the Big Bang to Black Holes*. London: Bantam, 1988.

Hoehn, Jack. "The Greater Controversy—How Ellen White's Great Controversy Theme May Help Coordinate Geologic and Biblical History." *Adventist Today* 23:1 (Winter 2015) 14–21.

Höver-Johag, I. "טוֹב." In *Theological Dictionary of the Old Testament*, edited by. G. Johannes Botterweck and Helmer Ringgren, 5:296–317. Grand Rapids: Eerdmans, 1986.

Jastrow, Robert. *God and the Astronomers*. New York: Norton, 1978.

Johnsson, William G. *In Absolute Confidence*. Nashville: Southern, 1979.

Kleinert, Andreas. "A Tangible Historical Lie: How Martin Luther was Made the Opponent of the Copernican World System." *Reports on the History of Science* 26 (2003) 101–11 (English summary). http://www.physik.unihalle.de/Fachgruppen/history/luther_sum.htm.

La Sor, William Sanford, et al. *Old Testament Survey: The Message, Form and Background of the Old Testament*. Grand Rapids: Eerdmans, 1982.

Lightman, Alan. *Searching for Stars on an Island in Maine*. London: Corsair, 2018.

Longman, Tremper III. "What Genesis 1 and 2 Teaches (and What it Doesn't)." In *Reading Genesis 1–2: An Evangelical Conversation*, edited by J. Daryl Charles, 103–28. Peabody, MA: Hendrickson, 2013.

Matthews, Kenneth A. *Genesis 1–11:26*. New American Commentary 1A. Nashville: B & H, 1996.

McIver, Tom. "Formless and Void: Gap Theory Creationism." *Creation/Evolution Journal* 8:3 (Fall 1988) 1–24.

Melott, Adrian L. "Intelligent Design is Creationism in a Cheap Tuxedo." *Physics Today* 55:6 (June 2002) 48–50.

Montgomery, James A. *A Critical and Exegetical Commentary on the Book of Daniel*. International Critical Commentary. Edinburgh: T & T Clark, 1927.

Moore, George Foot. *Judaism*. Cambridge: Harvard University Press, 1927. Republished Peabody, MA: Hendrickson, 1960.

Moule, C. F. D. "Ascension—Acts 1:9." In *Essays in New Testament Interpretation*. Cambridge: Cambridge University Press, 1982.

Murphy, Nancey. "Science and the Problem of Evil: Suffering as a By-Product of a Finely Tuned Cosmos." In *Physics and Cosmology: Scientific Perspectives on the Problem of Natural Evil*, edited by Nancey Murphy et al., 1:131–51. Vatican City: Vatican Observatory, 2007.

"Neo-Darwinism." In *New World Encyclopedia*. www.newworldencyclopedia.org.

Östring, Sven. "Our Miraculous Planet Earth." *Ministry* (December 2018) 6–10.

Pannenberg, Wolfhart. *An Introduction to Systematic Theology*. Grand Rapids: Eerdmans, 1991.

Pennock, Robert T. "Creationism and Intelligent Design." *Annual Review of Genomics and Human Genetics* 4 (2003) 143–63.

Porteous, Norman W. *Daniel: A Commentary*. London: SCM, 1965.

Provonsha, Jack W. "The Creation/Evolution Debate in Light of the Great Controversy." In *Creation Reconsidered: Scientific, Biblical and Theological Perspectives*, edited by James L. Hayward, 303–11. Roseville, CA: Association of Adventist Forums, 2000.

Rabin, Sheila. "Nicolaus Copernicus." In *The Stanford Encyclopedia of Philosophy*, edited by Edward N. Zalta and Uri Nodelmen. Standford: Stanford University, 2023. https://plato.stanford.edu/entries/copernicus/.

Redd, Nola Taylor. "Nicolaus Copernicus Biography: Facts & Discoveries." *Space.com* (2022). https://www.space.com/15684-nicolaus-copernicus.html.

Rogers, Lynden J. "Old Universe but Young Life?" *Christian Spirituality and Science* 10 (2014) 6–22.

Sarna, Nahum M. *Genesis* בראשית. JPS Torah Commentary. Philadelphia: Jewish Society, 1989.
Scott, Eugenie C. "The Creation/Evolution Continuum." *National Center for Science Education (NCSE)* (2016). https://ncse.ngo/creationevolution-continuum.
Singer, Peter. *Rethinking Life and Death: The Collapse of Our Traditional Ethics.* New York: St Martin's, 1994.
Skinner, John. *Genesis.* International Critical Commentary. Edinburgh: T & T Clarke, 1910.
Slatkin, Montgomery, and Fernando Racimo. "Ancient DNA and Human History." *Proceedings of the National Academy of Sciences of the United States of America (PNAS)* 113 (2016) 6380–87.
Stefanovic, Zdravko. *Daniel: Wisdom to the Wise.* Nampa, ID: Pacific, 2007.
Sterelny, Kim. *Darwin vs. Gould: Survival of the Fittest.* Cambridge: Icon, 2001.
Sundberg, Albert C. Jr. *The Old Testament Canon of the Early Church.* Harvard Theological Studies 20. Cambridge: Harvard University Press, 1964.
Thompson, Alden. *Inspiration: Hard Questions, Honest Answers.* Hagerstown, MD: Review and Herald, 1991.
von Rad, Gerhard. *Genesis.* Revised ed. Old Testament Library. London: SCM, 1972.
Wenham, Gordon J. *Genesis 1–15.* Word Biblical Commentary 1. Dallas: Word, 1987.
Wright, N. T. *Paul: A Biography.* San Francisco: HarperOne, 2018.
———. *Surprised by Hope.* London: SPCK, 2007.

Index

Abecassis Armand, 50, 51, 57
Accelerator mass spectrometer
    (AMS), 142, 143, 144, 146,
    150, 161, 164, 166, 170, 172,
    173, 175, 178, 179, 180
Alley Richard, 211, 212, 214, 220
Alter Robert, 6, 8, 12, 18, 27, 30
amino acid, 85, 160, 161, 163, 165,
    166, 167, 241, 250, 253, 257,
    260, 261
Apsu, 45, 46
Aquinas Thomas, 74, 278
Arnold Bill, 5, 9, 28, 30, 36, 39, 43,
    49, 53
Athrahasis, 45, 52
Atum, 43, 44
Augustine of Hippo, 276, 278, 312,
    313, 331, 332
Australian Antarctic Division, 213

Baker Lynne, 281, 320, 322, 323
Baldwin John, 271, 283, 284
Bandstra Barry, 8
Bar-Efrat Shimon, 12, 27
Barnola Jean-Marc, 211, 217, 218,
    223, 231
Barr James, 276, 324
Barth Karl, 285
Batten Don, 282, 304
Beauchamp Paul, 6, 17
becquerel (unit of radioactivity), 131
Becquerel Henri, 181
Behe Michael, 93, 94
Bimson John, 278, 279, 280, 282, 293
Bondi Hermann, 74

Bonhoeffer Dietrich, 98
Boyle Robert, 97
Brachylophosaurus canadensis, 248,
    249, 260
Bright John, 57, 65
Bristlecone Pine, 104, 105, 139, 140
Brueggemann Walter, 285
Brunner Emil, 274, 275, 326
Buber Martin, 6, 8, 26, 33
Bull Brian, 293

Camp Century ice core, 219, 228
Cassuto Umberto, 5, 8, 17, 20, 21,
    26, 30
Chicxulub Impactor, 242
Chlamydomonas, 217, 227
Chopineau Jacques, 26, 27
Colling Richard, 97, 98
Collins Francis, 80, 81, 82, 91, 92, 240
Continental drift, 193
Copernicus Nicolaus, 303, 307
Cordyceps fungi, 84, 90
Cornell Eric, 96, 97
Cotter David, 5
Coulson Charles A., 97, 98
Curie (old unit of radioactivity), 131,
    132
Curie Marie, 129

D'Elia Tom, 227, 229, 231
Dalley Stephanie, 45
Darwin Charles, xvii, 73, 77, 78, 84,
    99, 103, 239, 305, 306, 307
Davidson Richard, 272, 281, 287, 288,
Davies Paul, 79, 311, 329, 330

Index

Dawkins Richard, 305, 306, 308, 316, 321, 325
Day-Age Theory, 286, 287, 289, 305
De Fraine Jean, 6
dead carbon, 135, 151, 155, 156, 173, 176, 177
Delitzsch Franz, 6, 9
Dembski William, 93, 95, 186
Democritus of Abdera, 129
Dendrochronology, 104, 105, 107, 139, 140
Denton Michael, 92
Dome C, 217, 222
Doukhan Jacques, 289
Dowd Michael, 295, 309
Dye-3 ice core, 219
Dyson Freeman, 100

Eisenberg Josy, 50, 51
electromagnetic force, 78, 79, 81, 182
electroweak force, 130, 134
Enuma Elish, 45, 46, 49
EPICA (European Project for Ice Coring in Antarctica) ice core, 217, 222

Falk Darryl, 92
Faro Ingrid, 280, 282
Fokkelman Jan, 7, 27, 29, 31, 54
Foster Charles, 276, 290, 291, 292
Fraser Island, 110
Frendo Anthony, 42, 43

Galilei Galileo, 99, 303, 307
Gap Theory, 286, 304, 305
Geocentrists, 303
Giberson Karl, 80, 81, 82, 91, 276
Gilgamesh, 45
Gingerich Owen, 95, 96, 99
GISP2 (Greenland Ice Sheet Project 2) ice core, 219, 220, 225
gnammas, 112, 122, 123, 124
Gold Thomas, 74
Goldingay John, 6, 8, 17, 30, 54, 56
Goldstein Clifford, 271, 273, 274, 282, 318, 319
Gondwana, 199, 200, 201, 204
Gordon Cyrus, 54

Gosse Bernard, 54
gravitational force, 78
Gray Asa, 84
Grayson Albert, 42
Green River Formation, 117, 118
Greenwood Kyle, 8
GRIP) (Greenland Ice Core Project) ice core, 219, 220
Grudem Wayne, 282, 314
Guth Alan, 74
Guy Fritz, 293

hadron, 130
Hamilton Victor, 32
Hare Peter, 253
Hawking Stephen, 311, 312
Heidel Alexander, 50
Holmstedt Robert, 8
Houtman Cees, 54, 57
Hoyle Fred, 74, 81, 82, 83
Hume David, 75, 76, 77, 78, 99
Huon Pine, 105

IntCaL calibration curve, 105, 139, 140, 141
Intelligent Design (ID), 93, 94, 95, 96, 97, 186, 306, 315

Jagersma Henk, 6, 8, 26, 59
Jastrow Robert, 311, 312
Johnson Phillip, 93
Joüon Paul, 8
Jouzel Jean, 209, 230

Keil Carl, 6, 9
Kepler Johannes, 73, 74
King Leonard, 45
Kline Meredith, 272, 273, 280, 281, 287, 288
Kuhn Thomas, 262

Lake Baikal (Southern Siberia), 116, 125
Lake George (NSW, Australia), 116
Lake Malawi (Africa), 116, 120, 121
Lake Selina (Tasmania, Australia), 119, 120

INDEX

Lake St. Clair (Tasmania, Australia), 125
Lake Superior (USA/Canada), 116
Lake Tanganyika (Africa), 116, 125
Lake Titicaca (S. America), 116
Lake Turkana (Africa), 116
Lake Victoria (Africa), 116
Lake Vostok (Antarctica), 218, 227, 228, 229, 231
Lambert Wilfred, 45, 46
Laurasia, 196, 199, 200, 201
lepton, 130, 182
Lewis C. S., 98, 99
Libby half-life, 138, 147, 148, 185
Libby Willard, 128, 132, 138, 145, 147
Licht Jacob, 12
Lightman Alan, 306, 320, 329
limit of detection (*LOD*), 151, 152, 153, 155, 171, 172, 173
Link Christian, 69
Linnaeus (Carl von Linne), 239
Liverani Mario, 58, 63
Lods Adolphe, 57
Lucas Ernest, 68, 69
Lufengosaurus, 261
Luther Martin, 307
Lynch's Crater (Qld, Australia), 118, 119

Magnusson Eric, xvii
Marduk, 45, 46, 51, 58, 59, 63
Marsh Frank, 287
Mastodon, 248, 256, 257, 259, 260
McGrath Alistair, 92
Meese Debra, 219, 225
Methuselah Tree, 104
Milankovitch Variations, 211, 212, 224
Mississippi Delta, 108
moa, 250, 252
Moltmann Jürgen, 275, 285, 292, 293
Moreton Island, Australia, 110
Morris Henry, 117, 118
Morris Simon Conway, 92, 97
Muraoka Takamitsu, 8
Murphy Nancey, 319

Myall Lake (NSW, Australia), 113, 114

National Association of Testing Authorities, Australia (NATA), 148
Nebuchadnezzar, 56, 58, 61, 280,
Newton Isaac, 74, 98
NGRIP ice core, 234, 235, 236
Noth Martin, 65

Oard Michael, 212, 226, 232
Origin of Species, 78, 95
Osiris, 43

paleomagnetism, 219, 224
Paley William, 77
Pannenberg Wolfhart, 313, 314, 322, 323, 332, 333
Parker Simon, 45
Pascal Blaise, 74, 75, 80
Paul Shalom, 50
Paulien Jon, 289
Pelorosaurus, 243
Pennock Robert, 271, 272, 306
Periodic Table, 78, 129, 130
plumbum, 226
Polkinghorne John, 91, 92, 96, 291, 292
Porten Bezalel, 57
Pritchard James, 72
Provonsha Jack, 315, 318, 319, 320
Proxima Centauri, 272
Ptah, 43

quark, 130, 182, 183,

Ra, 43, 44
Rees Martin, 79
Rendtorff Rolf, 54
Renland ice core, 219
Rice Richard, 50
Ringgren Helmer, 43
Rogers Lynden, 304, 310, 311
Römer Thomas, 46, 52, 54, 55, 62
Rutherford Ernest, 130, 181, 182

Sagan Carl, 85

339

Index

Schweitzer Mary, 238–264
Scott Eugenie, 271, 302
Seybold Klaus, 27
Shuvuuia deserti, 257
SI System, 131, 132
Soggin Jan, 57, 62, 63
soil profiles, 105, 106
Sonnet Jean-Pierre, 27
specific activity, 131, 133
Speiser Ephraim, 6, 42, 50, 286
Spiekermann Hermann, 68
Standard Model, 130, 132, 182, 183, 186
strong force, 81
Super-Kamiokande, 184
Sydney Basin, 110, 111

Talon Philippe, 46
Tandem accelerator mass spectrometer, 143
Tarbosaurus bataar, 253
Tennant Frederick, 80
Tethys Ocean, 199
Tiamat, 45, 51, 286
Toba Lake (Sumatra), 121
transmutation, 130, 132, 134, 135, 136, 137, 138, 183
Triceratops horridus, 254

Tsumura David, 1, 8, 9, 50, 51
Tuggerah Lake (NSW, Australia), 114, 115
Turner Laurence, 6, 272
Tyrannosaurus rex, 245, 246, 247, 248, 255, 256, 257, 259, 260

Vostok ice core, 211, 218, 223, 226, 231
Vriezen Theodorus, 67

Wallace Alfred Russel, 203, 204, 239
Wallace's Line, 203, 204
Walton John, 6, 26, 30
weak force, 183
Wenham Gordon, 6, 26, 30, 47, 50, 66, 324
Wénin André, 6, 8, 17
Whitcomb John, 117, 118
Will Graham, v, vi, 106, 107
Wilson John, 43
Wright N. T., 330

Yiou François, 224, 231

Zenger Erich, 55, 59
Zinke Edward, 271, 274

www.ingramcontent.com/pod-product-compliance
Lightning Source LLC
Chambersburg PA
CBHW061423300426
44114CB00014B/1519